The Oxford
Children's History

The Oxford
Children's History

Volume 2 : The Making of the Modern Age

Peter & Mary Speed

Oxford University Press

Oxford University Press, Walton Street, Oxford ox2 6DP

Oxford   London   Glasgow
New York   Toronto   Melbourne   Auckland
Kuala Lumpur   Singapore   Hong Kong   Tokyo
Delhi   Bombay   Calcutta   Madras   Karachi
Nairobi   Dar es Salaam   Cape Town

and associated companies in
Beirut   Berlin   Ibadan   Mexico City   Nicosia

Oxford is a trade mark of Oxford University Press

British Library Cataloguing in Publication Data

Speed, P. F.
  The Oxford Children's History.
  Vol. 2: The Making of the Modern Age
  1. Great Britain – History – Juvenile literature
  I. Title   11. Speed, Mary
  941   DA30

ISBN 0-19-918187-X

Typeset by Tradespools Ltd., Frome, Somerset
Printed in Hong Kong

Contents

Contents

Chapter One   The Village and the Farm

1 The Open Field Village

Let us go back to the year 1760, and visit the village of Hillidon, near Nottingham. One of the farmers, John Fowler, will be our guide.

The village stands in the middle of its fields, the farmhouses and cottages huddling round the church. John's house is no more than a living room, a kitchen and two bedrooms. He has a wife and several children, so they do not have much space. The house smells dirty, especially as there is a heap of manure in the yard.

John has a stall for his cow, a barn for his corn and hay, and a shed for his farm tools. There is no plough, and John explains that he shares one with his neighbours. They keep it in the churchyard.

'How big is your farm?' we ask. 'About ten acres.' *'Well, that won't take us long to visit.'* 'Don't you believe it. If you want to see it all you must walk several miles.'

Rather puzzled, we follow John out of the village. 'There you are,' he says, pointing to a huge field of wheat, 'there is my bread for next year.' It is August and there is a sea of ripening wheat, stretching into the distance. *'But that can't be all yours. That field is hundreds of acres!'* 'No, I just farm half an acre in Holm-side Furlong, right over there, three-quarters of an acre in Old Mill Furlong in the middle, an acre in Wilsdon Furlong to our left, and a small piece just here.' *'But how can you tell which is yours?'* John laughs. 'Oh, I know all right. And if I tried to reap a neighbour's crop, he would remind me soon enough.'

On the other side of the village we find another field, just as big as the first, but it is growing barley, peas and beans. John has the same amount of land here. Again, it is scattered in small pieces all over the field. *'You like peas and beans for dinner then, John?'* 'Not I. They are for my cow and my sheep during the winter. They have most of my barley as well, but it looks a good crop this year, and I may be able to make a drop of beer.'

We go to a third field, again as big as the others. It has no crops at all, but we can see large grass patches in the dips. They are sikes, and are where the land is too damp to plough. 'My sheep are in this field,' ex-

plains John. 'They have been here since last autumn, eating the stubble and what grass they can find. They must come off soon, though, because we shall be ploughing for next year's wheat.' *'So you change the crops each year?'* 'Of course. Next year, the wheat field will grow barley, peas and beans, and the barley field will be fallow, like this one.' *'But why do you leave a field bare like this?'* 'Land needs a rest, or it is soon good for nothing.' *'But why not manure it?'* 'How should I get enough manure from one cow and six sheep?'

John now takes us to see his cow. It is another good walk, but at last we come to a long, narrow field that lies beside a stream. 'This is Stetchpool Meadow,' says John. 'I have a dole here, one a bit further along, and another at the far end.' Looking closely, we can see the field is marked out with stakes into patches no bigger than an ordinary garden. 'Of course, the meadow is really for hay,' John explains, 'but we must have all our hay cut, dried and carried by Lammas Tide. (August 1st.) We then graze our cows on the

ploughs

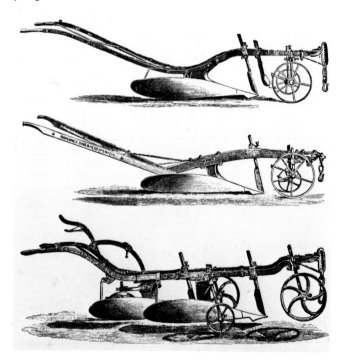

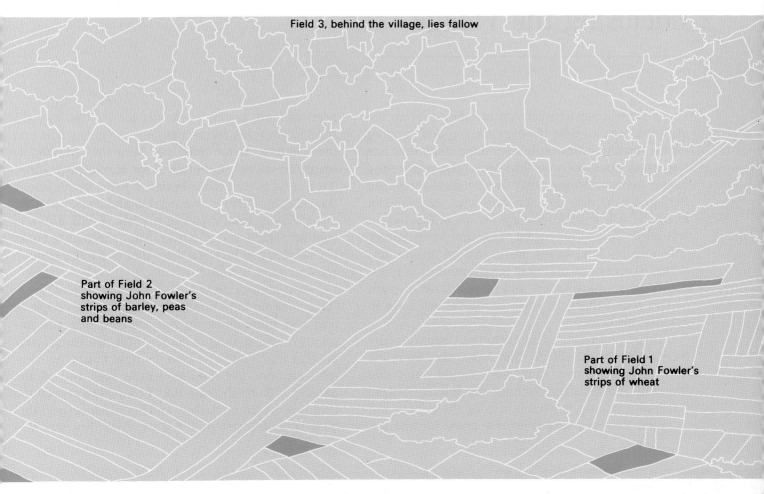

Field 3, behind the village, lies fallow

Part of Field 2 showing John Fowler's strips of barley, peas and beans

Part of Field 1 showing John Fowler's strips of wheat

aftermath. That is the grass which grows after we have cut our hay. Soon, we shall cut our wheat, and when it is all in, the sexton will ring the church bell, and we shall put our cows in that field for a time. We have to shift them around to graze where they can. I'm lucky because I have a bit of land. My animals can go all over the fallow field and the meadow. Villagers with no land have to put their beasts on the common. Grass doesn't grow in the winter, so they go hungry.'

He breaks off to point to a small, lean animal. 'There's my cow. She is happy enough now, but she won't be tomorrow. It's my turn for the plough, and she will have to help pull it.'

'Who sees you obey all the rules in your village, John?' 'The manor court, of course. We all belong to it, and take office in turn. I am a burlyman this year. There are four of us and we keep an eye on the fields. We see no-one ploughs the sikes, or anyone else's land. If they do, we tell the court and they fine them. They fined me last year because I didn't clean out my ditches.'

'Where do you sell your meat, John?' 'I don't sell meat, unless an animal drops dead. Dead animals are no good to me.' *'What about your crops, then?'*

'You must be daft. When the animals have eaten all they want, there is precious little left for the wife and children, let alone to sell. You must talk to Jack Hayward. He farms eighty acres and he has plenty to sell. He takes it to Nottingham, I think. I don't know. I never leave the village.'

2 Enclosing the Village

Today we will pay another visit to Hillidon. From the ale house we can hear the men arguing and banging on the furniture. Obviously something important has happened since we were last here. The squire, the parson and some of the richer farmers have persuaded Parliament to pass an Enclosure Act for Hillidon. Everyone will have to give up his land, and then it will all be shared out again. This time each farmer will have his land in one piece, instead of little bits scattered everywhere. He will have a number of fields, like those we have today, and he will have to plant hedges round them. In other words, he will have to 'enclose' his farm.

Three gentlemen called Enclosure Commissioners have arrived in the village. They have asked everyone how much land they think they should have, and have put up a list of the claims in the church. That, as much as anything, is what is causing the excitement.

John Fowler was puzzled. He knew he had ten acres of land, but that was not all. He also had the right to graze his animals all over the fallow field and the meadow. If he could not keep his animals, he would be ruined, so he asked for another five acres. 'Five acres to feed those beasts of yours?' says one of the villagers. 'Your cow is all skin and bone, she gives you no more than a couple of pints of milk a day in summer, and is dry all winter. Your sheep have backs like rabbits, and between them they don't give enough wool to make a waistcoat.'

'You aren't one to talk, Bill Finch,' replies John. 'You have no land at all. You only keep a couple of pigs and some geese on the common, but you are asking for three acres of land.' 'Yes, Bill Finch,' says another man, 'and you have no right to use the common anyway. We only let you to keep you off the parish.' 'Rubbish,' says Bill. 'I have always used the common, so did my father, and his father before him.' 'Lies,' says John. 'I shall tell the Commissioners you

are a liar, and you will have no land at all.'

Just then someone else comes into the room. He is much better dressed than the others. They all turn on him. 'It's a wonder you dare show your face here, Hayward,' someone shouts. 'You and the Squire have had this Act and it will ruin us all.'   'I don't think so,' Hayward replies. 'I am tired of being bossed by the manor court, and I am tired of having to farm like you.'   'What's wrong with our farming?'   'There's plenty wrong with your sheep for a start. Some of mine died of liver rot they caught from yours. And I have been telling you for years we should grow turnips and clover on the fallow field.'   'Who wants to poison their sheep with turnips or wear out their soil with clover?'   'A crop of clover does the soil good,' Hayward replies. At this, the villagers all roar with laughter. 'Well,' says Hayward, 'soon I shall be able to farm in my own way. Then you will see.'

The Enclosure Commissioners met the villagers one by one. John was worried because he had no papers at all to prove his farm really did belong to him. Luckily some of his friends were ready to swear he had always used the land and that no-one had ever challenged him. The Commissioners looked doubtful and

John was left for months wondering what would happen.

After nearly two years the Commissioners finished their work, and gave the parson their Award. It was forty sheets of parchment, each three feet by two feet. It said exactly who was to have every scrap of land in the village. The squire had the most with well over a thousand acres. The parson had about four hundred. Three of the wealthy villagers had two hundred acres each. Hayward had seventy acres. The poorest villagers who had kept beasts on the common were given half an acre each. No-one could feed a cow on that.

John only had eight acres. They were in one block of land, which was convenient, but they were part of the old common and were over a mile from the village. He had two years to enclose his land, that is, to plant a hedge round it. The hedge would give him a lot of work and expense, but worse was to follow. There was also a bill. Parliament charged £2,000 for the Enclosure Act, and the Commissioners charged £3,000 for their work. Everyone with land had to help pay. John's share was over £30, which was more money than he had ever seen in his life. How was he to find it? He was beside himself with worry.

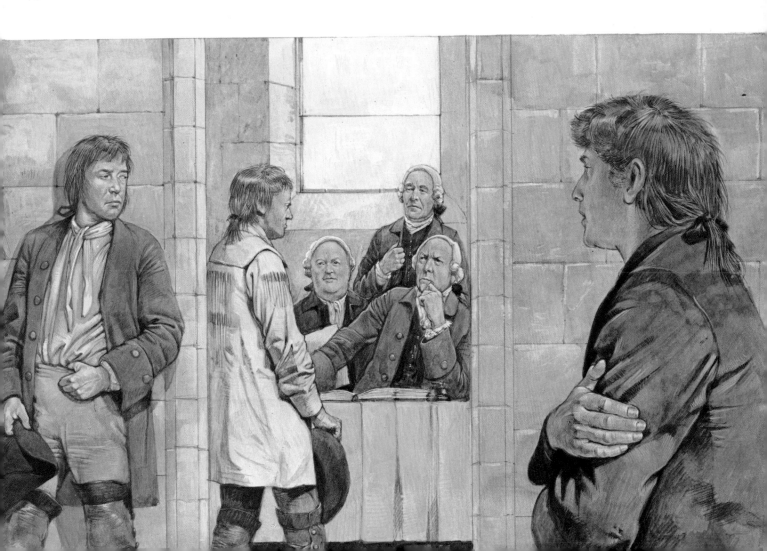

Enclosing the Village

In the upper picture you can see what Hillidon looked like before the Enclosure Commissioners arrived.

In the lower picture you can see what the village will look like after enclosure.

3 New Ways of Farming

Why was it that people like Hayward wanted to enclose their land?

For a long time the towns had been growing, and their people wanted to buy food. Farmers like John Fowler grew only enough for themselves, but men with more land had food for sale. They made so much money from it that they wanted to grow more and still more. They knew, too, that there were ways they could do this from the same amount of land.

Back in the 1560s, during the reign of Elizabeth I, some Dutch people fled from a terrible war in their own country and settled in Norfolk. Soon the Norfolk people were amazed at some strange plants the Dutchmen were growing in their gardens. They were turnips. Cautiously, the English tried them and soon they, too, were growing them in their gardens. Then someone, we do not know who, grew them in a field as winter feed for his sheep. Other farmers copied him, and within a hundred years turnips were a common crop in East Anglia. During the winter, grass does not grow, and a farmer may be short of hay. If he has turnips, though, he can give his animals something to eat.

The Dutch also brought new kinds of clover, much better than the wild sort found in England. Hayward was quite right about clover: it does do the soil good. Also, if clover and grass are sown together, they give heavy crops of hay.

After a time, farmers in Norfolk realised they could manage without fallow, and plant all their land if they grew the new crops in rotation with the old. They sowed a field with wheat in the first year, turnips in the second, barley, beans or peas in the third, and grasses with clover in the fourth. Usually, they let the grasses and clover stay for a few years before going back to wheat. We call this the 'Norfolk Four Course' system. A nobleman called Viscount Townshend was so keen on it, they called him 'Turnip Townshend'.

You will remember that John Fowler did not want to plant the fallow field because he did not have enough manure. Farmers who grew the new crops, though, had turnips and a lot more hay, so they kept more animals. The animals gave plenty of manure. The crops fed the animals, the animals manured the crops, and the farmers made a lot of money.

Also, there were new breeds of animal. A man called Robert Bakewell, of Dishley in Leicestershire, bred sheep which fattened so quickly that they were ready for the butcher in two years. Two brothers called Colling from County Durham bred some new cattle called shorthorns, which gave plenty of milk and meat. John Fowler's sheep would never have grown fat. He had them for wool and for dung. His cow was a poor little thing that he kept until she dropped dead from hard work.

the Norfolk four course system

this Durham shorthorn and the Leicester sheep are examples of the improved stock achieved by careful breeding.

We can now see Hayward's problem. He wanted to try new crops, but if he planted turnips on his part of the fallow field, John Fowler's sheep would eat them. Also, he wanted to try the Norfolk system, but it needed four, five, six, or even more fields. That was impossible at Hillidon, while Fowler and his friends insisted on having three fields.

Moreover, Hayward dared not buy expensive Leicestershire sheep and shorthorn cows. If he did, they would have to mix with animals belonging to the other villagers, and would catch diseases from them.

What Hayward wanted was to have his land all in one piece, fenced off from everyone else's. Only then could he grow the crops he wanted and keep the best animals. Unlike his neighbours he had travelled a bit, and had spoken to owners of enclosed farms. Some with no more land than he had were making twice as much money. He wanted to do the same.

4 The Squire

the old Squire builds his house

The Squire

We will now go forward seventy years and visit Hillidon in 1830. This time we will call on the squire, Sir William Courteney. He is a rich man, being squire of several villages, apart from Hillidon. His father had lived in a Tudor mansion. It was picturesque, but it was cold and draughty. He pulled it down and began an elegant new house. His son has just finished it.

Sir William is too busy to see us for the moment, but his agent, Mr. Starkes, meets us very politely. We ask him what work an agent does. 'I look after Sir William's estates. The most important thing I do is collect his rents, but that only takes a week or two at Michaelmas. I have to manage the home farm, which supplies the family and all the servants in the big house. We have an excellent herd of Jersey cows, so we are never short of milk, cream and butter. Then we have a brick works, a timber yard, a saw mill and a forge, all belonging to the estate. I have to keep an eye on them. If farm buildings need mending, the tenant has to do the work, but Sir William gives him the bricks and timber for nothing. It is my job to see them delivered. At the forge we mend the farm machines and make things like gate hinges, horse shoes and nails.

'My most difficult job, though, is to make sure the tenants take proper care of their farms. You see, each one has a lease, which is an agreement he has made with Sir William. Sir William promises the tenant he can keep his farm for twenty-one years, and a man could ruin it in that time. So that he does not, he must agree to grow his crops in the right way. We usually make tenants follow the Norfolk system – wheat, turnips, barley and then grasses for a year or two. We never let them take two straw crops one after the other. During the war, wheat was so dear they would have sown it on every inch of land. That would have ruined it, so we made them stick to the proper course. They grumbled at the time, but it paid off. The land is still in good heart.'

The big open fields, meadows and common have all gone, and in their place is a patchwork of smaller fields, just like today. There is no fallow land, but crops everywhere. The cows and sheep look much fatter than they did before, and we pass one or two farmers who look as fat and contented as their animals. There are, though, a lot of poor people in the village. Some of them are men who are out of work.

'This village grows a lot of food, Mr. Starkes.'
'Yes, since the Enclosure Act, everything has about doubled – crops, livestock and, I am pleased to say, Sir William's rents. He finds ways of spending the money, though. He has more debts than his father, and that is saying something. He can't resist buying land. Whenever there is a bit for sale, he snaps it up, whether he can afford it or not. The biggest worry, though, is the expense at the big house, with all those servants and all those parties.'

We return to the big house, passing through the huge iron gates into the park. Other guests are coming back from hunting, excited and happy. At the house we change into our best clothes and, when the gong sounds, go down to dinner. The house has a marble staircase, paintings on the walls and expensive furniture in all the rooms. In the dining hall the mahogany tables and sideboards are set with dishes of gold and silver. An orchestra plays in a gallery. There are servants dressed in livery everywhere.

The dinner is a dozen courses, with all the wine we can drink – too much in fact. At eleven o'clock the meal is over and the ladies go to the drawing room.

The men stay, drinking. They become noisy, telling rude stories and making unkind jokes. After a couple of hours they become bored and join the ladies. Groups of people play cards while others stand around gossiping. Towards two o'clock people begin to leave and we, too, stagger to our beds.

In the morning we wake up feeling dreadful. However can we make polite conversation? There is no need to worry. Sir William keeps out of the way, and none of the other guests wants to talk. Breakfast is set in the dining room, and we just help ourselves.

It is now time to say goodbye. We find Sir William in the estate office having a heated argument with Mr. Starkes, obviously about money. He breaks off, though, to wish us a kindly farewell, and says he hopes we will come and see him again before long.

5 Farmers

One of the best farms in the village belongs to George Hayward. He is the grandson of Jack Hayward, who was alive at the time of the Enclosure Act.

His farm is well away from the village. There is a large, square house, and a yard with fine, solid buildings round it. The largest is the great barn with two sets of double doors, big enough for a waggon. It has a threshing floor in the middle, though this is no longer used. Then there are the cow stalls, stables, cart sheds, pig sties, poultry houses and dog kennels. One building has a water wheel and inside is a powerful threshing machine. Everywhere there are animals – horses, cows, oxen, sheep, pigs, one or two goats, a donkey, hens, geese, ducks, turkeys, pigeons and even peacocks. Behind the house is a flower garden with beehives.

The Haywards have expensive furniture. There is a table and a sideboard of mahogany, comfortable armchairs, carpets and curtains. Mr. Hayward is proud of the silver cups his animals have won at cattle shows, and his wife is nearly as proud of her gooseberry wine, her home-made cakes, and her embroidery.

You are a rich man, Mr. Hayward,' we say. 'I do well enough, but I owe most of it to my grandfather. You see, he fought hard to have the Enclosure Act for this village, even though it made him unpopular. The Commissioners awarded him seventy acres, and he expected to make a good living from that. Then along comes Sir William, the father of the one we have now. "Jack," he says, "I will give you £30 an acre for your land." "Fine, squire," says grandfather, "but how does a farmer live without land?" "Don't you worry," says Sir William. "I shall soon have some farms ready of about 200 acres, each with its hedges planted, and with a new house and buildings. You shall have one of them if you want. I will give you a long lease and charge only £1 an acre rent for the year. Think of it Jack – a farm of 200 acres and over £2,000 in your pocket." My grandfather saw the squire was right, so they did the deal. The farm has done well ever since, especially during the war.'

'But you are only tenants now. Sir William could turn you out, if he wanted.' 'Not until my lease is up he can't. Even then he will give me a new one. Sir William never gets rid of a good tenant. We will just have to agree a new rent, that is all.'

'Sir William is a fair man?' 'Very fair. Back in 1823 when we could hardly sell our wheat he let me off most of my rent. I don't like Starkes though. He caught me selling a load of dung the other day – just a load of dung, but he stopped me and said he would fine me £5 if I did it again.'

Mr. Hayward takes us to see his water meadows. They are by a stream and from time to time he floods them. His grandfather had one crop of hay from his meadow, and grazed animals there for six weeks. George has three crops of hay and twelve weeks grazing. This is because the water helps the grass to grow. George is especially pleased since he wants to keep more animals and grow less wheat. 'During the war,' he explains, 'we had very good prices for wheat so we grew all we could – that is all Starkes would let us. Now wheat gets cheaper the whole time. Meat, butter and cheese hold their price, though, so I keep more sheep and cows.' *'Do you grow turnips for winter feed?'* 'Not the old kind. They couldn't stand the frost and rotted in the ground after Christmas. I have Swedish turnips now, and they last until the water meadows are ready for their first bite at the end of February. My animals grow fat, and my cows give milk all through the winter. Before enclosure my grandfather was lucky if he just kept his stock alive. I still go on making my farm better, like when I first tried swedes, and when I bought my threshing machine. Before enclosure no-one could change his farming like I do. The small farmers ate all they grew, so they didn't bother about prices. They never wanted change and they held back the better men. Things are different now, thank goodness.'

'But what happened to the small farmers after enclosure, Mr. Hayward?' 'You go into the village, and you will see.'

6 Farm Labourers

Back in the village there are a lot more people than there were in 1760. Most of the men are farm labourers, and among them is James Fowler, grandson of John Fowler. He lives in the same house, though he shares it with another family. It never was pleasant but now it is a dirty slum, with its walls crumbling and its thatch leaking. James Fowler has a sad story to tell.

'After the Enclosure Act, my grandfather was given eight acres of land. It was a mile from home, which didn't please him, and he had to plant a hedge round it, which pleased him less. His big worry, though, was the £30 bill he had for enclosure expenses. He asked the parson what to do about it, and the parson sent him to a lawyer in town. That man was as sharp as they come. He said he would give grandfather a mortgage of £30 on his land, and grandfather had to promise to pay him £5 a year for eight years. Grandfather thought that was hardly fair, but he had no choice. Anyway, he paid his £30 bill with the money the lawyer gave him. His troubles were just beginning, though. He had some land, but he had lost his common rights. In the old days, his animals had wandered all over the fallow field and the meadow. Now the land had been divided and fenced. He needed his eight acres to grow food for his family, so he sold his animals. He was much poorer and he could see it was going to be a struggle to pay his mortgage. Then one day the squire sent for him. "John," he said, "I will give you £25 an acre for your land." My grandfather was overjoyed. He saw he could pay his debts easily and have what looked like a fortune in ready money. He should have wondered what he was going to do when all the money was spent, but he never thought of that. Anyway, he bought himself and his wife new clothes, stood everyone drinks at the "Three Horseshoes" for a few nights and then went to pay the lawyer his £30. That man told grandfather he would be wise to put the rest of his money into Allen's Bank, which was what he did. The bank paid a bit of interest on the money for a few years, and then it went broke. Grandfather lost everything.' *'How did he make a living?'* 'He went labouring, of course. The Fowlers were yeoman farmers for generations. Since the enclosures they have been day labourers. It is all the fault of the enclosures.'

Other men in the village are just as unhappy. Dick Finch said that his ancestors had always been labourers, but in the old days life had been different. 'Most of them kept a pig or a couple of sheep on the common and their wives spun thread. Now the common is gone, and the beasts with it. All the spinning is done in factories these days, so the only time our women can earn a few pennies is during the harvest. As for the single men, they used to live in with the farmers. That meant they slept under a sound roof and ate good food. Nowadays, Hayward and his kind have bought fancy furniture and carpets. They don't want us in with them. We wear muddy boots and smell of dung. The worst thing lately has been the threshing machines. Not so long ago, four of us used to spend all winter in Hayward's barn, threshing out his wheat. It was hard, dull work, mind, but it gave us a wage through the winter. Now his machine finishes the work in a week. He turns us away then, and tells us not to come back until spring.'

Dick's wife tells us about her housekeeping. They are seven in the family, husband, wife and five children. She spends nine shillings a week on bread, a shilling a week on meat and cheese, and has to find sixpence a week rent. Nearly every year she either has a baby, or one of the children dies, so births and burials cost the family over £1 a year, or about sixpence a week. Candles, soap and a few other things come to a shilling. All together, then, they have to find twelve shillings a week, even if they spend nothing on clothes. Dick's wages are only nine shillings a week, when he has work.

'However do you manage, Mrs. Finch?' 'We go on the parish. A miserable life that is, too. We don't starve, but we come so close to it that at times it were better to be dead.'

21

7 The Poor

the overseers

Matthew Ramsden is one of the overseers of the poor at Hillidon. *'How did you become an overseer, Mr. Ramsden?'* 'I was elected. Every year those of us that pay rates, the farmers, the innkeeper and so on, meet in the church vestry. We choose the parish officers from among ourselves. It was Hayward's idea that I should be overseer. He doesn't like me. Still, I had my own back and named him as constable. Many a night he has had to come into the village to stop a fight at the "Three Horseshoes". It's less trouble than being overseer, mind. That takes me away from my farm a lot.' *'How much are you paid?'* 'Why, nothing, of course. The one comfort is, I can give up the job at the end of the year. I will try and see Hayward gets it.'

'What do you have to do?' 'Well, when I first took office, I sat down with the other overseer, Luke Chambers, and we tried to decide how much money we were going to need during the year. We looked at last year's expenses, and did a bit of guess work. Then we worked out how much each of the ratepayers owed, and went and told them. You can imagine how popular that made us. Poor rates this year were 15/- an acre, which is getting on for as much as we pay in rent. A man like Hayward can afford to pay, but others like Luke and me can barely keep our own families decently. It comes hard to give more than we can afford to keep a lot of paupers in idleness.'

'What do you do with the money?' 'We give it out to the paupers. They come along with their wives, all dressed in rags, and with their snivelling brats, and tell us how they suffer. Luke and I know there are several men who could work if they wanted.' *'Why not refuse to pay them?'* 'I don't want my ricks fired do I?' *'How do you decide what they should have?'* 'The Justices of the Peace, that's Sir William Courteney and his fine friends, say we must use the allowance system. Every family must have enough bread to eat, and if they don't have the money to buy it, the parish must give it to them. Say they need nine shillings for bread, and they only have seven shillings, well, the parish must pay them two shillings.' *'That way no-one need starve.'* 'True, but it runs away with the money. Take a man like Finch. His wife has a baby nearly every year, but he doesn't worry, because he knows the parish will feed them. He doesn't work,

either, no more than two or three days in the week. He knows that if he hasn't enough money, the parish must find it for him. Men like Hayward do well out of it, too. Hayward stands off most of his men in the winter, and the parish has to keep them. When they are in work, he only gives them eight or nine shillings

a parish notice-board

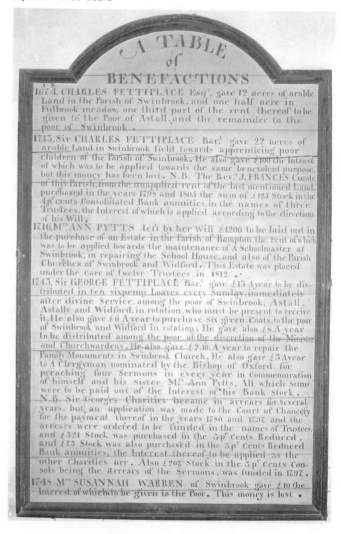

a week. They went to him the other day and asked for a rise. All he said was, "If your wages aren't high enough, the parish will make them up." It's people like Luke and me that suffer. We employ no labour, so we can't tell our men to live off the parish. Really, we are paying most of Hayward's wages for him.'

'*When we spoke to the poor, they blamed the enclosures. They said they would be all right if they could have their common back and keep a cow, or a pig or two.*' 'That's rubbish. The enclosed farms need much more labour than the old ones. Remember, there was no work done on the fallow field for a whole year, apart from ploughing it a couple of times. Now all the land is cultivated. No, the trouble is that we have too many labourers in Hillidon. The farmers can't employ them all.' '*Why don't some of them move?*' 'Sir William helped a few families to emigrate, and two or three more have gone into Nottingham. Only the best ones go, though. Men like Finch haven't the spirit. He and his kind are going to ruin Luke and me.'

Help was, in fact, on its way for Matthew and Luke. In 1834 Parliament passed an Act which changed the whole system of looking after the poor. Hillidon joined with fifteen other parishes to make a Poor Law Union. All the ratepayers elected a Board of Guardians, of twenty men. Matthew was one of them, but apart from four meetings a year, he had nothing to do. The Union was rich enough to pay full-time officers for the day-to-day work. In 1840, they opened a workhouse, and stopped giving the paupers money. If anyone was starving he could either go into the workhouse or stay hungry. Dick Finch tried it. He found he had to get up early in the morning, wear a uniform and live on plain food, like bread and watery porridge. He had no beer and no tobacco. His wife and children were taken from him and put in another part of the workhouse. What was worst, though, he had to spend the entire day smashing bones with a hammer. He soon decided it would be better to find a job.

Mrs. Fowler was unlucky. Her husband died and she had to go to the workhouse with her children. Most of the people there were widows and orphans. They had a miserable time.

Chapter Two   Famous Inventors

1 John Kay and James Hargreaves

It is the year 1780. Today we will visit a village in Lancashire where they make cotton cloth. It is no use asking the way to the factory, for there is none. Instead, people are working in their own homes. From some of the cottages we can hear a strange rattle — latitat, latitat, latitat. We go into one of these houses, which belongs to William Hobbs. It is small, but it is warm and comfortable, with good oak furniture. There is a dresser, with some expensive china, there is a clock on the wall, and a couple of pictures. This is not the home of a poor man.

The weaver is busy with his loom, which is making the 'latitat' noise. William explains how it works, but it is rather complicated. 'Well, I will try and make it easy for you. First of all, I put the warp threads in the loom. They are the ones that run the whole length of the cloth. Next, I weave in the weft. This thread runs from side to side. First I wind it on a bobbin. Then I put the bobbin in my shuttle and that carries the weft left, right, left, right, from one side of the loom to the other. I use a flying shuttle, of course.'   *'What is a flying shuttle?'*   'It is one that runs on wheels. I tap it from side to side by jerking this wooden peg. Otherwise, I would have to pass the shuttle through by hand.'

This flying shuttle was invented by a weaver called John Kay in 1733. It could be fitted to any loom, and was quite cheap. It did make a big difference, though, because a man could weave twice as quickly as before. Kay was pleased with his invention, and showed it to his neighbours. To his dismay, they were furious. They said that if one weaver could do the work of two, half of them would be unemployed. They were so cruel to Kay that he fled to France, where he died soon afterwards, poor and miserable. There came a time, though, when the weavers were able to sell all the cloth they could make. They were quick enough to use the flying shuttle then, and many, like William Hobbs, made a good living because of it.

'The flying shuttle did give us problems, though,' says William. 'When we first had it, we used up the yarn so fast that the spinners could not keep us supplied. They only had the old-fashioned wheels that spun one thread at a time. We used to bribe them with presents to work hard, but they couldn't keep up with us. Not that they tried very much. They had the advantage over us and gave themselves airs and graces, as well as charging dear for their work. It's

a flying shuttle

the spinning jenny

luckier than Kay, though. His mill did quite well and he earned enough to be comfortable, though he never became rich.

better now. They all have spinning jennies. The thread isn't a lot of good. It's uneven and soft, so we can only use it for weft. Still, there is plenty of it.'

William now leaves his loom. 'That's enough weaving for today. I have done four hours. Now I am going up to the Rose and Crown for a drink with my friends. This afternoon I expect I will do a bit of gardening, and I shall have to milk my cow.'

Next door, we find Jane Hudson busy with her spinning jenny. 'This is a fine machine,' she explains. 'It is a new one, that spins sixty threads at once. Some of the old kind only spun eight threads. Still, even that was a great advance on the one thread wheel. The only problem is, that we spin too much yarn. The weavers can't use it all. Mr. Hookham, our employer, pays them more and more, but all they do then, is to work less and less. Look at Hobbs. He's finished for the day already.'

The spinning jenny was invented by a Blackburn man, James Hargreaves. On the old-fashioned wheel, the piece that twisted the thread was the spindle. It stuck out sideways. One day, Hargreaves's wife knocked her wheel over, so that the spindle was up-right, but still turning round. Hargreaves at once thought, 'Why not put several spindles in a frame, and spin a number of threads at once?' It took him three years to perfect his machine, but he finished in the end. He then offered some models for sale. Instead of eager customers, though, a crowd of angry spinners invaded his home, and smashed all his machines. They were afraid of losing their jobs. Hargreaves fled to Nottingham, where he opened a spinning mill, using his jennies. Unfortunately he could not afford to take out a patent on his machine, so other men copied it, making a lot of money for themselves. Hargreaves was

2 Richard Arkwright

As we have seen, William Hobbs had his weft from housewives who worked with spinning jennies. He also needed warp. As warp threads run the whole length of the cloth, they have to be firm and strong. To see where they came from, we have to go into the Peak District, to the village of Cromford.

Cromford lies in the beautiful valley of the River Derwent. There are wooded hills all round, and trees overhang the water. In the village we find the usual things – a church, a public house, and rows of cottages. All the buildings, though, are new. The houses are clean and well built. They are in neat rows with lawns in front of them, and allotments behind. The cobbled street is shaded with trees. Almost everyone here works in the mill, a splendid building, with a huge water wheel. The whole village belongs to Richard Arkwright.

Arkwright was born in Preston in 1732. He came from a poor family, but he wanted to be rich. He was always saying 'One day I will ride in my carriage.' That is like saying, today, 'I will own a Rolls-Royce.' When he grew up, Arkwright became a barber, but he knew he could not make a fortune that way. Preston was a cotton town, so he decided to invent a spinning machine.

Many years before, a man called Lewis Paul had tried spinning with rollers. In spinning, you must not only twist the thread, but stretch it. Lewis Paul did so by passing it through two pairs of rollers, one pair going faster than the other. His machine had failed, but Arkwright thought he could succeed. He was not a craftsman, so he asked a carpenter and a clockmaker to help him. Soon, he could think of nothing but his machine. Sometimes, when he was shaving a customer, he had an idea. He then rushed off to his workshop, leaving the man sitting in the chair: one half of his face was shaved, and the other half was still covered with soap.

Mrs. Arkwright was worried. She thought her husband was going to lose all his customers, so one day she burnt his machine. Arkwright was furious. 'How much housekeeping money do I give you?' he shouted. 'Five shillings a week,' she answered. 'I promise you,' he said, 'that you will always have your

Cromford mill

five shillings a week. You will never starve.'

As we have seen, Lancashire people hated spinning machines, so, like Hargreaves, Arkwright moved to Nottingham. Here he was lucky. He met two rich stocking manufacturers, Jedediah Strutt and Samuel Need. They were already producing woollen and silk stockings, and wanted to make cotton ones as well. No-one, though, could spin cotton thread that was good enough. However, it looked as if Arkwright might, so they made him a partner in their firm. The machine was still far from perfect, and as time went by, Need grew impatient. He used to stump about, holding up some of Arkwright's thread, saying, 'Fine stuff this, to make a man ride in his carriage, all bumps and burs: fine stuff this.' Arkwright was not discouraged. Again he found a carpenter to help him. They slept in the same room, and if one of them had an idea in the night, he woke the other before he had time to forget. They then worked at it together. In the end, they had a machine that spun a smooth, strong, even thread. It was just what Need and Strutt wanted for stockings, and it was perfect for the warp threads in cloth as well.

The only problem left was that the machine needed a lot of power. They had to leave Nottingham, and build mills in the Pennines, where there were fast-flowing streams to drive water wheels. Because of this, Arkwright's invention was called the 'water frame'.

Soon, Arkwright left his partners and built his own mill at Cromford, the village we visited earlier. He built other mills as well. When he died, he had two and a half million pounds, and that would be worth thirty times as much today. The king knighted him, and he was made High Sheriff of Derbyshire. The humble barber had come a long way. He rode in his carriage, of course: in fact, he had several. However, he never forgot that his wife had burnt his first machine, and he punished her by keeping his promise! Every week, without fail, he gave her five shillings housekeeping money.

a water frame

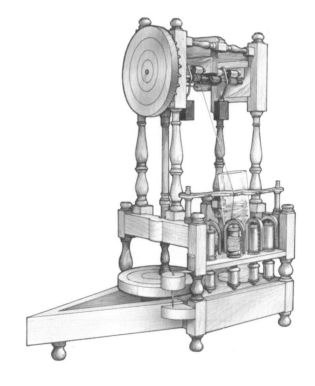

27

3 A Cotton Manufacturer in the Eighteenth Century

Francis Hookham is a cotton manufacturer. He lives in a splendid house in Manchester, and obviously he is a rich man. He has problems, though.

'My first worry is bringing my cotton from Liverpool. The Liverpool merchants unload it from the ships, and then it has to go into barges. In the estuary of the Mersey they often have trouble with the tides and headwinds. At Runcorn the boats join the Duke of Bridgewater's canal. The canal sometimes freezes in winter, and sometimes runs dry in summer. All the year round it is trying to carry more traffic than it should.

'Once the cotton is here, my men put it in my warehouse until we need it. I send some of it to my mill in the Pennines where they spin it into warp threads with water frames. That is the only part of the business which goes well. Most of my workers are scattered over southern Lancashire, and parts of Cheshire and Derbyshire. I have a depôt in many a village – a room in a pub, or something like that. We carry the cotton there on pack animals. Every Saturday, the spinners come and collect what they need from my agent. The next week, they bring back the thread they have spun and collect more cotton. My agent pays them for their work, of course.

'There are some lively arguments, I can tell you. The agent weighs the raw cotton, and the spinner must return the same weight of thread. Some of my agents are not very careful, though, and the spinners steal my cotton. There are good workers, who make fine, strong thread, but others make it too soft, too coarse, or, what's worse, quite uneven, and full of bumps and burs. Weavers can't use it, but if my agent refuses to pay, there is dreadful trouble. You can't rely on spinners to finish their work, either. Most of them are housewives, with a lot to do in their homes. At harvest time, the farmers need them, and they do no spinning for weeks. That is bad, when I have customers waiting for my goods. Lots of spinners are just lazy. They gossip all Monday and Tuesday, spin very little on Wednesday, and then try and do a week's work on Thursday and Friday. I pity their poor children on those days.' *'What about the weavers?'* 'They are even worse than the spinners. They come to the depôt on Saturday, as well, and my agent weighs out some yarn. It piles up in my warehouse, and I just cannot find weavers to take it all. I have tried paying them higher wages, but that's no good. If I give them more for each piece of cloth, they just do less work. Most of them have a bit of land, and a cow or a pig. They will cheerfully leave their looms to attend to them. They spend a lot of time drinking, as well. I think they are even more dishonest than the spinners, and steal a lot of my yarn. A good agent can always catch a thief, but not many of my agents are sharp enough. Another of their tricks is to make a good job of the few feet at the end of their roll of cloth, but take no care of the rest. What looks good work is often nothing of the kind.

'Well, in the end the finished cloth comes back to my warehouse. It is a dirty grey colour and we have to bleach it. That's a game, I can tell you. We soak it in water mixed with wood ash, we soak it in sour milk, and we peg it out in the bleach fields for the sun to do its work – that's when we have any sun. Usually, it takes six weeks. When it is pure white, we put it on pack animals and it goes all the way to London. The people down there print it. They know what colours and what patterns are in fashion, you see.' *'How far does a bit of cotton travel after it reaches Liverpool?'* 'That's hard to say, but some of it, two hundred miles, before it leaves my hands.' *'Why don't you bring all your workpeople into a factory?'* 'They would never come. No, they must have their freedom to stop work when they like, for a drink or a gossip. They have no sense of discipline.' *'But you have a mill in the Pennines.'* 'And do you know how I find the workers? I pay a few adults more than I can afford to persuade them to live in the wilds. For the rest, I have to go to the workhouses in the big cities like London and Birmingham. They give me orphan children as apprentices, and I send them out to the mill. As soon as they are twenty-one they can leave, and leave they do. It is really impossible to make people work regular hours in a factory.'

4 A Cotton Factory in 1835

Mr. Orrell in his factory

A Cotton Factory in 1835

We will now go forward in time to 1835, and visit a cotton mill near Stockport, belonging to Mr. Orrell. He is very proud of his mill and is pleased to show us round.

The building is three hundred feet long, and fifty feet wide. It towers above us, for it is seven storeys high. We go into the ground floor. The noise is overpowering. 'These are my power looms,' shouts Mr. Orrell. 'I have a thousand of them. We have to put them on the ground floor, or they would shake the building to pieces.' The machines are in straight lines, and each one is working perfectly. Above them are shafts with pulleys. From the pulleys, big leather belts run down to the looms and drive them.

We go to a corner of a room where there is a staircase and a lift. We take the stairs, because the lift is for materials. The machines on the next floor are quieter. They make a singing noise which is quite pleasant. 'These are my throstles,' says Mr. Orrell. 'We call them that, because they sound like song thrushes. My father used water frames. These spin warp just as the water frames did, and work on the same lines. They are much better, though. For one thing, they are made of iron, not wood.' The second floor is the same as the first floor.

The third floor is for preparation. 'We bring the bales of cotton here and open them. The cotton is packed very tightly, so we have to loosen it with scutching machines. We also have to take out things

like stones. The slaves in America who pack the cotton aren't too careful.' *'I thought the cotton came from Egypt and Turkey.'* 'A bit still does, but we could never have enough from there. They tell me that all the cotton cloth made in Lancashire last year would wrap round the equator eleven times.'

SCENE ON A COTTON PLANTATION. GATHERING COTTON.

'Before spinning, we have to comb the cotton. A woman wouldn't curl her hair before she had combed it, would she? Next, we draw it. Here you can see the drawing frames at work.' These machines are making the cotton into a long, loose roll, like a thin sausage, miles long. 'Now it is ready for spinning. Some of it goes down to the throstles, which you saw just now. The rest goes upstairs, to be spun into weft.'

printing cloth

On the fourth and fifth floors, Mr. Orrell has spinning machines called mules. Each one has a carriage, and a man pulls it forward about six feet. As he does so, hundreds of spindles turn busily, each twisting a thread of cotton so fine that it looks like cobweb. When the carriage is right forward, the man lets go, and it runs back of its own accord. The twisting stops, because the machine is winding up the length that it has just spun. 'These fine spinners are my most skilled men,' explains Mr. Orrell. 'They earn an enormous amount — about thirty shillings a week. They are a proud lot, too. Nearly every pub has a room for them with "Mule Spinners Only" on the door.'

We now go right to the top of the building. 'Here we do our finishing. Nasty smell, isn't there? That's chloride of lime. It's grand stuff for bleaching. We can make new cloth perfectly white in less than a day. Last of all, we print the cloth, and it is ready for the customer.' *'You don't send it to London for printing?'* 'We know as much about fashion as the London people, and with my new machines I can print the cotton at a fraction of the price, and in a fraction of the time that it took before. I buy bales of raw cotton, dyestuffs, and a few things like that, and I sell the finished cloth. All the work is done in my factory. My grandfather had spinners and weavers scattered over three counties. I don't know how he managed.' *'Do you have any problems with transport?'* 'It used to be hard bringing the cotton from Liverpool by canal, but we have a railway now. I hear

they are building another to London. That will be a great help.'

'Do you have trouble persuading people to work in your factory?' 'Most of the workers are women and children, as you saw. They do as they are told. The men are all highly skilled. I can afford to pay them good wages. They don't like the factory discipline though, especially when we are on a sixteen-hour day. We often work late. It is lucky we have gas lighting.'

Mr. Orrell now takes us down to the basement. Here two mighty steam engines are pounding and hissing away. 'Each engine is eighty horse power. I have two, because that gives a more even drive.' (If Mr. Orrell had known about bicycles, he could have explained that having one engine would be like riding a bicycle with one leg.)

Outside again, Mr. Orrell points proudly to his chimney. 'It is over 300 feet high. When it was new, and before we lit the fires, I took some of my friends up in the builders' hoist. I had a table up there, with some cakes and wine, as an extra surprise for them.'

33

5 Samuel Crompton

Samuel Crompton

Some of the most useful machines Mr. Orrell had in his cotton factory were his mules. The mule had been invented in the 1770s by Samuel Crompton.

Crompton was born in 1755, in Lancashire. His father had a farm, but it was not big enough to give the family a living. Like many others, they made up their income by spinning and weaving. Young Samuel had to do his share, and when he was sixteen his father gave him a spinning jenny. Samuel did not like his machine. As we have seen, jenny thread was soft, and full of 'bumps and burs'. Samuel, though, had heard about Arkwright's water frame, which used rollers. 'How would it be,' he thought, 'if I used the best ideas in both the spinning jenny and the water frame? I will make a machine better than either of them.' He did not find it easy, because he was not a mechanic. However, he was lucky in another way. The family lived at Hall i' th' Wood, a rambling old house with a big attic, which was just the place for Samuel to make his experiments.

After five years the machine was finished. Because it was part jenny and part water frame, Samuel called it a 'mule'. He took a pound of cotton and he spun some No. 40 thread. That meant he made 40 hanks from his pound of cotton, each 840 yards long. In all, it was nearly five miles of yarn. That may sound a lot,

mule spinning

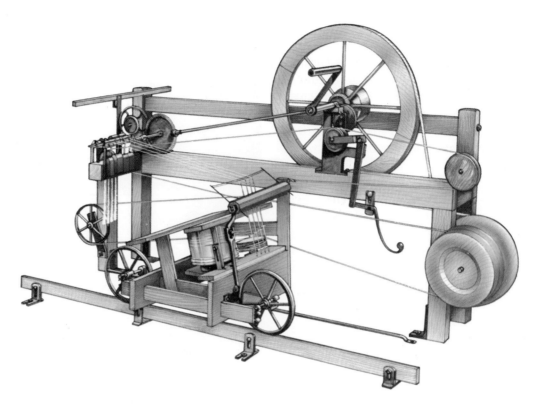

a mule

but any good spinner using a wheel or a jenny could do as well. What pleased Samuel, though, was that his yarn was smooth and strong, with no bumps and burs at all. The man who bought it was pleased, and a little puzzled. He was even more puzzled when Samuel came back later with some No. 60 yarn. In the end he was spinning No. 80 yarn, which is twice as fine as No. 40. Nothing like it had ever been seen before.

People now realised that Crompton must have a very special machine. Lots of visitors came to Hall i' th' Wood. Old Mrs. Crompton, she was by now a widow, tried to turn them away, but it was no use. Some even climbed the trees by the Hall, and looked through the attic windows with telescopes. Samuel wanted peace and quiet, so in the end he said that anyone could come and look at his machine on payment of one guinea. Several did so, and then went away and made mules of their own.

Later, other inventors improved the mule. Samuel's first machine spun forty threads at a time. Those in Orrell's factory each spun one thousand. Samuel worked his machine by hand, but the big machines needed steam power. By the 1840s most mules were 'self acting', which meant they worked all by themselves. A skilled mechanic had to stay with

them in case they went wrong, but the only other workers were a few children. Some of them were 'piecers' who joined any threads that broke: others were 'scavengers', who cleaned up the cotton dust. Samuel, as we have seen, was pleased to spin No. 80. The later mules spun No. 350. They made 165 miles of thread from each pound of cotton. No-one has ever invented a machine to spin better yarn than the mule. The only advantage modern machines have is that they are quicker.

What happened to Crompton? Between them, his visitors paid him about £50, and he used it to build a bigger mule for himself. He went on working in the attic at Hall i' th' Wood, but he did not earn a lot of money. In the meantime, men who had copied his machine were making fortunes. Some of Crompton's friends thought this was unfair, so they persuaded Parliament to give him £5,000. By now he was an old man, so he gave the money to his sons to start a business. They went bankrupt, and their father died in poverty.

What happened to all the women who had been working in their homes with spinning jennies? No-one wanted their yarn any more. The families had to manage as best they could without the wives' earnings.

6 Edmund Cartwright

After the invention of the water frame and the mule, there was so much yarn being spun, that it was hard to find enough weavers to make it into cloth. Employers had to pay weavers such high wages, that men like William Hobbs could afford expensive furniture for their homes. To show off, some went round with £5 notes stuck in their hat bands. Remember £5 of their money would be worth £150 today.

Then, in 1784, a clergyman called the Rev. Edmund Cartwright went on holiday to the fashionable little town of Matlock, in Derbyshire. At one of the parties, he met some cotton manufacturers from Manchester. They talked about the problems they had with their weavers. Cartwright knew nothing about making cotton cloth, but he said, 'You have spinning machines. Why doesn't someone invent a weaving machine?' They all laughed. 'Spinning is not too complicated,' one explained. 'Weaving is far more difficult. No-one could make a machine to do that.'

Cartwright had never seen a loom in his life, and he was no mechanic. Still, like many clergymen in those days, he had plenty of spare time. He decided to make a power loom, that is, a loom driven by a steam engine. A year later, he had finished his first machine. Sure enough, it worked, but it was clumsy, while the cloth it made was so coarse that it was only fit to make things like sacks. Cartwright now had a look at some ordinary looms, and was amazed to see how much better they were than his own. He studied them carefully, and copied many of their parts. Three years later, he had made a much better power loom, one that would weave good cloth. However, the machine had to be stopped so often that it was no faster than a handloom. If you had to adjust the chain of your

a handloom

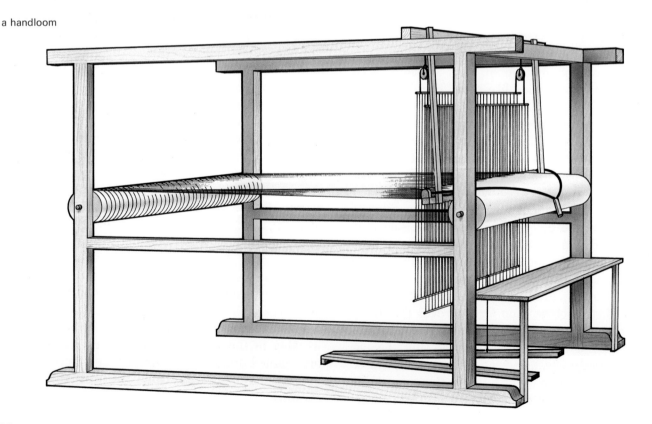

power looms

bicycle every hundred yards, you would find it quicker to walk. It was a bit like that.

In the end, Cartwright lost £30,000 on his loom, an enormous sum for those days. He then gave it up, but went on to make other inventions. None of them were much good. In the end, he did best as a farmer: he was never a good clergyman.

It was a long time before anyone else tried to make a power loom. However, in the 1820s a man called Horrocks succeeded. A boy or girl of fifteen could look after two of his looms and make four times as much cloth as a handloom weaver. It was Horrocks's machines that Mr. Orrell had in his factory.

We will now see what three different people thought of the power loom, and, indeed, all the new machines in the factories.

First, let us listen to a handloom weaver. 'When I was young, I could earn twenty-five or thirty shillings a week. Life was easy, too. I worked steadily enough from Tuesday to Friday, but I rarely did anything on Monday. Saturday was an easy day. I just went to the depôt to deliver my cloth, and collect more yarn. Now I can only earn seven shillings, and have to work fourteen hours a day, six days a week, even for that. My wages barely buy us enough bread. We can never afford new clothes. In the old days, my wife and I used to go out to the tea gardens or the theatre every Saturday. We always went to church on Sundays. Now, we cannot afford any amusements, and our clothes are so ragged that we are ashamed to go to church.'

An employer has something different to say. 'The handloom weavers are lazy and dishonest. When we employed them, they never did more than two or three good days' work in the week. I could not rely on them to finish their jobs to time. Many of them used to steal my yarn. Now, my machines work regular hours. I can tell my customers exactly when they will have their goods. No-one can steal from me, because all the work is done in my factory. We make twenty times as much as before. We have to sell the cloth a lot cheaper, but I still make handsome profits for myself. I can pay my skilled men good wages, too.'

Lastly, let us hear from a poor housewife. 'Now there are factories, cottons are wonderfully cheap. I can buy cloth in all sorts of pretty colours and patterns for less than a shilling a yard. I make my own dresses and I look as smart as any grand lady did thirty years ago. I can buy plain calico at threepence a yard for the children. That means I can afford to give them a change of clothing, so it is easy enough to keep them clean. My grandmother used to put her children to bed while she did the washing, and there they stayed until their clothes were dried.'

7 James Watt

None of Mr. Orrell's machines would have been any use without his two great steam engines. We must learn something about them.

The first man to build a steam engine that worked at all well was Thomas Newcomen, in 1709. It pumped water out of coal mines. At the top was a huge beam that rocked, like a seesaw. One end worked the pump, and at the other end was a piston in a cylinder. First, the weight of the pump rods pulled up the piston. At the same time, the boiler filled the cylinder with steam. Next, a valve cut off the steam and a jet of cold water shot into the cylinder. This condensed the steam, that is, cooled it, and turned it back into water. There was now a vacuum in the cylinder, so the weight of the atmosphere drove down the piston. This, in turn, pulled up the pump and sucked water out of the mine.

Newcomen's engines were useful, but they had a serious drawback. They burnt such a lot of fuel that only owners of coal mines could afford to run them. A man who had, for example, a copper mine, a cotton factory or an iron works badly needed a more economical engine. The man who invented it was James Watt.

James Watt's first experiment

Watt was born at Greenock, in Scotland, in 1736. He trained to be an instrument mechanic, and took a job at Glasgow University. He had to look after all their scientific instruments. One day, a model Newcomen engine went wrong, and Watt repaired it. He was puzzled because it burnt a great deal of fuel, but did very little work. Watt was friendly with one of the University professors, Dr. Black. Black explained that the engine used such a lot of fuel because it had to heat the cylinder at every stroke. Much fuel would be saved if the cylinder stayed hot. But how was it possible to cool steam inside a hot cylinder? It would be like making ice-cream in the oven. Watt puzzled

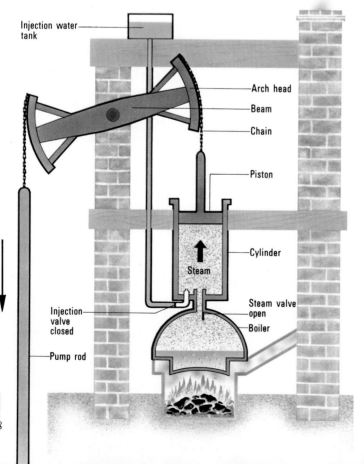

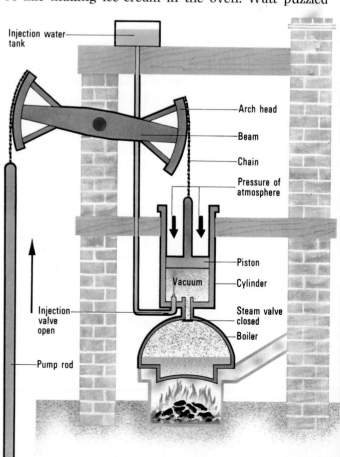

and puzzled and then, one day, when he was out for a walk, the answer suddenly came to him. He made a separate chamber which he called a condenser. When the moment came to condense the steam, a valve opened, and the steam rushed into the condenser. Here a jet of water cooled it, and made a vacuum, so that the weight of the atmosphere drove down the piston just as before. The piston remained hot, instead of being cooled and heated at every stroke. The result was that the engine burnt a lot less fuel.

So far, Watt had only made a model. He wanted, of course, to build a full-sized engine, but he did not have the money. Luckily for him, he met a rich man from Birmingham called Matthew Boulton. Boulton owned the Soho works, a factory that produced metal goods. He employed many skilled craftsmen who were able to make the complicated parts that Watt needed. Soon Boulton and Watt were producing pumping engines. Men who had tin and copper mines in Cornwall were especially pleased, because they had to bring all their coal from South Wales, and it was expensive.

Watt now wanted to make an engine that would drive machinery. He worked hard at his plans, and in the end he succeeded. These Boulton and Watt engines were a great help to people with factories. Mr. Orrell explains: 'Any mill needs 100 horse power to drive its machinery. We have water wheels as powerful as that, but there are not many places you can put them. You need large, fast-flowing streams to drive them. Before the steam engine, people like Arkwright and Strutt built their mills up in the Pennine valleys. You can imagine how hard that made transport. Besides, it was almost impossible to persuade workers to live in those out of the way places. Thanks to the steam engine, I was able to build my mill down here in Stockport. Lots of my friends have mills in and around Manchester. There is no problem finding workers in the big towns. Also, transport is easy, especially since the railways came. We are very grateful to James Watt.'

Watt was, indeed, a great inventor. Unfortunately, he was a mean, miserable man. But for Boulton, other men would have stolen his ideas, and he would have died a poor man, like so many inventors. As it was, he made a fortune, but he would never help the firm with his own money. It was always Boulton who found the cash. Watt was too selfish even to give his own son a large enough allowance. The young man knew better than ask his father for money. He went to Boulton, who gave him all he needed.

The picture on page 38 is of a Newcomen pump; the picture below shows James Watt's improved model.

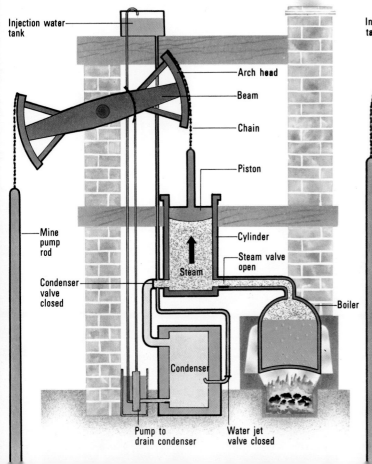

Injection water tank — Arch head — Beam — Chain — Piston — Mine pump rod — Condenser valve closed — Steam — Cylinder — Steam valve open — Boiler — Condenser — Pump to drain condenser — Water jet valve closed

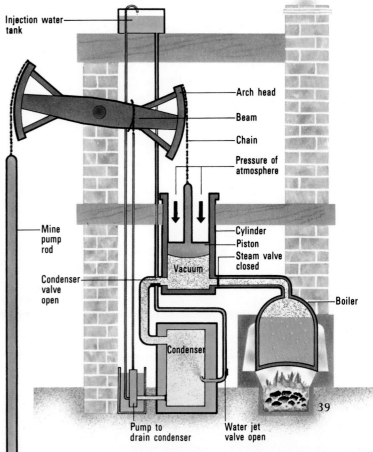

Injection water tank — Arch head — Beam — Chain — Pressure of atmosphere — Mine pump rod — Condenser valve open — Vacuum — Cylinder — Piston — Steam valve closed — Boiler — Condenser — Pump to drain condenser — Water jet valve open

The Village becomes a Town

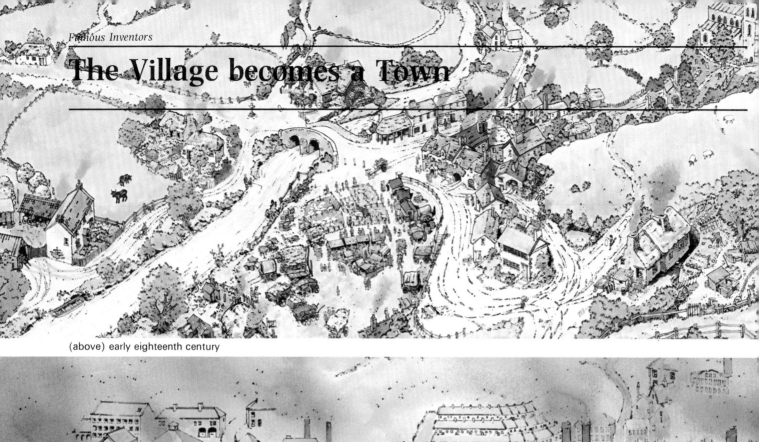

(above) early eighteenth century

mid-nineteenth century

(above) late eighteenth century

Chapter Three Transport

1 Transport in the Early Eighteenth Century

Until about two hundred years ago, most roads were like farm tracks. That was all they needed to be, since few people travelled long distances. Farmers drove their carts to and from their fields, and were happy to lumber along at two miles an hour. They did not worry if the roads were rough.

It was the duty of the people in each village to take care of their own roads. In 1555 Parliament made a law to say what they should do. The local farmers had to choose one of their number to be Surveyor of Highways. He could call on his poor neighbours to work on the roads for six days a year, without wages; he could make richer people lend their horses, carts and tools, free of charge.

The system did not work well. We can see why if we watch a gang road-mending. The Surveyor has sent for five men, and they have come most unwillingly. They lounge about and do as little as they can. A farmer was supposed to send some picks, some shovels and a horse and cart, but they arrived very late. There are not enough tools, while some of them are broken. The cart is worn out: the horse is old and tired. The Surveyor is not a trained Surveyor at all, but an ordinary farmer. He is angry because he has had to leave his own work, and he knows nothing about road building. His main problem is to drain away the water that makes the ground soft under the road. In some parts he has made the road very high in the middle, like the roof of a house. This lets the rain run off, but carts must keep to the centre of the road, otherwise they are in danger of tipping sideways. Even so, there is one patch that is always giving way, however much stone they put on it. Here the Surveyor decides to make the road as one switch-back after another, with a drain running across it at the bottom of each dip. It is lucky no-one wants to drive a cart at more than two miles an hour.

There were a few people who needed to travel long distances. You can imagine what it was like to go, perhaps, a hundred miles along cart tracks, and not

very good ones at that. There were stage coaches, but they ran only in summer. They had to be built very strongly, without springs, which meant they were most uncomfortable. It took a coach about ten days to go from London to Edinburgh. The only way to travel at all quickly was on horseback.

Some people had goods to carry. Woollen manufacturers, for example, needed to send sacks of wool and bales of cloth all over the country. They might use stage waggons, but they went at only half the pace of the coaches, and they, too, could only travel in summer. As with people, it was best for goods to go on horses. However, a pack-horse can only carry just over a hundredweight. If he has a cart on a good road, a horse can pull two tons.

The only way to move heavy goods long distances was by river. Even here there were problems. A Severn boatman will tell you about his work. 'My vessel is called a "trow". She is built like a proper ship, and is about sixty feet long and twenty wide. She has one big, square sail, though we can only use that when the wind is right behind us. We go up the Severn as far as Shrewsbury, but often we have to stay there for

days, or even weeks. The river runs dry and is too shallow. Sooner or later, though, down comes the rain, and we have a "fresh" which is a good rush of water. It will carry us merrily all down to Gloucester. Below Gloucester life is a bit easier, because there is a high tide every fortnight. We get by as best we can, with the current, the wind and the tides. They can't be against us all the time. They are often enough, though, and then my mates and I have to walk along the bank, pulling the boat. That's hard, slow work, I can tell you.'

One great problem was how to carry coal to London. Many people lived in the capital and there were not enough forests near at hand, to supply wood for fuel. Luckily, the Durham coalfield is close to the sea. Hundreds of little ships called brigs used to sail to the River Tyne for cargoes of coal. They carried it to London and, indeed, to places all along the coast as far as Lyme Regis, in Dorset. They were tough ships, with tough crews. The government was glad they were there because, in time of war, they pressganged the sailors into the Royal Navy.

2 Turnpike Roads

John Macadam

Thomas Telford

In the 1660s the people of Stanton in Hertfordshire were in despair. Every day large waggons came through their village, loaded with grain for London. As we saw in the last chapter, village folk did not expect many strangers to use their roads. At Stanton, though, strangers used them a great deal and damaged them badly. The roads became so bad that the magistrates fined the inhabitants and ordered them to work twelve days a year on their roads, instead of six. The people thought that the men who ruined the roads should pay for them, so they complained to Parliament. Parliament agreed with them. It allowed them to put up a toll gate and collect money from passing traffic to pay for repairs.

After 1700 there was more and more traffic everywhere, so many places had the same problem as Stanton. When that happened, important local people, like farmers and landowners, joined together to form a 'Turnpike Trust'. Parliament then gave them permission to put up gates and collect tolls, just as it had done for Stanton. The money paid for new roads called 'turnpike roads'. They had the name 'turnpike' from the 'pikes' or 'spikes' they put on top of their gates to stop people on horseback from jumping over.

By 1830 there were about 1,000 Turnpike Trusts in Britain. Most of them had about ten or twelve miles of road, though some had many more. The Bristol Trust looked after 173 miles of road.

Turnpike Trusts expected a lot of traffic, so they employed Surveyors who knew how to build roads properly. One such man was Thomas Telford. Telford prepared the bed of a new road carefully, making sure that every inch was properly drained. Roads collapse if the soil under them is wet and soggy. Next, he laid a good foundation of large stones. On top of those he put a layer of gravel, to make a smooth surface. Telford's most famous road was the one he built for the Government, from London to Holyhead. Holyhead was important, because it was there that the passenger ships sailed to Dublin. Telford built bridges as well. His most famous is the handsome suspension bridge over the Menai Straits. He was so pleased when it was finished that he kept riding backwards and forwards over it.

Another important road builder was John Macadam. Like Telford he drained his road bed carefully, but he did not put down heavy, expensive foundations. First came a layer of medium-sized stones and then a layer of smaller ones. The traffic finished the work. It ground the stones together making a fine powder that filled the gaps, and then pounded the road down so that the surface was waterproof. Macadam showed that as long as the ground below the road was dry, there was no need for foundations. His roads did not last as long as Telford's, but they were a lot cheaper.

Macadam employed women and old men to break stones. Doing it his way was not hard work. You sat down, and used a little hammer, with a long handle. A woman could crack as many stones like that, as two strong men using sledge hammers. It was important to make the stones the right size. Macadam told his workers that a stone should just fit in the mouth, so one day he was angry to see an old man making his stones much too large. He soon found the reason. The old man had no teeth.

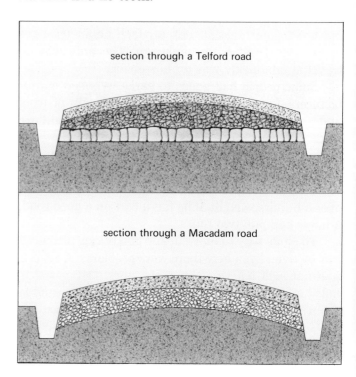

section through a Telford road

section through a Macadam road

When coach owners saw the new roads, they made much better coaches. They were light, well sprung, and comfortable. They would rattle along at twenty miles an hour and keep an average speed of twelve miles an hour. People could now go to places in a fifth of the time it had taken before. London to Edinburgh, for example, now took two days, instead of ten.

Coaching inns became important. It was at an inn that you bought your ticket, waited for the coach, had a meal, or slept the night. It was also the place where coachmen collected and dropped mail. Each inn, then, did the work of a railway station, hotel and post office. The most valuable job, though, was to change the horses. The ostlers had the four fresh horses ready before the coach arrived and could change them, with all their harness and buckles, in less than two minutes.

45

Turnpike Roads

a scene at a tollgate

3 Canals

In 1760, Francis, Duke of Bridgewater was an un-happy man. He was deeply in love with a young lady, but she did not like him at all. He felt he had to do something to help him forget how miserable he was. It so happened that he owned some coal mines at the village of Worsley in Lancashire. He sold the coal in Manchester. Unfortunately, there was a lot of water in the mines, which made them dangerous. Also, it was difficult to take the coal to Manchester, even though it was only seven miles away. There was no river, and the roads were bad, so they had to use pack-horses.

Then the Duke had an idea. Why not build a canal from Worsley to Manchester, filling it with water from the mines? He would drain his mines and have good transport for his coal, at the same time. But how was the Duke to build the canal? People knew about improving rivers by dredging them, making locks and building towpaths, but hardly anyone knew about canals. However, the Duke heard of a man called James Brindley. Brindley was a clever millwright. He knew how to make such things as mill dams, sluice gates, and leats. Leats are the channels which take water to the wheel. Brindley had no education, so when he had a problem he did not sit down with a pen

the Duke of Bridgewater

and paper. Instead, he went to bed and lay staring at the ceiling until he had the answer. It was Brindley who helped the Duke build his canal.

You can see from the map, that the canal ran from Worsley to Barton. Here it met the valley of the River Irwell. This was difficult, so the Duke asked Brindley what to do. Brindley built him an aqueduct over the river. You can see it in the picture. Later, aqueducts became common enough, but the one at Barton was the first and people were amazed. They were fascinated to see one boat sailing over the head of another.

When the Bridgewater Canal was finished, the people of Manchester were able to buy coal at half the price they had paid before.

Now other people wanted canals. One was Josiah Wedgwood, who made expensive pottery at Etruria, in Staffordshire. He used china clay which came from Cornwall by sea to the Mersey, and flintstone, which came from near Hull. He badly wanted a canal to join the rivers Trent and Mersey so he, and some other men, asked Brindley to build one. Brindley agreed, and in 1777 the Grand Trunk Canal, as they called it, was opened. It was much more difficult to make than the Bridgewater Canal, for it was 100 miles long, it had 76 locks and five aqueducts. There was also a tunnel two miles long at Harecastle. It had no towpath, so the boatmen had to lie down on boards that stuck out from the barges and 'walk' with their feet against the sides of the tunnel.

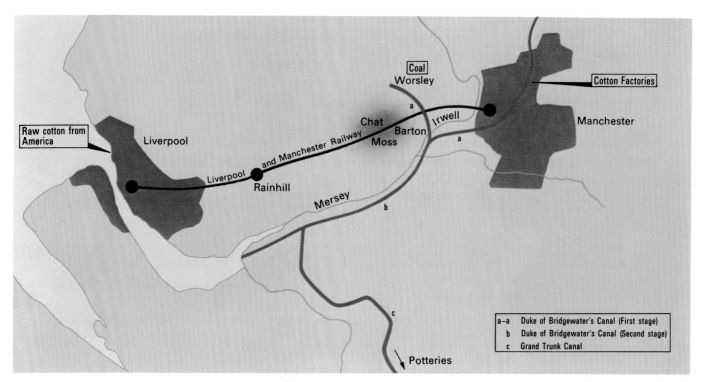

the Bridgewater canal and the canal system

Brindley died of work and worry, five years before the Grand Trunk was finished. Many other men were to die as well, from accidents. The work was so dangerous that two navvies were killed for every mile of canal made in this country.

Soon, other canals were built to join the Grand Trunk to the River Severn, and to the River Thames. You can see from the map how many places they joined. Then, in the 1790s, canals were built all over Great Britain, except where there were mountains. Nearly every big town had a canal to carry its heavy goods, especially coal.

There were problems with canals. Some of the boatmen were expert thieves. For example, they could open a sack of sugar, take out a few handfuls, replace them with earth, and then stitch up the sack, so that no-one knew it had been touched. The customer was the first to find out, for the small amount of earth, spoiled all the sugar. The weather made difficulties. In a long, hot summer, canals ran dry. In cold weather, they froze. Also, the boats were slow. The horses just plodded along at three miles an hour, so it was no use going by canal, if you were in a hurry. Passengers went by stage coach instead.

However, canals were ideal for heavy goods. One horse, pulling a canal barge, can move as much coal as 400 pack animals.

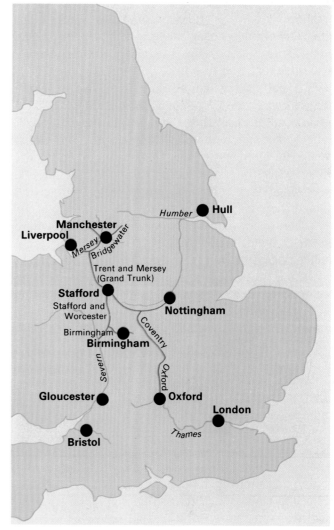

4 Early Railways and Locomotives

Have you ever tried to push a wheelbarrow? If so, you will know how difficult it is when the ground is soft, or when the wheel keeps hitting stones. However, if you put down a plank you can trundle your wheelbarrow along it quite easily. That is the idea behind the railway.

In the sixteenth century, men who owned mines and quarries laid wooden rails for their waggons. To keep the rails the right distance apart they nailed them to sleepers. To stop the sleepers from moving they packed stones between them, which they called 'ballast'. A modern railway is still made from rails, sleepers and ballast.

By the eighteenth century there were many waggon ways, some of them as much as twenty miles long. Their builders soon saw it was important to keep them as level as possible. In some places they made embankments, and in others, cuttings and tunnels.

To pull the waggons they used horses. On a waggon way, one horse could draw eight tonnes. On a bad road he could only manage a tonne and a half. Where there was a downhill slope, the waggon ran by itself. The man had a ride, keeping his hand on the brake, while the horse walked behind. At the top of a steep slope, they sometimes put a steam engine, that hauled the waggons up with a rope.

There were many waggon ways on the Durham coalfield. They carried the coal from the mines to the collier brigs, that you read about on page 45.

The trouble with wooden rails was that they wore out quickly, so in the late eighteenth century, they made them of iron. Some of the early iron rails were known as 'plates', because they were wide and flat We still call a man who puts down railway lines a 'platelayer'.

While some men were building waggon ways, others were making steam engines. The early steam engines were enormous and had to be bolted to the ground. They pumped water and drove machinery. Then, one day in 1784, the Vicar of Redruth in Cornwall was coming home in the dark when he heard a puffing and snorting. Next, he saw a dreadful monster, breathing smoke and fire, and he fled, quite sure the devil was after him. What he had seen was a steam

locomotive – that is, a steam engine that moves itself. It was the work of William Murdoch.

Another inventor was Richard Trevithick. His first steam locomotive went on the road, like Murdoch's, but he soon made one that ran on rails. It was for a coal mine in South Wales. He also amused the crowds in London with his 'Catch Me Who Can'. At first, the rails broke because they were not meant for anything as heavy as a locomotive. However, engineers made stronger rails, and the steam railway was born.

Perhaps the most famous railway inventor was George Stephenson. He built a number of locomotives for coal mines, and then came his big chance. In 1820 a woollen mill in the little town of Darlington burnt down. Many people lost their jobs, and a man called Edward Pease felt sorry for them. He thought that if he could build a railway to carry coal from the mines in South Durham it would help people start factories both in Darlington and in Stockton. The story goes that Stephenson tramped to Darlington to call on Pease. Pease nearly sent the stranger away, but he suddenly changed his mind and saw him. Pease was so impressed that he asked Stephenson to engineer the railway.

The Stockton to Darlington line opened in 1825. Above Darlington they used horses, stationary engines and gravity inclines, but between Darlington and Stockton they used locomotives.

the opening of the Stockton to Darlington line in 1825

Trevithick's locomotive

Stephenson did not know how far apart to put the rails, so he measured the local waggon ways to see what gauge they were. He found that, on average, they were 4′ 8½″, so that was the measurement he used. It is a very odd one, but most other railways in Britain copied it, and so did railways all over the world.

Many folk did not like the new line. Stephenson had to change the route he had planned because the Duke of Cleveland said the trains would drive away his foxes. People who owned plantations of pine trees were angry because the locomotives sent out showers of sparks. When the engines had no trucks to pull, their drivers went at top speed, which was twelve miles an hour. This frightened any horses that were near, so the drivers were ordered to go at no more than five miles an hour. Most people, though, were glad to have the cheap coal the railway brought them.

5 The Liverpool and Manchester Railway

On September 15th, 1830, a train set out from Liverpool to Manchester. It carried a lot of important people, including the Duke of Wellington, and a cabinet minister, William Huskisson. It was the official opening of the railway and Huskisson was delighted. He had done a lot to encourage the building of the line. The train stopped in a cutting, and Huskisson could not resist getting out to chat to people in other carriages. He was talking to the Duke of Wellington when someone shouted, 'The Rocket is coming!' Sure enough that famous locomotive was hurtling along the other track. Huskisson jumped to the side of the cutting, but did not feel safe. He jumped back again and tried to climb into the Duke's carriage. He was too late. The 'Rocket' ran into him, breaking his leg, and he died a little later. No-one was able to enjoy themselves after a tragedy like that. None the less, September 15th, 1830, was still an important day, for it saw the opening of the first modern railway. Why had it been built?

The Liverpool and Manchester Railway

In the early part of the nineteenth century, Manchester became an important town for the manufacture of cotton cloth. The raw cotton came from America to Liverpool, and then went the thirty miles from Liverpool to Manchester by barge. In summer, the canals sometimes ran dry and in winter they sometimes froze. What was worse, their owners charged high tolls.

In 1822, the merchants of Liverpool thought they had had enough trouble from the waterways so they decided to build a railway to Manchester. They formed a company and chose George Stephenson to be their engineer.

Stephenson's first task was to plan the exact route for the line, which meant he had to make a survey. Surveyors have to work carefully, with complicated instruments, and it is important to leave them in peace. Unfortunately, there were many people who did not want the railway, including two noblemen. They all objected, just as we do today if there is to be a motor-

the Olive Mount cutting

way close to our homes. They said that fields anywhere near the line would become black and useless, that cows would no longer give milk, and that sheep would no longer have lambs. Ignorant people believed these stories. Farmers turned bulls and dogs on the railway men. The two noblemen paid thugs to attack them. Instead of proper surveyors, Stephenson had to employ professional boxers! In the end, though, they finished their work, and Parliament passed an Act giving the company permission to build its line.

Now there were other problems. The people of Liverpool refused to have a noisy railway, so Stephenson had to build a tunnel, over a mile long, under the town. The workmen met a lot of water which threatened to drown them. There was also soft sand which fell on them, nearly burying them alive. However, engineers had learnt a lot about making tunnels from the canal builders, so they finished it eventually.

Near Manchester there was a marsh called Chat Moss. It was impossible to dig through it, and if you tipped in stone it just vanished away. Stephenson told his men to lay hurdles on the moss and pile stones on them. Then came more hurdles, and more stones, so that it was like making sandwiches, one on top of the other. The hurdles stopped the stones escaping, and although many layers sank into the marsh, in the end there was a good, firm bed for the railway.

a train crosses Chat Moss

The Directors of the Company had still not decided what was to pull their trains. Many of them thought they should have a number of stationary engines, drawing the trucks with ropes. Stephenson said they should have locomotives. How could they be sure, though, that the locomotives would be good enough for the work? The Company decided to hold a competition with a prize of £500, which would be about £15,000 in modern money. The trials were held at Rainhill in 1829, and many people came to watch. Their favourite locomotive was the 'Novelty', built by two London men, Braithwaite and Ericsson. It shot up and down the line at 30 miles an hour. This was the first time anyone had seen a machine go as fast as a horse could gallop, so the crowd was amazed. Unfortunately, the 'Novelty' kept breaking down. Then George Stephenson and his son Robert brought out their locomotive, the 'Rocket'. It, too, ran at 30 miles an hour and what is more, it did not break down. The Directors gave the prize to the Stephensons.

As we have seen, the Liverpool and Manchester line was finished in 1830. It was such a success that people began to build railways in many other places. By 1850 all our important cities were joined together, and Britain had the first public railway system in the world.

the *Novelty* and the *Rocket*

6 Sailing Ships

Quite likely you have visited the clipper ship *Cutty Sark* at Greenwich. If so, you will have seen her tall masts with their complicated rigging and long spars. They give you some idea of the great spread of canvas she carried. In all it was 32,000 square feet, and that was not a great deal for a clipper. The larger clippers had 50,000 square feet, which is bigger than a football pitch. You will also have seen the *Cutty Sark's* finely pointed bows, and graceful stern. Clearly, she was built for speed. Indeed, 'clipper' comes from a Dutch word 'klepper', which means a fast horse.

Sailing ships had not always been like that. In the eighteenth century they were rather like floating shoe boxes. Owners cared more about the amount of cargo their ships could carry, than how fast they could sail. The best of these old ships belonged to the East India Company. They were as well armed as men-of-war.

An East Indiaman once captured a French frigate, and another time a group of them fought with some French battleships. On the other hand, they often took six months to go to India, and up to a year to reach China.

There were few changes in the early nineteenth century until 1841, when an American called John Griffith designed a ship with fine lines and tall, sloping masts to carry a huge spread of sail. They were the plans of the first clipper. The New York shipowners were not interested. The hull was not roomy enough, and all the sails would have needed a large crew to work them. Within a few years, though, shipowners were begging Griffith to build them clippers. What had happened to make them change their minds?

For centuries, China had been unwilling to trade with other countries, but in 1842 she lost a war against Britain. Britain made her open her ports to

foreigners. The most important thing China had to sell was tea, and the ship that brought in the first of the new crop had the best price for its cargo. Griffith's ships were ideal for the tea trade. Then, about 1850, prospectors found gold in both California and in Australia. Men wanted to go to these places as quickly as possible, so they went on American clippers, because they were much faster than any British ships.

Not surprisingly, the British wanted clippers of their own. In 1852 an Englishman, Richard Green, built the *Challenger*. On her first voyage from China she raced the American ship *Challenge*, and beat her by two days. Soon there were many British clippers, most of them better than the Americans. The American builders used their native softwoods, which were cheap, but they became waterlogged, and the ships wore out in ten years. The planks moved so much the sailors joked that if you sat on the deck they would pinch your bottom. The British used teak or mahogany planks on iron ribs, so their ships lasted much longer. The *Cutty Sark* had a working life of 52 years.

A clipper ship in full sail was a wonderful sight, but the crew had a hard time. Sailing ships followed the winds, so they were often hundreds of miles out in the middle of the ocean. They could go for many days without sight of land, or even another ship. Often, storms battered them, especially off Cape Horn. To most of us it would be an adventure to climb the rigging of the *Cutty Sark* as she lies in dry dock. The sailors had to go aloft during gales and snowstorms while the top of the mast swayed as much as two hundred feet from side to side. They then had to work their way along the spars on footropes, to haul in enormous sails that might be sodden with water, or stiff with frost. At other times their ship could lie becalmed for days together in the heat of the tropics. For food, the men had little more than salt fish and ship's biscuits, though after 1850 they also had a ration of lime-juice each day, which stopped them developing scurvy. The sailor slept on a narrow bunk in the crowded forecastle. His mattress was stuffed with straw, so he called it a 'donkey's breakfast'. In spite of the hardship and danger he earned only £4 a month.

unloading tea

Sailing Ships

As more and more clippers were built, there was keen competition to bring the first cargo of tea to London. The winning ship had a valuable prize. In 1866 there was an especially exciting race when five ships left the Chinese port of Foochow within thirty hours of each other. The voyage was 14,000 miles, and took 99 days, but at the end the two leading ships, the *Taeping* and the *Ariel*, were racing neck and neck up the English Channel. *Ariel* reached Deal first. This was where clippers had to take in their sails, so that steam tugs could tow them up the Thames.

Taeping arrived just afterwards and was lucky to have the more powerful tug. She docked first by just twenty minutes. Her captain and crew were sportsmen, though, and shared their prize money with the men from the *Ariel*.

7 Steam Ships

Isambard Kingdom Brunel

One day in 1835, the Directors of the Great Western Railway Company met to talk about the new railway they were planning. It was to run from London to Bristol, which was over a hundred miles. This was in the early days of railways, and some of the Directors thought the line would be far too long. At this, the Company's engineer said, 'Why not make it longer? We could build a steamship to sail from Bristol to New York, and call her the Great Western.' The engineer's name was Isambard Kingdom Brunel.

Brunel's father, Marc, had fled to England during the French Revolution. Here, he became a famous engineer. Isambard was born in 1806, and he, too, became an engineer. When he was only twenty-three he designed the handsome suspension bridge at Clifton, near Bristol. In 1833 the Great Western Railway Company chose him as their engineer. This gave him an enormous amount of work, but he could not forget his dream. He was determined that one day, people should travel all the way from London to New York by steam.

There had been small steamships for a long time. By 1830 there were 300 of them in Britain. They took passengers around the coast and over to France and Ireland. Sailing ships with engines in them had already

the *Great Western*

crossed the Atlantic, but they had only used their engines part of the way. The problem in those days was that steam engines burnt a lot of fuel. A ship crossing the Atlantic would need more coal than she could carry. Brunel saw that the answer to the problem was to have bigger ships. A ship that is four times as large as another will use only twice as much fuel. It is a bit like buses and cars. A bus carries twenty times as many passengers as a car, but uses only five times as much fuel. Consequently, Brunel's *Great Western* was 1,340 tonnes, about twice the size of any other steamship.

The *Great Western* was launched at Bristol in 1837, and was then towed to the Thames to have her engines and all her other equipment fitted. Meanwhile, a rival company in Liverpool was also building a large steamer. They soon realized that the *Great Western* would be finished first, so they chartered a ship called the *Sirius*. She was only half the size of the *Great Western* but her owners thought that if she had some alterations, she might just cross the Atlantic. She, too, went to the Thames for changes to be made.

the *Sirius*

On March 28th, 1838, the *Sirius* was ready. She steamed past the *Great Western*, which was still not quite finished. Brunel did not lose heart, though. He knew the *Sirius* would have to lose a lot of time at Cork in Ireland, taking on coal. And he knew his own ship was much faster. Everyone worked hard, and on March 31st the *Great Western* set sail. Brunel was sure she would catch the *Sirius*. Within two hours, though, she was on fire. As Brunel rushed to the boiler room to see what was happening, he fell 28 feet and lay unconscious, his head in a pool of water. He would have been killed, but he landed on another man, who broke his fall, and pulled him out of the water. As it was, he was so badly injured that he had to go ashore.

The fire was put out, but it was twelve hours before the *Great Western* was sailing again. She went to Bristol where she took on coal, supplies and seven passengers. Fifty people had cancelled their bookings when they heard about the fire. At last, on April 8th, the *Great Western* set out for America. The *Sirius* had already left Cork on April 4th.

April 22nd, 1838, was an exciting day for the people of New York. In the morning, they heard that the first steamer had crossed the Atlantic from England, and they went to cheer her. She was a handsome vessel, with a figure-head of a dog holding a star – the *Sirius*. Then, in the afternoon another steamer twice the size of the first arrived, and was also cheered. For all her late start, the *Great Western* was only a few hours behind her rival.

Though he had lost the race, Brunel had proved that big steamers were better than small ones. It was not just that they were faster. The *Sirius* had burnt all her coal, while the *Great Western* still had enough for another 1,000 miles. She crossed the Atlantic regularly, while the *Sirius* was soon back where she belonged, on the Irish Sea.

Brunel was ambitious. In 1839 he built the *Great Britain* which was two and a half times as big as the *Great Western*. Even that was not enough. In 1859 he launched the *Great Eastern* which was 19,000 tonnes. She gave Brunel so much work and worry that he became seriously ill. However, he was sure his ship would be a success and he lay in bed waiting to hear good news of her maiden voyage. Instead, he was told that a violent explosion had blown off one of her funnels, and done a lot of other damage. Brunel had faced his problems with great courage all his life, but this was too much. Within a few days he was dead.

the *Great Eastern*

Brunel's work was far from wasted, though. In the early days, when the crew of a sailing ship saw a steamer, they used to jeer at the 'puffing kettle'. Sometimes they trailed a rope over their stern, suggesting the steamer needed a tow. After Brunel, though, it was clear that one day steamers would take the trade of the world from sailing ships.

Chapter Four Towns and Places of Work

1 Houses

a Glasgow court

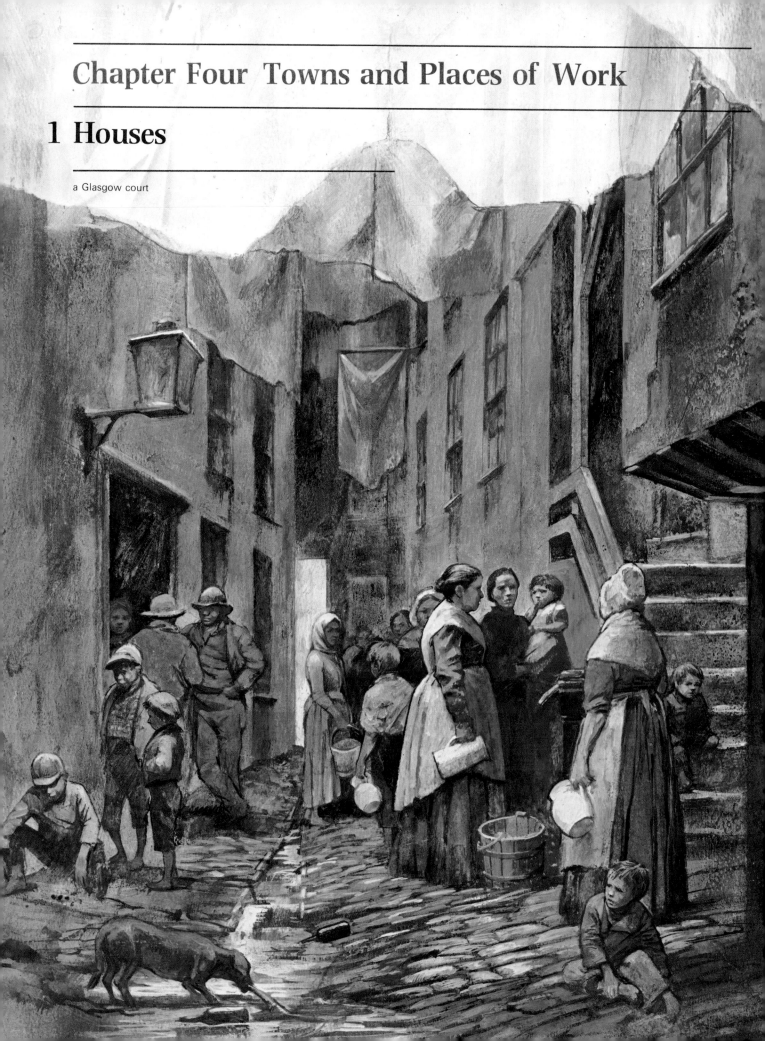

1 Houses

The previous picture shows you some houses that poor people lived in over a hundred years ago. It is in Glasgow, but it could have been in London, Birmingham, Liverpool or any large city. We are standing in what they called a court. Ahead, we can see an entrance which is not much bigger than a doorway, but behind us the end of the court is open, so that it is just possible for a cart to come in to collect rubbish. The people hang their washing on poles stuck from their windows, because they have no gardens. Next to this court is another, then another, and another. There are shopping streets in a different part of the town, full of people and horse-drawn vehicles of all kinds, making a tremendous clatter on the stones. This, though, is where the poor live, and this is where they will return, men, women, and children, after a hard day's work. They will have little energy for amusing themselves in the evenings, and on Sunday when they might have enjoyed some fresh air, there is nowhere to go. The countryside is too far away for them to walk, and there are no parks. All they can do is lounge around the court, gossiping, quarrelling and fighting, or else, if they have a little money, drinking in a public house.

If we visit one of these houses, we step straight into the living room. The first thing we notice is the smell for, if all the family are at home, the room will be crowded with people. None of them wash a great deal, and they are so afraid of fresh air that they stop every crack they can find, and stuff rags into any broken windows. The floor is brick – cold, hard and dusty. The builder has done nothing to make the house waterproof so the walls are black with damp. There is a coal fire burning, but that is more for cooking than for keeping the room warm. The children have to take turns to sit by it. The family keep their coal and their food in the same cupboard under the stairs. The furniture is a plain table, with some hard chairs, and some beds with grubby mattresses, full of bugs. Several share the same bed and some sleep under it. The family live, cook, eat and sleep all in the same room, so it is not surprising that they go drinking whenever they can.

The stairs lead directly out of the room to the ones above it. The family cannot use the extra rooms, though, for they have let them to lodgers.

If we could go into the attic we would see how badly the roof is made, with thin timbers, and signs of leaks. Some windows will not open, and some of the doors will not stay shut on their own. It is no use looking for a kitchen or a bathroom, since the house has neither, and the lavatories, which all the neighbours share, are outside, at the end of the court.

Like the rooms upstairs, the cellar is let to lodgers. Only the poorest will rent a cellar, for it is a dreadful place to live. It may have a fireplace, but no window, or, at best, only one at street level. As the family is poor, they cannot afford furniture and sleep on straw. The walls and floor are always damp, and water pours in after heavy rain. In the worst cellars the people have to take the door off its hinges and lay it on bricks, if they are to have somewhere at all dry to sit. In Liverpool there were many cellar dwellings that were so bad that the town council ordered the people living in them to leave, and filled the cellars with earth. It was not long, though, before the landlords had dug them out and let them to poor Irish families.

Not many places have underground sewers, but instead, deep, open drains called 'kennels' (channels). There is a kennel in the middle of the court in the picture. Not only rain water, but all the waste water from the houses runs in them, so they are most unpleasant. The barefooted urchins who live in the court do not mind, though, and jump in and out of them quite happily.

They call their lavatories 'privies', which means 'private places', but in fact they are very public because, usually, the whole court has to share one. A privy is a deep, brick-lined cess pit, with a wooden seat on top. When the cess pit is full, men are supposed to come and empty it. They make such a smell that they are only allowed to work at night, so they are called 'night men'. Often the privy overflows and the filth finds its way into the cellars.

On the left of the picture you can see the stand pipe from which they all draw their water. The water companies only turn it on once a day for about half an hour, so at that time there is always a crowd of people round the tap, arguing, pushing and trying to fill their tubs and buckets. Nor is the water pleasant, for the company takes it from the nearest river, which is where the town's sewage is dumped. One man who thought his water was tasting particularly nasty, took off his tap and found in the pipe the decayed body of an eel.

2 Disease

People living in slum houses, like the ones you have just seen, were bound to catch diseases.

The most frightening was cholera. Normally, only people in the Far East caught it, but during the nineteenth century great epidemics swept round the world from time to time. When the cholera was spreading, the newspapers followed its progress, and the British saw it drawing near, week by week. There was nothing they could do, but they knew that when the disease arrived, many people would catch it, and that at least half of those who did so would die.

The cholera patient has terrible cramp, and goes blue. He is sick so often, and has diarrhoea so badly, that he loses most of the water in his body. He is dehydrated, and that is what kills him. Cholera germs are usually carried in drinking water. Since much drinking water came from rivers, the disease spread easily. It attacked both rich and poor, and could appear in most unexpected places.

Another dreadful disease was typhus. The patient's face swells, his skin turns black, and he smells horrible. He also has a high temperature, so typhus was known as 'the fever'. It is carried by lice, insects that live in clothes and in the hair. If they have the disease themselves, they give it to their hosts when they bite them.

Smallpox was common, too. Usually it attacked babies. Quite large numbers recovered, but they had unpleasant little scars on their faces, and many went blind.

The disease that killed most people, though, was one they did not fear as much as the others. This was tuberculosis, or consumption as they called it. They were not afraid of it, because death came slowly, and there was not much pain. Tuberculosis germs attack the lungs and make cavities in them. Since the patient cannot breathe properly, he gradually wastes away.

What could be done about all these diseases? The answer was, not very much. Doctors did not understand them, for nobody knew anything about germs. They saw that dirt and disease went together, but dirt often makes a bad smell. They thought that since poisoned food killed you, so also did poisoned air.

Hospitals were dreadful places. There were no anaesthetics, so anyone who had an operation suffered terribly. Surgeons used to work very quickly, but even so, many of their patients died from shock. As they knew nothing about germs, they did not sterilize their instruments or use antiseptics. Often, people who lived through their operations died afterwards, because of gangrene in their wounds.

Jenner vaccinating against smallpox

DAY OF FASTING AND HUMILIATION IN EXETER.

AN Application having been made to me on the part of the Clergy and Laity of this City, the Sanction and Authority of the Lord Bishop of the Diocese having been previously obtained, that a Day of Fasting and Humiliation before Almighty God might be appointed, by reason of the fearful scourge of Cholera with which various Parts of this Country have been visited, and from which Exeter, although greatly favored, has not been entirely exempt, I have consulted the Council thereon, and, with their Sanction, have appointed **WEDNESDAY,** the *Nineteenth* Day of *September* instant, for the purpose. And I recommend to my Fellow Citizens, and to the Inhabitants of Exeter generally, to observe that Day by a Cessation from ordinary Business, and by Attendance on the Public Worship of God with those feelings of Submission and Devotion which become a Christian People under such an awful Visitation.

CHR. ARDEN, Mayor.

Dated the 12th Day of September, 1849.

NORTON, PRINTER, 247, HIGH-STREET, EXETER.

cholera posters

Some good things happened, more or less by accident. Cotton goods became cheap, so even poor folk could afford a change of clothing. When they washed their clothes, they killed the lice in them, so there was less typhus. The cholera did not come back to Britain after 1849, but we do not know why. Gradually, fewer and fewer people caught tuberculosis, and this is another mystery. A way of preventing smallpox was discovered in the 1790s. A Gloucestershire doctor, Edward Jenner, noticed that dairy maids did not usually have smallpox. Instead, they caught a disease from their cows, called cowpox. They felt slightly ill for a few days, and had some nasty sores on their hands, but that was all. Jenner thought cowpox made the girls immune to smallpox, and to prove it he made a daring experiment. He injected some pus from a cowpox sore into the arm of a boy. He at once developed cowpox. Later, Jenner injected him with smallpox, but the boy did not catch the disease. Jenner

called his treatment 'vaccination', from the Latin word 'vacca', meaning 'cow'. He vaccinated many people in a little hut, which is still standing, near Berkeley Castle. Other doctors copied him, and gradually smallpox died out. Today it is found hardly anywhere in the world.

By the middle of the nineteenth century, many people were trying to make their towns and cities better places. An important civil servant, Edwin Chadwick, will tell us about it. 'In 1848, after years of persuading, Parliament passed a Public Health Act. The cholera was on its way, and many M.P.s were scared. Now, I am a member of the new Board of Health under Lord Shaftesbury. Our duty is to persuade town councils to supply clear, fresh water, and to build sewers. In nearly every place there are people who object, because of the expense. We call them the 'dirty party'. We have shown, though, that a town can have proper sewers and water supplies for as little as $2\frac{1}{2}$d (1p) a week for each house. The average working man spends two shillings (10p) a week on drink and tobacco, so he can spend $2\frac{1}{2}$d on keeping healthy. Not many poor families have a flush lavatory or a sink with a tap that gives pure water. However, I look forward to a time when people will take these things for granted.'

BOARD OF WORKS FOR THE LIMEHOUSE DISTRICT.
COMPRISING LIMEHOUSE, RATCLIFF, SHADWELL & WAPPING.

In consequence of the appearance of **CHOLERA** within this District, the Board have appointed the under-mentioned Medical Gentlemen who will give ADVICE, MEDICINE, AND ASSISTANCE, FREE OF ANY CHARGE, AND UPON APPLICATION, AT ANY HOUR OF THE DAY OR NIGHT.

The Inhabitants are earnestly requested not to neglect the first symptoms of the appearance of Disease, (which in its early stage is easy to cure), but to apply, WITHOUT DELAY, to one of the Medical Gentlemen appointed.

The Board have opened an Establishment for the reception of Patients, in a building at Green Bank, near Wapping Church, (formerly used as Wapping Workhouse), where all cases of Cholera and Diarrhœa will be received and placed under the care of a competent Resident Medical Practitioner, and proper Attendants.

THE FOLLOWING ARE THE MEDICAL GENTLEMEN TO BE APPLIED TO:--
Mr. **ORTON,**
56, White Horse Street.
Dr. **NIGHTINGALL,**
4. Commercial Terrace, Commercial Road, (near Limehouse Church.)
Mr. **SCHROEDER,**
53, Three Colt Street, Limehouse.
Mr. **HARRIS,**
5, York Terrace, Commercial Road, (opposite Stepney Railway Station.)
Mr. **CAMBELL,**
At Mr. GRAY's, Chemist, Old Road, opposite " The World's End."
Mr. **LYNCH,**
St. James's Terrace, Back Road, Shadwell.
Mr. **HECKFORD,**
At the Dispensary, Wapping Workhouse.

BY ORDER,
BOARD OFFICES, WHITE HORSE STREET,   **THOS. W. RATCLIFF,**
26th July, 1866.   *Clerk to the Board.*

3 Police

In the big towns, there were not only dirty slums, with people dying of disease. There were lots of criminals as well. We will talk to Mr. Richards, a constable at Marylebone, in London, in 1750. We meet him in the street, on a winter's night.

'I was elected constable by the other ratepayers in the parish. I am a grocer, and I want to look after my shop. I have no money for being a constable, so I shall be thankful when my year is up. Someone else will take over then.' 'What do you have to do?' 'I am supposed to keep an eye on the watchmen. They are no good at all. They have such low wages that only poor old men will take the job. Here comes one of them now.' An old man shuffles past. It is a windy night, and he goes into a box like a sentry's, where he huddles out of the cold. 'That's old Jack,' Mr. Richards says. 'They made him watchman to keep him off the parish. Who is going to be afraid of him? Sometimes young people overturn his box, or attack him, just for

fun. They call it "milling a Charlie".' *'Charlie?'* 'That's the name we give watchmen. I don't know why.' *'What happens if there is any trouble?'* 'Old Jack runs away, of course.' *'Do you never catch any criminals, then?'* 'Nearly every one gets away. This last year we have had robberies, burglaries, and even one or two murders. Hardly any of the villains were caught. It's up to ordinary people, really. If you catch a dangerous criminal you have £40 reward. It's hard-earned money, though, for you not only have to arrest your man, you have to go into court and prove him guilty. Any time of the day or night his friends may come and threaten you or your family. No, it's safer to let criminals escape. The only police that are any good are Mr. Fielding's people. If you want to know about them, you must go to Bow Street.'

At Bow Street we go into a large, private house. It is the home of Mr. John Fielding, but on the ground floor he has a court room and some offices. In the

watchman   Bow Street runner   'Peeler'

court room, Mr. Fielding is trying a criminal. He has a bandage over his eyes, for he is blind. 'John Ray,' he is saying, 'you have been found guilty of stealing this lady's purse. Have you anything to say before I pass sentence?' 'It was the first time in my life I ever stole anything,' says the man. 'You are lying, John Ray. You were up before me for stealing, ten years ago, though you called yourself George Spenser, then.' The criminal's mouth drops open, but the man next to us grins and says, 'The "blind beak" never forgets a voice. He will remember a voice years longer than you will remember a face.'

We follow the man into another room. 'My name is Black,' he says. 'I am one of Mr. Fielding's Bow Street Runners.' *'You don't have a uniform.'* 'Some of our people wear uniform. They have blue coats and red waistcoats, so we call them Robin Redbreasts. They are the patrol men. No, a runner must not wear a uniform, or the criminals would know who he was.' *'You are a detective, then?'* 'That's right. It's an exciting life. I never know what I am going to earn, mind. Mr. Fielding has a bit of government money, and he pays me a guinea a week, come what may. There are rewards, of course. I haven't caught a man that weighed £40 yet, but I expect I shall get £20 for that fellow Ray. Then I do a bit of private work. Last month I was out in a big country house. They had had a burglary, and one of the servants was killed. I did not find who did it, but the gentleman paid me well for my help.'

We will now move on a hundred years, to 1850, and talk to Superintendant Thomas of the Metropolitan Police. 'Since 1829, London has had the best police in the world. That was when Sir Robert Peel started our force. People call us "Peelers", but we don't mind. They have a healthy respect for us. There are two Commissioners in charge of the Metropolitan Police, Sir Charles Rowan and Henry Mayne. They have their office in New Scotland Yard. They divided London into seventeen divisions. I have "E" Division. Under me are 160 men – sixteen sections, each of nine men and a sergeant. There are four Inspectors in the Division as well.'

Just then, a constable comes in. He is young and tall. He has a uniform with a blue coat and trousers, a wide belt and a tall top hat. 'Fine man, isn't he?' says the Superintendent. 'He is a good lad to have when there is a riot. Not that we have had one lately. Mobs used to run wild in London, for days at a time. If a crowd gives trouble now, we charge them with our truncheons, and they scatter fast enough.' *'You haven't mentioned detectives.'* 'There are a few at Scotland Yard, but our Commissioners don't believe in detectives. If a criminal knows there is a policeman about, he will behave himself. That's far better than trying to catch someone after he has done a burglary or a murder.'

4 Prisons

What happened to John Ray, the man who was brought before John Fielding? He was sentenced to be hanged, but, as usually happened, the punishment was changed to transportation. He was taken to Barbados, in the West Indies, where he worked as a slave on a sugar plantation. He was supposed to stay there for ten years, but the heat and the hard work killed him quite soon. One of John's friends who had been caught with him was flogged, and another was branded on the hand with a red-hot iron. In the eighteenth century it was unusual to send a criminal to prison. Most prisons were for debtors.

We will visit the Fleet Prison in London. Just inside the gate is a yard full of people – men, women and children. Some are enjoying themselves with a game that looks a bit like tennis, others are playing skittles, and the rest are sitting about, gossiping. There is a lot of noise from a room in one of the buildings, and, looking in, we see it is a bar, with people drinking, laughing and shouting.

A prisoner tells us his story. 'I used to be a ship-owner, but I lost nearly all my vessels. A few were wrecked, but most, the French took. I borrowed money and, in the end, owed £20,000. My creditors had me locked in here, but it will not do them any good. I will never be able to repay them.

Luckily, my parents are rich enough to send me money, so I live quite well. You can buy anything in prison that you can outside. It's just that the jailer takes his profit, so you pay a lot more. I have a couple of rooms, which means my wife and children can live with me. They are allowed to go in and out of prison as they like, and I can have friends to visit me. Sometimes I long to take a walk in the park, or go up the river in a boat, and it's miserable to think I may die in this place. Still, on the whole, life could be a lot worse.' *'But what happens if your parents stop sending money?'* 'Oh, I would hate to be a poor debtor. This is the masters' side. It is quite different on the common side, where the poor are. They are locked up together, and only come into their yard once in a while. They are filthy, and they have to live on bread and water. The jailer doesn't like them, because he can't make any money out of them. A while back, he chained one of them to a dead body, until a friend paid his admission fees.' *'Admission fees?'* 'Oh, yes, you have to pay to come in here, even though you are an unwilling visitor.'

A hundred years later, prisons were quite different. We will visit Pentonville, which was built in 1842. It is for criminals only, since debtors are no longer sent to prison. The governor shows us round. 'In the old days, no-one bothered much about criminals. They used to hang them, flog them, or send them overseas. We still send some to Australia, but more and more are going to prison, and we try and make better men of them. It isn't easy. The main thing is that we stop them speaking to each other. When a man is out of his cell, he must wear a mask, but most of the time, he is locked up on his own. We call it solitary confinement. It is wonderful what it will do. When they come in, some of them are big, boasting bullies. They swear and shout in their cells for a time, but after a few weeks on their own, they quieten down. I saw our chaplain talking to one this morning. The big thug was crying like a baby. The chaplain says he can make them think good thoughts, but I don't know.'

We follow the governor down one of the wings of the prison. Everywhere is spotlessly clean. From some cells comes a 'latitat' noise, and from others, a tapping noise. Prisoners are either weaving or shoemaking. Suddenly, a bell booms out, and warders move quickly from cell to cell, unlocking the doors. The convicts stream out, their heavy boots clanging on the iron galleries and stairs. Each one wears his mask, and they do not speak. They go into the prison chapel, where every man has his own cubicle, and cannot see his neighbours. The chaplain conducts a short service, and the men join in with good will. Probably, it is the only chance they will have of using their voices today. 'They have an hour's exercise in the yard, as well as chapel,' says the governor, 'but the rest of the time they are in their cells.' *'What happens if any of them misbehave?'* The governor shows us a punishment cell. It is completely dark, and completely silent. 'Bread and water and a few days in there will tame anyone,' says the governor.

5 Schools

We will now follow a child from one of the slum houses to school. His name is Alfred, and he is five years old. His parents only send him to school because they are at work all day. There is no law to say children must attend school, and as soon as he is eight or nine, Alfred will have to go to work himself.

Since it is Monday, Alfred takes twopence (1p) with him. That is his school fee for the week. All but the poorest children have to pay fees. Alfred's parents think they are worth paying in order to be rid of him. The rest of the money the school needs is given by the wealthier people in the town. They hope the school will teach the children religion, so that they will grow up into honest, law-abiding citizens. Apart from paying a little towards the salaries of the teachers, the government gives no help at all.

The school is just one big, gloomy room. The windows are high up, so the children cannot look out of them. The walls are stone, with no plaster. The floor is worn and dusty. The only heating is a brick stove. The children who sit near it are too hot, and the fumes make them cough, but most of the room is cold.

Alfred's first lesson is religion. The clergyman has come to take it himself. He has all the children, about sixty of them, and he tries to teach them their Catechism. The children stumble over the hard words. They can make no sense of them, and some begin to fidget and talk. The clergyman loses his temper. He tells them about hell fire and says that people who are wicked will burn for ever after they are dead. Alfred understands that well enough, and is very frightened. He often has bad dreams about hell.

After the clergyman has gone, Alfred has a writing lesson. He sits with his friends on an uncomfortable bench, and in front of them is a long tray, filled with sand. The children trace letters in the sand with their fingers. 'A', shouts the teacher, so they all try to draw a big, capital A. When they have it right, they smooth the sand. They then go to B, and so on through the alphabet. Older children have slates. They are supposed to clean them with damp sponges, but most use 'spit and shirt cuff'. Only the oldest have pen and paper. Some of them write beautifully. They do not write their own ideas, though. Most of the time they are just copying sentences from a book.

After writing, they have reading. The children stand in small groups round reading sheets. First comes the alphabet, next there are words of two letters, then words of three letters, and so on. In the end, they have sentences taken from the Bible. The oldest children read the Bible itself, though sometimes, as a rare treat, they are given a story book.

The only other subject is arithmetic. The younger children chant their tables, and the older ones do problems. Sometimes they work on their slates, but the master is fond of making them do difficult sums in their heads.

Alfred's teacher is only ten years old. He is one of the older boys in the school, who has been made a

monitor. He has to come to school every morning, one hour before the rest. The master tells him what he must teach Alfred and his friends during the day. Often he does not understand the work himself. Alfred learns little from him. The school has several monitors, each one with a class of ten.

In the school, there are also two pupil teachers. One is fifteen and the other is seventeen. Both became pupil teachers at fourteen. They teach all day in the school, and in the evening the master gives them lessons. They have to learn subjects like English, history and geography, and they have to pass an examinnation at the end of each year. If they do well, they go to a training college for teachers, when they are eighteen or nineteen.

The only adult in the school is the master. He has a difficult time. He has to teach his monitors every morning, and his pupil teachers every evening. Also, the school day is long. The children do not wash, and they are badly behaved. There is always a noise, because everyone is trying to work in the same room. The master often gives the cane, but he has some unusual punishments as well. Sometimes he ties a child in a sack. He also has a basket, with a rope and a pulley. If a boy is especially naughty, he puts him in the basket and hauls him up to the ceiling.

6 Factory and Workshop

In the last section you saw that only the youngest children went to school. As soon as they were about nine years old, their parents sent them to work. We will see what happens to a boy called Mark, who works in Mr. Orrell's cotton factory.

Mark has a long walk to the factory. He has to leave home at 5.00 in the morning to arrive on time. His house is like the ones on page 66-7. Compared with home, the factory is a palace. It is well built, with an iron framework and brick walls. Mr. Orrell keeps the rooms at the same temperature all the year round. This is important for the cotton. Mark likes it as well, for he is neither cold in winter, nor too hot in summer. In Mark's home parents and children are on top of each other, but in the factory there is plenty of space. There is a fresh air, too, most of the time. Even in winter Mr. Orrell says the windows must be open a little. The work people often shut them, however, because they do not like draughts. The factory is light, for there are plenty of windows, and after dark they have gas jets.

Mark does not like his work. He is a 'scavenger', and helps look after the mules. The cotton makes a lot of dust, which Mark has to sweep up. He must go everywhere in the room, even under the machines. They do not stop the machines for him, so he needs to be very careful. There have been some dreadful accidents. Once, a boy caught his arm in the machinery, Another time, a girl put her head too close to one of the big driving belts. The buckle caught her hair, swinging her up to the ceiling and over the pulley.

Mark's job is not hard, but it is boring. Some days he has to spend fourteen hours just brushing up dust. The spinners, that is, the men who operate the mules, are quite kind. They have to see the children do their work, though. At the end of a long day, Mark is sleepy, so his spinner keeps him awake by twisting his ears. Sometimes, he hits him with his belt, which is against Mr. Orrell's rules. If Mr. Orrell sees people doing wrong, he fines them. One day the overlooker caught Mark giving his friend a ride on his back. It was stupid and dangerous. At the end of the week, Mark found he had lost sixpence ($2\frac{1}{2}$p) from his wages. As he only earns 1/6 ($7\frac{1}{2}$p), that was a lot for him. His father beat him, because he always takes Mark's wages.

In Wolverhampton there is quite a different factory, belonging to a man called Hemingsley. Here they make iron washers. Mr. Hemingsley employs about fifty children including Anne Preston.

Anne is fifteen, but is small for her age. Her dress is no better than a piece of sacking. Her arms and head stick out through holes, making her look like a tortoise. She is very dirty. Anne cannot remember either of her parents. She was brought up in the workhouse, and still lives there because she has no home.

Anne has to be at the factory at seven in the morning. At nine o'clock she stops work for half an hour to have breakfast, and she has an hour for dinner, from one o'clock until two o'clock. After that, though, she has to work without stopping until 8 o'clock. Her only free day in the week is Sunday. Her wages are 4/- a week.

Mr. Hemingsley's factory is in a dreadful state. It's floors are so rotten they have to be held up with props, and its walls are cracked. None the less, it is full of heavy machines, so the whole building is shaking and groaning. One day a floor did collapse, killing several people, and it is likely to happen again.

We follow Anne into the factory. The noise is overpowering. We have to walk very carefully because the machines are close together. We could easily lose an arm if we fell into one of them. Anne has to work with two wheels whirring round a few inches either side of her head. In front of her a heavy hammer crashes down every two seconds. She has to feed it small pieces of metal, so that it stamps them into shape. If she is a little bit careless, the hammer will come down on her hand.

Mr. Hemingsley could easily box in the working parts of his machines, and put little guards in front of the hammers to keep the children's fingers from going under them. However, that would cost him money, so he will not do it. 'It isn't often they lose a hand', he explains. 'The machine just takes off the top of a finger. Anyway, they should watch what they are doing. It's just carelessness on their part — sheer carelessness.'

We will now go to Sedgley, near Birmingham. Here we meet George Brown, who is a nailmaker. George does not go to a factory, but helps his father make nails at home. They have a little workshop behind the house, where the whole family work together. It is a hut, about the size of a small bedroom. The walls are thin and the roof leaks. The floor is dug out, all round the edge of the room, and the family stand in this ditch. They use the centre of the room as a work bench. On it they put their tools, and in the middle is a coke fire. It fills the room with choking fumes.

Factory and Workshop

Every week a man delivers some long, thin bars of iron. The family heat the metal in the fire, then beat it into shape with hammers. The hut is full of noise, it is very hot, and everyone is crowded together. They are often cross with each other. George's father sometimes loses his temper. Once, he hit his daughter with a red-hot bar. Another time, he sent George what the people of Sedgley call a 'flash of lightning'. When a bar of iron comes out of the fire, it is covered with little bits of red-hot coke. The way to be rid of them is to shake them on the floor. What George's father did, was to shake them all over his son. They fell in his hair, on his face, and inside his shirt. They covered his body with tiny burns.

George's father can work when he likes, and his wife and children have to keep the same hours that he does. He takes Sunday as a holiday, and he usually spends most of Monday in bed. With a lot of grumbling he does some work on Tuesday afternoon. On Wednesday he may work for much of the day. On Thursday he is a worried man. All the iron must be made into nails by Saturday evening, and there are only three days left. Mr. Brown gets up at six, and drags his wife and children into the workshop. There they stay, hammering as hard as they can, for sixteen hours. Mr. Brown keeps them awake by shouting at them, and hitting them. Before he goes to bed, George has to make 1,000 nails.

When he collects the money for the nails, Mr. Brown keeps it all himself.

7 Coal Mines

Today will be exciting, for we are going to visit a coal mine in County Durham. Mr. Hudson will be our guide. He is a viewer, which is a kind of foreman.

While we are waiting at the top of the pit, Mr. Hudson shows us two steam engines. They are wheezing and banging away. 'This one is the pumping engine,' says Mr. Hudson. 'It pumps 70,000 gallons of water out of the pit every hour. It is a Newcomen engine. It has been here for a hundred years and still works well. The other is the winding engine, which means it lifts the coal out of the pit. It is a later design, by Boulton and Watt. Some pits still use a horse capstan to wind their coal, but we mine 800 tons a day. A horse could never lift all that. Well, here is our bucket now.'

The winding engine has drawn a huge, empty bucket to the surface. We get in rather nervously, and suddenly begin to drop. After a while we do not feel as if we are falling, but the hole at the top of the pit becomes smaller and smaller. In the end, it looks just like a star in the sky. After four minutes, there is a clanking noise, and the bucket stops. We get out, to find ourselves in a dark, damp tunnel, which they call a 'gate'.

'It is a mile to the coal face,' says Mr. Hudson. We go along the tunnel which, at first, is lined with bricks, and is quite high. After a while, though, we have to stoop. There are no bricks and we see loose stones in the roof. We cover the last part of the journey crawling on our hands and knees in dirty water. Everywhere, we are in a strong draught. From time to time we go through a door, and the air makes it bang behind us.

At last we reach the coal face. Here one of the hewers explains how he digs the coal. 'First I take my pickaxe and I cut a slot in the bottom of the seam, about three feet deep. That weakens it, you see. Next, I drive some wedges into the coal, and down it falls. All I have to do then is to shovel it into the corves. My wife and my two boys take them to the pit bottom.' These corves are big baskets, on wheels.

One of the boys describes his work. 'I am a hurrier, and I have to hurry, too. Father is paid for every corve he sends to the surface, and if I don't carry the coal fast enough, he beats me. In these narrow workings I have to drag the corve.' He shows us a belt he is wearing, with a chain. 'I hook the end of the chain to the corve, and pull it. In the main gates, though, there are rails, so I can go quite fast. I get behind the corve and push with my hands and head.' The little boy lifts his lamp to show us a bald patch right on top of his head.

'*Coal mining must be dangerous, Mr. Hudson.*' 'We have a lot of accidents. Most are because of the men's stupidity. I saw some the other day, smoking in a part of the mine where we have a lot of gas. Once, the engine boy did not stop the winding engine in

time, and drew a bucket with six men over the pulley. Several fell back down the shaft. Some accidents they can't help. A few years back, one of the gates collapsed, and some people were trapped. By the time we had dug through to them, they were dead. Most of our accidents, though, come from the odd rock falling out of the roof.' *'Do you have explosions?'* 'We take great care about that. They can be nasty. One near here blew twenty men out of the pit. It shot a great beam through the air like an arrow and it stuck in the side of a hill. Our men have safety lamps. We also ventilate the mine pretty well. There are two shafts, an upcast and a downcast. Under the upcast shaft we have a furnace. It draws air right through the workings. The doors make sure the air goes to all parts of the pit, otherwise it would take short cuts.' At each of the doors there is a little child, about five years old. We ask one of them what his work is. 'I am a trapper. When the hurriers come by with their corves, I have to open my door for them.' Mr. Hudson says, 'I am sorry for the little trappers. They sit in the dark, and the hurriers frighten them with tales of hobgoblins.'

We ride up the shaft and get out at the top, relieved that we have landed safely. *'One last question, Mr. Hudson, where does your coal go?'* 'We have a horse railway that carries it to the River Tyne, about twelve miles away. Then it goes by collier brig down to London. London people would be very miserable without Durham coal to keep them warm.'

Chapter Five   Britain and North America

1 Canada

To start with, in this chapter, we are going to visit some of the settlers in North America, in the eighteenth century. We will begin our journey in Canada, which belongs to France.

Early in the sixteenth century, fishermen from Brittany began sailing to the rich fishing grounds off Newfoundland. They said there were so many cod, that all they had to do was lower baskets into the sea, and pull them out, full of fish. Later, other Frenchmen wanted to go further. They hoped that they might find treasure, as the Spaniards had done in Mexico. In fact, there was no gold or silver, but they did discover wealth of another kind. In those days, it was the fashion to wear tall, wide-brimmed hats made of felt, and the best felt came from beaver fur. Beavers were common in Canada, so people found they could make a lot of money from trapping. Frenchmen began to settle along the banks of the St. Lawrence. In 1608 Samuel de Champlain built a little settlement which grew into the city of Quebec, and in 1662 the Sieur de Maisonneuve founded Montreal. These were the two most important towns in New France.

Each year, there was a fur fair at Montreal. Traders came from all over Canada, bringing goods the Indians wanted – axes, knives, kettles, blankets, ornaments and brandy. The Indians came too, in a great fleet of about 500 canoes laden with beaver pelts. The trading usually began quietly enough, but in the evening the Indians drank the white man's 'fire water'. They stripped naked and raced through the streets, whooping, screaming and waving their tomahawks. The inhabitants closed their shutters, barricaded their doors, and longed for the fair to end.

By the early eighteenth century there were perhaps 50,000 people in New France. The most important were the seigneurs, or gentry. Each one had been given land by the King, and all he had to do in return was to clear it and encourage settlers. Some seigneurs lived in log cabins, being no richer than ordinary farmers, but others were wealthy. One of them, Charles le Moyne, built himself a fortified house of stone just like a castle in France. It was surrounded by a high wall, two hundred feet by one hundred and seventy, with towers on the corners.

The seigneurs let their land to farmers, called 'habitants'. Each year the habitant had to pay his seigneur a rent of a small amount of money, along with some of his produce, such as wheat and live

a habitant's farm

chickens. A farm began on the river bank, which was important for transport. Next, came level, fertile land for grazing, and growing crops. At the far end was forest, where the habitant found timber for his buildings and fuel for the long, cold winter. The piece of land was perhaps two hundred yards wide and over a mile in length. Farms were long and narrow, because that way everyone could have his share of river bank, fertile soil, and forest.

The farmhouse was built of logs, with an earth floor. There was just one room, with a loft above it, where the children slept.

The habitants were honest and hardworking, but their lives were dull. A young man who wanted adventure became a 'coureur de bois'. This means, literally, 'a runner in the woods'. He would vanish into the forests for perhaps eighteen months or even four years. He might be killed by a grizzly bear or, much more likely, by Red Indians. His biggest problem, though, was to stay alive during the terrible Canadian winter. Many coureurs de bois were better hunters than the Indians, and even made better birch bark canoes. These men went into the forests to trap beavers, not just for adventure. They came home when they had enough pelts, but their dangers were not over. What they had done was against the law, and if the authorities caught them, they had them whipped and branded.

Jesuit missionaries had even more courage than the coureurs de bois. Any normal person, however brave, avoided hostile Indians when he could. Jesuits looked for them deliberately, hoping they could convert them to Christianity. Indians often tortured their prisoners to death, and could be especially cruel to 'Black Gowns', as they called the priests. Even the thought of dying horribly did not dismay the Jesuits. 'The blood of the martyrs', they said, 'is the seed of the Church.'

One Jesuit, Isaac Jogues, fell into the hands of the most terrible enemies the French had, the Iroquois Indians. They tortured him until he was badly maimed, when some Dutchmen, who were allies of the Iroquois, helped him escape. He went home to France, where he could have stayed, but he insisted on returning to Canada. He found that someone was needed to go on a mission to the Iroquois, and since he could speak their language, he volunteered. On his way he met fugitives who said the Iroquois were on the warpath, but he would not turn back. Again, the Indians tortured him, and this time they killed him.

a hunter

2 New England

We will now leave the French in Canada, and sail down the east coast of the continent, to Boston, in Massachusetts. The people are English. Indeed, this part of America is called New England.

The first settlers here were the Pilgrim Fathers, who arrived in 1620. They were strict Puritans. These were people who thought the Church of England had a great many faults, and wanted to 'purify' it. The government persecuted them, so they decided to go to America, where they would be free to worship as they pleased. Their ship, the *Mayflower*, arrived at Cape Cod, a rocky headland in Massachusetts Bay. Here they made their homes. Soon other Puritans arrived. They built the town of Boston, and settlers pushed inland, in spite of the Red Indians.

As the sea was full of cod, many New Englanders became fishermen. There were plenty of forests, too, so others were shipbuilders. Numbers of them were merchants, trading with Europe and the rest of America. First, we will meet a fisherman, who will tell us about his work.

'I have a schooner, with a crew of six men. We fish for cod on the Grand Banks, near Newfoundland. The round trip is about a thousand miles, but we go there and back three times in a good season.

'To catch the fish, we go over the side of the schooner in our dories. These are little rowing boats. Each man has a long line, with hooks. He baits these with bits of mackerel. The cod are greedy, and will swallow the bait readily enough. If I have done my

fishing for cod

job properly, and found a good shoal, the men are soon rowing back to the schooner with their dories full. The trouble with fish is that it goes bad quickly. We have to split the cod, throw away their insides and heads, and then drop them in barrels of brine. As soon as our barrels are full, we come back home to Boston. Here we spread the fish to dry. When that is done, we call it "stockfish". Stockfish will keep for a long time, even on a sea voyage to Europe, or the West Indies.

'It is fishermen like me that have made New England rich. The cod is the emblem of Massachusetts, so you can see how important he is for us.'

Now we will call on a merchant, Paul Green. He lives in a handsome house in a fashionable street. He has the best quality carpets, elaborate mahogany furniture, and gold and silver table ware. Mr. Green looks like a rich London merchant. His street and his house, too, could well be in London. 'How do you make your money, Mr. Green?' 'I trade with Europe and the southern colonies. I send tons of stockfish to Spain and Portugal. The inhabitants of those Popish countries eat it because of their religion. The British buy masts and spars for their ships. Our pine trees are just right for that. Then we have a lot of beaver fur from the Indians, up in the mountains, and we send that to Britain as well. In the southern colonies they have slaves, whose owners are glad to have our stock-fish to feed them. We also send them horses and, from time to time, a little corn. They sell us sugar, rum and tobacco, as well as hardwoods for our furniture.

'I prosper because I am a man of God. They have dancing these days in Boston, and folk even play with cards – the Devil's picture book. I waste no time on these things. I spend twelve or fourteen hours every day, in my counting house, save on Sunday. That is a day for prayer.'

Mr. Green is a stern father. He will not let his children play games, and on Sunday he takes them to the Meeting House. The preacher often gives a sermon that lasts for two hours. The children must listen carefully, the whole time, without fidgeting or whispering. Mr. Green is superstitious as well as religious. He is terrified of witches. At Salem, in 1692, it was men like him who had twenty wretches hanged for witchcraft. He is something of a hypocrite, too. He hates the Roman Catholic Church, and he thinks that slavery is wrong. However, he is quite happy to trade with Roman Catholics and slave owners. In fact, most of his money comes from them. But he is very honest in his business, and is hardworking. It is such men who have made Boston one of the richest towns in America.

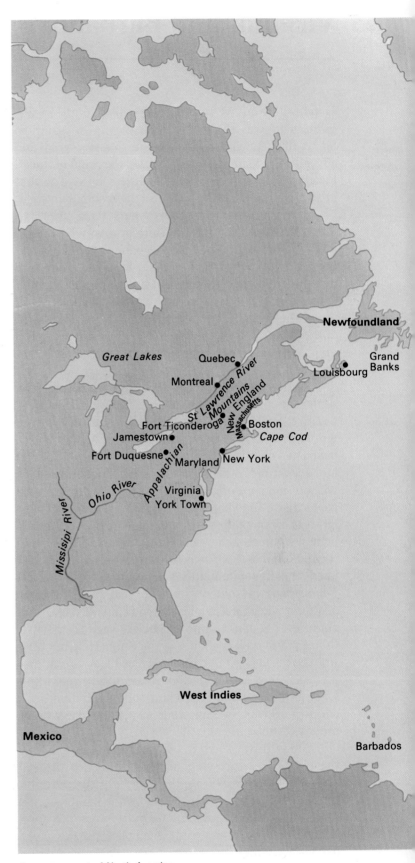

the eastern part of North America

3 Virginia and Barbados

Leaving Boston, we sail over 400 miles south, to Virginia. This was the first English colony in America. Sir Walter Raleigh had hoped to discover gold and silver, as the Spaniards had done. In the reign of Queen Elizabeth, he sent two lots of settlers here. The first group went home in despair, and the second vanished. Then, in 1607, some twenty years later, the ship *Susan Constant* brought 105 immigrants, who built a fort at Jamestown. They did not behave very sensibly. For example, when they wanted firewood, they tore down their homes, rather than do the harder work of felling trees. After two years only 38 of them were still alive. They packed, and set sail for home. At the mouth of the river, though, they met a ship bringing supplies and more settlers. They plucked up courage and returned.

Gradually, the new colony began to prosper. The settlers found no gold or silver, but they did discover a crop that was to make them richer than silver mines would ever have done. It was tobacco. The first Europeans in America were amazed to see Indians smoking, and even more so to find they could go for several days without food, as long as they had their tobacco. There was a Spanish doctor who thought tobacco could cure all sorts of complaints – rheumatism, toothache, headache, stomach-ache, chilblains, snake bites and wounds. James I of England, on the other hand, disliked smoking so much that he wrote a book called *A Counterblast to Tobacco*. In it he said that the body of a man who smoked a lot would be full of soot, like a chimney. People found tobacco very satisfying, though, and took no notice of the King. They not only smoked it, but also chewed it, brewed tea with it, and turned it into snuff. Virginians were soon making a lot of money growing and selling tobacco. In their own country it was so important that they used it for money, instead of coins.

The seed was sown in the spring, and all the time the plants were growing, slaves had to hoe the soil and pick caterpillars from the leaves. In the autumn, the leaves began to turn colour. That meant it was time to pick them, and hang them in bundles to cure. When the tobacco was ready, they packed it into huge barrels weighing half a ton. They rolled these down to the ships. Planters whose land was a little way from the water had to make special tracks called 'rolling roads'.

The planters were rich. Some of them owned thousands of acres of land, and lived in mansions, like the big country houses in England. They were very different from the poor habitants of New France. They were also very different from the Boston merchants, for they were no puritans. They left all the hard work to their slaves, while they enjoyed themselves. They squandered their money on luxurious furniture, clothes and carriages, they kept many servants, and they gave expensive parties. For all their large incomes many were deeply in debt, something which would have horrified a strict Bostonian.

Our last port of call is the island of Barbados, in the West Indies. Here, too, the inhabitants made themselves rich, and again, it was not from gold and silver. This time it was sugar.

The first Europeans to arrive were Spaniards, but all they did was to take away the natives to work in the silver mines on the mainland. Some English settlers arrived in 1625, and found the island deserted. Within a few years, they started to grow sugar cane. This was hard work, especially cutting the cane in the hot sun, so they bought negro slaves. After they had cut the cane, they crushed it between rollers to squeeze out the liquid. The rollers were driven by windmills. There were several hundred of these on the island. Next, they boiled the liquid to take out the sugar. This was a long, complicated job, lasting several months. As well as sugar, they produced a sticky treacle called molasses, and molasses could be made into rum. Sugar and rum were two luxuries for which the people in Europe paid high prices. The planters in Barbados became rich. Like the tobacco planters in Virginia, they lived in magnificent houses, with expensive furniture. They had expensive tastes as well, and often spent more money than they could afford.

The main town of Barbados, Bridgewater, was well built. The island had good roads made from broken coral. There were plenty of forts, with heavy cannon, to keep away the French and the Spaniards. Barbados is only thirty miles long, and twenty wide, so it is smaller than an English county. None the less, the people of Great Britain looked on it as their most valuable colony.

From just the few visits we have made, we can see how important North America had become to European people. In the north, the seas gave fish, and the forests, furs and timber. From the hot lands further south came luxuries like tobacco, sugar and rum. All this was worth fighting for, and there were some bitter wars.

4 The Slave Trade

You have seen in the last two sections that the planters in Virginia and Barbados used Negro slaves. This was true of all the English colonies south of Maryland, and in all the West Indies.

One of these slaves will tell us his story. He is from the Ibo tribe in Nigeria. 'My home used to be deep inside Africa. We had a hard life, but at least we were free. One day, a gang of black men attacked our village. We fought as best we could, but they had firearms and they soon overpowered us. They destroyed ten villages in our region, and took many prisoners. They put heavy collars round our necks and tied us in long lines. They then made us walk many miles every day.

They struck us with whips if we did not walk fast enough, but every so often someone would fall exhausted. They just shot him where he lay. We could not understand where they were taking us, but we were sure we were going to be eaten.

'At last we reached the sea. Here, I saw my first white men. They had red faces, straight, loose hair and they wore strange clothes. With them, they had bales of cloth, iron axes, iron pots, and some of those terrible firearms that had so frightened us when our village was attacked. They looked at each one of us carefully, prodding and poking, and they argued a lot with the black men who had captured us. Then I realized what was happening. We were being sold.

'We spent a few days locked in dungeons in a fort. Other captives joined us, from different tribes. My wife and children were taken from me, and I never saw them again. I was put with strangers, and we could not speak each other's languages.

'Then came the worst five weeks of my life. We were taken to a ship, chained together, and packed into the hold. The heat and the smell were unbearable. Many died from disease, and some just from despair. Each day the sailors collected a few more dead bodies and flung them over the side. One day, a number of people broke loose and jumped into the sea. I tried to kill myself by not eating, but some sailors forced my mouth open with a piece of iron, and made me take food. We still had no idea where we were going, but we were sure that there was a horrible death waiting for us at the end of our journey.

The Slave Trade

'At last the voyage ended, and we were more terrified than ever. We were taken to a market place, where we were sold once again. My new master brought me here. He did not kill and eat me. He whipped me once, when I disobeyed him, but most of the time he is anxious to keep me in good health. He treats me rather as he does his horse, and for much the same reason. He wants me to work. I have to toil for long hours in the heat of the sun. Cutting the sugar cane is especially hard.

'I have a new wife, but she is one my master chose, and I do not like her. We live in a little one-roomed hut, with wooden walls and a mud floor. Our food is mainly corn and salted fish. We dip the fish in flour, boil it, and then add hot peppers to give it some flavour. On Sundays, our master lets us rest. We dance and sing together and tell our children the stories that we learnt in Africa. Their favourites are the Anansi tales, about a man who was also a spider.

'Sometimes we talk of rebelling against our masters, and sailing back to Africa. We know in our hearts, though, that it can never be. We are going to be slaves, and so will our children and our children's children for ever more.'

No-one knows how many Africans were taken to America as slaves, but at least two million went to the British colonies alone. In 1700 they were sold for £15 each, on average, and by the 1750s they fetched £40. There was a lot of money to be made. Merchants in Liverpool and Bristol loaded their ships with cotton cloth and iron goods. They exchanged these for slaves in Africa, and sold the slaves either in the West Indies or in the southern colonies on the mainland. With the money they bought sugar or tobacco. The ships went out, then, with common, cheap goods, and came home with valuable luxuries. Men in the slave trade became rich, as did the planters.

After a time, though, more and more people saw how wicked the slave trade was. Men like Thomas Folwell Buxton and William Wilberforce spent years trying to persuade Parliament to make it illegal. Parliament finally did so in 1807.

TO BE SOLD & LET
BY PUBLIC AUCTION,
On MONDAY the 18th of MAY, 1829,
UNDER THE TREES.
FOR SALE,
THE THREE FOLLOWING
SLAVES,
VIZ.
HANNIBAL, about 30 Years old, an Excellent House Servant, of Good Character.
WILLIAM, about 35 Years old, a Labourer.
NANCY, an excellent House Servant and Nurse.
The MEN belonging to "LEECH'S" Estate, and the WOMAN to Mrs. D. SMIT

TO BE LET,
On the usual conditions of the Hirer finding them in Food, Clothing and Medical ance.
THE FOLLOWING
MALE and FEMALE
SLAVES,

ROBERT BAGLEY, about 20 Years old, a good House Servant.
WILLIAM BAGLEY, about 18 Years old, a Labourer.
JOHN ARMS, about 18 Years old.
JACK ANTONIA, about 40 Years old, a Labourer.
PHILIP, an Excellent Fisherman.
HARRY, about 27 Years old, a good House Servant.
LUCY, a Young Woman of good Character, used to House Work and the Nursery.
ELIZA, an Excellent Washerwoman.
CLARA, an Excellent Washerwoman.
FANNY, about 14 Years old, House Servant.
SARAH, about 14 Years old, House Servant.

Also for Sale, at Eleven o'Clock,
Fine Rice, Gram, Paddy, Books, Muslins,
Needles, Pins, Ribbons, &c. &c.
AT ONE O'CLOCK, THAT CELEBRATED ENGLISH HORSE
BLUCHER,

5 The British Conquer Canada

As we have seen, both France and Britain had colonies in North America. Each wanted to take the vast areas of land that remained. The British were hemmed in by the Appalachian mountains, and the French tried to hem them in even more. They built forts along the Mississippi and around the Great Lakes. Then, in 1753, they built Fort Duquesne in the valley of the Ohio. This annoyed the Virginians, who felt their enemies were coming far too close. They sent a force of militia, under Major George Washington, to drive them away. The French defeated Washington, as well as a British army under General Braddock, which came out later.

The war now began in earnest. However, there was fighting in Europe as well, and the French King was worried about his enemies in Germany. He only sent 3,500 men to Canada. On the other hand, the British Prime Minister, William Pitt, was determined to conquer North America. He sent 20,000 troops, and there were 22,000 colonial volunteers as well. Also, the British navy was there to help the army. The French only held on as long as they did, because they fought bravely, and because they had an excellent general, the Marquis de Montcalm.

Since he was heavily outnumbered, Montcalm fought on the defensive. In 1758 he defeated a powerful British force that attacked Fort Ticonderoga. However, the British army, helped by the navy, captured Louisbourg near the mouth of the St. Lawrence. Then, early in 1859, Montcalm decided he must concentrate his forces so he abandoned both Fort Ticonderoga and Fort Duquesne. Everything now depended on the defence of Quebec.

In June 1759, a British fleet of 50 warships and 120 troop transports anchored off the Isle of Orleans, near Quebec. They had been five weeks nosing their way up the St. Lawrence River. In charge was General James Wolfe. He was tall, but lanky, with sloping shoulders and he had a double chin. Also, he was young for a general, being only thirty-two. His appearance was misleading. Though he certainly did not look it, he was a man of great determination, and a brilliant soldier. He was going to need all his courage and skill.

Quebec stands on a headland, with cliffs facing the river, so it was impossible to attack it directly. Down-

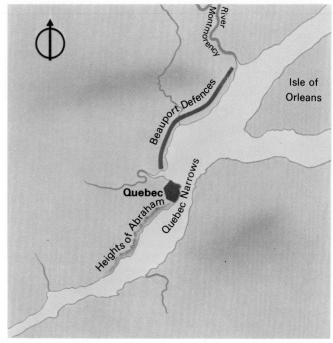

the attack on Quebec

stream, there were the strong Beauport Defences. As for going upstream, it seemed impossible to take ships through the Quebec Narrows, with their strong currents. Wolfe thought his best plan was to force the Beauport Defences. He landed his army by the River Montmorency, and attacked again and again. One day he lost 400 men in just two minutes. The French stood firm, and as the weeks passed, the British began to despair. By early August, Wolfe was ill and in bed. Then, in late August, he ordered his troops to abandon their camp by the River Montmorency and go to the south bank of the St. Lawrence. The French were delighted, for they were sure they were winning.

Wolfe, however, was not leaving. A British warship, the *Sutherland*, had sailed through the Quebec Narrows, showing it was possible to attack Quebec from the other side. However, the river bank was easy to defend, for there were cliffs all along it. Montcalm put groups of 50 men at likely places, and sent 1,000 of his best troops under Colonel Bougainville to patrol the area. The small groups would be able to hold off any landing party until Bougainville came to their aid.

Wolfe decided the only way was to cross secretly in the dead of night. At 2 a.m. on September 13th, nearly 2,000 men rowed ashore, using muffled oars, and in complete silence. A sentry challenged them, but a Scottish officer knew enough French to answer him. The leading men made their way up the steep face of the cliff and took the small French force at the top completely by surprise. Wolfe then ferried over more and more men, and when dawn broke, Montcalm was horrified to find 4,500 of his enemies on the Heights of Abraham, just outside the town. He had as many men himself, though, and he led them out to give battle.

The French advanced firing and shouting as they came. Wolfe's men lay down until the last minute, when they stood in line and waited in silence. The French came on, still firing and shouting. When they were only fifty yards away the British soldiers fired a tremendous volley. That was all that was needed. The one volley smashed the French army to pieces, and the survivors turned and fled.

The battle lasted only ten minutes, but when it was over Quebec was taken and soon afterwards, the

the death of Montcalm

whole of Canada. Many brave men died, though, on both sides. Among them were General Wolfe and General Montcalm.

The British
Conquer Canada

the death of General Wolfe

6 The American War of Independence Begins

During the conquest of Canada, Britain and her thirteen American colonies fought side by side against the French. A few years later they were fighting each other. Why was that?

A New England merchant will tell us what he feels about Britain. 'The British look on the American colonies as their back yard. We produce all sorts of things Europeans need – furs, timber, fish and tobacco. We want the best prices for our goods, but can we sell them where we like? Oh no! We have to send everything to Britain. Well, we need manufactured goods. Out in the New England countryside, for example, they want muskets, iron ploughs, knives, hoes and hundreds of thousands of nails to build their log cabins. Can we buy these things where they are cheapest? Not at all. We have to buy from Britain.' *'Can't you make them yourselves?'* 'The British will not allow it, otherwise we would have a flourishing iron industry in New England.

'Another thing, we fought the French to stop them taking the land beyond the Appalachians. There are thousands of square miles out there, inhabited by a handful of Indians. We need that land badly, and once we had beaten the French, we thought we could move into it. But what do the British say? They say that all territory west of the Appalachians is crown property, and we cannot take an inch of it.

'The worst thing, though, is their taxes. A while back, they suddenly decided that every legal document and newspaper must have a revenue stamp on it. Well, we put a stop to that. We burnt all the stamps, and one stamp master had to ride so fast to escape the mob, that his horse died under him. Then they tried taxing our imports, like cottons, wines and silks. We just refused to buy those things.' *'But everyone has to pay taxes!'* 'I know, but only if they agree. No-one is going to tax me without my consent, and all good Americans feel the same.' Now let us hear what the British Prime Minister, Lord North, has to say. 'Of all the ungrateful rascals in the world, the Americans must be the worst. They were in mortal danger from the French and the Indians, until we saved them. It cost us millions of pounds, and the lives of thousands of our soldiers. When we asked them to help us, all they said was, "We will come if you will pay our expenses." In the end we had to give them £1 million to fight for their own homes.

'Well, we decided that if the Americans did so little during the war, they could at least help when it was over. Their trade is useful to us. We need their goods and they need ours. What better to exchange with one another, rather than with our enemies? Then they have a long frontier to defend – some 2,000 miles. There are still some French settlements beyond it, as well as many hostile Indian tribes. That frontier has to be defended. We gave them a full year to make some suggestions, hoping they might raise an army of their own. They said nothing. "Very well," we told them, "we will look after the frontier, but you must help pay." We imposed some very light taxes, but they were so angry and vicious that we had to remove most of them.

'The main problem is that we have conquered Canada. The Americans are no longer afraid of the French. They think they do not need our help any more, so they are not bothered how much they annoy us.'

the Boston Tea Party

the Ride of Paul Revere

The troubles in America became really serious in 1773. The government tried another tax, this time on tea. Two hundred men from Boston decided to do something dramatic. Dressed as Red Indians, they boarded three ships in the harbour. They then poured £18,000 worth of tea into the sea. They called what happened the Boston Tea Party.

The British government was furious, and closed the port of Boston, so that there could be no more trade there. It was a savage punishment, and the Americans were furious in their turn. All the colonies sent delegates to what they called a Continental Congress. It was a kind of parliament. You probably know that Congress still meets today to make laws for the American people. The Americans prepared to fight, too. The young men formed armed companies. They called themselves Minute Men, because they were ready to fight at a minute's notice. Also, the colonists collected secret stores of weapons and supplies.

In 1774, the governor of Boston heard there was an arms store at Concord, eighteen miles away, so he sent a small force to destroy it. American spies heard of his plan, though, and a Boston silversmith called Paul Revere rode through the night, calling the Minute Men to arms. In the morning, they tried to stop the British at Lexington. The British scattered them, and went on to destroy the arms dump at Concord. They then went back to Boston, with the Americans firing at them from every rock and tree. The Americans lost eight men at Lexington, but their snipers killed nearly 300 British on their return march. The war had begun.

the battle of Lexington

7 The Americans Win Their Independence

George Washington

At the beginning of the war, there were plenty of Americans with fine words to say. One of their orators, Patrick Henry, exclaimed, 'Give me liberty or give me death.' When Thomas Jefferson wrote the Declaration of Independence in 1776 he included this famous statement:

'We hold these truths to be self evident, that all men are created equal, that they are endowed by their Creator with certain inalienable Rights, that among these are Life, Liberty and the pursuit of Happiness. That to secure these rights, Governments are instituted among men, deriving their just powers from the consent of the Governed.' Many of the men who signed this document owned slaves!

Congress issued the Declaration on July 4th, which the people of the United States still celebrate as Independence Day. The first congressman to sign, John Hancock, wrote his name large and clear, saying that King George III must be able to read it without his spectacles.

So much for fine words, but when it came to fighting the rebel Americans did not do very well. All sorts of men joined the army. There were farmers, lawyers, labourers and criminals. All were hard to discipline. A German officer who tried to help them complained that he had to give the reason for every order before his men would obey. Their Commander in Chief, George Washington, said in despair, 'Never was such a rabble dignified by the name of army.' British regular soldiers, on the other hand, were the best in the world. In an open battle, they were almost sure to win. For example, at Guilford Courthouse in 1781, a British force of 1,900 beat 4,500 Americans. Most of the rebels fired one shot and ran.

A big problem was that Congress found it hard to raise money. The American taxpayer was as mean during the war as he had been before it. In the winter of 1777 Washington's army was camped at Valley Forge. They were in rags, dying of disease, and living on 'a leg of nothing and no turnips'. When Washington asked Congress for supplies, they told him to plunder the local farmers. Washington refused.

Why, then, did Britain lose the war?

In the first place, Congress chose the right man to be Commander in Chief. As we have seen, he was George Washington. Washington was a planter and slave owner from Virginia. He was not a brilliant general, but he was brave and determined. He thought that if he could hold on long enough, he might one day have the chance to win a great victory, and end the war.

Secondly, though they were not much good in battle, many of the rebels were splendid guerrilla fighters. Lots of them were frontiersmen who were excellent marksmen. They had been shooting wild animals and Red Indians all their lives.

Thirdly, the American colonies covered a vast area. The British had only a few thousand troops, and though they might win battles they could not hold the land they conquered. The best they could do was to occupy the most important towns on the coast, like New York. Here, they were fairly safe, as long as they had the Royal Navy to help them.

Most important of all, though, the Americans found allies. The French wanted revenge for the loss of Canada, but they did not wish to lose another war. Then, in 1777, a British general, John Burgoyne, blundered into the forests of New England. He was surrounded by a much larger force of Americans, and had to surrender at Saratoga. He lost 6,000 men, which was bad enough. What was far worse, his defeat encouraged the French to help the Americans. Soon afterwards Holland and Spain joined them. Britain was on her own. Her enemies attacked her colonies in the Far East, they attacked her islands in the West Indies, and the Spaniards besieged Gibraltar. There was even talk of invading Britain herself.

the battle of Bunker Hill

French money, French supplies and French soldiers poured across the Atlantic. Even more important, the Americans now had a powerful navy on their side. Washington saw that if the French would attack places like New York from the sea, while his army attacked from the land, the British could be defeated. Twice Washington tried to persuade the French to help in this way, and failed. Then, in 1781, he heard that the French Admiral de Grasse was going to Chesapeake Bay. Here, General Cornwallis had a force of 7,000 men in Yorktown. After six years of waiting, Washington's chance had come. He marched as fast as he could to Yorktown.

Cornwallis found himself besieged by an army of 16,000 French and Americans, while there were twenty-four French warships out in the bay. He fought as long as he could, but, in the end, he had to surrender. His men laid down their arms and marched out of the town. As they did so, their band played an old tune, 'The World Turned Upside Down.'

Yorktown need not have been the end of the war, for a few months later Admirals Rodney and Hood smashed the French fleet at the Battle of the Saints, in the West Indies. However, Yorktown made it seem the

the British land troops in New York

war might drag on for years. The British were tired of fighting, so in 1783 they made peace, giving the thirteen colonies their freedom. They became the United States of America.

Chapter Six   The War Against Napoleon

1 France Under Napoleon

It is 1812. We will go to Paris to visit Monsieur Lebois, who is a banker. He has a handsome house in a brand new street called the Rue de Rivoli. His furniture is expensive, with a great deal of rich, gold ornament. The walls are hung with silk, while the emblem of the eagle is everywhere. The eagle reminds us that France is ruled by an Emperor, Napoleon Bonaparte.

Both Monsieur Lebois and his wife are small, round, plump and very rich, *'You have a fine house, Monsieur.'* 'It was not always so. We have had a terrible time in France.' *'What happened?'* 'It all began in 1789. The King, Louis XVI, was desperate for money, so he asked the Estates-General* to meet and help him rule the country. We were all pleased, because we thought that at last bankers, merchants, and other people like myself were going to have a say in the government. Until then, it was just the King and nobles who counted. The only time they had any use for us was when they wanted to borrow money. It all went wrong, though.' *'Why was that?'* 'It was the leaders of the Paris mob, the Jacobins, who seized control, not respectable citizens at all. The mob was completely out of hand.' 'They *were* starving,' says Madame Lebois. 'That may be, but there was no need to behave as they did. First they tore down the Bastille,** and then the executions began. I could hardly feel sorry for the King and the nobles when they lost their heads. Before long, though, they were killing quite ordinary people – anyone they thought might be an enemy. The tumbrils used to rattle

* They were a bit like the British Parliament.
** A royal fortress, like the Tower of London.

the execution of King Louis XVI

through the streets taking the victims to the scaffold. The guillotine was busy all the time. My wife and I went to see it one day, but once was enough. We knew our own turn might come quite soon.' Monsieur Lebois's double chin quivers at the thought.

'That wasn't all,' Madame Lebois goes on. 'These men, the Jacobins, plunged us into war with the whole of Europe. Austria and Prussia attacked us by land, and Great Britain by sea. At one time we thought Paris itself would fall.' *'How did it all end?'* 'We were saved by Napoleon,' replies Monsieur Lebois. 'He became a great general, and then used his position to make himself Emperor. He was crowned in 1804. He has done wonders for France. We now have gold coins in our pockets. It just used to be worthless, paper notes. There is plenty of trade and industry, so my bank is doing well. France now has the best secondary schools in the world. We have a new code of laws as well.' 'Think of the improvements to Paris,' says Madame Lebois. 'We have gas lighting in the streets, pure, fresh drinking water in the homes, and there are all the marvellous new buildings, like our street, the Rue de Rivoli. The Emperor has even thought of a new way of numbering houses – even numbers down one side, and odd numbers down the other. It makes finding an address so easy. I like the Opera, too. There were no entertainments during the Revolution, but Napoleon himself enjoys the Opera. We have seen him there several times with his new Empress. He is especially fond of Italian music. He is Corsican, you see, so he is practically an Italian himself.'

'He gave us back our Sunday, too,' says Monsieur Lebois. *'What do you mean?'* 'My wife and I are Catholics, but no-one was allowed to go to church

during the Revolution. They even crucified some peasants in La Vendée, because they refused to pull down a cross. The churches are open again now.' *'So you have no complaints about Napoleon?'* Monsieur and Madame Lebois look at each other uneasily, and then Monsieur Lebois says, 'Well, we do not like the war. It seems the Emperor wants to rule the world. He hates the British, but he can't conquer them, because their navy is too strong. There is a dreadful war against the Spaniards. If those people capture a French soldier, they torture him to death. Now, Napoleon has invaded Russia.'

Tears come to Madame's eyes. 'Our only son, François, is an officer in the Imperial Guard,' she says. 'It is a great honour, but we would rather he was at home, helping in the bank. Just now, he is with the army, on the way to Moscow. We do not know if we will ever see him again.'

coronation of Napoleon

2 The British Navy

When France declared war on Great Britain in 1793, her army was many times larger than our own. All that stopped a French invasion was the British Navy. It was enough. Admiral Jervis said proudly, 'I don't say the French can't come: I say they can't come by sea.'

the *Victory* under full sail

Today, one of the old battleships, H.M.S. *Victory*, is in Portsmouth Harbour. She is 227 feet long and weighs 3,500 tonnes. You can compare this with a modern aircraft carrier, which may be 900 feet long and weigh 50,000 tonnes. A battleship was a floating fortress. *Victory* carried 100 guns, which were on three decks, as you can see from the picture. They are nearly all at the side. In battle, a ship fired her guns, one after the other, very quickly, so it was like a roll of thunder. This was called 'firing a broadside'. The weakest part of a ship was her stern, because the officers' cabins were there, and they had glass windows. The best position was to have your broadside to your enemy's stern. Then, you could fire all your guns into her and she could reply only with a few. Some of your shot might go the whole length of the other vessel and do terrible damage. This was called 'raking' an enemy.

Victory at the time of Trafalgar

1 Mizzenmast   2 Quarter Deck   3 Mainmast   4 Fo'c'sle
5 Foremast   6 Upper Gun Deck   7 Nelson's Day Cabin
8 Nelson's Sleeping Cabin with his cot   9 Middle Gun Deck
10 Wardroom   11 Entry Port   12 Lower Gun Deck   13 Orlop
14 Sick Bay   15 Midshipman's Berth – here Nelson died
16 Powder Room   17 Shot Locker

The British Navy

What was it like to be a sailor? A midshipman called Edward Power will teach us. *'How old are you Edward?'* 'I am twelve.' *'That is young to go to sea.'* 'Not at all. There are many midshipmen younger than I am. We want to be officers as soon as possible, so we start young. I hope to be a lieutenant by the time I am eighteen. The ordinary sailors are grown men, of course. Sometimes, I have to command a boat's crew. The men don't like taking orders from a boy, but they have to do as I say. It's not often that I give orders, though. I have lessons from the school-master, and the officers teach me how to manage the ship. Also, I am Lieutenant Jones's servant. I have to look after his cabin and clean his equipment. If he is not pleased with me, he sends me to the masthead.' Edward points to a small platform, high in the rigging. 'You can imagine what it's like to stay up there for three hours in a gale. Still, that's not as bad as the punishments the men have. They are flogged with the cat o'nine tails. One was hanged, even, last year.'

Next, we talk to one of the seamen, George Evans. 'I am a master gunner. I have three men to help me. To load our gun we first ram in a bag of gunpowder, and after it, a wad, to hold it tight. Then we put in the shot. Next, my mate lays the gun. That means he points it at the correct angle. We fire when ordered. As the gun goes off, it leaps backwards, so we have to be well to one side of it. Before reloading, we swab out the barrel with a damp sponge, to make sure there are no sparks left. We have to be quick, because the enemy will not wait for us. *Victory* can fire three broadsides

the battle of the Nile

in under four minutes. If an enemy ship gets all three, she is finished. We always fire into their hulls. The French, they fire into our rigging, hoping we won't be able to chase them.' *'How did you join the navy, George?'* 'I used to work on a collier brig, so I was a good sailor. I volunteered to get away from my wife. Lots of the crew, though, were taken by the press

the Press Gang

gang. Many a man has been out walking, had a crack on the head, and woken up on this ship. Once on board, you don't leave until the war is over. I have been five years on "Victory". None of us likes it. There is danger from shipwreck, or having an arm or a leg shot off by the French. If we are at sea for a long time, all we have to eat is salt beef and ship's biscuits. Discipline can be hard. Nelson is a good man – strict but fair. On some ships the officers enjoy having the men flogged. What bothers us most, though, is our pay. We only have nineteen shillings a month, and mostly it is in arrears.'

This, then, was how Britain treated the men whom she expected to save her from the French. It is not surprising that in 1797 there was a mutiny in the fleet. The sailors wanted all sorts of things, but mainly more pay. As the government was expecting a French invasion at any time, it at once raised the pay of the ordinary seaman to twenty-nine shillings a month. The King also gave a royal pardon to everyone who had taken part in the mutiny. Most of the sailors went back to their duties willingly enough.

3 The Battle of Trafalgar

Napoleon won many battles, and by 1803 he had only one important enemy left. That was Britain. He determined to conquer her, so he gathered a large army at Boulogne. From there, on a clear day, he could see the white cliffs of Dover. He could have taken his soldiers across quite easily if it had not been for the Royal Navy. He said, 'Let us be masters of the Straits for six hours, and we will be masters of the world.'

The French had a good navy, but it was scattered. There were ships in Brest, Rochefort, and Toulon. Spain, who was France's ally, had ships in Ferrol and Cadiz. Outside each of these ports was a British fleet, blockading it. Napoleon's plan was that the French should escape from their harbours and sail to the West Indies. That would frighten the British, because their West Indian islands were important for their trade. Doubtless, the British would send a large fleet to defend them, much as you would rush to protect your money box if someone was after it. When the French ships met, they were to hurry back across the Atlantic and seize control of the English Channel. With any luck, Napoleon's soldiers could invade England before the British fleet returned from the West Indies.

At first, Napoleon's plans went well. The French Admiral at Toulon was Villeneuve, and the English Admiral blockading him was Nelson. Nelson allowed Villeneuve to escape and then wasted time hunting for him in the Mediterranean. Villeneuve, though, headed across the Atlantic, and it was some weeks before Nelson realised where he had gone. He then chased after him. None of the other French squadrons joined Villeneuve, so he came back to Europe. He hoped he might help his friends escape and join with him to sail up the Channel. What happened though, was that he met a British fleet under Admiral Calder, off Cape Finisterre. Calder drove him away, so he went to Cadiz, where he joined the Spaniards. He now had a fleet of thirty-four French and Spanish ships, but in the meantime, Nelson had returned. He was off Cadiz with twenty-nine British ships. What was Villeneuve to do? He decided to come out and fight.

The French Admiral drew up his ships in line of battle. He thought the British would form a line of battle, too, and fight broadside to broadside. His gunners would fire at their enemies' rigging, so that his ships could escape quite easily, if they wanted. Nelson was determined they should not. He divided his fleet

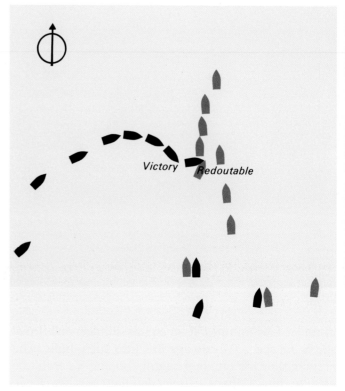

the *Victory* breaks the French line

into two. One part he commanded himself. He put it in line behind his flagship *Victory*, and cut the enemy fleet in half. He engaged the middle of their line and the wind made it difficult for their leading ships to join the battle. Meanwhile, Admiral Collingwood with the other half of the British fleet destroyed the remaining third of the enemy. Nelson ordered his captains to sail between the enemy ships and not to fire until they could rake them. This was dangerous, because it meant they had to take the French broadsides as they came up. However, their raking fire did terrible damage. Even more important, the ships that broke through were behind the enemy and stopped them escaping.

Nelson's plan worked, but the British did not win easily. One of the heroes of the battle was a little man only 4' 10" tall. He was Jean Lucas, captain of the French ship *Redoutable*. His ship engaged Nelson's *Victory*. They fired broadsides at each other and then grappled. Lucas called out his boarding parties. He had trained them well, so they were good shots and experts at throwing grenades. These men swarmed into their

Nelson falls during the battle of Trafalgar

rigging and swept *Victory*'s decks with musket fire. They also threw some 200 grenades into her. The English sailors fled below, and the French began to board. Just then, though, the *Temeraire* came to the rescue, pouring one broadside after another into the *Redoutable*. Lucas fought on, but now he had two enemies. Soon all of his guns were out of action, 500 of his crew of 640 were killed or wounded, and his ship was sinking. Only then, did he surrender.

During the attack on *Victory*, a French musketeer shot Nelson. The bullet smashed through his chest and broke his backbone. He died three hours later, but not before he had learnt that the battle was won. The French and Spaniards lost 4,400 dead, 2,500 wounded, 20,000 prisoners, and twenty ships out of their thirty-four. The British lost 450 killed, 1,200 wounded and no ships at all. Napoleon gave up all hope of invading Britain.

4 Wellington's Army

the Duke of Wellington

In 1807, the French invaded Spain and Portugal. The following year, the Duke of Wellington took a British army to help those countries defend themselves. We will visit his camp to talk to some of his soldiers.

First of all we meet Bob, a man from the artillery, who takes us to see his gun. The gun barrel is just like the ones we saw on Nelson's *Victory*. The carriage, though, has large wheels which make it easier to move on land. 'This is a field piece,' explains Bob. 'That means we can use it in battle. It's quite light, you see. For a siege we would want a much heavier gun – a twenty-four pounder, at least.' '*What ammunition do you use?*' Bob picks up a cannon ball that weighs about six pounds. 'At long range we use this round shot. If the ground is at all hard, it will bounce along like a marble, and kill quite a lot of men. Sometimes we use shells. A shell is filled with gunpowder, and has a fuse.' '*How do you light the fuse?*' 'The blast from the gun does that. If we time it right, the shell will burst over the heads of the enemy. One of their shells fell near me once. It lay on the ground, fizzing away. I just had time to dive into a hole before it exploded.' '*What are these cans?*' 'That's case shot. The canister is full of odd scraps of iron that fly through the air like a handful of loose stones. We can do terrible damage to the enemy with case, but only at short range.'

Next, we meet a cavalry officer, called Charles. He is a proud young man with black, curling moustaches. His horse is a handsome grey charger. 'The cavalry is the most important part of the army,' he says. 'One man in the cavalry is worth three in the infantry.' He draws his sabre to show us. It is curved for slashing, and is as sharp as a razor. 'One blow with that, and I can take off a man's head,' he boasts. 'My most important weapon, though, is my horse. If I came charging at you on Betsy here, I don't think you would stay

to argue.' *'When did you learn to ride?'* 'Almost before I could walk. My father has an estate in Leicestershire, which is grand hunting country. Just now, I chase Frenchmen instead of foxes. It is much more exciting. We go out scouting most days, often very near the enemy. Our horses are so good that the French gave up trying to catch us long ago.'

The last man we meet is a sergeant in the infantry, called William. 'This is my Brown Bess,' he explains, picking up a musket. He shows us how to load it by ramming a cartridge down the barrel. The cartridge is a tube of paper, with gunpowder and a musket ball inside. *'That takes a long time, William.'* 'Not at all. We can load and fire four times a minute, which is four times as fast as the French.' *'How far will your musket shoot?'* 'About three hundred yards, but we don't open fire above one hundred yards. At that range we usually hit someone, even if it's not the man we aim at.' *'The cavalry don't seem to think much of the infantry.'* 'They are a conceited lot. They are all right for scouting or chasing the enemy when he is defeated, but they aren't much use in a battle. Their trouble is that they think the war is one big hunting party. I overheard "Nosey"* himself complaining about them the other day. It seems Major-General Slade had been soundly beaten by a French force no bigger than his own. "They gallop at everything," he

* The soldiers' name for Wellington.

was saying, "so they fall straight into any trap the French may set for them."' *'Surely you infantry can't stop a cavalry charge.'*

For his answer, William draws his bayonet and clips it on his musket. He then thrusts it towards us. 'You imagine our battalion, eight hundred of us three ranks deep, standing so, in a square. There is no horse born that will jump a hedge like that. I have been fighting in the Peninsula for five years now, and I haven't seen French cavalry break a British square yet. What's more, I haven't seen our cavalry break a French square, either.'

107

5 A Day with Wellington's Army

It is the summer of 1813. Wellington has led his army into the heart of Spain. He has won a great victory, the Battle of Vitoria, and now the French are retreating to their own country. We will spend a day with the British army, which is moving after them.

At 5.00 in the morning the bugles sound, and the soldiers wake up, grumbling and cursing. In the half light, they take up their muskets and haversacks, and form ranks three ranks deep, ready to march. First, a body of light cavalry canter away. Next comes a detachment of light infantry in smart, dark-green uniforms. Almost at once, we hear the rumble of wheels, and a dozen light guns roll past, the horses drawing them at a quick trot. These three groups make up the advance guard. They have a busy time ahead of them and it will be exciting, too, if they meet any French.

Now comes the main army, moving much more slowly. Heavy cavalry lead, their steel helmets shining. Long columns of infantry tramp by, raising clouds of dust. Next come the supplies. There are herds of bullocks, for live meat travels easier than dead; there are strings of mules, laden with baggage; there are clumsy Spanish carts, whose wheels make a squeak like a knife edge being drawn over a plate. The men in charge of them are colourful, but villainous-looking Spaniards.

The road is already churned into ruts, but now the heavy guns appear. They are twenty-four pounders, for use in sieges. Long teams of straining oxen draw them, and we wonder how they manage in the mountains. More infantry follow. These are Portuguese, but they are as well disciplined as the British soldiers we saw earlier. From time to time we see little groups of women, for one soldier in twenty is allowed to bring his wife. An officer's wife goes past, riding a donkey, and carrying a pink parasol. A servant, on a mule, is nursing her baby, and tied behind the mule is a tired, unwilling goat. A body of cavalry brings up the rear. It is several miles from the head of the column.

A Day with Wellington's Army

The troops march for half an hour, then the bugles sound and they fall out for breakfast. This is a large, dry biscuit, and a piece of cold beef. Fifteen minutes later they are off again. They now march for an hour, rest for five minutes, and keep going like that until the midday break. They have more biscuits and beef, and rest through the worst of the heat. Then the march begins once more. With his musket and haversack, each man carries a load of sixty pounds. Their faces are caked with dust, save where trickles of perspiration wash it away. They are used to the discomfort, though, and keep up their spirits, laughing and joking. At last, the bugles sound a halt. The day's march is over. They have covered twelve miles at an average speed of two miles an hour.

The Quarter Master has chosen a good place to stay the night. The ground is flat, there is a stream, and there are trees nearby. Soon the men are busy making themselves comfortable. Some go to fetch water, some to collect wood, and others to draw rations – biscuits and beef again, but this time, a little rum as well.

We join a group who have lit a fire to brew tea. *'That was a hard day's march!'* we say. 'About average. We can cover thirty miles in a day, if we need to,' replies one of the soldiers. 'The worst march we ever did was the retreat from Madrid, last year,' says another. 'It was winter time you see, and usually we are snug in our billets at that time of year. The rain poured down and sometimes the mud was up to our knees. We had no tents, either, so we had to lie in the mud to sleep. What's more, the officer in charge of the supplies had sent them by another road. He made sure the French didn't eat our food, but neither did we. All we had for three days was acorns. Several of my friends died on that march.'

The men finish their supper, and lie down for the night. A few, fresh from England, twist and turn, but not the others. A mule starts braying, then another, and another, until dozens of them are making a hideous noise. The men sleep soundly until early morning when, at the first notes of the bugle, they are on their feet at once.

6 Napoleon in Russia

In 1811, Napoleon quarrelled with the Russians. Their ruler, Tsar Alexander I, had refused his offer of friendship, they were threatening his friends the Poles, and they insisted on trading with Britain against his will. Napoleon decided to invade Russia. He gathered a force of over half a million men. They came from twenty nations, including Italy, Poland, Germany, Holland and Switzerland. Only one-third was French. You will remember that Napoleon had 300,000 troops fighting in Spain.

As Napoleon advanced, the Russian armies fell back. They drove away the cattle, destroyed the crops and burnt the villages. The country is an enormous, grassy plain, and Napoleon's men began to think they were going to march for ever through vast, empty spaces. Napoleon was making for Moscow. The capital was St. Petersburg, but Moscow was larger, and was in the heart of Russia. The Tsar ordered his army to save it. Their commander was General Kutuzov. He had lost an eye in a battle with the Turks, he was so fat that he could not ride a horse, and he was 68 years old. For all that, he was an excellent soldier. He decided to make a stand at Borodino, a village 70 miles from Moscow.

When he realized the Russians were going to fight, Napoleon was delighted. He was not so pleased, though, when he saw where they were. Kutuzov had chosen a piece of country broken up with ravines and woods. They made it impossible for Napoleon to manoeuvre his men, using the clever tactics that had helped him win other battles. Also, the Russians had had time to build themselves trenches, and protect their artillery with mounds of turf.

Each side had about 600 guns, so the battle opened with the roaring of well over a thousand cannon. Napoleon had a plan, but it did not work. All he could rely on was the courage of his troops. They attacked the Russian positions again and again until, in places, the dead lay eight deep on the ground. The Russians fought like tigers. They were used to doing battle with the Turks, who always tortured and killed their prisoners. Russian soldiers never surrendered, but went on fighting to the end. Napoleon's army was the better, though, so they took the Russian positions one by one. General Kutuzov decided to retreat. He led away two-thirds of his army, having lost 44,000

men. Napoleon could not pursue him, for he had lost 33,000 himself. Dead and wounded lay everywhere. The senior surgeon in the French army sawed off 200 shattered limbs during the day, and his assistants were just as busy. However, the road to Moscow lay open.

Though Napoleon entered Moscow in triumph a few days later, he was soon a disappointed man. He had expected wealthy citizens to come and greet him, but they had left. All that remained were criminals and beggars. Next, soon after the French arrived, the Russians set fire to the city. They had taken away their fire engines, so four-fifths of it was destroyed. Worst of all, though, the Tsar showed no signs of wanting peace. Napoleon sent him several messages, but he just ignored them. In the end, Napoleon saw it was hopeless: he decided to leave Russia. He had wasted valuable time, though. The first snows fell as the French left the blackened ruins of Moscow, and soon their army was in the grip of a terrible winter.

the battle of Borodino

Men struggled through blizzards, their faces frost-bitten. Any that fell behind were killed by Cossack cavalry. The most difficult problem was to find food for the horses. One soldier kept his alive by creeping into the Russian camp, and stealing their hay. Few horses were as lucky, though. Most of them died, and later, so did the men. Only a few thousand staggered home. One of the last to arrive was a giant of a man, all in tatters. He was one of Napoleon's most famous generals, Marshal Ney, but some sentries who stopped him did not recognise him. 'Who are you?' they asked.

Ney replied, 'I am the rearguard of the Grand Army.'

After a while, Napoleon had abandoned his soldiers, and raced on in a sleigh. Back in France, he raised more troops. He fought on for another two years, but his old enemies, Prussia and Austria, had taken heart and joined the Russians. Meanwhile, Wellington was invading the South of France along with the Spaniards and Portuguese. In 1814, the Prussians under General Blücher captured Paris, and Napoleon surrendered.

7 The Battle of Waterloo

In 1814, after Napoleon had been defeated, he was given the little island of Elba in the Mediterranean to rule. This was generous treatment from his enemies, but in 1815 he decided to return to France. By then a brother of the King who had been guillotined was on the throne. He was Louis XVIII. Louis ordered soldiers to arrest Napoleon. When he saw them, Napoleon stepped forward and opened his greatcoat to expose his chest. 'I am your Emperor,' he said, 'kill me if you like.' 'Shoot him,' ordered the officers, but the men cheered Napoleon and ran to join him. Soon all his old soldiers were with him— the ones that were still alive— and Louis XVIII fled.

Napoleon was still in great danger, though, because there were powerful armies all round France, including the British and the Prussians who were in Belgium. He started by attacking the Prussians who were under Blücher at Ligny. He defeated them, but most of them escaped, and Blücher managed to hold them together. Two days later, Napoleon met the British at Waterloo, just south of Brussels. It was to be the first time he ever fought them. 'It will be a picnic,' he told one of his generals who warned him to be careful.

To the joy of the English soldiers, Wellington had been put in charge. 'Nosey has got the command,' said one of them. 'Won't we give them a beating now!' Wellington, though, was far from happy. Nearly all his best soldiers had been sent to fight in America, and

the ones he had were raw recruits who had never been in battle.

All Wellington could do was to stay on the defensive and hope that Blücher would come and help him. He put most of his men behind the brow of a hill, so that the enemy gunners could not see them, and sent some of his troops forward into some farmhouses, which they hurriedly fortified. He hoped they might break up the French attack before it advanced too far. Wellington kept his nerve, though. At the worst moment in the battle he was carefully studying the French army through his telescope, while his second in command, the Marquis of Anglesey, was sitting on his horse beside him. Suddenly, a cannon ball struck the Marquis, who yelled to Wellington, 'By God, Sir, I have lost my leg.' Wellington looked at the shattered, bleeding limb. 'By God, Sir, so you have,' he said, and turned back to his telescope.

Napoleon, on the other hand, was not at his best. He had piles, so it was painful for him to sit on his horse. At one point his officers were astonished to see him waddle off behind some bushes with his legs wide apart. He had gone to change his bandages.

The battle began with a splendid attack by some French infantry, and it might have succeeded had not the English cavalry charged and scattered them. Unfortunately, the English horsemen, who did a lot of hunting at home, chased the fugitives as if they were foxes. They rode much too close to the main French army, where they stuck in the mud and many of them were killed.

The French came back to the attack, captured one of the farmhouses, and pressed on to the main British army. The fighting was now so fierce, and men were falling so fast that one English officer wondered if everyone was going to be killed on both sides.

Most of the attacks came from French cavalry. The English infantry formed squares. The men fresh from England were terrified, but they soon saw that if they stood firm the horsemen could not ride into them. Napoleon thought, though, that if he made a really determined effort, the battle was his. He turned to his best soldiers, the cavalry of the Imperial Guard, and said, 'Follow me!' He led them to the weakest point in the British line, then, standing aside, ordered them to attack. They made a magnificent charge, but they could not break the British squares. Volley after

the French capture the farmhouse

a British square under attack

volley crashed into them so that the ground was heaped with dead and wounded. The survivors fled. A cry of dismay went up from the French, 'The Guard is retreating!'

Then, at last, the Prussians began to arrive. Blücher had promised Wellington he would join him early in the morning, but his first men did not appear until four in the afternoon. It was almost too late, but not quite. The Prussians wanted revenge for the Battle of Ligny, and the sight of this new enemy was too much for the weary French. Soon the whole of Napoleon's army was in full flight.

Some days later, Napoleon surrendered to the British, who sent him as a prisoner to the little island of St. Helena, in the middle of the Atlantic. There he died in 1821. Wellington went back to England in triumph, but he did not boast about his victory. When someone asked him what he thought of Waterloo, all he said was, 'It was a damned close-run thing.'

the Old Guard retreats

The Battle of Waterloo

Napoleon leaves the battlefield

Chapter Seven Transport and Exploration

1 Ocean Liners

1897 was the year of Queen Victoria's Diamond Jubilee. There was a grand review of the fleet at Spithead. One hundred and sixty-five battleships were drawn up in three lines, each thirty miles long. The Prince of Wales took the salute, sailing near the battleships in the royal yacht. Suddenly, a small boat appeared and began dashing in and out among the lines of ships. Fast Admiralty launches at once chased after her, but the small boat shot through the water at nearly 35 knots (40 m.p.h.) and the launches could not go nearly as fast. The boat was called the *Turbinia*, and belonged to Sir Charles Parsons. He had invented a new type of engine and he was determined that everyone should see how good it was. This engine was a steam turbine. It was much simpler than an ordinary steam engine, but it was also much more powerful.

The *Turbinia* certainly attracted a lot of attention. It was not long before shipbuilders were using turbines in much larger vessels. Then the Cunard Company became interested. The ship that crossed the Atlantic in the shortest time was awarded a prize called the 'Blue Riband'. At that time the Germans held the record but the Cunard Company was planning to build two gigantic liners, the *Mauretania* and the *Lusitania*. Perhaps Parsons's turbines would help Cunard win the Blue Riband for Great Britain? No one knew how turbines would work in a vessel weighing 31,000 tons, but Cunard was willing to try. The *Mauretania* made her maiden voyage in November

the *Turbina*

1907. It was a terrible crossing, but she won the Blue Riband for Great Britain. The liner was in service for twenty-eight years, and she held the Blue Riband for twenty-two of them.

We will pay the *Mauretania* a visit, and one of her stewards will show us round.

'You will see the *Mauretania* has four funnels,' he says. 'That's very important to the passengers. They think it means a ship is among the best afloat. Some liners even have a dummy funnel to make up the four because some passengers won't sail on a ship that has fewer than four funnels.'

The ship has seven decks. We go from one to the other in an electric lift. Some people think of a liner as a floating hotel but the *Mauretania* is more like a floating town! There are many cabins, of course, as well as various public rooms: a library, a writing room, a drawing room, a lounge, a smoking room and a grand saloon for meals and entertainment. There are so many flowers and plants that gardeners are needed to look after them.

'One of our main problems is to stop the passengers becoming bored,' continues the steward. 'There are all sorts of games they can play, like shuffleboard and deck tennis. In the evening there is dancing, or sometimes a show. I dread the shows. The passengers take part themselves, you see. Some of them think they can sing or dance or tell funny stories, but usually they can't and it's embarrassing to watch. When there is nothing else to do, they can go for a walk. Four times round the promenade deck is a mile. Some people who never go for a walk on land do so at sea. One man covered a hundred miles between Liverpool and

the promenade deck of the *Lusitania*

New York. The passengers get most excited at noon, when our captain says how many miles we have sailed in the day. They lay bets on it, you see.'

'*How far do you usually sail in one day?*' 'Over six hundred miles – quite often.' '*Do the passengers enjoy their voyage?*' 'Not as much as they think they will. We spend five days at sea, and most passengers spend the

the first-class lounge of the *Lusitania*

Ocean Liners

a cross-section of the *Mauretania*

first two days being sick. For the next three they still have to put up with the pitch and roll of the ship. The first-class passengers are amidships, so it's not too bad for them. The third-class passengers are at the front where it is nothing for them to rise and fall fifty feet in rough seas.'

'*How do you enjoy life at sea?*' we ask the steward. 'I have to put up with silly questions from passengers. They ask the same ones every voyage — Do you carry any sails in case the engines break down? How does the captain know the way? How

do the brakes work on a ship like this? Still, many of them tip quite well, so I don't complain. If you want to know what it's like for some of the crew though, come and see the "Black Gang".'

The steward leads us to the boiler room where the stokers are at work. The noise, heat and smell are overpowering. A stoker opens a furnace door and rakes out a shower of red-hot ashes. He then spreads four or five shovels of coal over the fire and shuts the furnace door with a clang. He is caked with dust and sweat.

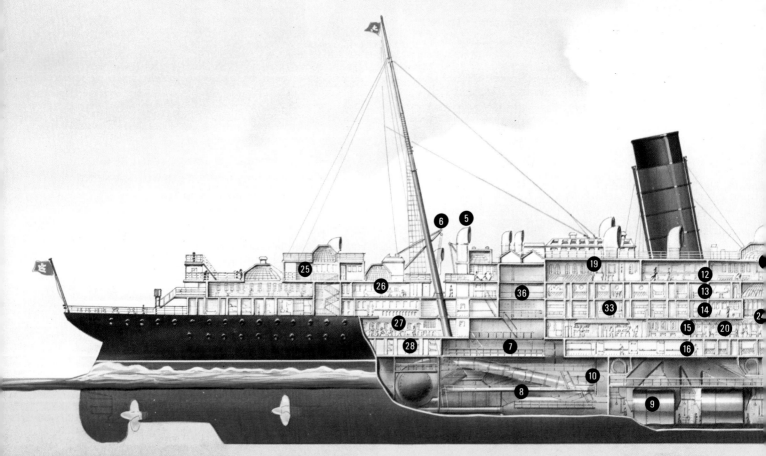

'He has to do that every seven minutes,' says the steward. 'You can imagine what it's like in a gale. These men are really hard. I have seen that one brought on board in a wheelbarrow, dead drunk. There are dreadful fights, too. Usually it's when they are on land, but we have had fights at sea. The only thing to do then is to slam down the hatches and let them get on with it. I heard of an officer on another ship who interfered in a fight and was never seen again. They split open his head with a shovel, and then flung him into the furnace.'

1 bridge   **2** wheel house   **3** captain's cabin   **4** officers' accommodation   **5** ventilators   **6** cargo hoists   **7** engine room   **8** turbines   **9** boilers   **10** control platform   **11** wireless room   **12** 'A' or boat deck   **13** 'B' or promenade deck   **14** 'upper C' or shelter deck   **15** 'C' or upper deck   **16** 'D' or main deck   **17** 'E' or lower deck   **18** 1st class lounge   **19** 1st class smoke room   **20** 1st class dining saloon   **21** 1st class staircase and lifts   **22** 1st class library   **23** 1st class accommodation   **24** musicians' gallery   **25** 2nd class lounge   **26** 2nd class drawing room   **27** 2nd class dining saloon   **28** 2nd class accommodation   **29** 3rd class dining saloon   **30** 3rd class public rooms   **31** 3rd class accommodation   **32** nursery   **33** hospital   **34** bank   **35** bathrooms   **36** engine room hatches   **37** regal suite   **38** printing offices

2 The First Motor Cars

Who invented the motor car? It is really impossible to say, for many people had a hand in it. It all began thousands of years ago when someone invented the wheel. Much later, people learnt how to make light, fast carriages with proper axles, springs and comfortable seats. By the early nineteenth century there were carriages driven by steam engines. Some worked quite well, but were unpopular and soon went out of use.

There was a big step forward in about 1860 when a Frenchman called Lenoir invented a gas engine. His engines provided power for factories and workshops. People were glad to have them because they were so easy to start and stop. There was no need to light a fire and wait for water to boil as with steam engines. Lenoir also used his engines to drive carriages but they did not work very well.

At about the same time, companies were beginning to drill for oil. From the crude oil they made lubricating oil, and paraffin for lighting. They found that the liquid they were left with burst into flames very easily. They thought it was too dangerous to use,

an 1898 Benz

so they threw it away. It was called 'benzine'. We know it as petrol.

Then someone said, 'Benzine turns into a gas very easily, so why not use it in an engine like Lenoir's?' Several people tried to make petrol engines. In the 1880s two Germans, Gottleib Daimler and Karl Benz succeeded. They started firms which are still making motor cars today. Other Germans copied them. The French were not far behind.

What was happening in Britain? Here Parliament had made a law for the big steam tractor engines used on farms. It said that each one must have three men to drive it, that it must not go over three m.p.h. and that someone must walk in front of it to give warning, usually with a red flag. No one had dreamt of motor cars when this law had been made. But people who bought French or German cars found they were expected to obey it. In 1896 Parliament at last changed the law and made motoring legal. The few people who owned cars celebrated by driving from London to Brighton.

We will now visit the village of Midsomer Norton, ten miles from Bath. It is 1906 and we go to see the local doctor, Dr. Bulleid. He is the only man in the village to own a car. It is a Panhard, made in France. It has black shining bodywork, a polished brass radiator and lamps, and seats of red leather.

'Why did you buy this car, Doctor?' 'It's convenient for visiting my patients, but I still keep my horse and carriage because the car is quite likely to break down. Mainly, I like it for amusement during my spare time. If it's fine this afternoon I will go out on the Bath road.' *'You mean you will go to Bath?'* 'I mean I will go in that direction,' laughs the doctor. 'If I arrive, it will be a pleasant surprise.' *'What can go wrong?'* 'A puncture is the most likely thing. I once punctured all four of my tyres in ten miles. Our roads were made for carts, not motor cars. I hear that in some places they have a new kind of road surface called tarmacadam. I hope we will have it on our roads soon. The engine often goes wrong, of course. I have learnt a lot about car engines by putting this one right and helping other motorists. If we see someone in trouble on the road we always stop and try to help.'

'What do the local people think of your car?' 'Most

Dr. Bulleid and his new Panhard

the London to Brighton race today

the London to Brighton race today

of them just come out of their houses and gape when I drive by. They are amazed to see a horseless carriage. Farmers don't like cars, because they frighten their horses. I startled a milkman's horse the other day. The animal bolted and there were upset churns and milk all over the road. The police are a nuisance; they are always setting speed-traps. They hide behind hedges with stop-watches. The A.A. Scouts are a great help in spotting speed-traps. They used to wave a red disc or salute as a warning, but the magistrates said this was against the law. Now, the Scouts only salute when the road is clear and are careful *not* to salute if there is a police trap. A man can hardly be fined for doing nothing, can he?'

'*Have you had any accidents, Doctor?*' 'The car ran away once when I parked on a steep hill. The brakes are not very good, you see, so now when I stop on a hill, the first thing I do is put a brick behind one of the wheels. My coachman hurt himself and the car rather badly a few weeks ago. He is more used to horses than to motor cars. He came up the drive rather fast and forgot to brake or turn off the engine. We heard him crash through the garage doors shouting, "Whoa, you devil, whoa!" '

3 The Austin Seven

In the early 1920s a new car appeared in the show-rooms – the Austin Seven. We will visit a family who have just bought one. *'Are you pleased with your new car, Mr. Brown?'* 'Delighted!' *'It's not very big, is it?'* 'It's just right for us. My wife and I sit in the front. We lift the two children over the seats and put them in the back where they are out of harm's way. I know a farmer who drives his fat wife to market in his Austin Seven, and he takes two large friends as well. The engine just about copes, but the body of his car is beginning to crack. It's his own fault. He puts too much strain on his car.'

'How fast does she go?' 'Once we went over fifty miles an hour, but it frightened my wife so I haven't tried that again. The car nips up hills easily. Richer motorists laugh at the Austin Seven and call it a "bath tub on wheels" or a "motorized pram", but we often overtake bigger cars. We wave at them as we go past! If you have paid £500 for a car it upsets you to be passed by one that only costs £165!'

'Do you have any trouble with it?' 'Well, I have to watch the oil pressure. I keep an eye on that little knob. If it sticks out I have to stop the car, take out four little plugs and poke some holes clean with a bit of wire. It doesn't take long, and hasn't happened often. No, we can rely on our Austin Seven to take us anywhere.'

'What do you think of the car, Mrs. Brown?' 'I can't tell you how pleased I am. My husband used to talk about buying a motor bike and sidecar, but you would never get me on a pillion in all winds and weathers. I wouldn't like the children cooped up together in a sidecar, either. They would certainly be uncomfortable and they wouldn't be able to talk to us. We often looked longingly at the cars in the show-rooms but we never thought we'd be able to afford one. Now, we can go out every weekend, either into the country or to the seaside. We are going on holiday in it this summer. Think how much easier it will be than on the train!'

'It's good for my work, too,' adds Mr. Brown. 'I don't have to cycle or catch the bus, so I am home much earlier than before. In fact, we are thinking of buying a new house, right out of the town. It will be much nicer for the family, and I will be able to drive to my office quite easily.'

'Do you drive, Mrs. Brown?' 'I tried once, but after what my husband said to me, never again!' 'She had trouble with the clutch!' explains Mr. Brown. 'She just couldn't let the clutch pedal out smoothly enough. She made the car jump like a kangaroo. Goodness knows what damage she did. She nearly shook the children out of the back seat.'

Now we will visit Mr. Tupton, who helps to make Austin Sevens. *'Where do you work, Mr. Tupton?'* 'At Longbridge, near Birmingham. It is hard to believe there was only a derelict factory there less than twenty years ago. I joined the firm when Sir Herbert Austin started it. We only made Austin Twenties then. Beautiful cars they are, but expensive. During the Great War we had to go over to making munitions. Of course, the plant covered acres of ground by then. There were over 20,000 of us working there at one time. Soon after the War ended, when the big cars didn't sell any more, it looked as if we were going to lose our jobs. Then Sir Herbert had this bright idea

one of the first Austin Sevens

later version of the Austin Seven

the Austin Seven production line

of making a cheap, little car that ordinary folk could buy. Everyone laughs at the Austin Sevens, but they sell like hot cakes!'

But Austin Sevens could do more than take a family out for a weekend drive. In August 1978, holiday makers on the roads of Scotland were surprised to see convoys of Austin Sevens, many still in good condition, heading towards the town of Fort William. About eighty of the old cars were making their way to a special rally in the town, which is at the foot of Ben Nevis, the highest mountain in Great Britain. Fifty years before, a Mr. George Simpson drove to the top of Ben Nevis, in an Austin Seven fitted with a specially low first gear. The car reached the top in 7 hours, 23 minutes and came down again in 1 hour, 55 minutes, a time which still stands in the *Guinness Book of Records*. This was a great triumph for the little Austin. Even today, no other ordinary car has ever reached the top of Ben Nevis.

4 The First Aeroplanes

For thousands of years men watched birds soaring through the air and longed to do the same. The obvious way to fly seemed to be to make a pair of wings and flap them, but this idea never worked. No one is strong enough to carry his own weight into the air. There was another way to fly, though, and that was by balloon. Ballooning became quite a popular sport, but it is not really flying like birds. You can only go where the wind takes you.

During the nineteenth century, many inventors tried new ways of flying. One of them was Sir George Cayley, who showed that flapping wings would never be any use. A better idea was to have fixed wings and

the Lilienthal glider

drive the aircraft with a propellor. Several people built models that flew quite well, and others made gliders. A German called Otto Lilienthal managed to pilot a glider for three hundred yards. He made many flights but in 1896 his glider crashed into a hillside and he was killed.

A big problem was to find a suitable motor. At first, only steam engines were available, which were far too heavy. Then, in the 1880s Benz and Daimler developed the petrol engine. They had used it to drive a carriage. Would it be possible to make it drive a glider? Several people decided to try, including two American brothers, Wilbur and Orville Wright.

The Wright brothers were brought up in Dayton, Ohio. They were both very ingenious inventors. As young lads they made a printing press from scrap metal and an old tombstone. When they grew up they started a small business, mending and making bicycles. In 1896, the same year that Otto Lilienthal was killed, Orville Wright nearly died from typhoid fever, and as he was recovering he had plenty of time to think. He and Wilbur had been interested in flying for a long time. They decided they would try and make an aeroplane.

The two brothers went to work carefully. They realized that the first thing they had to do was to learn to glide. They left Dayton and went 400 miles away to Kittyhawk. This was a little village on a narrow sand bar, just off the coast of North Carolina. Here the wind blew steadily and there was a bare hill called Kill Devil Hill which was just right for launching a glider.

They built three gliders, each better than the last. Between them they made over 1,000 flights, and learnt how to control their craft in the air. Then, in 1903, they built another machine, this time with a motor and two propellors— the first aeroplane. On Kill Devil Hill they made a sloping track. Their aeroplane had skids, so that it would slide down the track like a toboggan, and gain enough speed to take off. By December 14th, 1903 everything was ready. The two brothers tossed a coin to decide who would try to fly first, and Wilbur won. He started the engine. The aeroplane raced down the track and began to rise. Almost at once its nose shot through the air. The

the Wright brothers' first flight

aeroplane stalled, dropped back to the ground and fell sideways. Luckily, Wilbur was not hurt and there was little damage to the machine. By December 17th they had repaired it and now it was Orville's turn to take the controls. Again the aeroplane shot down the track. Wilbur ran beside it for a few seconds, but then it rose gently and left him behind. Orville stayed in the air for twelve seconds and flew 120 feet. This was the first flight ever made in a powered, heavier-than-air machine.

Delighted with their success, the brothers at once made some more flights. On the last one Wilbur was in the air for 59 seconds and flew over 850 feet. He crash-landed in the sand, damaging the machine slightly. They carried it back to the hangar, but on the way a gust of wind turned it over and smashed it to pieces. So ended one of the most important days in the history of flight.

Wilbur and Orville Wright had worked almost entirely on their own among the sand dunes of Kittyhawk. Only a handful of friends came to see their first flight. Hardly any newspapers reported it and few of the people who did hear of it believed it had really happened. The two brothers went on quietly with their experiments, making better and better aircraft and making longer and longer flights. Meanwhile, other people were also making aeroplanes.

The French were especially proud of their inventors and pilots. In 1907 Wilbur Wright came to France to demonstrate his aeroplane. It had to be carried in pieces in packing cases and then put together. Wilbur took so long over the work and was so quiet and shy that people began to laugh at him. However, on August 8th, 1908 thousands came to the race course at Le Mans to watch his test flight. He soared into the air, circled twice round the race course, did a figure of eight and came gracefully back to land. The crowd was amazed and delighted.

Back in the United States, Orville was also giving demonstrations. He flew over 250 feet high, and stayed up for well over an hour at a time. From then on the two quiet, modest brothers were famous, and they soon became rich as well.

What did Wilbur and Orville think their machines would do? For one thing, they hoped they would prevent wars. They thought that because generals would be able to fly over enemy lines and discover what was happening, they could ruin each other's plans quite easily, and no one would bother to fight any more. In fact, the aeroplane was to make war more horrible than it had ever been.

127

5 Across the Atlantic by Aeroplane

During the First World War aeroplanes had improved greatly. By the time it was over, there were thousands of military aircraft. Could aeroplanes be useful in peacetime? For a time it looked as if airships might be better. With their huge cigar-shaped envelopes full of gas, they carried much heavier loads than aeroplanes could. Passengers and crew travelled in comfort. If an engine failed the airship did not crash at once as an aeroplane did.

However, there were plenty of men, and even women, who were willing to take aeroplanes on long, dangerous flights. One of these was John Alcock. He had an exciting time as a pilot during the War. He shot down several enemy planes, but in the end he crashed on enemy territory and was taken prisoner by the Turks. He did not return home until the War ended in 1918. At that time, the Daily Mail was offering a prize of £10,000 to the first man to fly non-stop across the Atlantic. Alcock decided to try to win it, so he went to the firm of Vickers and

Alcock and Brown

persuaded them to give him one of their 'Vimy' bombers which had been built to bomb Berlin. In theory, the Vickers-Vimy could fly the Atlantic. But would it? So much depended on how well the aeroplane was built and how reliable its two Rolls Royce engines were. Alcock felt he was able to pilot the plane but he also needed a good navigator. One day, when he was at Vickers, a quiet, shy young man came into the room. He was Arthur Brown. Like Alcock he had been a pilot during the War. The two men began talking and, almost at once, Alcock knew that Brown was the right man to be his navigator.

The shortest distance across the Atlantic is from Newfoundland to Ireland. It was easier to fly from the American side, because then the prevailing westerly winds would help them. The Vimy bomber had to be taken apart and shipped to Newfoundland. Once there, mechanics worked hard to put it together, hindered much of the time by spectators. Some of them prodded the fabric of the aeroplane with umbrellas and one even tried to light it with a cigar! Another problem was to find an airstrip, for the country was wild and rocky. Alcock and Brown found a reasonable piece of land 400 yards long, but it was barely enough.

By June 14th, 1919 everything was ready. The aeroplane had made two test flights. Its petrol tanks had been filled and food had been packed for the journey — sandwiches, chocolate and thermos flasks of coffee. The passengers also went on board. They were two black cats called Lucky Jim and Twinkletoes.

Alcock and Brown were anxious to leave. A Major Brackley was also in Newfoundland busily preparing a big Handley Page aeroplane ready to attempt an Atlantic crossing. Alcock and Brown got up at 3.30 a.m., only to find a strong cross-wind was blowing. They waited for it to die down until finally they lost patience. At 5.28 p.m. they decided to go. Alcock raced the Vimy along the short runway and at the last second took her into the air. They just missed a fence, but beyond that was a wood. From the ground it looked as if they brushed the trees, but they cleared them by several feet. The long flight had begun.

the Vickers Vimy over the Atlantic

The two men sat side by side in their little cockpit. They were so cramped that at the end of the journey they said they wanted to stay standing for the rest of their lives. The whole time Alcock had to keep one hand on the joystick and both feet on the rudder bar. Brown had to concentrate on his charts and instruments and make difficult calculations. They could not speak because of the roar of the engines and the noise became even worse when an exhaust pipe melted away. They had a strong following wind, but in every other way the weather was unkind. They had rain, snow, sleet and hail. Several times Brown had to climb out of the cockpit and kneel on the fuselage to wipe snow from a gauge. The clouds shut out the sky so Brown could see neither sun nor stars to help him navigate. They climbed through a bank of cloud to find another above that and another above that again. Once they had to climb to 11,000 feet for a look at the sky. At that height the sleet jammed some of the controls and one of the engines made an alarming pop-pop-popping noise.

Their worst moment was when they suddenly hit a bank of fog. It was impossible to tell whether they were level or straight. The aeroplane stalled, then went into a spin. They knew they were falling simply because they were pressed against the backs of their seats. If the fog had gone down to sea level, they would certainly have crashed. Suddenly they broke clear of the fog and there was the sea, standing upright, or so it seemed. The aeroplane was flying on its side. Alcock straightened the plane just in time. They could even hear the sound of the waves above the noise of the engines.

At 8.15 the next morning they saw two small islands and soon they were circling round the little Irish village of Clifden. Alcock saw what he thought was a beautiful stretch of green field, and brought the aeroplane down for what would have been a perfect landing. Suddenly the machine jarred to a stop and its nose stuck in the ground. The beautiful green field was, in fact, an Irish bog. The time was 9.25 a.m. They had come 1,800 miles in just under sixteen hours.

Until then, hardly anyone had heard of Alcock and Brown, but now they were heroes. However, as Arthur Brown crawled out of his cockpit, dazed from the crash, and so stiff he could hardly walk, he was sure of one thing. If people were going to fly across the Atlantic, it would be far better to travel by airship.

6 Airships

In 1783 two Frenchmen, the Montgolfier brothers, made the first hot air balloon. They were too scared to go up in it themselves, so on its trial flight the balloon carried a sheep, a duck and a cockerel. In front of a large crowd, which included King Louis XVI and his Queen, these animals took off from Versailles near Paris. They were in the air for eight hours and flew two miles. Soon people found that hydrogen was more effective at lifting than hot air. During the nineteenth century there were many successful flights in hydrogen balloons. But the trouble with a balloon is that you have to go where the wind takes

the Montgolfier hot air balloon

you. People tried 'rowing' their balloons with huge, canvas covered oars. Then they tried propellors turned by hand. When they found that men were not strong enough to do this, they tried steam engines, but these were far too heavy. Then, in the 1880s Daimler made his petrol engine. Here, at last, was a machine that was powerful enough for air travel and not too heavy. At about the same time, scientists discovered how to produce aluminium cheaply. Now it was possible to make an airship. Instead of one balloon, they had several in a row. To stop them flopping all over the place, they put them in a huge framework of aluminium and covered it with fabric. Beneath this envelope, as it was called, were the motor and the 'gondola' which carried the passengers.

The most famous of the airship builders was a German, Count von Zeppelin, but the man we are going to meet is called Hugo Eckener. He worked for Zeppelin until the old man died in 1917. Then he became Chairman of the Company. We will visit him in 1935 and talk about his airship the *Graf Zeppelin*.

'*Why are you so keen on airships, Herr Eckener?*' 'Because they are the best way to travel. In the *Graf Zeppelin* we can go at 80 m.p.h. which is three times as fast as an ocean liner. The passengers are just as comfortable, too. There is plenty of room for them to stretch their legs, and there is always something interesting to see from the windows. The world looks wonderful from up there. I shall always remember a sight-seeing trip we made in 1928. We went to the South of France and from there to Rome. Then we flew over Crete, Cyprus and Palestine. We flew very slowly whenever we saw anything of interest. I took the ship low over the Dead Sea. The passengers were amazed when I told them we were flying 1,000 feet *below* sea level! We came back to Germany over the Austrian Alps. We had travelled for three days without stopping. Everyone was delighted.'

'*Flying over the sea cannot be very interesting.*' 'No, but we can cross the Atlantic in a couple of days. We have an orchestra to keep people amused and an excellent kitchen so we can serve very good meals.' '*What happens in a storm?*' 'That can be exciting. Rain or hail beating on the envelope makes a tremendous noise, and the ship pitches and rolls. The cups and

building an airship

the Hindenburg

plates often fly off the tables. Still, it's no worse than being on a liner.' *It's more dangerous, surely.'* 'We could never have an airship disaster as great as the sinking of the *Titanic*, because airships couldn't carry so many passengers' replies Herr Eckener. 'And airships are much safer than aeroplanes. If the engines of an aeroplane fail, it crashes at once. An airship will at least stay up if the engines fail. If we have a fault on the *Graf Zeppelin* we can sometimes put it right without landing. If we can't put it right, we can just float gently down to earth.'

'Yes, but several airships have crashed, and if the hydrogen explodes everyone aboard is killed. The British haven't flown airships since the R.101 crashed.' 'Well, we have overcome those problems in our new ship the *Hindenburg*. We shall fill her with helium, which is much safer than hydrogen. The only problem is that we have to get helium from America. I don't know whether America will let us have any more. They

don't trust Germany now that Hitler is in power. I can't blame them. I don't like Hitler myself.'

This new airship, the *Hindenburg*, was the finest ever built. She was 800 feet long, with four huge diesel engines, each over 1,000 h.p., and she could carry fifty passengers. The *Hindenburg* had a lounge, a library, a promenade deck, a dining room and luxurious cabins, each with a bathroom. Unfortunately, as Hugo Eckener feared, the Americans refused to sell helium to Germany. The *Hindenburg* had to use hydrogen after all. She began flying in 1936, and made several trips to the United States and South America. Everyone said she was a great success. Then, on May 6th, 1937 she arrived at Lakehurst near New York. A radio commentator called Herb Morrison was there to broadcast what was happening although it was not expected to be very exciting. This is what he said: 'Passengers are looking out of the windows waving. The ship is standing still now. The vast motors are just holding it, just enough to keep it from . . .' Suddenly he shouted, 'It's broken into flames. It's flashing! Flashing! It's flashing terribly! It's bursting into flames and falling on the mooring mast. This is terrible. This is one of the worst catastrophes in the world. Oh, the humanity and all the passengers . . . I told you . . . it's a mass of smoking wreckage. . . I . . . I . . . folks, I'm going to have to stop for a moment because I've lost my voice. This is the worst thing I have ever witnessed.'

There were 97 people on board and 35 of them died. After the loss of the *Hindenburg* no one wanted to travel by airship again. No one knows for certain why the *Hindenburg* exploded. Possibly a charge of static electricity ignited the hydrogen, which is a highly inflammable gas.

131

The Hindenburg

7 Scott of the Antarctic

The southern continent of Antarctica is a huge plateau, covered almost entirely with snow and ice. It is terribly cold, there are howling blizzards, and for four months of the year there is complete darkness. In the early twentieth century, people began to explore Antarctica. Why was this? For one thing, scientists wanted to study the rocks, the weather, the movement of ice, the earth's magnetic field and the strange creatures, such as the Emperor Penguins, which lived there. The main reason, though, was to find adventure, and to go where no one had been before. Above all, they wanted to reach the South Pole. The first person to do so would certainly become famous.

One of the most enthusiastic explorers of the southern continent was Robert Falcon Scott, a captain in the Royal Navy. In 1901 he led an expedition in the *Discovery*. Quite possibly you have seen her, for she is now moored on the Embankment in London.

Captain Scott

Scott did not try to reach the South Pole on that expedition, but he did learn a lot about living and working in Antarctica. In 1910, he set sail again, this time in the *Terra Nova*. She was a whaling ship which had been built for the Southern Ocean, so she was just right for the expedition.

If you look at the map of Antarctica, you will notice a huge bay by the Ross Sea. It looks as if it is possible to sail quite close to the South Pole. But this bay is covered with ice hundreds of feet thick. Explorers called it the Great Ice Barrier. The *Terra Nova* could go no further than Ross Island. Scott and his men built themselves a wooden house at the foot of a smouldering volcano they named Mount Erebus. Here they spent the winter. They found plenty of scientific work to do and they thought about the problems and dangers of the journey that lay ahead. Their biggest worry was that they were not alone. On one of their scientific trips the crew of the *Terra Nova* were amazed to find another ship. She was called the *Fram* and she carried an expedition led by the famous Norwegian explorer, Amundsen. Amundsen was determined to reach the South Pole before Scott.

Scott's route to the Pole

McMurdo Sound
Ross Island
Cape Crozier
ROSS SEA
Biscoe Bay
Cape Evans
Mt.Erebus
Hut Point
Bay of Whales
THE GREAT ICE BARRIER EDGE
KING EDWARD VII LAND
One Ton Camp
Last Camp
Scott, Wilson & Bower d.
Oates d.
ROSS BARRIER SURFACE
VICTORIA LAND
Mt.Markham
Lower Glacier Depot
Beardmore Glacier
Evans d.
King Edward VII Plateau
Captain Scott Jan. 18th 1912
SOUTH POLE

Mount Erebus from Hut Point, a watercolour by Dr. Wilson

Scott and his friends waited impatiently for the summer, which of course comes to countries south of the equator during our winter. At last, on November 1st, 1911, they set out. The plan was to start with a large party carrying as many supplies as possible. Every 65 miles or so they made a depot of stores that could be used on the return journey. The further they went, the less there was to carry, so Scott sent back

Captain Scott writing his diary in the hut

three groups of men at different times. They were bitterly disappointed because they were not allowed to go to the Pole. To pull their sledges Scott's team had ponies, dogs and two tractors with petrol engines. The motors broke down after only fifty miles. The wretched ponies struggled through the snow until they were too weak to go any further, and had to be shot. With the journey about half finished, Scott sent back the dog teams. There was now only one way to pull the sledges. The men had to do it themselves.

By this time they had travelled 450 miles over the Great Ice Barrier to reach the foot of the plateau. A great river of ice, the Beardmore Glacier, lay ahead. The glacier is twenty miles wide in places and it is 120 miles long, rising to 10,000 feet at the top of the plateau. All over the glacier are great ridges, so hauling the sledges was very hard work for Scott and his men. It was dangerous as well, because of crevasses. These are wide, deep cracks in the ice, and it is usually impossible to see them because the snow makes a kind of bridge over the top. On an earlier trip, Scott had seen a whole team of dogs vanish into a crevasse, one after the other. This time a member of his party fell through one and found himself dangling

7 Scott of the Antarctic

Manhauling a sledge over the ice-cap

at the end of his harness with an 80 foot drop below him.

It took the expedition three weeks to climb to the top of the glacier, and then Scott sent back his last return party. He pressed on with only four men, Dr. Wilson, Captain Oates, Petty Officer Evans and Lieutenant Bowers. Tugging the heavy sledges was hard, tiring work and their strength began to fail. However, the thought of being the first men at the South Pole kept them going. At last, when they were only a day's march from their goal, one of them saw a black dot on the horizon. As they drew nearer, they soon realized the worst. It was the Norwegian flag they could see. Amundsen had placed it there thirty-three days before. The five tired, disappointed Englishmen now faced the 800 mile tramp back to their base camp.

The biting winds tore at their faces until they were covered in sores. Petty Officer Evans's finger nails began falling off. Edward Wilson suffered from snow blindness, and strained a muscle in his leg. Scott fell and hurt his shoulder. In three weeks they managed to reach the top of the Beardmore Glacier. Then began the most difficult part of their journey, picking their way among the great ridges and crevasses. Petty Officer Evans was a giant of a man, full of good humour, but he was worn out and so confused as the result of a fall that he could not even do up his boots properly. He died on February 17th.

Scott's exhausted party at the Pole *left to right* Oates, Bowers, Scott, Evans, Wilson

the Great Ice Barrier *right* the last entry in Scott's diary

we shall stick it out to the end but we are getting weaker of course and the end cannot be far.

It seems a pity, but I do not think I can write more —

R Scott

Last Entry —

For Gods Sake look after our people

The rest of the party struggled to the foot of the glacier and then a further 250 miles over the Great Ice Barrier. At last they made camp, not knowing that a relief party was only eleven miles away. Captain Oates was now very ill, and knew he was a burden to the others. While a blizzard was raging, he left the tent saying, 'I am just going outside and may be some time.' They never saw him again. The blizzard lasted for eight days, and when it was over Scott and his companions were too weak to move. They died where they lay.

Eight months later, a search party noticed a dark speck in the snow. It was the top of the tent. Inside were the bodies of the three explorers and also the diary that Scott had faithfully kept. It told the dreadful story of all the hardships and disappointment.

8 Everest

Everest from the air

If you tried to climb Everest you would find it rather like storming an enemy fortress. What problems would you face?

In the first place, there is the height. Everest is 29,002 feet high, which is more than six times as high as Ben Nevis. Up there, the cold is biting. If you are caught without shelter for the night you would certainly die. However, you can only carry a light tent which gives you barely enough protection from the cold. In addition, the air is thin. There is a good chance that you will suffer from 'anoxia' which means 'oxygen shortage'. This makes you violently sick and too weak to move. Even if that does not happen, you find that every step you take needs a great effort. You take two steps and have to rest, two steps more and have to rest again, and every ten steps or so you will fall down exhausted. You may behave very strangely. A member of the expedition in 1953 went to sleep with a sardine hanging out of his mouth! Your mind does not guide your body properly. At sea level you can light a stove and boil water in a couple of minutes. Up on Everest it may take you half an hour. You need a lot of liquids, too, because your body loses moisture very quickly. Everything freezes solid, so you have to heat all your drinks. At least the melted snow is pure water!

The weather is certain to be bad for much of the time. You will have such severe snow storms that you will be unable to leave your camp, and if you are caught in a storm you may be lost for ever. The wind will howl almost without ceasing, and at night your tent will bang and thrash like the sail of a ship in a gale.

Now let us look at the mountain to see what you have to climb.

the Khumbu icefall

the route to the summit

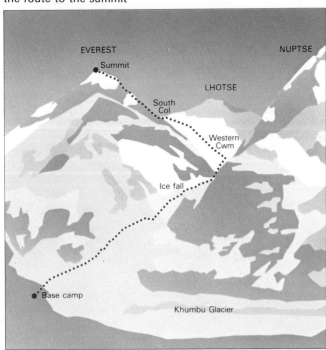

Everywhere in the Himalayas there are rivers, but they are rivers of ice, called glaciers. In places they are hundreds of feet thick, and up to two miles wide. They have gouged great valleys, and at their sources they have bitten back into the mountains, much as you would bite into an apple. A 'bite' like this is called a cwm, and there is one on Everest called the Western Cwm. On leaving it, the glacier drops suddenly into the valley below. It is not a waterfall, but an enormous icefall 2,000 feet high. The ice moves only a few feet a day, but it is alarming when it does. Sometimes there are cracks and groans, sometimes dull thuds, and sometimes a roaring like an express train, all caused by the movement of the ice. Everywhere there are huge boulders of ice, and even cliffs. Towering above you are ice pinnacles, some of which are likely to fall at any minute. At your feet you are likely to find a crack, or a crevasse. As the glacier leaves the cwm it has to bend, so it cracks open, just as your rubber does if you bend it over the corner of your desk. A crevasse can be a hundred feet deep. It may be so narrow that you can step over it quite easily, or it may be thirty feet wide.

Once you are in the Western Cwm you will find it is fairly flat, but at the far end is the Lhotse face. It is 4,000 feet high and almost as steep as a wall. Once up there, you come to the South Col. Here you will find a small area of flat land where you can camp. But the Col is a desolate and windswept place. From here you must climb to the South Summit, where you will see the way to the very top of Everest. It is above a knife-edge of rock with a drop of thousands of feet on either side.

How can mountaineers overcome all these problems? The most important things they need are great courage and determination. Next, they must have a lot of equipment and porters to carry it. Lastly, they must plan everything with immense care.

Several expeditions went to Everest, and in 1952 some Swiss mountaineers nearly reached the top. In 1953, Colonel John Hunt took a British party to the mountain. There were thirteen men altogether. Among them was a tall, lanky New Zealander called Edmund Hillary. Hillary kept bees for a living, but he was an expert mountaineer who had done a lot of climbing in New Zealand and in the Himalayas.

To help them carry all their food and equipment the British hired no less than 350 Sherpas. The Sherpas are a people who live in the mountains near Everest. Most of them are small, but they are courageous, very strong and are used to the cold and bad weather. They are also cheerful, loyal and hard-working. But the Sherpas lead a simple life and are not used to mechanical things. They found it impossible to learn how to use oxygen sets. They could light a paraffin stove, but the tea they brewed tasted horrible and was often thick with grease. On Everest, though, any warm drink is welcome.

Of course, not all 350 Sherpas were going to climb Everest. Most of them just carried their loads to the foot of the mountain and then went home. A few hand-picked ones who were expert climbers stayed. Among them was Tensing who had climbed with the Swiss party the year before. He and one of the Swiss had nearly reached the top.

The first stage of the journey was a hike of 170 miles through Nepal. It is beautiful, thickly wooded country but there are no roads, only a path which led the party over one mountain ridge after another. When they caught their first sight of Everest, some of them were so excited they climbed trees to have a better look. At last they arrived at the monastery of Thyangboche which has a grandstand view of the mountain. From here it was only a few days trek to the foot of the icefall.

a camp en route to Everest

Everest from Thyangboche Monastery

Everest

Hillary

Tensing

The only way to climb the mountain was to attempt it in stages. They had to set up camp after camp, each higher than the one before. The last camp had to be close enough to the top for the climbers to reach the summit and return safely in a day.

The first problem was to find a way up the icefall. Edmund Hillary led a party to do this. They picked their way among ice boulders and tottering ice pillars. They crossed, or dodged round, gaping crevasses and they scaled ice cliffs. All the time, the ice groaned and grumbled. They named various places – Mike's Horror, Hillary's Horror, Hell Fire Alley, Atom Bomb Area and Ghastly Crevasse. But in the end, they reached the cwm. Getting back to camp was unpleasant, but now it had been climbed once, the icefall did not seem to be so terrible after all.

Some members of the party then made the path as easy as they could. They bridged crevasses with wooden planks, they chopped steps, they fixed ropes to the sides of cliffs, and, at one point, they hung a rope ladder. They also marked the path with flags. The movement of the glacier and fresh falls of snow kept spoiling their work, but the Sherpas were able to carry load after load of supplies into the Western Cwm. Here they set up their advanced camp.

The next step was to find a way up the sheer wall of the Lhotse face. After several days they managed this and again they prepared the way with fixed ropes and steps. Not surprisingly, it was hard to persuade some of the Sherpas to carry their loads up there. But on May 21st, they finally pitched Camp 8 on the South Col.

Hunt had chosen two assault teams for the final attack. The first was Charles Evans and Tom Bourdillon; the other was Edmund Hillary and Tensing. On May 26th, Evans and Bourdillon set out. At first all went well, and the men below watched them with excitement. Only Tensing was silent. He thought a Sherpa should be one of the first men to climb to the top. By one o'clock Evans and Bourdillon had reached the South Summit. They could now see the very peak of the mountain and it was only 400 yards away. Should they go on? Unfortunately they were already tired and they were fast running out of oxygen. Probably they could have reached the top, but they knew that if they did so they would die on their way back down. At six o'clock they staggered into Camp 8, barely able to walk, with their faces covered in frost. It was now the turn of Hillary and Tensing.

On May 27th the weather was so bad they could do nothing. But on the following day they set out. Three other men came with them to carry their tent, spare oxygen and food. The five men climbed until mid-afternoon and then looked for a place to camp. The slopes were so steep that it seemed impossible to find one, but in the end they discovered a ledge, a tiny shelf on the face of a precipice, thousands of feet high. The three companions turned back, leaving the equipment they had carried, including a large cylinder of oxygen. This was the supply Hillary and Tensing needed for the night. It is impossible to sleep at that height without oxygen.

The ledge had a slope of 30 degrees, so Hillary and Tensing levelled it as well as they could, prising rocks out of the frozen ground. The ground was too hard

climbers on Everest

a high camp on Everest

for tent pegs, so they stuck oxygen bottles in the snow and used those. When they had put the tent up they had supper of soup, sardines on biscuits, dates and pint after pint of sweet lemonade. They also ate a tin of apricots which Hillary had kept hidden until then. It was a great treat.

The night was miserable. Every now and then a gust of wind threatened to blow them off their ledge. They also found that one of their helpers had taken back the adaptor for the large bottle of oxygen. They only dared use their climbing oxygen for four hours, so they had little sleep.

At 6.30 the next morning they set off. It was a hard struggle to reach the South Summit, and after that came the dreadful ridge that had defeated Bourdillon and Evans. The only way was to chip steps all the way up it. They went over one hump after another, hoping each would be the last, but the ridge seemed to go on for ever. At one point they reached a sheer wall forty feet high. It looked impossible, but it had a crack in it and they were able to force their way up that. At 11.30 a.m. they finally reached the summit.

What do you do at the top of Everest? Hillary and Tensing shook hands, like the English, then hugged one another like Sherpas. Tensing buried a few sweets and chocolates as an offering to the gods that live on the mountain, and Hillary buried a little white crucifix. Hillary next took some photographs of the mountains all around, then three of Tensing. There is no photograph of Hillary on the summit because Tensing did not know how to use a camera and Hillary thought it was hardly the time to teach him. After a quarter of an hour they made their way down. They reached the South Col by the evening, just as the oxygen ran out. The following morning they arrived in the Western Cwm, so all

Tensing on the summit

they had to do was to go down the icefall for the last time and make the long hike through Nepal.

The expedition had been a great success, and everyone had shown tremendous skill and courage. Both Hunt and Hillary were knighted. But why had they wanted to reach the top of Everest in the first place? The only answer Sir John Hunt could give was, 'We climbed it because it was there.'

Chapter Eight   At School and at Work

1 The Elementary School

We are back in the 1890s and Weymouth House School in Bath has just had a new building. It is plain, but so solid that it will last for a hundred years or more. It has three storeys. The ground floor is for infants, the first floor is for girls and the top floor is for boys. On each floor there is a large hall as big as a modern gymnasium. This is called the school room and Mr. Swanson, the headmaster of the boys' school, says there are three standards in this room.

'What are standards, Mr. Swanson?' 'They are classes. There are about forty boys in each. Standard One is for boys aged seven, Standard Two is for boys aged eight and so on. A boy has to pass an examination before he can go up a Standard. Some boys spend their whole school life in Standard One. A bright lad can jump a standard. Pupils are allowed to leave as soon as they have passed Standard Four, otherwise they have to stay at school until they are twelve. Many play truant, of course. Some parents send their sons to work in their last year. The magistrates fine them, half-a-crown perhaps, but the boys' wages soon pay that.'

a new school in the nineteenth century

'Don't the classes disturb each other, Mr. Swanson?' 'They do a little, but this way I can keep an eye on the boys and on the teachers. We have two classrooms as well. Standard Four is in one of them and Standards Five and Six are in the other.'

The two classrooms have glass screens, so in fact Mr. Swanson can see what is happening in them nearly as well as he can in the schoolroom.

'Your teachers look young, Headmaster.' 'They are not as young as they would have been in years gone by. At one time a headmaster had only monitors to help him, and they were children of twelve or so. Mr. King, Mr. Budd and Miss Edwards are all over eighteen. The youngest here is my pupil teacher, Stephen Dunton. He is only fourteen, but I don't give him much to do. I take two standards myself, and he helps me.'

'What subjects do you teach?' 'This is a Church school, so religion is very important. The trouble is that religion does not earn grant, so I teach it first thing in the morning when all the latecomers are arriving. Then I mark the register. What really matters are the three Rs — reading, writing and arithmetic.' *'What is this grant?'* 'Every year we have a visit from an inspector. He gives the boys an examination, and if they do well the Government gives the school managers money. A good boy can earn the school over a pound a year. The rich people of Bath still give money to the school, but most of it comes from the Government these days. If the grant is too low, the managers might not have enough cash to pay my salary. I make the boys work, believe me.'

'Do you teach only the three Rs?' 'Oh no. We can earn grant for singing, drawing, and what we call class subjects. In this school the class subjects are history, geography and object lessons.'

'You have no piano for teaching music, I notice.' Mr. Swanson takes a tuning fork from his desk. 'The boys can earn the music grant if they can sing a couple of easy songs by ear. All I have to do is start

them on the right note, and I don't need a piano to play one note.'

'*What are object lessons?*' Mr. Swanson takes us into one of the classrooms where Standard One is listening to the pupil teacher, Stephen Dunton. He is sharpening a pencil and telling the children that he can cut the wood quite easily. He then asks if anyone knows what kind of wood it is. A few boys give wrong answers so Stephen tells them that it is cedar wood and that cedar trees grow in the Lebanon. One of the boys asks what that is, but Stephen pretends not to hear and goes on to talk about the pencil lead.

'Object lessons teach the boys to observe and reason,' says Mr. Swanson. 'Here are the object lessons for Standard One. There are all sorts of things on this list: a bucket, a camel, rain, an orange and so on.' *Are object lessons a kind of science, then?*' 'You could say that,' replies Mr. Swanson.

He now shows us some drawings. They are the most intricate patterns and beautifully drawn, but all copied from a book, so we ask if the boys do any imaginative work. 'The purpose of drawing is to train the hand and the eye,' says Mr. Swanson. 'The imagination is something we have to keep in check.' At this moment a boy appears. He stands to attention and salutes, saying that Mr. King had sent him for the cane. Mr. Swanson canes him twice on each hand, and a hush falls over the school. '*You believe in being firm, Headmaster!*' 'If the boys behave badly they will not learn their lessons properly. Besides, there is a grant of 1/6d per head for discipline.'

2 The Boarding School

Charles Walker

Charles Walker, who is fourteen, lives in Bath but he goes to a boarding school at Blandford in Dorset. It is quite easy to get there because it is near the Somerset and Dorset Railway which runs from Green Park Station in Bath to Bournemouth.

In those days everyone admired the old and very famous schools, such as Eton and Harrow. They are called public schools, though in fact they are so expensive that only rich people can afford the fees. Charles's school is neither old nor famous. but it tries to copy them. For one thing, it is divided into houses. You may have a house system at your school, but in this boarding school the boys really do live in separate houses. A housemaster has charge of each one and does all he can to see that his boys are the best in the school at work and at games.

First, we will meet the headmaster who will tell us about his ideas on education.

'My main aim is to train the character of my boys. I have to turn them into gentlemen and leaders. I don't believe in being soft with them. We have discipline here and if a boy misbehaves, I give him a good hiding. We have no fancy food, just good plain meals. To harden the boys we make them take a cold bath every morning, winter and summer. They have games most afternoons, rugby in winter and cricket in summer. If they cannot play because of the weather, then we send them for a good long cross-country run. I believe in team games because they teach boys to take knocks and to be unselfish. The

house system helps a lot. Boys are keen for their house to win, so they play hard. We have prefects, of course. They have their own bedrooms, a special table in hall, their own uniform and other privileges. They help with the discipline of the school and I allow them to cane the younger boys, if they think it necessary. Every senior boy has a junior to fag for him. The senior learns how to give orders, and the junior learns how to obey them. I am a clergyman of the Church of England, so I take chapel every morning, and Communion and Evensong on Sundays. My sermons do much to guide and inspire the boys. We have to train their minds as well as their characters, of course. The boys learn useful subjects, like English and mathematics, but their real education comes from the Classics, Latin and Greek.'

'Isn't it important to learn science these days, Headmaster?' 'Oh, we do teach some science, but that is strictly for boys who are not very bright. Science is all very well for those who are unfortunate enough to have to work in industry, but our glorious Empire is ruled by men trained in the Classics.'

We will now see what Charles says about his school.

'I hate it here. Papa says that school days are the best days of your life but I don't believe him. What would he say to a cold bath on a January morning? The food is dreadful, not much more than bread and butter with some meat and potatoes at lunch. Luckily there is a tuck shop in Blandford. We go there whenever we can and have steak and onion, ham and eggs, mushrooms on toast and puddings and cakes. I quite like cricket in the summer and rugby isn't too bad, except that we get caked in mud and have to wash in cold water. There is too much fuss about which house wins. What I like best are the boxing and fencing in the gymnasium. We have an army sergeant who takes us and I think he is a better teacher than the masters.'

'What do you think about the prefect system?' 'I hate prefects. They are sneaks and bullies. They have their own rooms with fires in the winter, while we sleep in a cold dormitory. I have to fag for Jones, which means I have to tidy his room, make him scrambled eggs on toast and that sort of thing. If he wants a bit of fun he twists my ears, or holds me close to his fire until I scream. But I will have my own fag one day. Then I will get my revenge.'

'Do you enjoy your lessons, Charles?' 'Not at all, as we don't do much but boring old Latin and Greek. We are translating reams of Virgil at the moment.

Luckily one of my friends has a crib.' *'What is that?'* 'It is an English translation. We just copy it and make a few mistakes so that it looks like our own work. But the most boring thing is having to go to chapel and listen to old Porky's sermons. I try to sit where he can't see me dozing off.'

'What do you want to do when you leave school?' 'I want to be an engineer. I want to design steam turbines, like Parsons. His name is Charles, the same as mine. Papa and Mama won't hear of it, though, and I dare not tell anyone at school. The trouble is that the things they are teaching me here will not be the least bit of use. But I must go now. Mama promised to send me a hamper, and with any luck it will be waiting for me in the porter's lodge.'

3 Secondary Education for All

A middle aged man will tell us about his school days. He came from a poor home, but he is now a wealthy solicitor. He has done well in life because he went to a secondary school. Today, everyone has a secondary education, but when this man was young, only a few children had the opportunity. They were the lucky ones who had passed a difficult examination, or whose parents could afford school fees.

'One winter morning, back in 1937, I was just leaving for school when my mother called me. She told me to open my mouth, and then gave me a spoonful of Glucose-D. This was a sickly-sweet white powder which clung to the inside of your mouth. On the tin, it said it gave you strength and energy. Normally, we only took it when we were ill, so I was surprised. But this was no ordinary morning. I was going to sit my scholarship examination.

'There were three schools in our little town – Brookside, High Street and Weston Hill. The first two were much the same. I went to Brookside, which was an old building with pointed gables, a slate roof, and a turret with an iron bell. The bell rope had been broken for years, but that did not matter because the teachers used whistles. There was a central hall, with classrooms around it. The floors were so worn it was

Poole's Park School football team in 1938

impossible to clean them. When we stamped applause at Christmas concerts the air filled with dust. The school was cold. Every winter playtime rows of boys clustered round the huge iron pipes that carried lukewarm water round the building. There were no laboratories, no workshops, and no domestic science rooms. This was an elementary school, built in about 1860 to teach the children of the poor their three Rs – reading, writing and arithmetic; even in 1937 little more was taught. I had started at Brookside when I was five. I was now eleven and I expected to stay until I was fourteen. The only question was whether I could "pass my scholarship".

'The only children who had a chance of passing were in Miss Evitt's scholarship class. She had worked hard with us, but even so, we knew that only five or six could pass. Her way of teaching mental arithmetic was to stand us round the room while she barked questions at us in turn. If we answered wrongly, she swished us with her cane. She had the best scholarship results in our part of the county and meant to keep it that way.

'The scholarship examination had three parts. There was an English test, an arithmetic test, and a test on general knowledge. I went home without hope, and the rest of the term passed quietly. Then it happened. During the Easter holidays a letter came from the County Council which told my parents I had been awarded a Free Place at Weston Hill Secondary School. I went upstairs, knelt by my bed and said a prayer of thanks to God. I should have thanked Miss Evitt as well.

'As a pupil at Weston Hill, I was rather superior. My grandfather bought me a new bicycle – a shining "Hercules" which cost at least £3. My parents bought me the school uniform, and a big, strong leather satchel. My father painted my initials on it in small, neat black letters.

'Weston Hill was a very different school from Brookside. The floors were polished, and the brass door handles shone. There were a dozen well-heated classrooms, an assembly hall, and a gymnasium. Behind the main school was a brand new concrete building which housed laboratories, physics down-

nearly as difficult. We called it the "eleven plus", because children took it when they were eleven or just over. My younger brother failed this selection test. In the old days my grandfather would probably have paid his fees to Weston Hill, but this was no longer allowed. However much the family disliked the idea, Dennis had to go to Brookside Secondary Modern. When I asked him what it was like, he said that it was the same old gang teaching the same old rubbish. Most people felt things were much as before. Miss Evitt coached and caned children for the "11 +", just as she had done for the scholarship. In fact, she continued to talk about her "scholarship winners" until the day she retired.

post-war schoolboys

stairs and chemistry upstairs. There were also rooms for woodwork and housecraft, but no one took these subjects seriously. Latin, French and science were going to be far more important in our lives. At first, we couldn't see much sense in learning Latin, but I am glad I took it, because I needed it to go to university.

'The children came from elementary and private schools from miles around. One girl rode to school on a horse. The "scholarship winners" were placed in Form One Parallel. We were told we were the brighter pupils but that if we did not work hard we would go down to Form One. The children in Form One had not passed the scholarship examination so their parents had to pay fees. Many of them had come from a small private school in the town where pupils did not learn much, but they did not have to mix with the miners' children in the elementary schools. For their parents this was more important than anything else.

After the War and the Education Act of 1944 the schools changed, especially High Street and Brookside. All the younger children went to High Street, which was made a Primary School. The older ones went to Brookside, which was called a Secondary Modern School. As for Weston Hill, it became a Grammar School and still took the best pupils. There was no "scholarship examination", it is true, but there was a "secondary selection test" which was

'It is different today. Weston Hill Grammar School has become Weston Hill Comprehensive School and the old red brick building is surrounded with extensions. Brookside has handsome new buildings on a new site, and is also a comprehensive school. Pupils attend one or the other, depending only on where they live and not whether thay can pass an examination. However, those of us who were pupils at Weston Hill would still prefer our children to go to that school.'

147

4 The Trawler Skipper

It is 1960. We will go to Hull to talk to George Hume, who is the skipper of a trawler. He has just come back from a voyage. His ship, the *City of Nottingham* is nearly 200 feet long and carries a crew of twenty. You can see from the diagram how she catches fish. The map shows you where the fishing grounds are. The best ones are in the shallower waters, near land.

'*How long have you been at sea, Mr. Hume?*' 'We have had an average trip – about three weeks. We have been to Iceland. It usually takes us seven days to go there, and seven days to come home, and we spend seven days on the fishing grounds. We have two or three days ashore, then off we go again.' '*Did*

a fishing fleet in harbour

you catch many fish?' 'Enough. This cargo is worth about £6,000 – that's about 150 tons of cod.'

'*What is it like on voyage?*' 'Well, the trip out isn't usually too bad. The crew have no more to do than if they were on a cargo boat. The work really begins when we start to fish. We work round the clock, and no man has more than six hours sleep in twenty-four. Usually we trawl for about two and a half hours, then up comes the net, full of cod, with any luck. We tip them all over the deck, and the men have to work frantically to get the net back over the side. Sometimes it's quite badly torn. As soon as we are trawling again, the deckhands gut the fish and pack them in ice in the hold. That's a terrible job in rough weather. I have seen men go flying into a pile of fish and icy water. I have even known them swept overboard. Much of the time the wind is bitterly cold. The fish start to freeze solid, so it is hard to gut them. The spray that falls on the men freezes, too. All they have on their hands are rubber gloves. They gut the fish fast enough, I can tell you, in the hope that they can snatch half an hour in the warm cabin before we winch the trawl in again.'

'*Where are you all this time?*' 'I am on the bridge. It's heated and I am out of the weather, but there is no rest for me once we start fishing. The trawl must stay in the same depth of water, so I have to listen to my echo sounder and study my charts. I have to tell the helmsman which way to turn and shout orders down to the engine room. All the time I have

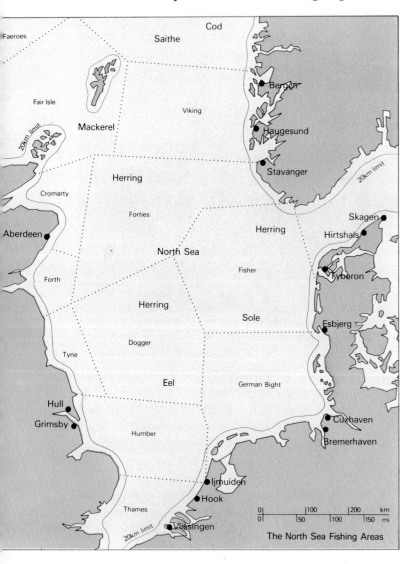

The North Sea Fishing Areas

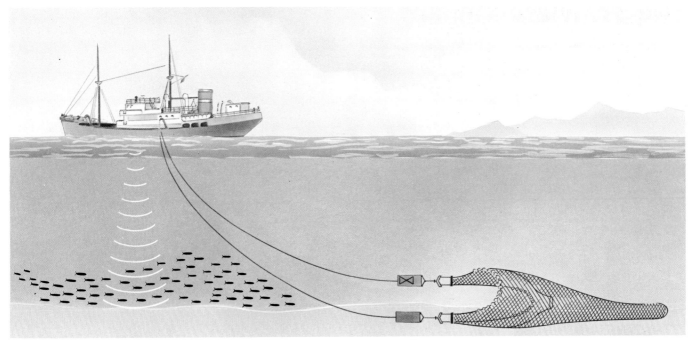

a trawler using sonar to locate fish

to watch the weather, the birds, and, especially, the other ships. If I see one of them make a good haul, we go over and join her. If we make a good haul ourselves, we try to hide it. The game is to catch all the fish you can, and rob the others. It's cut-throat competition all the time. Then I have to drive the men to their work. I find myself shouting and swearing at them more and more. I get tired, too. Some skippers let their mates take over for a few hours, but I can't sleep while we are fishing. I eat very little, too.

'At last it's all over and we sail for home. That's a blessing, I can tell you. Sometimes I sleep for a whole day and a night. I can't count on that though, because if the weather turns bad, I have to go back to the bridge and see the ship safely through the storm. One of my friends who was a skipper was found dead in his bunk. I wasn't surprised. He was going nearly mad with worry.'

'*But why is it so important to catch fish?*' 'Well, for a start, I get no regular pay. The owners of the trawler give me ten per cent of the profits of each trip. The trip costs £3,000, so if we only catch fish worth that amount, I have nothing. We need to double that amount for it to be worthwhile. More important, if I didn't bring home good catches regularly, the owners would take me off this fine new ship. If I had an old tub, built before the war, I should have no chance of making a good living. I might even have to go back to being a deck hand.'

'*How dangerous is fishing?*' 'More dangerous than almost any other job. Quite often we have to sail in a Force 10 gale, and on land that would take the roof off your house. Ice is the big enemy though. If the weather is really cold, the spray freezes as it falls. We hack it off the decks and turn hot water hoses on it, but if we can't work fast enough, the trawler becomes top heavy, and over she goes. You don't live long if you fall into the icy waters of the Arctic Ocean: just thirty seconds, I believe.'

149

The Trawler Skipper

bringing the catch on board in rough seas

5 The Production Line Worker

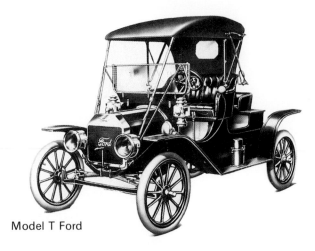

Model T Ford

Do you think you could put together all the parts that make a motor car? There are 16,000 of them! Possibly you could learn how to do this enormous puzzle, but it might take you years. However, if there are several hundred people then each one could take a different job. You might do no more than fit wheels. You could learn to do that very quickly. This method of breaking a big, complicated job into a large number of small, easy jobs is called mass production. The first man to make motor cars that way was an American called Henry Ford. Until then every car had been built by a handful of skilled craftsmen. Cars took a long time to complete and were expensive. Henry Ford's 'Model T' was so cheap that many more people could afford one, and soon car manufacturers in England were copying his way of making cars.

We will visit an imaginary car works in the 1960s to see what is happening. It belongs to the Bridge Motor Company.

We can have a good view from the catwalk. This is like a footbridge which runs the whole width of the factory. The building is enormous. Pipes snake all over the floor, there is a lot of banging and the machinery is whining. The cars stand on a huge belt,

about two feet from the ground, and the belt is moving steadily forward. This is the 'production line'. At the beginning, each car is just a skeleton: at the end it is finished and ready to drive away. All along the line, men are working. There are hundreds of them, each doing one job, over and over again. We can see a man fitting carpets. He turns a piece of carpet over, spreads glue on it, then puts it in place. By the time he has finished, the next car has arrived. The man does not have to hurry, but neither does he have time to waste.

It is now the tea break, so we will go and talk to Fred, one of the workers.

'What is your job, Fred?' 'I fit gearboxes. I have a supply of them beside me and when a car arrives I drop one in a hole in the engine and fix it down with a couple of bolts, I fit forty gearboxes every hour — that's three hundred and twenty a day.' *'Do you like the work?'* 'I hate it. It's so boring. How would you like to do the same thing day after day, week after week? You have to keep going, you know. If you are too slow you are carried on to the next man's patch and get all tangled up with him. Some mornings I have a headache, and would love to take it easy. The line never has a headache, though. At first I didn't think I could stick it, but I have been here for two years now.'

'Why do you do the job?' 'I do it for the money, of course. I've got a wife and a couple of children, and £17.00 a week isn't bad pay. There are plenty of men around here with no job at all. Anyway, it's better than on the building site. I was a builder's labourer before I came here. At least the factory is warm and dry.' *'What training did you have when you started?'* 'Training? What training do you need? The foreman just took me over to Bill and told him to show me what to do. Bill wasn't too pleased, but I

T Ford production line

soon learnt the job and now I can fit a gearbox without thinking.' *'What do you think about while you are working?'* 'I don't think about anything at all. I just make my mind go a blank. It's the only way to get through the day.'

'Does the Company look after you?' 'Well, we have a canteen and a sports club, but they are only for show. We don't care about the Company, and the Company doesn't care about us. We are only numbers to them, not people. They just get all the work out of us that they can, in order to make money for themselves. If I had a problem it would be no use going to any of the bosses here. They wouldn't be interested.' *'Aren't you proud, though Fred, to see all those new shiny cars come out of the factory, and to know that you had a hand in making every one?'* 'I don't often see the finished cars as they come off the belt right down the other end, and even when I do, I can't say that I feel all that proud. I know how the lads put them together. Don't ever buy a Bridge car. You will be lucky if you find a good one. The chances are you will buy a

"Monday car", a "Friday car" or a "tea-break car", made when we're all tired or fed-up, and a whole lot of trouble will go with it.'

At the end of the shift we stand by the gate and watch the men come out. They are all in a great hurry to leave. Some walk, some have bicycles, and some have cars. Among them is Fred. He is driving a handsome, new 'Bridge Consort'.

The Production Line Worker

6 The Office Girl

As you know, difficult sums can take you a long time if you have to do them on paper. However, for hundreds of years people have been making machines to help them with their arithmetic. One of the first of these was the abacus. It is very efficient, even though it is only rows of beads on wires. Later, there were more complicated machines. In 1801, a Frenchman called Jacquard made punched cards to help weavers put patterns in their cloth, and soon other inventors were using cards like Jacquard's in arithmetic machines. People had to work such machines by hand, but in 1949 some scientists in Cambridge made the first modern electronic computer.

A computer is rather like a pocket calculator. If you are lucky enough to have one of these, you can ask it any sums you like, and it will work them out in no time at all, using electricity. Of course, full-sized computers are much more complicated. All sorts of people use them in all sorts of ways. Gunners in the army have them, as well as doctors in hospitals and astronauts. We are going to see how they have changed the work of people in offices.

We will talk to June. She is a middle-aged woman now, but back in the 1940s, when she was a girl, she started work in the general office of a small glove-making firm. There were no computers then.

'What was it like in an office in those days, June?' 'The wages were much lower then. I only earned £2.50 a week. The hours were longer too. We started at 8.30 a.m. and worked until 5.30 p.m. and had only two weeks' holiday a year. I was in a general office which meant that all of us did different jobs in the same room. I helped the chief wages clerk. It took us four days to work out the wages. We used calculating machines, of course, but we had to work them by hand, and it was a slow business. Then on Friday mornings everyone in the office helped with paying out the wages. At 9.30 a.m. the office manager and a van driver went to the local bank to collect the cash for the wages. They were for all the firm's employees: the factory workers, the office staff and the "out-workers" who made gloves in their own homes. We cleared all our papers from the desks and we each had a pile of wage slips, another of small brown packets with typed names on the outside, and bags full of pound notes, and silver and copper coins. It was very important to check the amount of money we were given and to make sure that we put the right number of notes and coins into the packets. If there was not enough money to match the wage slips, or if there was any left over at the end, then we knew we had made a mistake. We had to empty all the packets and

making up the wages in the 1940s

start again. We enjoyed this work, though, because it was a change from our other duties.'

'*Were there ever any mistakes in the wages, June?*' 'Sometimes there were and then the men and girls from the factory would come straight to the office and complain. Quite often they complained even when we hadn't made any mistake. We could check their pay slips and time cards and sort out any problems straight away. I can only remember one man who got very angry and threatened to hit the office manager.'

'*What is your work like today, June, now that you have the computer?*' 'At present I work in the wages section of a large office block in London. In this firm all the wages are worked out by the computer.' '*What does the computer do?*' 'We tell it all it needs to know about each of our employees – rate of pay, how many hours worked, tax code, and so on. We can't speak to it in the ordinary way, of course. There is a special computer language. You can't even hear it, because it is holes punched into a paper tape. The computer uses all this information to work out how much each of our employees has earned. Then it takes away tax and national insurance payments, leaving the amount the employee will actually have to spend. After the computer has finished its sums, it prints out the information on a pay slip which we send to the employees. We don't send them any actual money. Instead the wages are paid into their own bank accounts by what we call "credit transfers".'

'*Why did your firm buy a computer?*' 'To save time and money. Five years ago we had three separate departments dealing with pay, with eighty staff and twenty supervisors. When the computer was put in we only needed one office and forty people. That meant that lots of us had to change our jobs or be retrained. The supervisors all kept their jobs, of course!'

'*Is the computer efficient?*' 'Oh yes. It prepares pay slips for thousands of our workers all over the country. It only makes mistakes if we feed it the wrong information. After all, you wouldn't expect your pocket calculator to get your sums right if you gave it the wrong numbers.' '*What other differences are there between office life now and in the 1940s?*' 'Our hours are shorter than before, holidays are longer, our wages are higher and office buildings are more comfortable. But today people work in separate sections. I hardly know what is happening in other departments of the firm. I only know about wages. In some ways it was more interesting in a general office where you knew more about other people's jobs. It was fun, too, putting the wages into the pay packets. These days, of course, we should need bigger packets for the wages and I don't suppose it would be safe to bring such large amounts of money into the office. It would be too much of a temptation for criminals.'

left a modern IBM computer
top typists in a modern office

157

7 North Sea Oil

Today we will talk to Michael Higgins who works on an oil rig in the North Sea.

'*What exactly is an oil rig?*' 'It's a huge, floating platform used to drill for oil.'

'*What is it like to be on one?*' 'In some ways it is like being on a ship. There are about 200 of us. We have comfortable cabins, cinemas, games rooms, TV rooms and rest rooms. There are mess rooms as well, of course. The food is excellent. We can have as much as we like of anything we like – steak, scampi, smoked salmon – anything.'

'*You make it sound like a holiday cruise.*' 'Don't you believe it. For one thing, the North Sea isn't the Mediterranean. Sometimes we have fog, sometimes we have hurricane force winds with waves 60 feet high, and at other times it is bitterly cold.

'There is danger, too. The worst disaster was in 1980 when the rig Alexander L. Keilland broke a leg in a gale and capsized. There were 230 men on her, and 140 were drowned. Also, some of the individual jobs can be dangerous. Mine is the most dangerous of the lot. I'm a diver.'

'*Tell us about it, please.*' 'For shallow work I go over the side in a diving suit. If we are working at any great depth, though, six of us go to the sea bed in a decompression chamber. This is like a little room. Air is pumped into it until it is the same pressure as the sea outside. That means we can go in and out of the chamber without noticing any difference. We can read and play chess or cards, but it's very cramped. Sometimes we are down for three weeks. At the end of that time we have seen quite enough of each other.

'We spend up to ten hours a day working. There are all sorts of jobs that have to be done under the sea. We photograph equipment, we inspect it and we clear the rubbish that has collected around it. We install equipment too, and repair it. I do under water many of the jobs that a skilled engineer would find tricky on dry land.

'Many things can go wrong, of course, and that can be serious. Five or six divers are killed every year in the North Sea. Apart from the danger, the worst enemy is the cold. On top of that you run a chance of developing bone disease or ear trouble.

'When we are brought up to the surface we can't

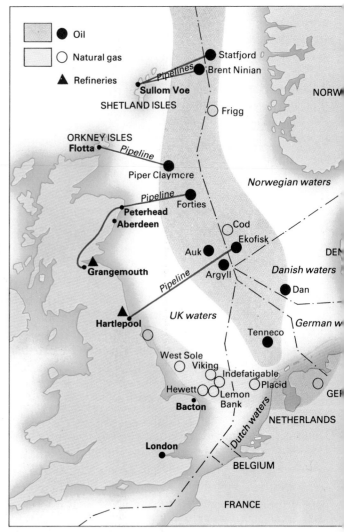

North Sea oil fields

oil rig

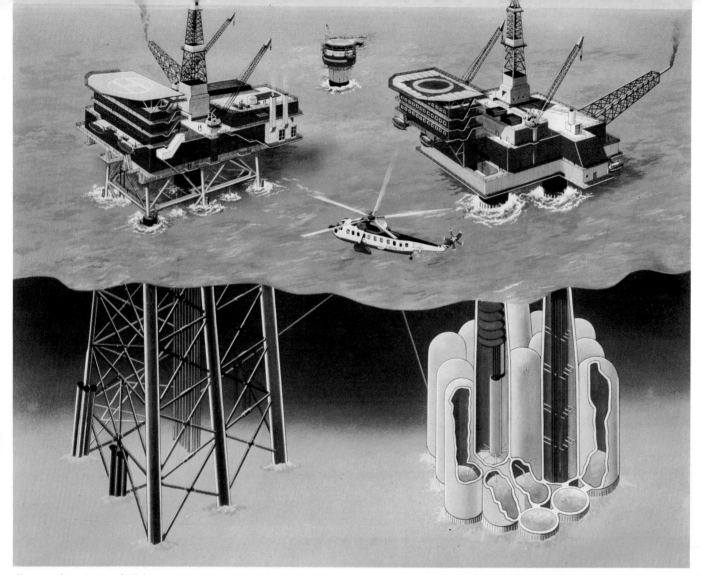

diagram of two types of oil rig

just step out of our decompression chamber. They have to let the pressure down very slowly, otherwise we get a horrible complaint called "the bends". It can kill you. For every 30 metres we have been down, we have to spend a day in decompression, and sometimes we have to work at a depth of 150 metres.'

'Whyever do you do the work?' 'For the money, of course. There can't be many jobs that pay as well. But I know this. I earn every penny of it.'

We will now talk to a Member of Parliament about North Sea Oil.

'Why is it that men like Mr. Higgins have to risk their lives to find oil?' 'North Sea oil is very important for Britain. Oil itself is vital. Without it our cars, lorries and trains would stop running, our ships would not put out to sea, our factories would cease working and a great many buildings would have no heat. The whole country would grind to a halt. Until recently we bought nearly all our oil from the Middle East, which is

a very unsettled part of the world. In 1973 the countries there suddenly put up the price of their oil four fold and they have gone on putting up their prices ever since. The Middle East states had us at their mercy, which was most unpleasant. Now, thanks to North Sea oil, we produce all we need ourselves and don't have to worry any more.'

'North Sea oil should make us rich, shouldn't it?' 'Of course it should. It saves us hundreds of millions of pounds that we once paid for foreign oil. The industry has created thousands of jobs. Also, the government collects enormous sums of money in oil taxes, but I'm afraid that much of it is wasted. A couple of national-ised industries like British Steel and the National Coal Board can lose money as fast as the government collects it in taxes. My hope is that more and more of the tax will go to creating new industries, like micro-electronics. If that happens, who knows? We might even overtake Japan and West Germany!'

8 British Industry, 1891 and 1981

British Industry in 1891

In this section we will talk first to a Lancashire cotton manufacturer, living in 1891.

'What do you think about British industry today?' 'It's the best in the world. No other country can touch us. Take my industry, cotton. Did you know that 70% of the cotton cloth sold in the world was made here in Lancashire? There are $12\frac{1}{2}$ million spindles in Oldham alone, nearly as many as in the whole of the United States of America. Then there's shipbuilding. Of every ten new ships launched in the world, eight are built in British yards. On top of that, a quarter of the world's coal is mined in these small islands.'

'Why do you think Britain is doing so well?' 'Partly it's our geography. Here, we are on islands where foreigners can't invade us. We have hundreds of miles of coast line with any number of good harbours. We have all the coal we want. Factories need steam

engines and steam engines need coal. That is why Britain's industries are in the north, on the coalfields. We leave it to the southerners to keep cows and grow turnips.

'What's more, the industrial revolution began in Britain, didn't it? You mention any of the world's greatest inventions – James Hargreaves's spinning jenny, Edmund Cartwright's power loom, James Watt's steam engine, George Stephenson's railway locomotives, Isambard Brunel's steamships. What do you notice about the inventors? They are British to a man! They gave us a lead we will never lose to foreigners.

'But I think our success today is mainly due to the people we have in this country. There are thousands of business men like me. I am in my counting house until all hours of the night and I do business with traders all over the world. Then there are our workers. It's a real joy to watch the lads and lassies in my factory tending their machines with such skill. As for the engineers in the textile machinery works up the road, it's amazing

nineteenth century production line – men making guns

what they can do. They are craftsmen to their fingertips.

'The government has the right ideas, too. It lets us get on with our jobs. We don't want it to tell us what to do, but we do want it to police the streets of our towns and the seas of the world. This it does. We have no riots in British cities and thanks to the Royal Navy, our ships can sail where they like. If the Chinese, say, decided to interfere with some of our traders the government would soon send a gunboat to bombard Canton. We'll have no nonsense from any foreign Johnnies.'

British Industry in 1981

Now we will go forward ninety years and talk to an economist living in 1981.

'*What is happening in British industry today?*' 'The most important thing to realise is that everything is changing so quickly. Before the Second World War factories gave up steam power and went over to electricity. That meant all sorts of industries grew up in the south, electronics – radios, washing machines and so forth – aircraft and, most important of all, motor cars. Change is even faster now, micro-electronics, for example.'

'*Tell us about that, please.*' 'You know that if you

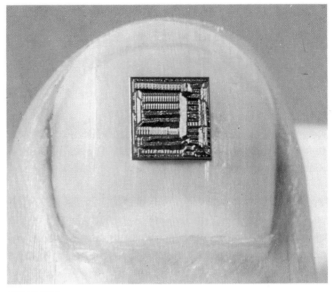

silicon chip

look into an automatic washing machine you will find a control box which tells it what to do, and a whole tangle of wires. Today, we can put all that on a silicon chip a quarter of an inch square and 1/50th of an inch thick. But that's nothing to what the chip has done for

1982 production line – robots assembling cars. How many men can you see?

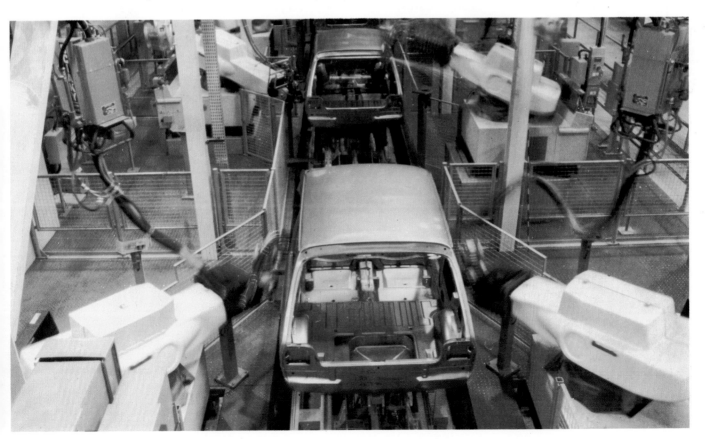

British Industry, 1891 and 1981

computers. The first computer, made in 1950, was the Ferranti Mark I Star. It needed a large room to hold it. Inside it had six miles of wire, 4,000 valves each nearly as big as a light bulb and 100,000 soldered joints. Also, it used as much electricity as thirty electric fires. Today, a single chip will do 100 times as much work and will use hardly any electricity at all. As a result, modern computers are so small and economical anyone can have one. That's what micro-electronics means. Equipment that was once too big, and too expensive to buy and to run, is now small and cheap. It is also much more reliable. The old-fashioned computers were always breaking down, but modern ones hardly ever go wrong.'

'*What can we use computers for?*' 'For all the difficult calculations you have to make if you run a factory or a business. Sums which would take a man hours, a computer will do in seconds. Also it will store information for you. Instead of having hundreds of filing cabinets, you have a computer on your desk and instead of spending ages looking through cards, you just press a few buttons. Up comes the answer on a screen. If a secretary has a word processor, she can type three times as many letters and the typing will be much better.

'In a factory you can use computers to guide robots and they will make your cars, your cardboard boxes, your ballpoint pens or anything else you want. What's more, robots don't chat to their mates, or take tea breaks and they work as well on Monday morning and Friday afternoon, as they do during the rest of the week.'

'*Can micro-electronics help us in our daily lives?*' 'You've got a pocket calculator, haven't you? That will have a silicon chip in it, and so, quite likely, will your watch. Chips can control your washing machine, your dishwasher, your oven, your central heating system and help you drive your car. There are chips in all sorts of toys. They will even play chess.'

'*It sounds as if we are having a new Industrial Revolution.*' 'We certainly are, but this time Britain is not in the lead.'

'*Why is that?*' 'For one thing, micro-electronics began in the United States. The Americans were determined to be the first to put a man on the moon, but everything in a space craft must be as small as possible. You could hardly fit one with a Ferranti Mark I Star! That set the American scientists thinking. Their discoveries in micro-electronics were not only useful for space craft, but for thousands of other things.

computer 1950

computer 1981

Prestel

'Countries like Japan, West Germany and France were quick to copy the United States. Britain has done so too, but she is limping behind the leaders. We know about robots, for example, but last year we only had 370. The Japanese had 7,000. We know about micro-electronics, but only half our factories use it. The most modern things many firms have are electric typewriters.'

'*That doesn't speak very well for our scientists, does it?*' 'There is nothing wrong with our scientists. They have always been the best in the world and they still are. If you go to San Francisco, the very home of micro-electronics, you will find that one-third of the scientists are British. They have emigrated so that they can earn decent salaries and escape from crippling taxes.'

'*Whose fault is it that we are so behind in micro-electronics, then?*' 'I would blame almost everyone. Take the workers, for example. They will fight tooth and nail to stop their firms buying new labour saving equipment. They say it will cost them their jobs. What they must realise is that unless Britain keeps up with other countries we will be out of business. Then no one will have a job. I'm not all that impressed by British managers, either. They don't welcome new ideas and they think more of their golf than they do of their work.

'Mainly I blame the government. No matter what party is in power, it doesn't have a proper plan. The governments of West Germany, France and Japan do make plans. Those countries are like schools with proper time-tables. But can you imagine a school with no time-table, and staff and pupils wandering round not knowing which classrooms to use or what subjects to study? Britain is a bit like that.

'Then again, our government wastes a terrible amount of our money. You can say that our industries are of two kinds. There are the old no-hope industries like steel, shipbuilding and motor cars. Then there are the new "sunrise" industries as we call them, like micro-electronics and robotics. Which should the government help?'

'*The sunrise industries, surely.*' 'Yes, of course. They are the ones we need if we are to keep up with the foreigners. Well, the government does give them money, but only in tens of millions of pounds. At the same time it gives thousands of millions to the no-hope industries. The Japanese do just the opposite. Not only are they ahead of us, but they are forging further ahead the whole time. I'll give you just one example. You go out and try to buy a video tape recorder which was wholly made in Britain. You will be out of luck. Every single one on sale in this country was made in Japan.'

'*What makes the British government behave like that?*' 'We already have nearly three million un-employed and if the no-hope industries closed we should have several million more. Also the govern-ment will have serious problems with the trade unions if help isn't given to the older industries. The trouble is that while giving money now seems to help, in fact it is just making things more difficult for the country in the future. We are just losing the race in micro-electronics and that means losing the race in trying to sell our products abroad.'

163

Chapter Nine Home Life and Leisure

1 The Poor Family at Home

Bath is one of the more pleasant towns in England. It has hot springs which some doctors think may help to cure rheumatism and other illnesses, so wealthy people come to the city to drink or bathe in the water. There are good hotels for them and a magnificent Pump Room. There are Roman remains, an abbey church and some splendid streets built in the eighteenth century. But not everything about Bath is pleasant. We will talk to Mr. Jardine, an inspector employed by the N.S.P.C.C.

'*What is your work, Mr. Jardine?*' 'I visit poor people who we think may be ill-treating their children, and try to persuade them to stop. If they will not listen to us, I have them prosecuted.' '*Surely you don't have much to do in a town like Bath?*' 'You are wrong, I'm afraid. You see, Bath is a place where rich people

come when they retire. There are army and navy officers, clergymen, gentlefolk and we even have a dowager duchess here. These people need a lot of servants, and they mainly employ women and girls. There is little work for men. Wages are low, except for skilled cabinet makers and coach builders. There are slum areas by the river, like the Dolemeads. The houses are poor, and in some winters they are flooded. The other day, I visited a house down there. The plaster was coming off the walls, the windows were broken and the roof leaked. No one had cleaned the grates for weeks, so there were ashes piled right into the room. Upstairs, they kept pigeons and the room was full of their muck. The bed was just a heap of filth, and crawling with bugs.' '*What were the children like?*' 'There was a baby lying on a heap of rags with

maggot flies buzzing all round him. He could hardly breathe because of bronchitis. There was a little boy of five in a torn shirt and an old pair of trousers. He had gangrene in a cut in his leg. There was also a girl of about eight. She had on a bodice and a bit of sacking for a skirt. All the children were covered with fleas and lice. I could hardly find a spot on the boy's back that didn't have a flea bite. The trouble with this family was that the mother was a drunkard. Things are bad when the father drinks, but if the mother drinks, there is no hope!'

Outside we find a group of boys playing, and we talk to one of them. His clothes are poor, but he is wearing shoes and is quite well fed. He must come from a better home than the one Mr. Jardine has described. He tells us his name is Frank. He is twelve years old and his father works for a builder.

'*How are things at home, Frank?*' 'Not too bad at the moment. Father has work now that the spring has come. I still have to do my bit to help, though.' *What do you do?*' 'I am a newsboy. I sell newspapers in the streets. I earn 2/6d (12½p) a week but I have to work hard for it. I am usually on my stand for about five hours after school and it's often ten o'clock before I've sold out. It's bitterly cold in winter and it's hard on the voice. Folk won't buy unless you shout out loud and clear. I like it best if there's been a good murder or something like that, I sell my papers quickly then.'

'*What happens to your wages?*' 'Mother has them, of course. Still, I can sometimes make a bit for myself. I scoop up horse muck from the streets and sell it for a farthing a bucket. (A farthing is about one-tenth of a penny.) I don't tell mother about that.'

'*Do you have time to play?*' 'Only on Saturdays and during the school holidays. In the summer I go off with my friends. We go into the woods, and if it's hot we undress and bathe naked in the river. That really annoys the smart young men taking their lady friends for a row. Most of the time we lark about in the streets. Sometimes we play marbles and sometimes we bowl our hoops. It makes the ladies very angry when we run into them, but it serves them right for wearing such stupid dresses. We have some good sport, especially after dark. The other night we daubed our faces with luminous paint and frightened the life out of a drunk. Once a rich old geezer who lives near here sent for the police because we were making a bit of noise outside his house. We came back later and tied a cat to his bell pull. The best part was watching the maid trying to untie the cat. We had a

a street game in East London

rare bit of good luck last winter. The Rector of Walcot went into his church and left the key in the lock. We locked the door and ran off with the key. He had to ring the bell for ages before anyone came to let him out.'

'*Haven't you anywhere to play except the streets? Can't you go into the park?*' 'No, the police chase us out of the Victoria Park, except when we have our school treat. Each boy has to march along carrying a cup slung over his shoulder on a strap. At the park we run races against other schools. When it's over we get a free tea of buns and lemonade. We look forward to that all the year. Boys who go to Sunday School get taken to Weston-super-Mare on the train, but I can't be bothered with Sunday School just for one day a year at the seaside.'

2 The Rich Family at Home

Mr. Walker is a solicitor. He makes a lot of money from many of the rich, retired people in Bath. They are glad to have a clever lawyer to look after their affairs so he is always busy. He is in his office at eight o'clock every morning and quite often he does not leave it, except for lunch, until eight o'clock in the evening. His wife, though, has no work to do. We will see how she spends her day.

The Walkers live in Queen's Square. It is not quite as grand as the Royal Crescent, but the houses are very elegant. They were built in the eighteenth century, and little has been done to bring them up to date. Mr. Walker sees no point in spending money to make the house easier to look after. There are plenty of poor women and girls in Bath who have to work as servants, though they earn very low wages. The main rooms are on three floors. On the ground floor is a drawing room, a dining room and Mr. Walker's study. On the other two are bedrooms. Under the roof are the attics where the servants sleep. In winter these attics are cold. In summer they are unbearably hot. Beneath the house is the basement where the servants work. There is a scullery for washing up, a larder and a kitchen. The basement is always dark

Queen's Square, Bath

Mr. Walker

and gloomy although the kitchen is always hot. The living rooms and bedrooms are always comfortable because their thick walls keep out the summer heat and in winter the servants light a fire in every room. There are thick carpets, heavy velvet curtains, expensive furniture and many ornaments and nick-nacks. To us it all looks very elaborate, cluttered and fussy. But the Walkers are proud of their fine things, which help show other people how wealthy they are.

Mrs. Walker wakes up at eight o'clock, when the maid taps on her door and brings in the breakfast tray. It may be bacon and eggs, boiled eggs, grilled kidneys or fish. Sometimes there is kedgeree, an Indian dish made from rice, eggs and fish. Next the maid makes up the fire so that it blazes merrily, and brings in a hip bath. She puts it near the fire and then fetches several cans of warm water from the kitchen. There is no bathroom in the house, but for Mrs. Walker a bath in front of the fire is very pleasant. It is not so pleasant for the maid who has to carry the water!

After bathing and dressing, Mrs. Walker goes to the drawing room and rings for the cook. Between them they decide what to serve at lunch and at dinner. Mrs. Walker has an annoying habit of changing her mind after the cook has begun to prepare a meal. For the rest of the morning Mrs. Walker hasn't very much to do. She reads a little,

plays the piano a little or does some embroidery. She usually finds the time drags until her husband comes home for lunch.

After lunch, Mrs. Walker begins what is for her the serious business of the day. She makes her 'calls', and goes round to see her friends and neighbours. She takes a little ivory case with her in which she keeps her visiting cards. She might leave a card at a house to say thank you for a dinner party, or perhaps to say she was sorry to hear someone was ill. Mrs. Walker bends one corner of each card to show she has called in person. Now and then, she may ask to see the lady of the house. Again, she will leave a card if the maid says, 'Not at home.' When she has paid all her calls, she returns home, anxious to see if anyone important has left a card for her.

On many afternoons Mrs. Walker attends an 'at home' and sometimes she gives one herself. These are elegant little afternoon parties. The maid announces each visitor by name and they all sit in the drawing room, drinking tea and eating very thin slices of bread and butter and tiny cakes. Perhaps someone will play the piano to entertain them.

In the early evening Mrs. Walker sees her children for half an hour. She finds them noisy and tiresome, so she is glad when the nurse takes them away. She now dresses for dinner, the most important event of the day. First she puts on a cotton shift, and then a corset. The idea of the corset is to hold her waist in and give her an 'hour-glass' figure. Mrs. Walker holds the back of a chair while the housemaid and tweeny, or junior maid, pull the corset laces as tight as they can. Next comes the bustle (a bone framework which makes the dress stick out at the back). On top of the bustle comes a petticoat and then comes the dress itself, a beautiful pink silk one trimmed with white lace.

For dinner there are a large number of French dishes, which are really too complicated for the cook to make properly. When it is over the family and the guests go into the drawing room where they drink coffee, play cards and gossip, until it is time for bed.

167

3 Domestic Servants

In the 1890s, over a million women and girls worked as domestic servants. A rich nobleman might employ as many as three hundred servants, but even a solicitor, like Mr. Walker, had four. They were a nurse, a housemaid, a cook and a tweeny. The nurse looked after the children. The housemaid saw that the house was clean and tidy, as well as doing other jobs such as receiving callers and helping her mistress to dress. The cook prepared all the meals. The tweeny, or between maid, helped the housemaid in the morning and the cook in the afternoon. We will talk to the tweeny, who is called Eliza.

'*Where do you come from, Eliza?*' 'I was born in Gurney Slade, about fifteen miles away.' '*How did you become a servant?*' 'There were eight children in our

family and father thought it would be a good idea for me to go into service. There was precious little else to do. When I was eleven I started as a slavey with a shopkeeper at Gurney Slade.' '*What is a slavey?*' 'I was the only servant they had, so I did all the work — the fires, the cleaning, the washing up, looking after the children and the washing and ironing. The only thing the mistress did was the cooking, and a fine mess she used to leave for me to clear up! Then the rector heard that Mr. Walker wanted a tweeny, so I came to work in Bath.' '*Are things better for you now?*' 'Not a lot. I still have to get up at six in the morning, though I can usually go to bed by ten. It used to be midnight more often than not.'

'*What work do you have to do?*' 'I am first up in the morning. I have to creep down, making sure I don't wake anybody, and then I light the range. First of all I have to clean out the ashes and polish the top of the stove until it shines. When the kettle boils I take Jane the cook and Ellen the housemaid a cup of tea. When Ellen gets up I help her lay breakfast and take the mistress her breakfast in bed. I have to go round and make sure there is a good fire in every room. The family doesn't like to be cold. I also have to take them their hot water. I am up and down stairs all the time it seems, carrying heavy buckets. The master once lifted my bucket of coal and said it must weigh about thirty pounds, but he didn't offer to carry it for me.

'After the family has dressed we do the bedrooms. I have to do the dirty jobs, of course. I see to the fires and I empty the chamber pots. They have to be rinsed and wiped out. Sometimes that makes me feel sick. To clean the carpets, I scatter tea leaves everywhere and then brush them up. That picks up the dust you see. Making beds is a game! Each one has three mattresses. There is a straw one at the bottom which we only turn once a week. Next there is a wool one that we turn every day. Lastly, there is the feather one which we have to shake until it's all puffed up. There are the living rooms as well, of course — grates, carpets and the dusting. The floors have to be spotless, even under carpets. The missus once hid a shilling under a carpet, just to see if we cleaned underneath and if we were honest.

'In the afternoon I have to help the cook. There is the washing up from lunch, and there are all the vegetables to prepare for the evening meal. Cook is old and bad-tempered and often has a drop too much to drink. I have to make the fire roar away so the kitchen gets as hot as a furnace. It's dreadful in summer. Ellen usually waits at table, but if the family has friends to dinner I help her. I hate that. They all sit there in their finery, talking posh. I feel scared I am going to drop something. Once, someone said something which made me giggle and I couldn't stop. The missus was furious. We aren't supposed to listen to the conversation. She wouldn't hear my excuses. "I allow no answers," she said.

'After dinner there is a mountain of washing up – everything from delicate wine glasses to great sticky copper pans. I once counted sixty knives and forks, forty spoons and a hundred plates. It was well after midnight before I finished all that.'

'Do you ever leave the house?' 'Only to wash the doorstep and as I'm from the country I do miss the fields and woods. This house is like a prison. I have a half day on Sunday, but they make me go to church. Once a month I have a full day, and can go home to see my family – that's if missus doesn't find me a job so that I miss my train.'

'How much do you earn for all that work?' 'I get ten pounds a year and have to buy my uniform out of that.' *'Do you have any boyfriends?'* 'Followers, do you mean? I'm no dolly mop, but there is a boy back home who rather likes me. He walked all the way to Bath to see me, but I had to send him away at once. If the family knew I had a follower, they would sack me on the spot.'

4 Washday

Mr. and Mrs. Cox and their eight children live on the outskirts of Bath. Mr. Cox owns a lock-up shop in the centre of town and the family are comfortably off. They are not rich, but they can afford to have someone to help Mrs. Cox with the housework. Mrs. Parsons comes in from a nearby village every Monday. Both women dislike Mondays and even the Cox children are glad when Monday is over. We will ask Lily, one of the daughters, why she does not like Mondays.

'None of us likes Monday because it's washday and that means a scrappy cold lunch of leftovers and nothing very nice for tea and supper either. Mother is so busy all day that she doesn't have time to bother with cooking. By the evening she is always tired and cross. One of us is usually in trouble before bedtime. You can hardly get inside the kitchen on Monday evening anyway, because it is always full of drying clothes and piles of ironing.'

Now let us see what Mrs. Cox herself thinks about Monday. *'Please tell us about washday, Mrs. Cox.'* 'First of all, before my husband leaves to open the shop, he lights the fire under the boiler. By the time Mrs. Parsons arrives to help me the water is very hot. The boiler uses quite a lot of coal but I boil all my whites in the copper and get them really clean, the way I like them. When they are finished we lift them out with a boiler stick and put them into baths of water: a bath of rinsing water, one of starch and then a bowl of blue. When the clothes have been through the baths we lift them out for mangling.' *'How do you fill the boiler and the baths with water, Mrs. Cox?'* 'I'm lucky because there is a tap and a low sink in the corner of the wash-house. We fill up with buckets of water from the tap and empty them into the sink. It's sometimes difficult to get every drop of dirty water out of the boiler, but I have a special little round bowl with a wooden handle. It's very useful for scooping out the last drops of water.' *'Do you put all your clothes into the boiler, Mrs. Cox?'* 'Dear me, no, I certainly don't boil my coloured things. I wash those in a dolly tub. First of all I pound away at the washing with a dolly, which is rather like a three-legged stool with a tall handle in the middle. I rub the really dirty clothes on my rubbing board with some good strong

yellow soap.' *'Do you use soap powder, Mrs. Cox?'* 'What's soap powder? All I need is soap, soda and lots of elbow grease. The soda is a bit hard on the hands and Mrs. Parsons and I usually have raw, red hands by Monday evening. We have to put soda in the water to make the soap lather well.'

'What happens next?' 'We put the clothes through the mangle, which is the hardest work of all. I have a large mangle with heavy beech rollers. The handle is hard to turn. Luckily, Mrs. Parsons is strong. I can only just manage it and when the children are at home in the holidays it takes two of them to turn the handle while I guide the sheets through the rollers. The water drains straight into the sink which is just above floor level. A heavy mangle is best because it squeezes most of the water out of the washing and then it does not take too long to dry. As I have a garden, I can dry my washing easily when the weather is fine, but in bad weather it is often hanging on clothes horses around the kitchen stove for days.'

'What do you do when the clothes are dry?' 'Well, I mustn't let some of the things get too dry or they are very hard to iron. It usually takes me most of Tuesday to finish ironing which I do on my big wooden table in the kitchen. It's hard work and it gets very hot because there has to be a good fire in the stove to heat up the irons. I have two big cast iron ones and while I am using one iron, the other is re-heating on the trivet in front of the fire. I also have a polishing iron which I use for my husband's stiff collars. Ironing shirts is bad enough, but it takes ages to do my daughters' cotton petticoats and long frilly drawers because there is so much material in them.'

As we have learnt from the Cox family, washing and ironing in Victorian times meant hours of

drudgery. As you know from your own homes, it is different today. What helped to bring about this change? Mrs. Cox's only source of power was coal, but during the twentieth century another important source of power was developed – electricity. At first there were lots of separate electricity companies and they were not always well organized. Then, between 1926 and 1935, workmen were busy all over the country building the huge pylons that can be seen everywhere. They carry a network of cables that we call the National Grid. This joins together all the different power stations, so that each one is helping to supply the whole country with electricity. The National Grid is the responsibility of the Central Electricity Generating Board and the country is divided into twelve areas, each with its own board.

Electricity has brought many changes into people's lives. It has certainly altered washday. In the 1930s Mrs. Cox's young daughter Lily was the first person in her road to own an electric washboiler.

Compared with today's washing machines it was a very simple affair. All the mangling still had to be done by hand. But the neighbours thought Lily was very lucky. 'You won't know yourself now,' they said.

5 Sundays and Holidays

Mr. Fussell keeps a grocer's shop in Bath. We will see how he and his family spend their time.

For his three sons, Sunday is the worst day of the week – much worse than school days. They have to be dressed by eight o'clock, wearing their best black suits and white shirts with stiff collars. They have to shine their shoes and plaster their hair down with macassar oil. After breakfast they go to Sunday School until eleven o'clock when they join their parents in church. They listen to the sermon carefully because they know their father will question them

about it later. After church the whole family goes for a walk in Victoria Park. Mr. and Mrs. Fussell like to show off their best clothes and see what their neighbours are wearing. The boys feel uncomfortable in their suits and bowler hats.

After lunch the boys go to Sunday School again and when they return home they have to read religious magazines until their parents take them to Evensong. After the service Mr. Fussell gathers his family together and reads to them from the Bible until bedtime.

Mr. Fussell's shop is open six days a week, from early in the morning until late in the evening. On Sundays the family must go to church, so the only time they can enjoy themselves together is on bank holidays and these are rare. Sometimes they go for walks. A favourite one is to Winsley, then home through Sally-in-the-Woods, a distance of ten miles. If they want something more peaceful, they can take a canal barge to Bradford-on-Avon. The boys like to hire Canadian canoes and paddle up the River Avon. They often capsize, but that is all part of the fun. In Victoria Park traders sell sweets, toys or balloons. Local farmers sell curds and whey and there are donkey rides for the smaller children.

Sometimes for a special treat the Fussells go to Bristol. They have lunch in a restaurant in Broadmead. It costs 9d (just under 4p), but it is a good meal. Afterwards they may go for a boat ride down the Avon Gorge under Brunel's famous suspension bridge. They may visit the Zoo on Clifton Down.

Once a year, Barnum and Bailey's circus visits Bath. Many children play truant from school to watch the men put up the big tent and to hear the lions roaring in their cages. Going to the circus is the greatest excitement of the year.

There is a theatre in Bath, and the Fussells often go on a Saturday evening. The plays are real 'blood and thunder' shows. It is great fun to cheer the hero and boo or hiss the villain. Mr. and Mrs. Fussell do not have evening dress, so they must sit in the tradesmen's circle. The theatre manager would not allow them into the dress circle. From the tradesmen's circle, they can look down on the wealthier people of Bath, who are wearing their fine clothes and

jewellery. Sometimes Mr. Fussell will nudge his wife and say, 'There's Colonel Bright. He owes me £10.' Or 'That large lady in blue is Mrs. Reader. She hasn't paid her bill for three months.' Mrs. Fussell gets very annoyed with her husband.

Once Mr. Fussell took his wife to a music hall in Bristol. The famous Marie Lloyd was on tour, and he badly wanted to see her. He will tell us about it:

'The show began with the usual sort of thing, performing dogs, jugglers and comedians. It was good fun, but we were all waiting for Marie. Then, at last, they ran her number up at the side of the stage. The band played her music and there was a hush, but there was no sign of Marie. They played her music again, a spotlight came on, and there she was. She is a tiny woman you know, and not very pretty – her teeth stick out. But on the stage she was magic. I have never laughed so loudly or clapped so much in all my life.' 'She sang a most vulgar song,' snaps Mrs. Fussell. 'A vulgar song?' says her husband. 'You tell me a rude line, or just one rude word that

was in it.' 'It was not *what* she sang,' replies Mrs. Fussell. 'It was *how* she sang it. That wink of hers was quite disgusting.' What is certain is that Mrs. Fussell enjoyed Marie Lloyd's song nearly as much as Mr. Fussell did.

The Music Hall

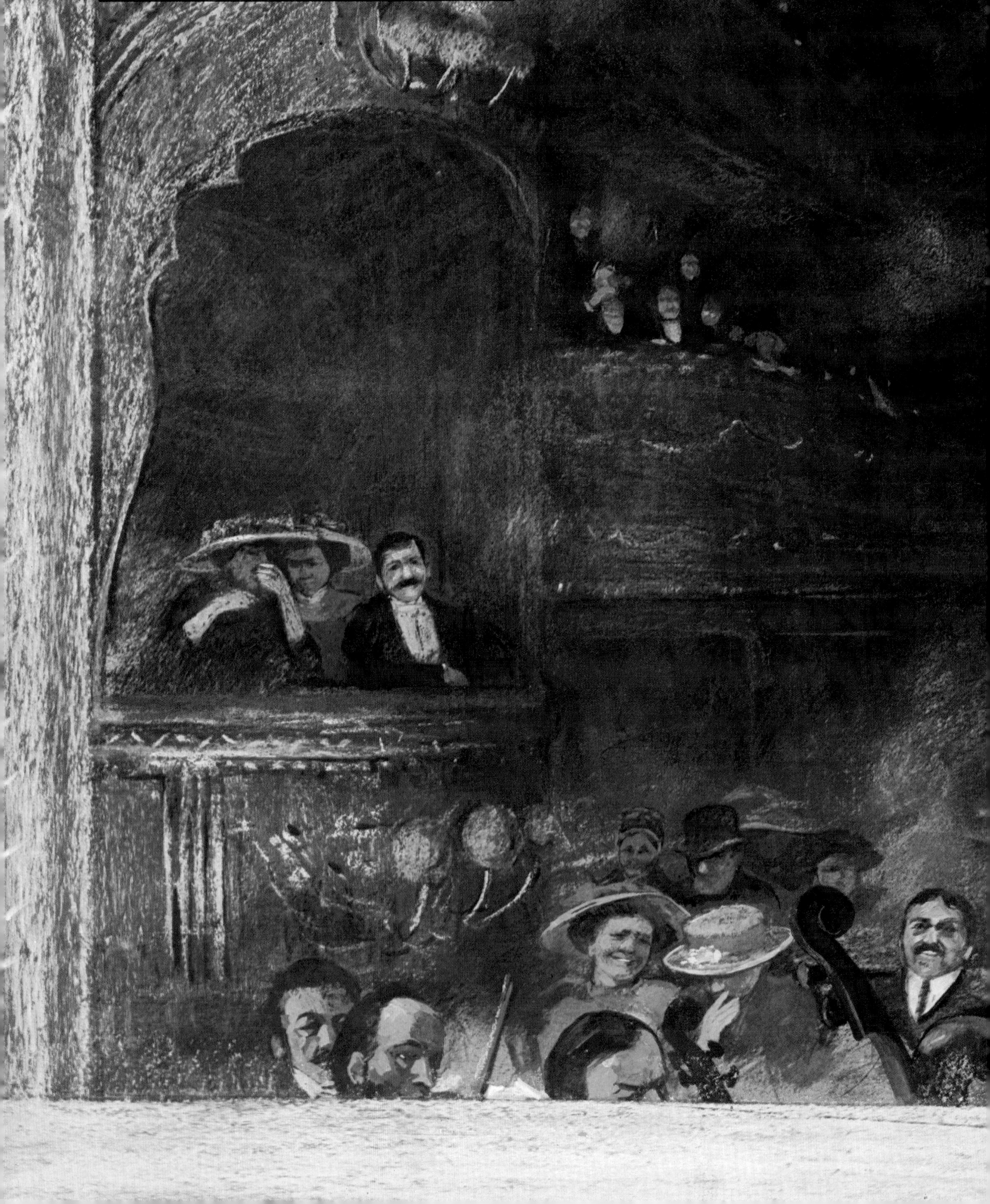

6 Radio and Cinema

In 1896 an Italian called Marconi discovered how to send Morse code messages through the air. People were already sending such messages, but along telegraph cables. Thanks to Marconi they could manage without the cables, so they called his invention 'wireless telegraphy'. It was especially useful to ships.

Then, on Christmas Eve, 1906, the wireless operators on ships near the coast of America were amazed. Their sets should only have sent them the dots and dashes of the Morse code, but they were talking and playing music! It was one of the world's first radio broadcasts.

In Britain, the British Broadcasting Company started regular programmes in 1922 and four years later two million families owned wireless sets or 'radios' as some called them. The mother of one of these families will tell us about it.

'The radio is wonderful entertainment, of course. We have the Children's Hour, which keeps the little ones quiet for a while. My older boy laughs at it. "It's kids' stuff," he says, "with all those soppy uncles and aunties." What he likes is "Radio Dance Band". I like classical music myself. We could never go to a concert because we are so far from town, but now we have the concerts in our own home. My husband is interested in feature programmes which are often very realistic because they use music and sound

a live broadcast in 1923

effects. I wish they would broadcast in the mornings as well. Some nice music would cheer up the housework.'

'Has the radio given you any problems?' 'Well, sometimes I have trouble getting the children to bed. I find, too, that some of our neighbours drop in more often than they used to. They can't afford their own radios, so they come and listen to ours. They expect tea and biscuits as well!' *'Do you find the radio keeps your family at home?'* 'I suppose the children spend less time in the streets, but I'm afraid it would take more than the wireless to keep my husband out of the Red Lion on a Saturday night.'

We will now ask a teacher about school broadcasts. 'A waste of time. They are never relevant to our work. How can a machine replace a teacher? I would never have a wireless in my house, let alone in my school. As for my pupils, they just listen to "the voice" these days and never think for themselves. It's a bad influence, too. I caught a boy hammering out jazz on the school piano the other day, and two girls dancing the Charleston. What really worries me, though, is this man Baird who has invented television. If people have the confounded cinema in their homes it will be the ruin of everything we do in school.'

While wireless sets became a part of life in the home, the cinema became the most popular form of public entertainment. The very first film performance in England was in 1896. Soon films were being shown all over the country. For the first time people outside London were able to see important events, such as the funeral of Queen Victoria and the Coronation of Edward VII.

The early films, of course, had no sound at all. The words the actors spoke were printed on cards which came up on the screen every few seconds. A pianist played music to suit the action of the film — fast exciting music for fights and chases and soft, sweet music for love scenes. The first film to use sound was *The Jazz Singer* in 1927, in which Al Jolson sang, but did not speak. The following year brought the first talking film.

The new 'talkies' were a great success. Almost every small town had one cinema, and there were a

number to choose from in the larger towns. Probably the cinema was most popular during the 1930s and the early 1940s. The films and stars from Hollywood were known and loved all over the world. We will visit a small town in the West of England to talk to a shop assistant called Shirley.

'*How often do you go to the pictures, Shirley?*' 'There are two separate programmes at the Palladium every week, so I always go on Monday evenings. On Saturday night my boyfriend takes me to the late performance. Sometimes we go to Bristol on Sundays if there is a very good film showing. It's not very expensive when you think of how much we enjoy the films – only 1/6d (7½p) for the ordinary seats and 3/– (15p) for the best ones. Anyway, there's nothing else to do here, particularly in the winter.'

'*What kind of films do you enjoy?*' 'Well, I like almost all kinds really, but I particularly enjoy love stories and musicals, although my boyfriend's favourites are the Westerns. We enjoy funny films too. Laurel and Hardy always make me laugh. My favourite stars, are Joan Crawford and Clark Gable. I wrote to Hollywood once and they sent me their autographs. I'd queue all day to see any film that starred either of them. Life would be miserable without the cinema, I think. Going to the pictures is a really good night out and it's something to look forward to when I'm at work.'

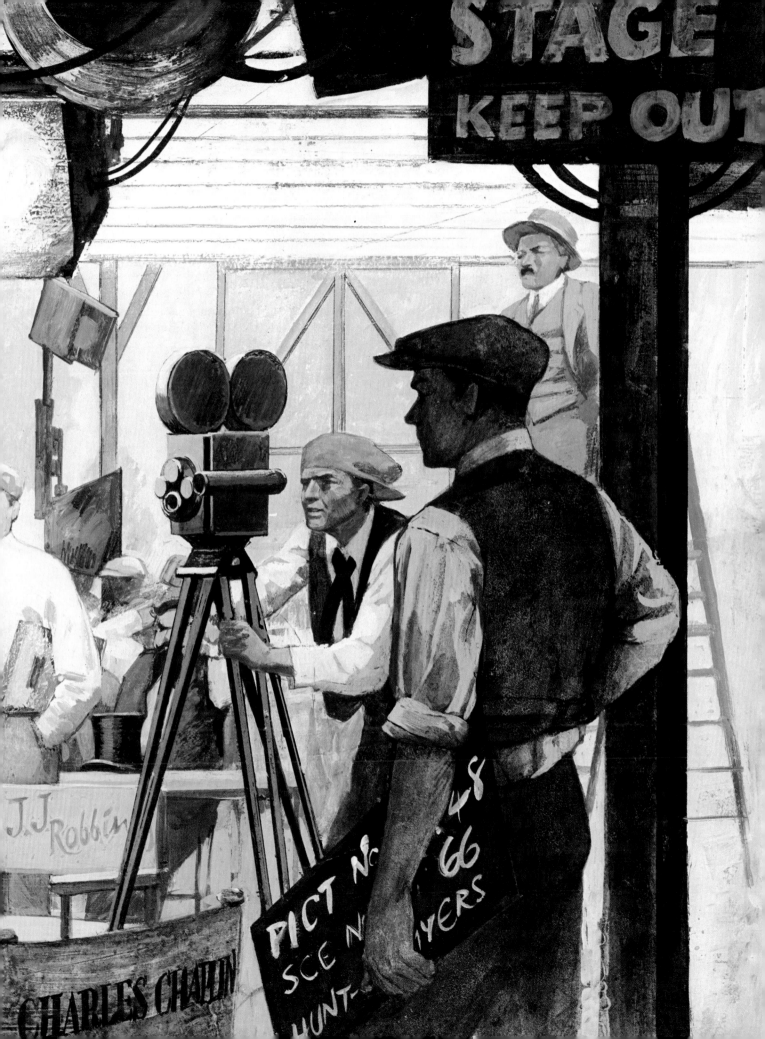

Chapter Ten   The Countryside

1 The Farm Worker and his Family

Today we will visit Gurney Slade, a small village on the Mendip Hills fifteen miles south of Bath. We will travel by the Somerset and Dorset Railway – the S. & D. Some people call it the 'Slow and Dirty', but girls from the village who work in Bath are very glad it is there, because otherwise they could not go home. The same railway takes wealthy Bath families to Bournemouth for their holidays. The village farmers are also grateful for the railway because it carries their milk to Bath. Their grandfathers had been unable to send fresh milk to market so they had to turn all the milk into cheese and butter.

We will leave the train at Binegar station and walk a mile to the home of the Woodget family. The lane has a surface of loose stones and is damp and muddy. In one place the hedges are so tall and overhang the lane so much that it is like walking through a tunnel. Near the village there are stone walls, and the wide grass verges are yellow with primroses. It is peaceful and beautiful.

The Woodgets live in a tiny cottage. There is one room downstairs which has a stone floor. It is only twelve feet square and the ceiling is so low that we can touch it. The stairs are not much better than a

ladder. They lead to a small bedroom where the parents and four children all sleep together. It is not surprising that the family are pleased because Eliza, one of their daughters, has left home to work in service in Bath. She is the tweeny you met in Chapter Three.

Mrs. Woodget cooks over the living room fire. There is a hook for roasting joints. It hangs down from the chimney and has a clockwork device that makes it turn. There is a kind of tin oven for baking which has to stand open in front of the fire. There is also an iron plate with a number of little hooks. This is for roasting sparrows. The most important thing though, is a large iron pot in which a whole supper can be cooked. There may be bacon, beans, potatoes and roly-poly pudding. Mrs. Woodget puts each type of food into a separate net and drops it into the pot at a different time. She uses the same pot to boil the clothes on washday.

Mrs. Woodget is a tall strong woman wearing a long dress that reaches to her ankles. The dress is coarse and plain, but her apron is sparkling white. Her hands are brown and hard but her face is not at all sunburnt. She spends many hours outside but she is always careful to wear her bonnet. All the women think that a sun tan would spoil their looks.

'What do you do during the day, Mrs. Woodget?' 'I am very busy looking after my home and my family. I get up at half past five and make breakfast and dinner for my husband and oldest boy. I tie the food up in handkerchiefs. Sometimes the boy gives me a bit of trouble. His boots dry out, you see, and the leather gets very hard. He doesn't want to put them on because they hurt his feet. He goes off to work in the end and I have a bit of bread and lard for breakfast. Then it's time to see the younger children off to school. I spend the morning fetching water from the pump in the village and cleaning the house. In the afternoons I garden or have a couple of hours with my friends drinking a cup of tea. Then I must make up my fire and cook supper for the family.'

'How much housekeeping money do you have?' 'My husband earns a gold half-sovereign a week. That's ten shillings (50p). I give him back one shilling for pocket money. My boy, George, earns two shillings. I have to pay the rent of the cottage which is one shilling and sixpence (7½p) a week. Sometimes I buy some biscuits and an orange or two, but mainly I buy tea, sugar, cheese and bread – especially bread.' 'Is that all you live on?' 'Goodness no. We have a big allotment and that grows us enough potatoes to last us the year, and some oats as well. Then there is the garden. That gives us cabbages, celery, onions, beans, cauliflowers, and fruit too in the summer. And where do you think that comes from?' (Mrs. Woodget points to some bacon hanging on the wall.) 'Better than any picture, isn't it? We fatten and kill a pig every year. We never go hungry, but clothes worry me. My husband earns a bit extra at hay making time. I work on the farm then for a few weeks too. Still, that doesn't pay for much more than our boots. It's lucky our girl is in service with a good family. They let her have their cast-offs to send us. The vicar's wife helps, too. She runs some charities and often gives me a bit of cloth when one of the children needs a dress.'

Mr. Woodget is a large, brawny man. He is wearing heavy boots, corduroy trousers and a coarse, cotton jacket, but no shirt. As it is Sunday, he is going to have a shave, but he hasn't done that yet, so his face is covered in stubble. He is still quite young and is very strong. He has never known a day's illness, but one day he will suffer for the life he is spending outside in all kinds of weather. Most of the old men in the village are crippled with rheumatism.

'Tell us about your work, Mr. Woodget.' 'I work on Mr. Dando's farm. There are the cows to be milked every day, but the rest of the work depends on the season. Hay making is the busiest time, of course. We have a reaper to cut the grass, but Mr. Dando doesn't have a tedder, so we have to turn the hay with pitchforks. It's an anxious time watching the weather. Too much rain washes the goodness out of the hay, and turns it mouldy. As soon as it's dry we have to get it into the yard and stack it. The waggons go to and from the fields from dawn until dark. We enjoy the hay harvest, though. Mr. Dando gives us plenty of cider to help us keep working. That's better than the cold tea my wife gives me the rest of the year.' 'What about the corn harvest?' 'Farmers round here don't grow a lot of corn. They used to in the old days, my father told me, but now we just have a few acres of oats and barley for cattle feed.'

1 The Farm Worker and his Family

harvest-time

'*Your work must need a lot of strength, Mr. Woodget?*' 'Strength, yes, but it needs skill too. You see that little silver cup? I won that for ploughing. I drive a straighter furrow than anyone else in these parts. How would you get on with thatching a rick, do you think? My ricks are thatched as neat and snug as any house. Did you see that hedge as you came up the lane? I cut and laid that this winter. There's no townsman born could ever do a job like that.' '*Does the weather interfere much with your work?*' 'We have to stop in very heavy rain, but otherwise I just fling a sack over my shoulders and carry on. Mr. Dando says "Plough when the north-east wind is in the air. That's what kills the germ in the soil." He doesn't seem to worry about killing his ploughman as well!'

Soon, George Woodget comes home. He is twelve but is small for his age. He is wearing a shirt with no collar, a coat several sizes too big with no buttons, and torn, baggy trousers. They are so stiff with meal and mud that they look as if they would stand up on their own. He wears a shapeless hat with a wide, tattered brim that falls over his eyes. He has no socks, and on his feet are huge boots, caked with mud. It is now twelve o'clock and he has already been working for six hours but as it is Sunday he has finished for the day. He has a job on a dairy farm and cows need milking and feeding every day. He tells us about his work during the week.

'I have to be at the farm by six o'clock. First, I clean out the stable and water the horses. Next, I go into the cow-shed to help with the milking. Mr. Gough, the farmer, has thirty cows, but several of us work together and we usually finish by half of eight o'clock (7.30). Then I can snatch a few minutes for breakfast. Mother gives me bread and cold tea. After breakfast I drive the cows to the fields, and then come back and help clean out the cow-shed. We pile the dung in the yard. When it is rotten we load it in a cart and take it to the fields. One of the men throws it out of the cart, while I lead the horse. I do all sorts of other jobs too. I have to carry hay and clean straw to the cow-house and stable, chop sticks for firewood, and collect the eggs from the hen-house.

When we have calves, Mr. Gough boils up meal and I feed it to them. I spilt a whole lot down my trousers today and got a beating. The cows need milking again in the evening, of course. Mr. Gough gives me an hour for dinner. I usually go up in the hay loft. It's bread and cold tea again, but I generally have a bit of cheese as well – that's if I didn't eat it for breakfast. Usually, mother gives me a bit of pudding from last night's supper.

'After dinner, I have to work until nightfall, and walk home in the dark. I don't like that very much. Sometimes gypsies camp by the lane and there are ghosts in the woods. I have to pass Mother Giddings's cottage, too. She's a witch. It's good to get home on a winter's night, I can tell you. Mother always has a hot meal for us, even if it's only potatoes and cabbage.'

'How do you enjoy yourself, George?' 'I don't have much time for playing. I can't even have a lark with the two other boys at the farm. Mr. Gough won't let us work together. He says "A boy is a boy: two boys are half a boy: three boys are no boy at all." '

left threshing wheat by steam power

2 The Farmer

It is time to visit George Woodget's employer, Mr. Gough. His house is set near the road and has a hedge of neatly clipped yew. It is no use knocking on the handsome front door because that is only opened for weddings and funerals. Instead, we will go round to the back of the house and into the kitchen.

The kitchen has a floor made from flagstones. It is uneven and cold, but perfectly clean. There is one small window with the farmer's rocking chair beside it, so that he can see to read his newspaper. The fireplace is huge, and has chimney corners with little stools in them. There is a wooden settle (a kind of bench), a deal table well worn with scrubbing, and some Windsor chairs.

There is a parlour, too, which has a carpet, velvet curtains, wallpaper, a settee and some easy chairs. But the parlour is used as seldom as the front door, and for the same reasons. All the life of the house takes place in the kitchen. A hundred years before the farmer's wife fed the workers there. The cowman, carter and the labourers used to clump in, wearing their heavy, muddy boots, and have huge meals of bread, cheese, bacon and cider. That has not happened for a long time and now the men eat at home or, during the day, out in the fields. Mr. and Mrs. Gough eat and live in their kitchen and also entertain friends there.

Beside the kitchen is a scullery. Here, Mrs. Gough and her maid prepare the food and do the washing up. It is a low, dark room. The sink is old and worn. There is one great luxury though. The pump is inside the room. The maid still has to pump water, but at least she does not have to go outside. This maid is unhappy. She does not like Mrs. Gough, and still less does she like being 'in service' in a farm. She hopes that she will soon find a place in a smart house in Wells, or even in Bath.

The farmers in the district visit each other quite often during the winter evenings. They sit round the kitchen table and play cards by the light of an oil lamp. To make it more interesting they gamble, but only with pennies or halfpennies. No more than a few shillings change hands during the evening. They drink big mugs of cider, and in cold weather they sometimes dip a red-hot poker into the cider to warm it. Mrs. Gough keeps the fire blazing, so it is hard to go out into the cold at the end of the evening. Most people travel by dog-cart. They button their overcoats and wrap rugs round their knees because they have to sit up in the biting wind, the rain or the snow. The horse clip-clops through the lonely lanes, and the only light comes from two feeble lanterns flickering on either side of the cart. But there is not much danger, because the horse knows every bend and pot-hole in the road. It is not often that a farmer is so drunk that he does not know where he is going, but, if by any chance he is, then he can count on his horse to take him home.

Most of the time people have to make their own amusements, but once a year there is a sheep fair at Priddy, and a horse fair at Binegar. Farmers buy and sell animals at the fairs, but there are side-shows as well. Friends from miles around meet to gossip and drink together, and in the evening there is dancing on the village green. Priddy is a few miles away, but Binegar is the next village. The horse fair brings worries as well as pleasures. Gypsies and tinkers as well as all sorts of ruffians come, and there is always a chance that a drunken gang may attack a lonely

farmhouse. Mr. Gough usually has some gold coins in the house, kept in a big oak chest, so he is afraid his money might be stolen. He also has a big, old sword in the chest. On the night of Binegar Fair, he takes it out, and puts it on top of the chest. It is rusty with age, and not at all sharp, but he feels safer when he has it ready. Luckily, he has never had to use it.

On Sunday Mr. and Mrs. Gough, with their two grown-up sons, walk across the fields to church. Mrs. Gough wears a large bonnet, a shawl, and a long, flower-patterned skirt with a bustle. Bustles are now out of fashion in the towns, but the country women still think they are smart. The men wear black suits, in place of their week-day jackets, breeches and gaiters. Mr. Gough has a pew near the front of the church. He sits close behind the squire. Most of the other farmers are behind him, and the tradespeople like the grocer and the innkeeper are behind the farmers. The few labourers who come sit right at the back of the church. Mr. Gough is a churchwarden. More than that, he has just given a lot of money to pay for new pews. He feels his neighbours should be grateful. In fact they are rather jealous and say the new pews are not nearly as comfortable as the old ones.

The Farmer

Now let us see what is behind the farmhouse. It has been raining and the farmyard is a sea of mud. Around the yard are the buildings. The most important is the cow stall, with room for thirty cows. Above it is a hay loft, with trapdoors, so that the hay can be tossed into the mangers down below. The farm cat lives in the hay loft with her four kittens. Then there are stables for the horses, and sheds for the carts as well as for Mr. Gough's mowing machine. The only other piece of modern equipment is the cream separator. One of the women pours milk in at the top, while another turns a handle. Cream then comes out of one spout and skimmed milk from another. The cream goes to make butter, and the skimmed milk is fed to the pigs. The wives of the farm workers can have a jug of skimmed milk for a penny, but they do not usually bother with it. Beyond the yard is a paddock with several large horses. They are fine animals and we stop to admire them. Last of all, we visit the dairy which is cool and spotlessly clean. This is Mrs. Gough's department and she is pleased to show us round.

'We churn a little butter, but mainly we make cheese. In this part of Somerset it is Cheddar, of course. First we heat the milk until it is warm. We used to do that by guesswork, but I have a thermometer now. Then we put in rennet, if you know what that is. Well, whenever we kill a young calf, we are careful to keep the stomach because inside there is some half-digested milk, all curdled. That's rennet. If you put a couple of spoonfuls into twelve gallons of warm milk, it soon divides it into curds and whey.' *'Do you mean it goes sour?'* 'It looks rather like that. Next we have to separate off the whey, break up the curd and put it in the press. We press it several times to squeeze out all the whey, and make the cheese nice and firm. Then the cheeses must stay for a while on the shelves to cure. We have to turn and wipe them every day. It's hard work in a dairy. When my mother was an old lady her hands used to shake all the time, so that she couldn't even hold a teacup. The doctor said that was because she worked too hard in her dairy when she was younger.'

We go back into the kitchen and Mr. Gough talks about his farm. *'You seem to be earning a good living,*

making cheese

Mr. Gough.' 'I'm not doing too badly, thank you. But times are not as good as they were. Back in the 1860s farmers lived like gentlemen. A lot has happened since then. There's all this wheat they bring in from America. Our farmers can't grow it at double the price. They bring frozen lambs in from New Zealand and beef from South America. It's nothing like the home-grown meat, but it's dirt cheap.' *'But you don't produce wheat or meat.'* 'That's right. Somerset farmers used to think themselves unlucky because it is too wet here for corn or beef cattle. We have always produced milk. Now we are in luck, because milk is the one thing they can't bring in from abroad.' *'Do you make a lot of cheese?'* 'A fair bit, but most of my milk is sold fresh. We take the churns down to Binegar station, first thing in the morning. Some goes north to Bath, some goes south to Bournemouth. All of it reaches the customers the same day. I don't know how we would manage without the railway.'

'Don't you grow any crops at all, Mr. Gough?' 'Only a few oats and a bit of barley. None of it leaves the farm because I use it all as cattle feed. But don't you forget that grass is a crop. I have to chain harrow it, and manure it to make it grow. Making hay is a big job, too.' *'You don't have much machinery.'* 'I have a

a modern demonstration of threshing by steam power

mowing machine, and my men say I should buy a tedder. I say they can turn the hay just as well with a pitch-fork. A dairy farmer doesn't need much machinery. Why should I buy expensive machines when the men will work for ten shillings a week?'

'Don't you think you should pay your men more?' 'Certainly not! How would they spend the money? They all have houses and some of my best workers live in them rent-free. I never knew one of them go hungry. What use would fancy food be to them? A man does better on bread and bacon than on beef steaks and pies. To work hard you must live hard. They all look happy enough when each has his golden half-sovereign on pay-day.' *'But how do you manage to thresh your oats and barley?'* 'A contractor comes round with a threshing machine and a steam engine. He can finish my lot easily in a day.' *'You seem to have a lot of horses, Mr. Gough.'* 'Yes, that's a useful sideline of mine. I breed shire horses.'

Mr. Gough proudly shows us some cups he has won at the Bath and West Show. But Mrs. Gough says her husband frightens the life out of her because whenever he sees some horses in a field, he must go and look at them. He lifts their hooves, looks in their mouths, then cracks his whip to see how they gallop. She is afraid he will be kicked to death one day.

'Horse dealers have a bad name, don't they, Mr. Gough?' 'Well they do get up to all sorts of dodges. For instance, if a horse limps you can cut a nerve in

his leg, so he doesn't feel any pain and walks evenly. It will be days before the customer sees there is something wrong. I don't do that sort of thing. I only stooped to dishonesty once and that was when I was a young man. My father sent me to London to buy some horses and I had to put them in a field with lots of others. In the morning all of mine had gone. I knew the old man would half-kill me, so I took someone else's horses and got away as fast as I could. I was frightened, I can tell you. I would have spent a long time in prison if I had been caught.'

horses at work on the land

3 The Village Wheelwright

Now let's see what happens in the village wheelwright's shop. We will talk to one of the men who works there. *'What kinds of things do you make, Mr. Maggs?'* 'We make anything the farmers want, from milking stools which cost them sixpence ($2\frac{1}{2}$p) to four-wheeled waggons worth £50.' *'It must be skilled work.'* 'It is indeed. I had to do a seven-year apprenticeship, and even then it was a long time before I was any good at my trade. You need a lot of skill and strength to use the tools, and you need to know about wood. The best made wheel will fall apart in no time if you put just one bad bit of wood in it.'

'How do you make a wheel?' 'We call the piece in the middle the stock. I turn that on the lathe so that it's nice and round. Then I cut holes in it with my chisel for the spokes. The stock is made of elm wood,

but the spokes must be heart of oak. I chop them roughly to shape with an axe, just as you do firewood. Next, I make each one smooth with a plane and a spoke shave. I put one end against the bench and hold the other with my stomach.' Mr. Maggs opens his shirt and shows us a hard patch of skin, where he has pressed against hundreds of spokes. 'The spokes have to fit tightly in the stock – so tightly that I have to drive them in with a sledge-hammer. I can't hit them just anyhow, though. They have to go in at just the right angle. The rim of the wheel is made of felloes.' (Mr. Maggs pronounces this 'fellees.') 'These are separate curved pieces of wood. Each one forms part of a circle. I chop them into shape with my axe, and then one of the boys planes them smooth. Each felloe takes two spokes, so I have to drill two holes in

hammer. The wheel makes noises like whips cracking.

The owner of the business, Mr. Cole, now shows us round. There is a yard surrounded by workshops, a smithy and sheds for storing timber. The planks of timber are laid with small gaps between them so that they will dry. That may take five years or more. Mr. Cole never gives his men unseasoned timber, and they would refuse to use it if he did.

In a corner of the yard is a brick-lined pit, about six feet deep. 'This is the saw pit,' explains Mr. Cole. 'One man goes into the pit and pulls the saw down, while one stands on the top and pulls it up. I was bottom sawyer as a young man. My face ran with sweat and was caked with sawdust, and all I had to look at was the brick wall. It's worse for the top sawyer though. His work is much harder, and he has to guide the saw.'

There is a smell of timber in the workshops and there are chippings and shavings on the floor. All

it. I then shape the ends of the spokes, and put on the felloes.' *'Is the wheel finished then?'* 'Not at all. We have to put on its tyre. If you like you can watch us do that in the morning.'

At six o'clock next morning we go to the wheelwright's shop. One man is lighting a furnace with a huge iron hoop in it. This is the tyre. It is six feet across and weighs about fifty pounds. Two men are fixing a wheel to the tyring platform. The platform is just a large iron plate on which the men clamp down the wheel. The boys trudge backwards and forwards from the pump, filling water buckets. There are several watering cans nearby.

The blacksmith has made the tyre about an inch and a half smaller than the wheel, so how will they fit it? The answer, of course, is that the tyre expands when it is red hot, and if everyone has done his work carefully, it should just slip over the rim of the wheel.

Soon everything is ready. There is a blast of hot air as Mr. Maggs opens the furnace. Three men grip the tyre with iron 'dogs', drop it into place and, working as fast as they can, drive it on with sledgehammers. The wood catches fire, so the boys spray it with water from the cans. The air is full of steam and smoke, and the men's eyes run. They still have to be very careful or they will spoil the wheel. When they finish, one of them trundles the wheel into a trough of water and there is a loud hissing. As the tyre cools it shrinks, forcing the spokes into their joints even more tightly than Mr. Maggs could with his sledge-

sorts of hand tools lie on the benches. The windows have no glass, just wooden shutters, which can be opened to let in the light. What must it be like in winter?

Mr. Cole tells us that the smith and the wheelwrights earn twenty-five shillings a week and the other men less than a pound. They work from six in the morning until seven in the evening. The men are proud of being craftsmen but they use the old ways which Mr. Cole thinks are too slow. He says he is losing money and will have to buy some machines or he will go out of business.

The Village Wheelwright

fixing the rim to a waggon wheel

4 The Wartime Farm

It is the year 1942. The Second World War has been raging for three years. German U-boats are sinking more and more shipping and Britain cannot import all the food she needs. It is essential that her farmers should produce all they can. We will visit a farm in Essex to see what is happening.

In the farmyard two girls are loading a trailer with manure. Suddenly a rat appears. They chase it into a corner and one of them kills it with a broom. Then she picks it up and throws it on the manure heap. *'Country girls aren't afraid of rats, then?'* 'We aren't country girls,' says one of them. 'We are typists, and we come from London.' *'What are you doing here?'* 'We are land girls for as long as the War lasts. We left our usual jobs to come down and work on this farm.' *'How do you like it?'* 'It's not bad once you get used to it. We were scared of mice in the beginning, but even the rats are scared of us now.'

The two girls hitch their trailer to a tractor and chug off to the fields. We go into the house to talk to Mr. Roe, the farmer. *'What are you doing to help the war effort, Mr. Roe?'* 'Trying to grow more food for the country, of course. This farm was in a shocking state when the War began. The ragwort grew so high you could get lost in it. Some of the hedges were thirty feet wide and twenty feet tall. Well, we have burnt the weeds, and we gained thirty acres, just by cutting back the hedges.' *'You are doing well, then?'*

Mr. Roe

'I could do a lot better if I were left alone, but the County War Agricultural Committee likes to tell us what to do. One of their men called to see me. He went over the farm and told me I would have to plough a lot of my land. But this soil is heavy clay, fit only for grass, as I explained to him. He replied that ploughed land feeds ten times as many people as grassland so I must plough it. When I told him my team of horses couldn't draw a plough through this clay, he promised to send me a tractor and some lime and some fertilizer to improve the poor soil. Then when I grumbled that I didn't have any labour because two of my men had joined the Army, he agreed to send me some labour. Well, the tractor, lime and fertilizer arrived, but do you know what the labour amounted to? Two London office girls, all dolled up with their silk stockings and nail varnish!'

'I still wasn't going to plough my fields, so they took me to court. I took a lump of clay and banged it on the table. "Who in their right mind would plough that?" I asked. The magistrate just said I must plough my land or he would have my farm taken away. I did plough it then. The clay turned up like putty, and then baked like bricks in the sun. It was a terrible job to break it down for sowing.' *'What happened?'* Mr Roe looks uncomfortable. 'Well,' he says, 'we did manage to grow a fair crop of oats.'

'How are the land girls managing?' 'Let's be fair,

they have come on very well. They do most of the farm jobs now. They grumble a bit, because they don't have much fun, but they don't know how to enjoy themselves in the country. They ought to come hunting with the rest of us.' *'Do you hunt in wartime?'* 'Why not? We've got to keep the foxes down somehow. People say hounds are too expensive to feed and we should spend the money on Spitfires. But what about the dogs townspeople keep? I say that the time to destroy the hounds is when all pet puppy dogs have been made into glue.'

'*Are you making a good living on the farm, Mr. Roe?*' 'Not too bad, thank you. It won't last, though, not once the War finishes. I can remember the First World War. "Grow all you can," they said, "and when the War is over we will make sure you always get a fair price for your goods." But almost as soon as the War ended they forgot their promise. The country was flooded with Canadian wheat, New Zealand lamb and Danish bacon. We just couldn't make a living. When I went into town I used to cross the road rather than go near my bank. I knew the manager was after me. One of my neighbours begged me to buy his land for £1 an acre, but I couldn't find the money. I would be a rich man now if I had. No, I just let this place become a wilderness as long as peace lasted. It will be the same again when this War ends, you mark my words.'

5 The Village Today

The village of Tarrant Upton is in West Dorset. The countryside around it is pleasant, but the village itself is unattractive. There is no manor house, no picturesque cottages, and the church is a very ordinary building, not much more than a hundred years old. Normally, tourists do not come here, and if any stray this far, they drive straight through.

We will walk along the village street in the middle of a summer day. Everything is still. There is no sign of life. Several of the houses must be empty, because their windows are boarded. The village pub is closed and there is a 'For Sale' sign outside. Further down the street is the church. It looks neglected, for the gravestones are nearly hidden in long grass. Here at last though, is someone to whom we can talk, for a little old lady is arranging flowers at the altar.

'*Whatever is wrong with Tarrant Upton?*' 'It's dying, that's what is wrong with it.' '*But why is it happening?*' 'Take this church for a start. When I was a girl there was a good congregation here for three services every Sunday — yes, and ringers to give us a peal of bells. Now the rector comes once a month and preaches to about four of us. The village school was closed because it was down to one teacher with a class of ten. Now there is a bus to take the children into Weymouth. Of course there are no tradesmen here, like plumbers, carpenters or painters. It's very difficult to get any jobs done. When my television broke down I had to telephone a man five miles away. He refused to come, because it wasn't worth his while.

'It was terrible when we lost our Post Office and general stores. Mrs. White who ran it said she just could not make a living. Now you can't even buy a postage stamp or a pound of sugar in Tarrant Upton. A few of the people have cars, so they shop in Weymouth, but I can't drive. Luckily one of my neighbours does my shopping for me.' '*Can't you go to Weymouth by bus?*' 'We used to have a bus three times a week. Then it came only on Saturdays. Now there isn't one at all.'

'*What other problems do you find about living here?*' 'The thing that really frightens me is that we have no doctor. Mine lives six miles away. If I was taken ill on a winter's night, I could be dead before he reached me. It's very difficult, too, when you need to get

medicines in a hurry.'

'What causes all these problems?' 'It's the farmers. They buy these huge machines, so they don't need so many men. A farmer can manage a big farm with his son and a couple of workers. The young men want jobs, so they move into town with their families. We old people are the only ones left. The farmers are ruining the countryside. When I was a girl, the banks were yellow with primroses, and you could sit in a field full of buttercups and celandines, with any number of pretty butterflies fluttering around. The farmers have killed all the flowers and insects with their horrid sprays. What's more, their great bulldozers are pulling up miles of hedges every year, and that destroys the wild life.'

We will now visit one of the farms. It is at the end of a long, private road, well made of concrete. The farmhouse is brand new. Behind it is a jumble of buildings and some new, expensive-looking machines. Mr. Hooper, the farmer, shows us round.

'You have spent a lot of money on machinery, Mr. Hooper.' 'Yes, indeed. That combine harvester alone cost me £14,000. It's worth it, though. You see, now I can manage this farm with three men. In the old days we needed a dozen.' 'But that means you are driving families from the village!' 'They insist on high wages, so I can only afford to pay a few.' 'An old lady in the village told us your sprays are killing all the wild flowers and insects.' 'I have to make a living from my farm, not keep it looking pretty for old ladies. Cows can't live on primroses and butterflies.' 'Why are you uprooting hedgerows?' 'They take up a lot of land and it makes a lot of work lopping them every year. Besides, I need big fields for my big machines.'

The saddest sight on Mr. Hooper's farm is the battery house. Here hundreds of hens are crowded three at a time in little cages. Mr. Hooper explains that this is the only way to make them lay enough eggs.

'Your farm seems very efficient, but it is certainly not very pleasant.' 'Now listen! British farmers could quite well scrap their machines, employ more men than they need, grow pretty hedgerows, and let their chickens run wild. And if they did, you towns-men would have to pay twice as much for your food as you do now.'

Chapter Eleven   People and Their Rights

1 Care of the Poor

Mr. Walker is one of the Guardians of the Poor in Bath. He will tell us what he does. *'How did you become a Guardian, Mr. Walker?'* 'I was elected with about twenty other men. The ratepayers voted for us. We have a meeting once a month.' *'Is it a bit like being elected to the City Council?'* 'Yes, except that the City Council deals with all sorts of things. Guardians just look after the poor, nothing else.' *'What have you done for the poor in Bath?'* 'We have built a fine workhouse on Combe Down. We pay a workhouse master to run it, we pay a local doctor to visit it regularly, and we even pay a schoolmaster to teach the children.'

'Why is it that so many poor people in Bath would sooner starve than go to the workhouse?' 'We do nothing to make the workhouse comfortable. The paupers have to wear a uniform, we give them only the plainest food, mainly bread and gruel, and the men and women have to live separately. No one has any beer or tobacco and we will not let relatives send in things like cakes or puddings. We find the inmates plenty of dull work. The men crack stones and the women wash clothes. Life must be made more unpleasant in the workhouse than outside, or people would flock there in their hundreds. The workhouse costs the ratepayers enough as it is.'

'Is that all you do for the poor in Bath?' 'Oh no, there are plenty of charities as well. I give money to a soup charity myself. When food is scarce, as it was last winter, we open a soup kitchen in Walcot. Those of us who have paid money towards the kitchen give out tickets to poor people of our choice. They can go to the kitchen and exchange the tickets for soup. We only give tickets to the deserving poor, of course. We do not aim to feed drunkards and idlers. There are other charities for milk, bread and coal. You can be sure that the wealthier citizens of Bath look after their poor.' *'But we have found families in the Dolemeads living in slums, and starving.'* 'That is their own fault. They drink too much and throw their money away on stupid things. They never

Dr. Barnado

think of saving. Most of them are wicked and their unhappiness is God's way of punishing them. Besides, it is quite a good thing for some of the lower classes to live in misery. The others see them, and it makes them work harder. It is quite certain that there will always be some poor people. It says in the Bible, "The poor ye have always with ye." '

Luckily, not everyone was like Mr. Walker. In 1866 a young Irish medical student came to London. He opened a school for poor boys in an old donkey stable at Hope's Place, World's End, in the East End of London. During the evenings he taught there while the other students enjoyed themselves. One day, a wretched, starving boy called Jim Jarvis refused to leave when the lessons were over. He had nowhere to go. The teacher took him home and while Jim was enjoying the first good meal he had ever eaten, he told his life story. He could not remember his father but could just remember his mother as she lay dying. Jim had been taken to the workhouse but hated it so much that he ran away. For a time he lived in a garden shed belonging to an old woman. Then, when he was about seven, he worked for a bargee called Swearing Dick. Dick was a drunkard who beat Jim cruelly. He had a fierce dog and threatened to send him after Jim if he ever tried to escape. Jim did escape in the end, and for the next three years he lived in the streets of London. By begging and doing odd jobs he managed to stay alive, but nearly every night, winter and summer, he had to sleep in the open.

At first the medical student refused to believe that there were children who had no homes, but Jim took him out into the night. They came to a dark street and climbed a high wall. At the top was a tin roof, and on it were eleven boys, just like Jim, all fast asleep. The student was horrified. He found somewhere for Jim to live and decided that he must spend the rest of his life doing the same for other homeless children. He needed money, of course, and the first person to give him any was a servant girl who let him have all her savings, twenty-seven farthings (about three pence). By the time he died in 1905, he had raised three million pounds and helped 168,000 boys and girls. His name was Doctor Barnardo.

a homeless girl   same girl after rescue by Dr Barnardo

There came a time, too, when the Government saw that it could not leave the care of the poor to Guardians like Mr. Walker. It was arranged that money should be paid to people when they were ill or unemployed, and in 1908 pensions were given to old people. A pensioner had to be seventy years of age and received only five shillings a week. Even so, many old people could not believe their good luck. All they knew was that they were very grateful. Some of them took flowers for the postmistress when they went to collect their pensions.

2 The Welfare State

In the last section you saw that during the Victorian age very little was done for people who were hungry or homeless. They either had to go to Poor Law Guardians, like Mr. Walker, or ask for charity. You also saw that early in this century the Government began to help a little by giving old age pensions.

During the Second World War the Government realized it should do a great deal more. It thought that if everyone could work together to beat the Germans, they could work together to make Britain a better country when peace came. In 1941 they asked a man called Sir William Beveridge to prepare a plan. We will ask him to tell us about his ideas.

'I believe that we have to fight a number of great giants, and the worst of these is "want". The trouble with Britain has been that while some people have had more money than they needed, others have been near to starvation. Now, if a man is fit and has work, we can expect him to look after his family. But if he is ill or loses his job he must be given help so that he,

slums before the Second World War

his wife and children have enough money to live on.'

'*Where is all the money to come from?*' 'We will have a National Insurance fund. It will be like a huge savings bank. The Government must pay into it, and so must employers. Every working man, rich or poor, must pay something every week as well, provided he has a job. That way we will have plenty of money to help those who are in need. We can give them "unemployment benefits" or "sickness benefits".' '*Do*

you think people will be willing to pay this money?' 'Oh, I think they will. Until now, ordinary men and women have been very worried about becoming ill, or losing their jobs. With National Insurance they will at least have enough to live on if they are not earning wages. In addition, we will be able to give them better old age pensions than before the War and pay for their funerals when they die. I think we must help parents with young children, too. We will give money to women when they have babies and we will pay family allowances.' '*Do you think all that will make Britain a better and fairer country, Sir William?*' 'It will be a good start, but it will only defeat the giant "want". There are five other giants as well.' '*What are they?*' 'First there is the giant "disease", and to conquer him we must see that everyone can have free medical care. The second giant is "ignorance", which means we must have more and better schools for all our children. Then we must fight "squalor". We will build decent houses so that no one need live in a

modern council houses

slum. Lastly, we must defeat "idleness" and make sure there are jobs for everyone. If we really want a better future, I am sure we can fight together to get rid of all these giants, in time.'

As soon as the War ended, Parliament made some new laws to carry out Sir William's ideas. On July 5th, 1948, the welfare state was born. The idea behind it is that the Government looks after all the people in the country from the day they are born to the day they die.

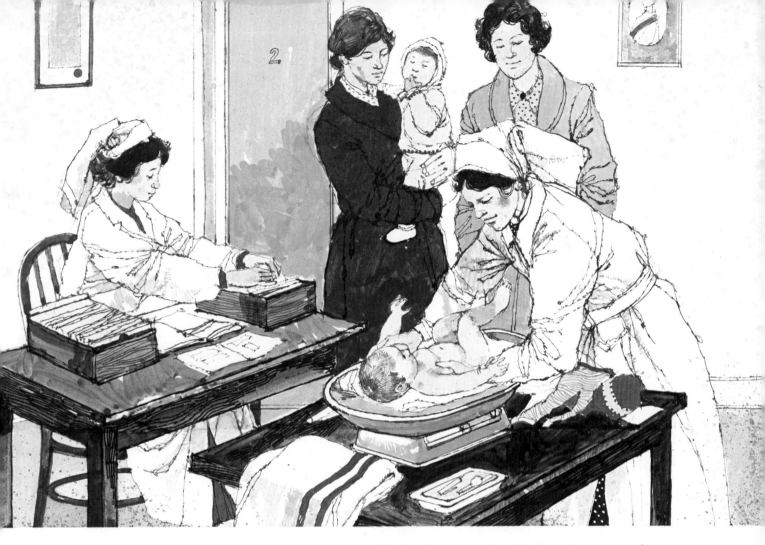

No one need be afraid of any of the giants Sir William described.

To find out how the welfare state is beating the giants we will talk to Mrs. Groves, a miner's wife who lives in a small town in South Wales. It is 1949. *'Is life easier for you since the creation of the welfare state, Mrs. Groves?'* 'Oh yes, indeed. I think it's a wonderful thing. We were very poor when I was a girl and it was terrible for all of us when my father didn't have any work.' *'Tell us about some of the help you get today.'*

'There are so many things. Of course I get the family allowance for my three younger children – the oldest in the family doesn't get any money you see. I save this for clothes, especially shoes. There is free milk too for the children and orange juice from the clinic for the baby. What's more, the older children get a good, cheap meal at school. When the children are unwell I take them to the clinic or to the doctor. The baby was immunized against diphtheria last week and now my older boy needs spectacles because he is shortsighted. It's lucky we can get them free on the National Health. I'm glad to say there is plenty of work in the mines these days, but my husband had an accident underground early in the year and was

at home for a month. The benefits meant that we could just about manage to pay all our bills.'

'Does this mean you are satisfied with the way you live now, Mrs. Groves?' 'Well, this house is too small for us and needs lots of repairs. We are hoping to move into a new council house next year. It will be lovely to have more space, a modern kitchen and a real bathroom. My widowed mother will come and live with us there. She has a pension, so although she is getting old, she will be able to pay her way. She is very proud and would hate it if she had to live on us. Things are so much better for me than they were when my mother was young. I wonder what they will be like for my children and grandchildren?

3 Votes for Women

You will remember reading about the Walker family in Chapter Three. Their maid, Eliza, was treated little better than a slave. However, in a certain sense Mrs. Walker was a slave as well. For one thing she was a slave to her clothes. To dress fashionably she wore very tight corsets to give her a 'wasp waist'. Her long full skirt came down to her feet and her underclothes were also long and bulky. It is not surprising that she always walked sedately and never tried to run.

Mrs. Walker was even more of a slave to her way of life. She always had to remember to obey the rules of polite behaviour. She had to be careful about the things she chose to discuss. A lady could be interested in embroidery, music and books, but it was not considered proper to be interested in business or politics. As a result, women were not allowed to vote when there was an election. Most men thought that women did not have enough brains to understand Parliament, the Government, or Britain's place in the world.

To see how one lady felt about this, we will call on Miss Christabel Pankhurst. It is 1912, and she is living in Paris. She is a 'suffragette'. The suffrage is the right to vote and a suffragette is a woman who wants that right.

'Why are you living in Paris, Miss Pankhurst?'
'Because if I went to England, I would be sent to prison. Ten years ago, my mother Emmeline founded the Women's Social and Political Union, and since then our cry has been "Votes for Women". We even had a newspaper of that name. We did all sorts of things

suffragettes outside Buckingham Palace

a suffragette poster

to persuade Parliament to give us the vote. We printed leaflets by the thousand, we had processions and we made speeches. Making a speech was often quite an adventure. Hooligans in the crowd often pelted us with mud, rotten eggs and live mice. My mother was knocked unconscious by a mob at Newton Abbot. We fought back though. We went to election meetings and interrupted the speakers. They locked us out, so one of our members had herself lowered through the skylight. Some of us chained ourselves to the railings outside No. 10, Downing Street and shouted "Votes for Women" until the police cut us free. We wrote our slogan with acid on the putting green at Birmingham. Later we tried smashing windows. Lots of us were sent to prison, of course. I have been to prison myself. We went on a hunger strike but the warders made us take food. They pushed tubes right down our throats, into our stomachs and then poured in soup or some other liquid. They nearly killed some of us, feeding us like that, so they had to stop doing it.

'Early last year it looked as if Mr. Asquith's Government was going to let us have our way, but he let us down at the last minute. He is called "Wait-and-see Asquith", because he will never make up his mind. Some of our members wanted to give up, but I said we must fight even harder. We have burned the letters in pillar boxes and also grandstands, empty houses and schools. I have just heard from England that Emily Davison, one of our members, has thrown herself under the King's own horse, Anmer, while it

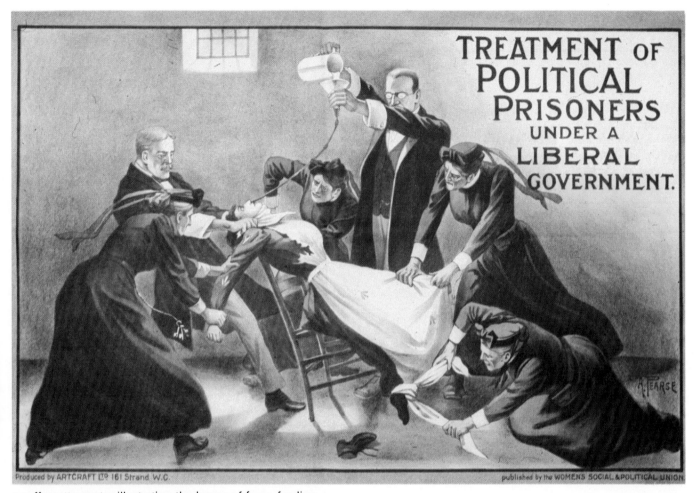

a suffragette poster illustrating the horror of force-feeding

was running in the Derby. She was badly injured, but as they carried her away to die, she was nearly mobbed by a crowd of men who had backed Anmer to win. That shows how determined we are and what sort of people we are fighting.'

The violent things the suffragettes did turned many people against them. Parliament made a new law. It said that people who made themselves ill in prison, by going on hunger strike, could be released, but then they were sent back to prison when they were well again. Suffragettes called this the 'Cat and Mouse Act'.

It might have been many years before women were given the vote, but in 1914 the Great War began. As men went away to fight the Germans, women had to take over their jobs. They worked as bus conductresses, railway porters, shipbuilders and in fire brigades. They worked in munition factories, where they handled dangerous explosives and unpleasant chemicals which turned their skin yellow and their hair green. Thousands of them joined the Women's Land Army to work on the farms. Thousands more joined the Army while others went into the Navy and Air Force. These women showed that they could do men's work and do it well. Even 'Wait-and-see' Asquith agreed they should have the vote and in 1918 Parliament at last gave it to women who were thirty years old or over. It was not until 1928 that all women over the age of twenty-one were given the vote and therefore had the same right to vote as men.

The women's struggle was not over, however. There were many jobs which women were not allowed to do and, even where they were doing the same work as men, employers paid them less money. But now the law says that men and women must have equal pay for equal work. As for jobs, Britain had her first woman engine driver in 1978 and her first woman Prime Minister in 1979.

Votes for Women

Emily Davidson throwing herself in front of the King's horse in the 1913 Derby

4 The General Strike

On May 2nd 1926, some three million men in Great Britain went on strike. They were in all sorts of jobs, but the trouble had started with the coal miners. One of them, Bill Evans, will tell us how it happened. He is a leading member of their trade union, the Miners' Federation of Great Britain.

'Coal mining is a terrible job. Down in the pit it is dark, hot, wet and very dirty. We have to slave away with our pickaxes in cramped little tunnels, breathing coal dust the whole time. The worst thing is the danger. Over a thousand miners are killed every year and thousands more are injured. For these reasons, we think that miners should have a decent wage. Things weren't too bad during the War. The Government took over the mines and the country needed coal so they paid us well. But after the war the Government handed the mines back to the owners. They are men like the Duke of Northumberland. He gives his men hovels to live in, and won't do a thing to improve them even though he has £80,000 a year in rent. What he and his kind want to do now is to make us work longer hours for lower wages. We won't have it, of course. We say, "Not a minute on the day, not a penny off the pay."

'The employers' excuse is that the price of coal has fallen so much since the war that they simply must cut our wages. If that is true, then we say the Government must help. We would like the Government to nationalize the mines, and take them over completely, but if they won't do that, then they must give the coal owners a few million pounds a year to make up for their losses. Then we could be paid a decent wage.

'We are very pleased that the Trades Union Congress has called on the other unions to help us. The railwaymen, lorry drivers, bus drivers, dockers, gas and electricity workers, builders, printers, engineers, and many more are all on strike in sympathy with us. We have brought this country to a stand-still. The Government will have to give in.'

Now we will go to a London bus station and talk to Mr. Brown. He is very much against the strike and is doing all he can to help defeat it. Usually he is serving customers in his grocer's shop but at present

he is driving buses. He explains why.

'Mr. Baldwin, the Prime Minister, saw some time ago that this trouble might come. He called for people to learn to drive buses, lorries and trains and so a lot of us volunteered. I can just about manage a bus, and I will go on driving until this strike is over.'

'Don't you feel sorry for the miners, Mr. Brown?' 'I suppose I do. But this strike isn't really about miners' pay at all. There are some trade union leaders who are trying to make the Government do something it doesn't want to do – that is pay a subsidy to the mines. I think Parliament should rule this country, not the trade unions.' *'Do you think volunteers like you can keep things going?'* 'Well, there are problems, of course. A friend of mine drove a bus down a subway and I heard of one express train that arrived at Waterloo with some level crossing gates hanging on its bumpers. Still, we aren't on our own. Soldiers and sailors are helping as well. I must say that the Government is well organized. They have beaten the printers' strike by publishing their own news sheet and by broadcasting on the wireless. Mr. Baldwin himself is going to speak to us tonight. Have you seen Hyde Park? They have set up a milk depot there. Still, even the strikers are not trying to stop food supplies. They have to eat themselves.'

Just then a bus comes in. Everyone cheers. There is a policeman beside the driver, but several windows are broken. A notice reads: 'The driver of this bus is

a student at King's College Hospital. The conductor of this bus is a student at King's College Hospital. Whoever interferes with this bus will be a patient at King's College Hospital.' 'That's the spirit,' laughs Mr. Brown. 'That's how we will beat this strike.'

Mr. Brown was right. The Trades Union Congress soon realized that most people in Great Britain were against the general strike, so after just nine days they called an end to it. Bill Evans and the other miners were very angry. They felt their friends had betrayed them, but they were still determined they would not be beaten. They carried on striking.

As the weeks dragged by, the miners suffered more and more. The men had a little strike pay from their union. In some areas wives and families had poor relief. But if you have read the first section of this chapter, you will know how mean Poor Law Guardians were. One little girl was in school during the winter without shoes or a coat. Her dress did not even have any sleeves, because her mother had used them to patch the skirt. For weeks she had lived on tea and dry bread. There were many children like her among the miners' families.

After seven months, the miners decided to end their strike. They had to work longer hours for less pay, just as the employers had demanded. Some of the smaller pits had closed because of the strike. They did not reopen, so many of the strikers lost their jobs altogether.

The General Strike

5 Immigrants

Many of the people of Bedford are immigrants. They have come from the West Indies, India, Pakistan and various parts of Europe. In 1970, there were 7,000 Italians in the town. This was ten per cent of the population. A manager of the local brickworks will tell us about them.

'Bedford stands on a thick layer of clay. It is perfect for making bricks, but the work is very hard and unpleasant. We have always found it difficult to persuade people to do it. Well, back in 1950 we heard there was a lot of unemployment in Southern Italy, so some of us went to Naples to see if there were any Italians who would like to work in the brickfields. When they heard what good wages we were paying, they were very keen to come. We were glad to have them. They were used to a rough life and they didn't complain about the work. The only trouble was that the best ones left after a while. Some have started their own businesses. A few sell ice-cream, and others are hairdressers or grocers.' *'How did the Italians get on with the people of Bedford?'* 'Very well, on the whole. Italians are clean and hard-working, and they keep out of trouble. What more do you want?' *'Don't you think you ran a big risk, bringing so many foreigners to an English town?'* 'English people would soon complain if there were no bricks to build houses. If they won't make the bricks themselves, foreigners must

Italian brickmakers in Bedford

do it for them.'

We will now talk to a Roman Catholic priest who is himself an Italian. *'What work do you do for the immigrants, Father?'* 'I have to help in all kinds of ways. I don't think the English understand half the forms they have to fill in, so you can imagine how difficult strangers find them. I do my best to see they have jobs, and houses, and I act as interpreter when necessary. They must not forget they are Italians, so we have a youth club for the young people and another club for the grown-ups. That one has a bocca court, so they can play a real Italian game. My main task is to see that they are good Catholics, and bring up their children in the Faith. We have built a beautiful church dedicated to Saint Francesca Cabrini. She spent her life working for emigrants. There is plenty to do. Twenty-five million Italians left their country in the last hundred years.' *'Why was that?'* 'Most of them came from Southern Italy and Sicily, and they were desperately poor. They lived in little hovels, in villages almost cut off from the rest of the world. The soil is thin and poor, there is hardly any rain, and it is as hot as North Africa in the summer. The men who came here only wanted to make

a village in Sicily

money. They didn't mind working in the brickfields as long as they could scrape together enough money to bring over their families. At first they crowded together in lodgings, but most of them have their own houses now.'

'How do the Italians get on with the people of Bedford?' 'There were problems at first. You see, Italians can hardly ever talk quietly. They shout and wave their arms around. They don't stay inside on summer evenings, but flock into the streets. They love to have their radios playing loudly, so the air is full of noise, to say nothing of the smell of cooking. That's how people behave in Italy, but English neighbours found it hard to accept. Fortunately there have been no serious problems, such as violence.' *'Is that because the Italians have learnt English ways?'* 'Not at all. They keep out of trouble, by keeping themselves to themselves. They have their own part of the town. Mostly they only talk to each other. Not many speak English at all well – just enough to get by.'

We will now meet an Italian boy called Marco. He is fifteen and was born in Bedford. *'Do you want to go back to Italy, Marco?'* 'My parents have taken me back on holiday, but I could never live there. The village in Italy was so boring because there was nothing at all to do. I am hoping to get an engineering apprenticeship when I leave school but there are no jobs of that kind in my parents' village.' *'Do you enjoy life in England?'* 'I can't say it's easy. I am at school with English boys, and I like to go around with the gang. They go to football matches, they smoke and drink, and one or two are trying drugs. If I don't do the same, they call me "chicken". They don't understand how easy it is to upset Italian parents. My father thinks his word is law. If I want to go out he asks where I am going, what I am going to do and who I am going with. He always wants to know when I will be back. Sometimes he just sits in front of the television and tells me I must stay in. My English friends don't have to put up with that. They come and go as they like and they laugh at me because I am scared of my father. But it's even worse for my sister. She is eighteen and works in an office, but my parents only let her go out one evening a week. On the other evenings she must stay in and spend her time helping with the housework. My parents even say that when she marries it must be to a boy they choose. They are scared she will do like one of my cousins who went off to live with a man who isn't even a Catholic. My mother says she has disgraced the whole family – grandparents, uncles, aunts, cousins, everyone.' *'How do you feel about her, Marco?'* ' "Good luck to her", is what I say!'

four generations of the Spadaccino family, originally from Italy, now settled in Bedford

Chapter Twelve   Britain in the Modern World

1 Introduction: The British Empire

It is 1898. The Colonial Secretary, Joseph Chamberlain, talks to us about the British Empire.

'How does the British Empire compare with others, like the Roman Empire, for example?' 'It is the greatest the world has ever seen.'

'Why do you say that?' 'There is its size, for a start. It covers one fifth of the surface of the earth, and its people make up a quarter of the human race. We have possessions in every part of the world, so we can say with truth, that the sun never sets on the British Empire.'

'Sheer size does not make a great empire, surely.' 'Of course not. The way we govern it is even more important.'

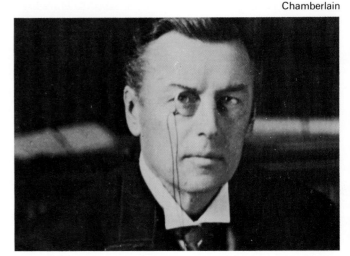
Chamberlain

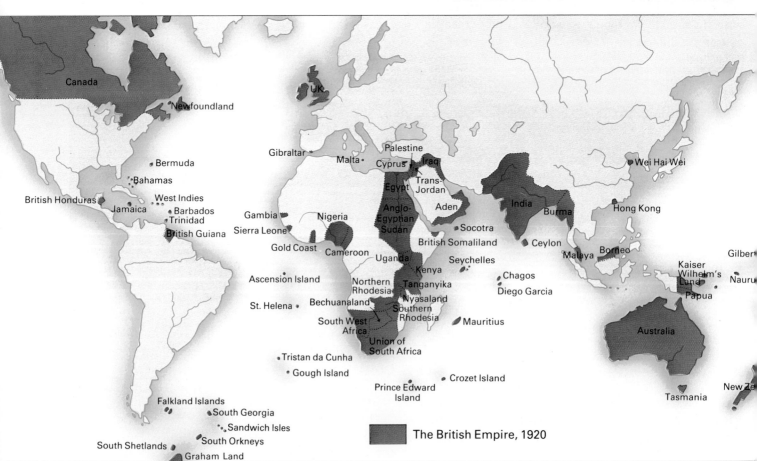

The British Empire, 1920

Empire Day parade

'*How is that done?*' 'The countries of the British Empire are of two kinds. There are the ones where most of the people are white, and others, where most of them are coloured. The most important of the first kind are Canada, Australia and New Zealand. They are what we call "Dominions". That means they are equal with Great Britain. They have their own parliaments and their own governments, and look after themselves entirely.

'The countries with coloured inhabitants are backward, so we British govern them, for their own good. After all, it is better for an African to take orders from a Christian Englishman, than from one of his own witch doctors. We help these people improve their farming, and we build roads, railways and harbours. We keep law and order and stop tribes fighting each other. We stamp out any evil we find. For example, in India the Hindus used to burn widows alive: in East Africa there was a flourishing slave trade: in the Gold Coast they used to make human sacrifices. We have put an end to all these terrible things and many more like them.'

'*What are the advantages of having this Empire?*' 'They are enormous. Here we are, 40 million people in these tiny islands where we can grow only a fraction of what we need. Because of the Empire we can have wheat from Canada, wool from Australia, lamb from New Zealand, cotton and tea from India, sugar from the West Indies, cocoa from the Gold Coast – the list is endless. On the other hand we are a great manufacturing nation. We make engineering goods, like railway locomotives and farm machinery. We produce thousands of miles of cotton and woollen cloth each year and we mine huge quantities of coal. We can send all these things to our colonies in return for what they send us. It is a splendid partnership.'

'*Do you think the British Empire will fall, as the Roman Empire did?*' 'I see no reason why it should. I am trying to persuade our government to encourage even more trade with the Empire. If this and future governments will do so, I think our Empire should last for ever.'

Unhappily, foreigners did not see the British Empire as Joseph Chamberlain did. They called the British 'Imperialists' which means people who will conquer any country which they want for themselves. Someone once sneered, 'If the sun doesn't set on the British Empire, it's because God doesn't trust the British in the dark.'

Nor was the later history of the British Empire at all as Joseph Chamberlain had hoped. The coloured people objected to British rule, and after the Second World War they won their freedom.* Also Britain herself gave up all idea of having an Empire and, in 1972, joined the Common Market.

*For what happened in India, see Chapter 19.

2 The Suez Crisis, 1956

Eden   Nasser

After the First World War Palestine became part of the British Empire. There were both Jews and Arabs living there and they made trouble for each other and the British. For example, in 1946 Jewish terrorists led by Menachem Begin blew up the King David Hotel in Jerusalem, which was the British Headquarters. In 1948, the British left and at once there was war between the Jews and the Arabs. The Arabs living in Palestine were helped by their friends in the countries nearby. The Jews won, they drove out most of the Palestinian Arabs and they created the state of Israel. After that, there was bad feeling between Israel and her Arab neighbours and in 1956 Britain and France tried to take advantage of it. A Jewish soldier will tell us what happened.

'Our Arab neighbours are all Muslims. They hate us for our religion and they have been trying to destroy us ever since we won our freedom from the British in 1948. Things became especially difficult for us after

Israel and her Arab neighbours: the Suez crisis

1952 when Gamal Abdel Nasser became President of Egypt. He organised armed groups which raided our country, burning homes and murdering. He called them "Fedayeen" or "men of sacrifice" and said they were fighting a holy war. In fact, they were just terrorists.

'It was not only Israel that Nasser upset. He annoyed France and America too. The Americans refused to give Nasser some money they had promised him. Nasser needed that money badly. He had told his people he was going to increase the height of the dam at Aswan to give them more electricity and more water to irrigate their fields. What could he do? Then he had an idea. Running right through Egyptian territory is the Suez Canal. It did not belong to Egypt, but to an international company. This made a lot of money by charging tolls to ships that went through the Canal. Nasser thought, "I could use these tolls to build the Aswan Dam, so why not seize the Canal for Egypt?" In July 1956 that was exactly what he did.

'Now it was the turn of the British to be angry. A lot of their trade passes through the Suez Canal, including oil from the Middle East. They were afraid Nasser might one day close the Canal to their ships. Their Prime Minister Anthony Eden said "Nasser has a thumb on our windpipe."

'Britain, and indeed, France, both wanted to take control of the Suez Canal, but they needed an excuse to attack Egypt. What they did, was to hatch a plot with us. We were to invade Sinai – which we had good reason to do because of the Fedayeen. Britain and France were then to order both us and the Egyptians to leave the Suez Canal so that they could protect it. We would agree, of course, but everyone knew the Egyptians would not. The British and the French would then send their armies to seize the Canal.

'The big worry was what the Russians might do, for they were friendly towards Egypt. Eden hoped they would be too frightened to do anything. After all, the Americans hated the Russians and were the allies of Britain. He felt America would surely support Britain.

Israeli paratroopers seize the Mitla Pass

"We hope," he said to them, "that you will take care of the bear."

'We launched our attack on October 29th. As our army swarmed over the border, our paratroopers seized the Mitla Pass. The Egyptians ran like rabbits. In a week we had taken the whole of Sinai. Meanwhile, what were the British and French doing? They had decided the nearest point at which they could gather their forces was Malta, over 900 miles away! Now a great convoy lumbered its way across the Mediterranean going at the pace of its slowest ship, which was some old merchant vessel. The whole world looked on in amazement. Well, the convoy did arrive in the end – after we had defeated the Egyptians – and the British and French did take Port Said. But by then other things had happened.

Anthony Eden had hoped the Americans would back him, but to his dismay, President Eisenhower said Britain had acted badly and should leave Egypt alone! Eisenhower wanted to please countries like India. They remembered the days of the British Empire when Britain had bullied *them*, so they were very angry about the attack on Egypt. They said the British were behaving as imperialists, just as they had always done.

'The Russian leader, Khrushchev, also had something to say. He warned the British and French that if they did not leave Egypt he might – he just might – drop nuclear bombs on London and Paris. I think the French would have called his bluff, but Anthony Eden lost his nerve. He agreed to withdraw his troops, so the French had to do the same. The Americans and Russians now ordered us to leave Sinai. We had to go, of course. You will hardly believe this, but the British also ordered us to leave! A lot of notice we would have taken of them on their own!

'The man who did best out of this was Nasser. He was the hero of his people and the whole Arab world. As for Britain and France, they were completely humbled. I cannot think they will ever try to be imperialists again.'

213

3 Britain and the E.E.C.

De Gaulle refusing Britain's entry to the Common Market

In this section we will talk to an English woman who works for the E.E.C. in its capital, Brussels. She is an economist.

'What do the letters E.E.C. stand for?' 'The European Economic Community. These are difficult words so we usually talk about the Common Market.'

'How did the Common Market begin?' 'For centuries the countries of Europe had been fighting each other, and then came the Second World War. That brought almost complete ruin. Sensible people saw it would be far better to work together. The United States of America was a great success, so why not try a United States of Europe?

'There were one or two false starts, mainly because Britain was against the whole idea. We still thought our Empire was important for us. How could we abandon Australia, New Zealand and Canada who had fought beside us during the war? Anyway, we didn't like the Europeans. We used to laugh at the French and Italians, though I can't think why. As for the Germans, we hated and feared them. In the end, the European countries decided to carry on without us. Six countries, West Germany, France, Italy, Belgium, the Netherlands and Luxembourg formed the Common Market in 1958.

'After a time Britain realised she was doing more trade with Europe than with her Empire. There wasn't much Empire left, anyway. We decided we had better join the Common Market after all, and in 1961 we asked if we could.

'In 1958 we would have been welcome, but by 1961 General de Gaulle was President of France. He hated Britain and would not let us in. We had to wait until he retired.

'Britain finally joined the Common Market in 1972. Eire and Denmark did so at the same time and Greece joined in 1981. That means ten countries are now members and together we do more trading than even the United States.'

'What does being in the Common Market mean?' 'It means that all the countries in it sell goods to each other, without any interference.'

'How does that help?' 'You know that a shop in a big town will probably make more money than one in a village. That's because it has more customers. If this

Common Market countries, showing when they joined

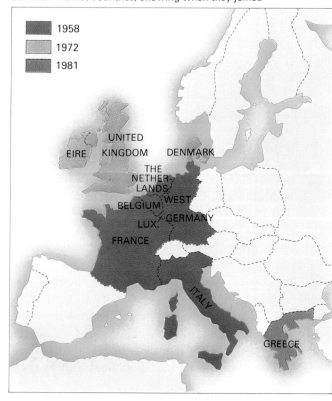

1958

1972

1981

UNITED KINGDOM
EIRE
DENMARK
THE NETHERLANDS
BELGIUM
WEST GERMANY
LUX.
FRANCE
ITALY
GREECE

country were on its own, our manufacturers would only have the people of Great Britain as their customers, about 55 million of them. As it is, we are in the Common Market with a population of 270 million. That is bound to be good for business.'

'Why do you so often hear people grumbling about the Common Market?' 'That is because of the Common Agricultural Policy. In many of the European countries there are a lot more farmers than in Britain. Their governments are determined that the Common Market shall help them as much as possible. If they grow more food than people need, the Common Market buys it from them. It then goes into store. There are "butter mountains", "meat mountains", and "wine lakes". When there is too much to keep it is sold abroad for next to nothing. Usually the Russians have it.'

'Why can't it be sold cheaply at home?' 'Because food prices would fall. The farmers wouldn't like that.'

'Where does all the money come from to pay the farmers?' 'Each country has to find a certain amount each year. The way it was worked out meant that Britain, one of the poorest countries, was paying more than any other – £1,000 million a year! We made them charge us less after a great deal of argument, but I still think we give far too much.'

'It sounds as if we are being swindled. Why don't we leave the Common Market?' 'Some people think we should. But you must remember that every new project has its teething troubles. They will be overcome, I'm sure. In the meantime, they are a small price to pay for belonging to the Common Market. Our partners buy 60% of all the goods we export. Where else could we sell them if not in Europe?

'No, it was all right for us in the old days, before the First World War. Then we were at the head of a huge Empire. Today that Empire has gone. Britain is now just a part of the Common Market, and by no means the most important part, at that. We shall just have to give up a lot of our traditions and accept the fact that we are Europeans.'

French peasants. One result of the Common Agricultural Policy is to keep backward farmers like this in business

4 Britain and Northern Ireland: Bad Memories

In 1130 Richard de Clare, Earl of Pembroke, known as 'Strongbow' went to Ireland with an army. Dermot Macmurrough, King of Leinster, had asked him for help against his enemies. Strongbow gave it, but he also married Macmurrough's daughter, and made himself King of Leinster when her father died. Strongbow was the first of many invaders, so that by the reign of Queen Elizabeth I, the English ruled the whole of Ireland. At this same time the English became Protestants, while the Irish remained Roman Catholics. That gave the Irish even greater reason to hate their enemies. Soon worse still was to happen in the north, with the 'Plantation of Ulster'.

For a long time the men who came from England were nobles, looking for estates, and those estates were no use without people. English lords chased away the Irish chiefs, but the Irish peasants could at least keep their farms. But early in the seventeenth century large numbers of ordinary people, all of them Protestants, arrived in Ulster. Many of them came from Scotland,

some from England. London merchants found much of the money they needed, so the town of Derry became Londonderry. To make way for the settlers, Irish peasants were driven from their land. This made them very angry, and the Protestant newcomers were afraid for their lives. They had good reason to be.

In 1641, the Catholic Irish rose in rebellion. They tortured and killed many Protestants. At Portadown they herded 100 of them on to a bridge and flung them into the river. They then shot the ones who could swim, or knocked them on the head as they struggled to the bank. It was said afterwards, that from time to time the ghost of a woman would rise out of the water screaming 'Revenge!'

Revenge came in 1649. Oliver Cromwell led an army to Ireland where he sacked Drogheda and Wexford. At Drogheda, some of the defenders fled to a church tower. Cromwell's soldiers set fire to it, shooting any who tried to escape the flames. There were many other cruelties as well, so the Catholic Irish have never forgotten the 'curse of Cromwell'.

Some forty years later there were other important happenings. In 1685 James II became King of England. He was a Catholic and by 1688 he had made himself so unpopular that the English deposed him. They asked his Protestant brother-in-law, a Dutchman called William, Prince of Orange, to be their king. But in the Irish James had subjects who were Catholics like himself. They were glad to help him, so in 1689 they formed an army which marched on Londonderry. They ordered the citizens to let them in, and the town council was about to agree when thirteen apprentice boys slammed the gates shut. The Catholics then laid siege to the town, and before long its people were dying of starvation. When they were invited to give up, though, they replied, 'No surrender'. Finally, they were rescued by a British fleet but it was months before its commander found the courage to sail up the River Foyle under fire from King James's guns. The citizens of Londonderry were disgusted, and since then the Protestants of Ulster have never been sure how far they can rely on the British.

The war ended the following year, 1690, when William of Orange came to Ireland with an army, and defeated James at the Battle of the Boyne.

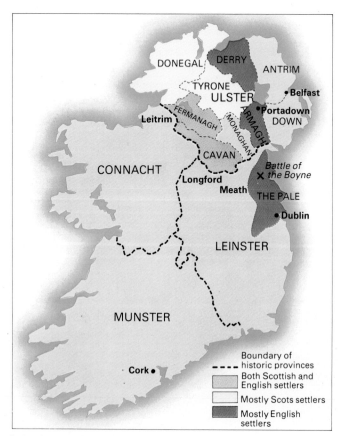

Ireland

apprentice boys closing the gates of Londonderry

Ireland had many troubles after 1690, but the greatest tragedy by far was the famine which lasted from 1845 to 1849. In 1800 the population was about 4½ million, but by the 1840s it had risen to 8 million. There was very little industry so all these extra people had to make a living by farming. Particularly in the west, farms were divided again and again until many a family had no more than an acre of land. Only potatoes would give them enough food from such a small plot, so that was all they grew. Then, in 1845, peasants were horrified to find that their potatoes were rotting in the ground. Even the ones they dug which appeared sound, soon turned into a black, stinking mess. This was 'blight', a new disease which no one understood. Thousands of people, faced with starvation, looked to ·Britain for help.

They were disappointed. The British government had few ideas on what to do and none of them were much good. It was determined the Irish should not live on charity, so hungry men were sent to earn their keep doing 'public works'. Usually that meant building roads which were not needed. However, there were not nearly enough public works, and often even those men with jobs had to wait for weeks until they were paid. Meanwhile there were parts of Ireland where farmers grew oats and kept cattle, but they had to pay their rents. That meant selling their goods in England. While hundreds of thousands of Irish starved, shiploads of grain, meat, butter, and cheese left their country every day.

The potato blight returned in 1846 and again in 1848. Probably 800,000 people died of hunger and disease, while many others fled to Britain or America. In the end 1½ million emigrated.

No one, of course, could blame the British for the potato blight, but many blamed them for the famine which followed it. To this day there are people in Ireland who believe that the British hoped it would destroy the Irish nation.

Irish peasants emigrating because of the famine

5 Britain and Northern Ireland: Modern Problems, 1981

As time went on the Catholics of Ireland became more and more determined to break away from Britain and have their own independent country. They made so much trouble that in 1913 the British government gave way and Parliament passed a Home Rule Bill to give Ireland her freedom. At once there was a problem. Sir Edward Carson, the leader of the Protestants of Ulster made it plain that his people were not going to join a Catholic Ireland and would fight rather than do so. They organised an Ulster Volunteer Force 100,000 strong, while friends in Britain sent them 24,000 rifles. In reply, the Catholics formed the Irish Volunteers*, but they were much fewer in number and had only 1,500 rifles. The only answer was to divide Ireland which was done at last in 1921 after even more troubles. Twenty-six counties became the Irish Free

*The Irish Volunteers later became the Irish Republican Army – the I.R.A.

the division of Ireland 1921

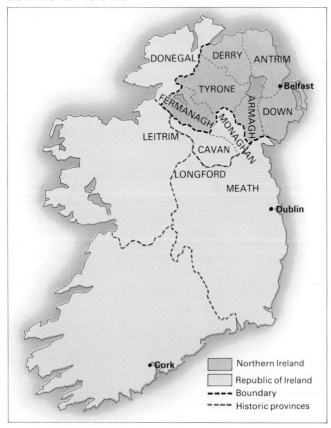

Northern Ireland
Republic of Ireland
---- Boundary
---- Historic provinces

Orange Day procession

State, which was quite independent of Britain. Today it is the Republic of Ireland, or Eire. The six counties in the north-east remained part of the United Kingdom, but they did have their own Parliament, so that they could look after themselves to quite an extent.

The division of Ireland in 1921 did not bring an end to all the unhappiness. The main problem is that one-third of the people of Northern Ireland are Catholics and they and the Protestants have been unable to live together in peace. There was so much disorder that in 1969 the government of Northern Ireland asked the British government to send in the army. It is still there and has a very difficult time. An officer will tell us about it.

'*What do you think is wrong in Northern Ireland?*' 'One thing is that the people know too much history. You ask an English child what was happening in 1689 and he hasn't a clue. An Irish child, though, will tell you all about the siege of Londonderry and the Boyne. They just can't forget what they have suffered in the past. But the main trouble is religion.'

'*How is that?*' 'Some of the Catholics will go to any lengths to get what they want, especially the I.R.A. In prison they will even starve themselves to death on hunger strikes, hoping to force the government to give way to their demands. As for the Protestants, they aren't like our Church of England people. They are descendants of Scottish settlers, so they are strong Presbyterians and have extreme views. They just hate Catholics in a way that we find it difficult to understand. They are frightened, too. They are scared that Northern Ireland might become part of Eire which would put them at the mercy of the Catholic Irish. That fear led them to be unfair to the Catholics in their own province.'

'*What did they do?*' 'For one thing, they always managed to fiddle elections so that they won more seats than they should. A third of the people are Catholics, but they never won more than a quarter of the seats in Stormont – that's their Parliament. In Londonderry there are more Catholics than Protestants, but the Protestants always had a majority on the town council. The law was such that the poor couldn't vote, and most Catholics are poor.

'As the Protestants were in charge, they took care of their own people. Catholics found it very hard to find council houses or even jobs. Today there are twice as many Catholics unemployed as Protestants.

'Well, in the 1960s the Catholics decided they had had enough. They formed a Civil Rights Association to demand equal treatment with the Protestants. One of its leaders was a very lively young lady called Bernadette Devlin. In January 1969 they went on a march from Belfast to Londonderry. It was peaceful enough until they reached Burntollet bridge. There a Protestant mob waded into them hurling bricks, and wielding iron bars, broken bottles and planks studded with nails. The police did hardly anything until it was nearly over. Then they arrested eighty Catholics. There was so much trouble afterwards that the British army had to go in. We have been there ever since.'

'*You have hardly mentioned the I.R.A. yet.*' 'They didn't matter much until the 1970s. You see they

British troops in Belfast

want the whole of Ireland united immediately, but they are about the only people who do. The Ulster Protestants are certainly against it, while the government of the Republic doesn't want a million unwilling Protestant subjects on its hands. Even the northern Catholics wouldn't have bothered, if they had been treated fairly. Things changed when we arrived. We saw it as our duty to put down all the rowdies, Protestants as well as Catholics, and that was what we did. But the Catholics have always hated the English and they had it firmly in their heads that we were on the side of the Protestants. If ever we searched Catholics or their houses they were sure we were picking on them. Then there was "Bloody Sunday" in January 1972 when our men shot down thirteen Catholics in Londonderry. They asked for it. They were taking part in an illegal march and began to pelt us with stones and shoot at us, but the Catholics didn't see it that way. All this gave the I.R.A. their chance. They said to the Catholics "We will protect you if you will help us." Today, nearly every Catholic in Northern Ireland is on the side of the I.R.A. and that makes it impossible for us to defeat them. It is equally certain they will never defeat us, so we have a war neither side can win.'

'*If they can't win, why don't the British take their army out of Northern Ireland?*' 'I wish they would. I hate being over there. But there would be civil war at once. Hundreds of people die every year as it is. If we left, I firmly believe they would kill each other in their thousands.'

1 How the First World War Began

It is August 1914 and Great Britain has just declared war on Germany. We talk to Sir Edward Grey, the British Foreign Secretary.

'*Why did this war start, Sir Edward?*' 'Mainly because many of the countries of Europe hate each other. Look at France and Germany. In 1870 there was a war between them. Germany won and took from France the two provinces of Alsace and Lorraine. Imagine how we would feel if she had taken Kent and Sussex from us! The French have been waiting for a chance to win back their lost provinces, and the Germans are determined to stop them.

'Also, there are problems in South-eastern Europe. Once, Turkey had quite a large empire there but, as a result of wars and rebellions, she has lost it, a bit at a time. Russia has always wanted Constantinople and the straits that join the Mediterranean to the Black Sea. Because Turkey was growing weaker, she thought she had a good chance of taking them. Austria–Hungary is determined to stop this, so she and Russia are enemies.'

'*Do all the European countries hate each other?*' 'By no means. Germany and Austria–Hungary have been allies for a long time, and so have Russia and France. That means that if any two of them started a war, the others would join in.'

'*What is Britain's position?*' 'We have grown to dislike Germany, because she is a threat to us.'

'*Why is that?*' 'The ruler of Germany, Kaiser William II, is very jealous of our empire, which is the largest in the world. Germany does have a few colonies, but would like a lot more. In the hope of winning them she has been building a powerful modern fleet. We were afraid that one day it might be strong enough to challenge the Royal Navy.'

'*How did the war actually start?*' 'In June of this year the heir to the throne of Austria–Hungary, Franz Ferdinand, was assassinated at Sarajevo. Austria–Hungary said this was the result of a plot hatched in Serbia and attacked her. Russia is friendly towards Serbia, so she prepared to defend her. Because

Sir Edward Grey

arrest of Franz Ferdinand's assassin

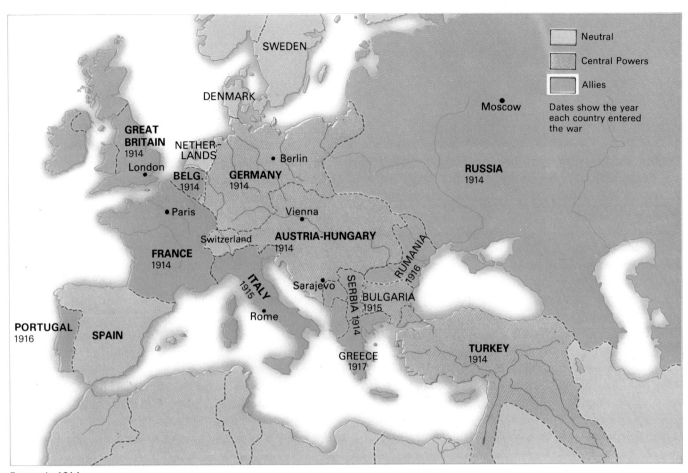

Europe in 1914

of the alliances, Germany then had to help Austria–Hungary, and France had to help Russia. What began as a little war, spread all over Europe.'

'*Why did Britain join in?*' 'Nearly a hundred years ago Britain promised to defend Belgium against any country that attacked her. It seems that the German army had to go through Belgium if it was to carry out its plan to defeat the French. In any case, when we asked the Germans to leave Belgium alone, they refused, so we declared war on them.

'It was not only that we wanted to help Belgium. It was in our own interests to fight the Germans. As I explained we did not like the navy they were building. We knew that if they defeated France and Russia they would have us at their mercy.'

Austria–Hungary. Austria–Hungary was unusual in that she was really two countries, but with the same ruler. He was the Emperor Franz Josef. Also, in earlier times, the Austrians had conquered the Slav peoples to the north, while the Hungarians had conquered other Slav peoples to the south. Both groups of Slavs wanted to break away and form their own independent states. The Southern Slavs also hoped they could join Serbia, which was why Franz Josef disliked that country.

2 The First World War, 1914–1918

When the war began, the Germans hoped to defeat France in six weeks. Their armies swept through Belgium and on through northern France until they were dangerously close to Paris. At last the French, helped by the British, were able to stop them at the Battle of the Marne.

After the Marne, both sides began to dig trenches which, before long, ran in an unbroken line from the English Channel to the Swiss frontier. The men in the trenches had rifles and machine guns and in front of them they put up miles of barbed wire fences. It was almost impossible for enemy soldiers to reach a trench without being killed. What is more there were usually three rows of trenches, one behind the other. The whole system was five miles deep. Generals on both sides thought the only way to break through was to destroy the enemy trenches with gun fire and there were some tremendous bombardments. For example, at the Third Battle of Ypres in 1917 the British fired $4\frac{1}{2}$ million shells over 19 days. Even then their attack failed. The guns did a lot of damage to the German trenches, but the ground was a mass of shell holes, which soon filled with water. When the British troops went forward it was impossible to send them enough food and ammunition. The Germans brought up reinforcements and soon drove them back.

The one hope was a British invention, the tank, for neither machine guns nor barbed wire could stop it. However, the first tanks broke down very easily and, more important, the British did not have enough of them until the end of the war.

The Germans, the British and the French all made desperate attacks and lost hundreds of thousands of men. Neither side was able to make much progress until 1918.

On the Eastern Front the Russians began well in 1914, by advancing into Germany but soon Generals Hindenburg and Ludendorff drove them back. In 1915 the Germans defeated the Russians thoroughly, capturing one million prisoners.

The Russians tried again in 1916 when General Brusilov attacked Austria–Hungary. He was quite successful, until the Germans came to the rescue of their ally and defeated him. After that, the Russians did very little fighting. In 1917 there were revolutions in their country which overthrew the government, and early in 1918 Russia made peace with Germany.

There was fighting at sea, too. In 1916 the British and German fleets fought the Battle of Jutland. Both sides claimed a victory, but, in fact, it was a draw.

battlefield

the German army marches home, 1918

fighter planes destroying observation balloon

Then, in 1917, Admiral Tirpitz decided he could win the war for Germany, by ordering his U-boats to sink all ships sailing to Britain and France. Without food and war supplies the two countries would have to surrender.

At first the U-boats were very successful but before long the warships of the Royal Navy protected the merchant vessels by sailing with them in convoys. The Germans also sank a lot of ships belonging to the United States. That made the Americans angry, so in 1917 they declared war on Germany. The Germans had made an enemy of the richest country in the world. At first America was not ready for war, but by 1918 she was pouring men and weapons into France.

After Russia made peace in 1918, the Germans moved many soldiers to the west. General Ludendorff was able to make several powerful attacks on the British and French. He hoped to defeat them before too many Americans arrived. The Germans advanced a long way in several places, but in the end they were

stopped. These defeats, coming after four years of bitter fighting made them lose heart. By August it was the turn of the British and the French. Helped by their tanks and by their American allies they drove the Germans back the way they had come.

The German people at home had also lost heart. The British navy was stopping any food reaching them from overseas so they were starving. There were strikes and riots in many German cities, and there was even a mutiny in the fleet. The German government decided it must surrender. On November 9th the Kaiser fled to Holland, and on November 11th an armistice was signed.

The German soldiers then marched home. They went proudly and in good order, for though they had retreated they had never broken and run away. The people who saw them refused to believe this splendid army had been defeated in the field. Instead, they were sure it had been 'stabbed in the back' by traitors at home.

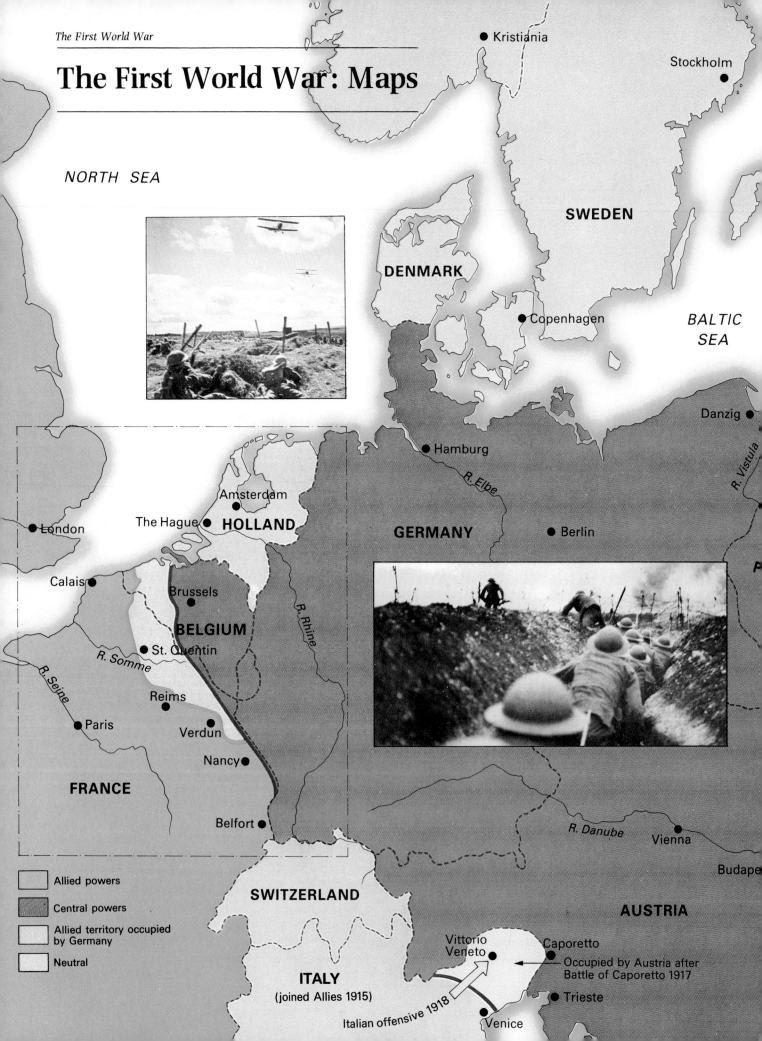

The First World War: Maps

NORTH SEA

SWEDEN

● Kristiania

Stockholm ●

DENMARK

Copenhagen ●

BALTIC SEA

Danzig ●

● Hamburg

R. Elbe

R. Vistula

GERMANY

Berlin ●

Amsterdam ●

The Hague ● **HOLLAND**

● London

● Calais

Brussels ●

BELGIUM

R. Rhine

R. Somme ● St. Quentin

Reims ●

R. Seine

Paris ●

Verdun ●

Nancy ●

FRANCE

Belfort ●

R. Danube Vienna ●

Budape

Allied powers

Central powers

Allied territory occupied by Germany

Neutral

SWITZERLAND

AUSTRIA

Vittorio Veneto ●

Caporetto ●

← Occupied by Austria after Battle of Caporetto 1917

ITALY
(joined Allies 1915)

Italian offensive 1918

● Trieste

Venice ●

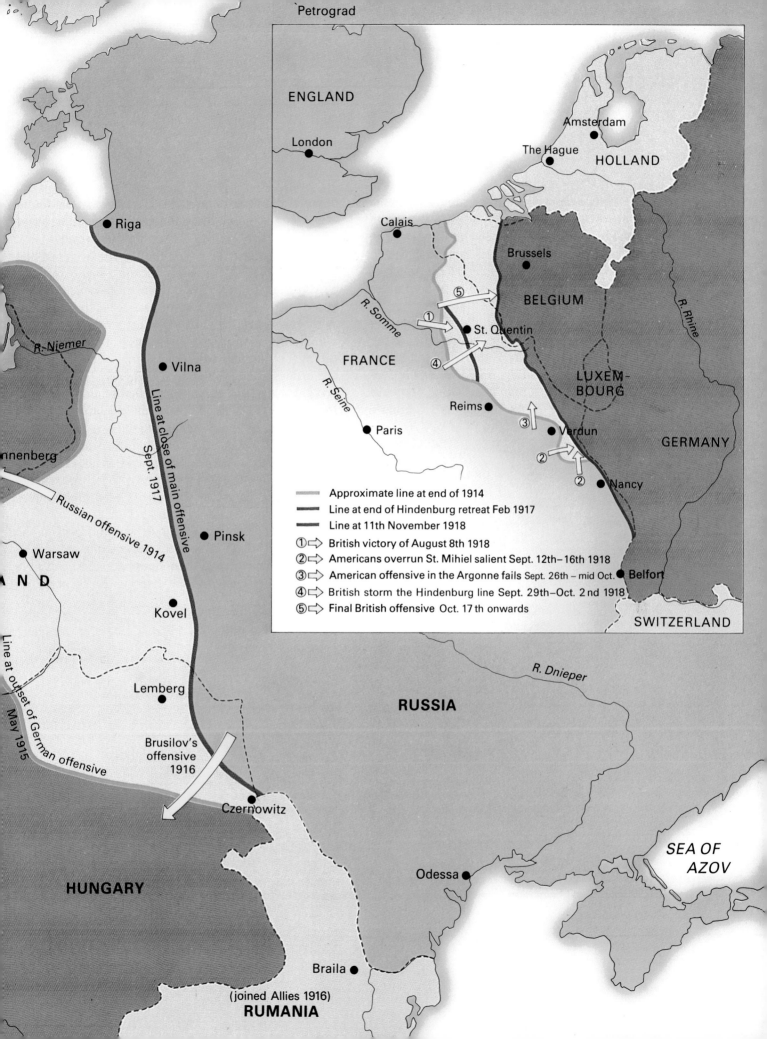

Petrograd

ENGLAND

London

Amsterdam

The Hague · HOLLAND

Calais

Brussels

BELGIUM

R. Somme

⑤

①

St. Quentin

FRANCE

④

LUXEM-
BOURG

R. Rhine

R. Seine

Reims

③

Verdun

GERMANY

Paris

②

②

Nancy

Approximate line at end of 1914

Line at end of Hindenburg retreat Feb 1917

Line at 11th November 1918

① ⇨ British victory of August 8th 1918

② ⇨ Americans overrun St. Mihiel salient Sept. 12th–16th 1918

③ ⇨ American offensive in the Argonne fails Sept. 26th – mid Oct.

④ ⇨ British storm the Hindenburg line Sept. 29th–Oct. 2nd 1918

⑤ ⇨ Final British offensive Oct. 17th onwards

Belfort

SWITZERLAND

Riga

R. Niemen

Vilna

Line at close of main offensive Sept. 1917

Russian offensive 1914

nnenberg

Pinsk

Warsaw

AND

Kovel

Lemberg

Line at outset of German offensive May 1915

Brusilov's
offensive
1916

Czernowitz

RUSSIA

R. Dnieper

HUNGARY

Odessa

SEA OF
AZOV

Braila

(joined Allies 1916)
RUMANIA

3 Life in the Trenches

For some time after the War began in 1914, the people of England went on living the same kind of life they had always known. The men went to work, the women cooked and cleaned their homes and the children went to school. Now and then, the people of Kent and Sussex heard a rumbling, like thunder. It was the guns firing in France, barely a hundred miles away.

The War was so close, that if anyone sent a soldier a letter, his favourite newspaper or a magazine, it arrived within a day or two. Wealthy mothers sent their sons hampers, just as they had done when they were at boarding school. A man could come home on leave quite quickly. He might be shooting Germans one evening, and going to the theatre in London the next. At the beginning of the War, at least, he found everything at home the same as ever. When he went back to the fighting, he was in another world.

In the first few weeks of the War, the Germans had won several battles, but soon the French and the British had stopped their advance. Now neither side could move. There were two reasons for this — barbed wire and machine guns. You can imagine what it would have been like to try to pick your way through a tangle of barbed wire under a hail of bullets. When the armies attempted to blast their way through with artillery, the soldiers dug trenches to protect themselves. The front ran for 400 miles from the Belgian coast down to the Swiss frontier. Each side dug at least three rows of trenches. There was such a maze of trenches that the soldiers gave them place-names, such as Piccadilly and The Strand. Where the trenches met and formed cross-roads they called them names like Hyde Park Corner or Marble Arch.

You can see how a trench was made from the diagram, although they were never quite as neat as that. One soldier called them 'lousy scratch holes'. We will talk to a soldier called Barry, who is home on leave.

'*How does it feel to be home, Barry?*' 'I can't believe it. Only yesterday I was shooting at Germans.

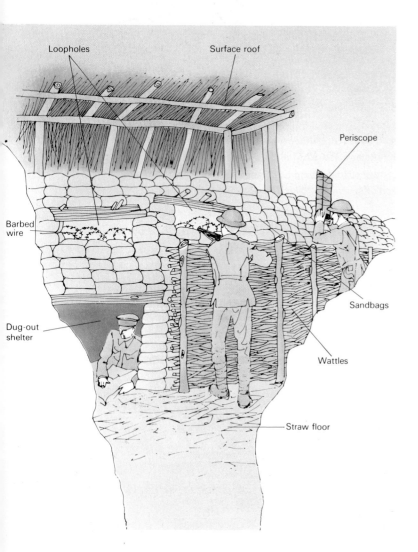

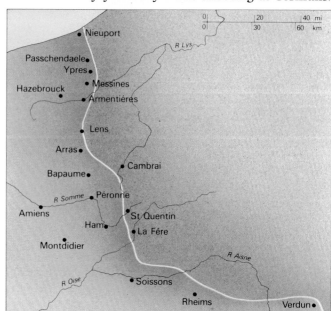

sentry duty on the front line

Now I am back here and everything is like it always was. I feel as if I had suddenly come out of hell.' '*What is it like in the trenches?*' 'The first thing you notice is the mud. It is often up to my knees and has been up to my waist. They say the Germans can make it rain whenever they want. Well, that seems to be all the time. There is a foul smell too, from the bodies of the dead men and horses. They sprinkle chloride of lime on the bodies, but it doesn't do much good. Something you soon realize is that it's not only soldiers that live in the trenches. Within a few days I was crawling with lice. There are rats, too. Big, fierce things they are. One night we shut a cat in a dug-out, hoping it would kill a few. In the morning the cat had vanished, bones, fur, flesh, everything.'

'*What food do you eat?*' 'Mostly it's bully beef and Maconochies. That's corned beef and tinned stew. We have big biscuits, like dog biscuits, sometimes with a bit of jam on them. Once a day we have a ration of rum. We really enjoy that. With all the rain and mud our big problem is fresh water. Usually there is enough to drink but not always enough to wash our mess tins. Usually there is no chance of washing ourselves. The shelling is worst of all; it never seems to stop. Several times I have had to help take the dead and wounded out of a trench that has been hit. Unless I am very lucky my turn will come.'

'*How do you spend a normal day?*' 'We start before dawn, with a stand-to. That means we take our rifles and watch. Dawn is a good time for an attack you see. We strain our eyes, looking into the half-light for a line of grey figures to appear. I have seen some beautiful sunrises but I will never feel the same about sunrises again. One morning one of our chaps lost his nerve and seemed to go mad. The officer just took out his revolver and shot him. During the day I may clean

Life in the Trenches

my rifle, write a letter home or just sleep. Sometimes I sit and look at the earth wall of the trench and sometimes I look up at the strip of sky above me and wonder if a shell will come whistling out of it. We do most of our work at night. We have to carry our supplies from the rear – ammunition, duck boards, barbed wire – that sort of thing. The unlucky men have to go into No-Man's Land, the strip of land between our trenches and the enemy trenches. We have to mend the barbed wire fences broken by shelling. We may even raid the German lines. Sometimes the Germans

send up flares and it is as bright as daylight for a few moments. The only thing to do then is to freeze where you are and hope a machine gunner doesn't see you.'

'*How long do you think the War will last?*' 'Well, both sides have made some desperate attacks and lost thousands of men. The front doesn't move. The only hope of winning is to find some way of picking your way through a tangle of barbed wire, under a hail of machine-gun bullets, without being shot. That's almost impossible, of course. As far as I can see, the War will last for ever.'

Over the Top by the war artist, John Nash

WHAT IN THE END WILL SETTLE THIS WAR? TRAINED MEN IT IS YOUR DUTY TO BECOME ONE ENLIST NOW

13th May, 1916.

ARMY RESERVE

WHEREAS by a Proclamation dated the 4th of August, 1914, His Majesty in exercise of powers conferred upon him by the Reserve Forces Act, 1882, ordered (The Right Hon. Herbert Henry Asquith) one of His Majesty's Principal Secretaries of State from time to time to give, and, when given, to revoke or vary such directions as might seem necessary or proper for calling out the Army Reserve or all or any of the men belonging thereto.

And Whereas by a Royal Warrant dated the 20th day of October, 1915, His Majesty was pleased to order that men enlisted under the terms thereof might with their consent be transferred to the Reserve.

I, Field-Marshal the Right Hon. Earl Kitchener, K.G., K.P., one of His Majesty's Principal Secretaries of State, now therefore do hereby direct as follows:—

That men who have been enlisted and passed forthwith to the Army Reserve under Royal Warrant dated 20th October, 1915, and classified in the group mentioned in the subjoined Schedule, are required to report themselves on such date and at such place as may hereafter be directed for the purpose of rejoining the Army.

If they do not receive any such directions within 30 days from the date of attaining 19 years of age they will report by letter to the Recruiting Officer at the Recruiting Office where they were attested, or to the Office the address of which is entered on their card Army Form W.3194. The necessary instructions as to their joining will then be given.

N.B.—The publication of this Notice in the Parish in which the last registered place of abode of a man belonging to the undermentioned group is situate shall be sufficient notice to such man, notwithstanding that a copy of such notice is not served on him.

SCHEDULE.

Group.
All men of the 24th Group as and when they attain 19 years of age.

Date on which the Group will commence to be called up.
13th June, 1916.

WHICH? HAVE YOU A REASON— OR ONLY AN EXCUSE— FOR NOT ENLISTING NOW!

(4856.) Wt. W2941/P429. 100,000 Pads. 12/17. H. W. & V., Ld. (E. 2825.)

"B" Form. MESSAGES AND SIGNALS.

Army Form C2122.
(In pads of 100.)
No. of Message.........

Prefix........Code........m.		Received		Sent		Office Stamp.
Office of Origin and Service Instructions.	Words	At........m.		At........m.		
		From...		To...		
		By...		By...		
TO						

Sender's Number.	Day of Month.	In reply to Number.		AAA

From			
Place			
Time			

* This line (except AAA) should be erased if not required.

Army Form W. 3431.
MESSAGE PAD.

........DIVISION.
Map reference or Mark on Map at back.

1. I am at.................. {and am consolidating. / and have consolidated.}
2. I am held up by M.G. at ....
3. I need :—Ammunition. / Water and rations. / Bombs. / Very lights. / Rifle bombs. / Stokes shells.
4. Counter attack forming up at ....
5. I am in touch with.............. on Right/Left at..........
6. I am not in touch on Right/Left
7. Am being shelled from..................
8. Present strength..........rifles. Reinforcements required :— ....Platoons. ....Sections rifle bombers. ....Sections riflemen. .... „ Lewis gunners. .... „ bombers.
9. Hostile ... {Battery / Machine Gun / Trench Mortar} active at..................

Time.............. m. Name..................
Date................... Platoon..................
Company..................
Battalion..................

W1843—R1643 150,000 5/17 HWV(P1139)
7253—M2951—200,000 8/17

17th NOVEMBER, 1914.
100,000 MEN
ARE NEEDED AT ONCE
To add to the ranks of the New Armies.
JOIN FOR THE WAR.

Extension of Age Limit and Reduction of Height to the Normal Standard.

Age on Enlistment—19 to 38 years
Height for Infantry—5ft. 3ins. and upwards
Chest—34½ ins. at least

PAY AT ARMY RATES.

SEPARATION ALLOWANCE under Army conditions is issuable AT ONCE to the wife of a married man who signs the necessary form at the time of enlistment, and in certain circumstances to the dependants of other soldiers. Pamphlets with full details from any Post Office.

Enquire at any Post Office, Police Station or Labour Exchange for address of nearest Recruiting Office.
GOD SAVE THE KING.

some of the documents used in the war

4 The First Tanks

The first man to have the idea of building a tank was Colonel Ernest Swinton. This is what he said:

'In the autumn of 1914 I was worried about the way the War was going. We were sending men through barbed wire fences to attack machine guns and they were being killed in their thousands. Then, one day, I saw a Holt caterpillar tractor. This was an American machine. It was being used to pull a big gun. I believe the Americans built it for use in the swampy lands of Louisiana where tractors with wheels just stick in the mud. I thought to myself, "Why not put a box of armour plate on caterpillar tracks? Men could sit inside it and then neither bullets nor barbed wire would stop them." I spoke to the generals in charge of our Army but they just laughed at me. I had friends in London, though. They saw all sorts of important people, and, in the end, Sir Winston Churchill took up my idea. He was First Lord of the Admiralty at the time, so the most important new land weapon of the War was developed by sailors!

'The next thing I heard was that a firm called Fosters of Lincoln were going to build this new fighting vehicle. They asked me what to call it. We wanted to keep it secret, so they had to say they were building something harmless. I said they should call it a "tank". After all, it was a big iron box, so it looked like a tank, and what could be more harmless than a container for water?'

The first tanks went into battle in September 1916, but we are going to talk to a tank driver at the end of 1917.

'This is one of the new Mark IV tanks. It is a male. You see it has two six-pounder guns, and only four machine guns. A female has six machine guns. Our job is to destroy the German defences. Female tanks are man-killers.'

'*How many men are there in a tank crew?*' 'There

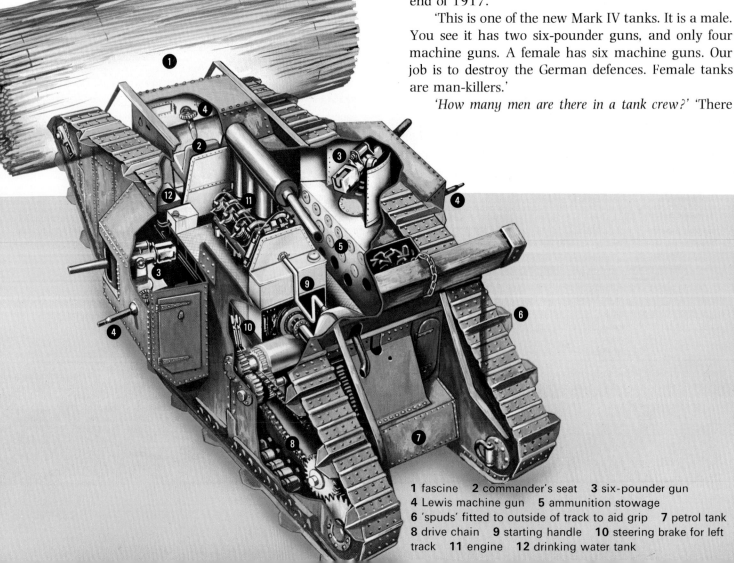

a Mark IV male tank

1 fascine   2 commander's seat   3 six-pounder gun
4 Lewis machine gun   5 ammunition stowage
6 'spuds' fitted to outside of track to aid grip   7 petrol tank
8 drive chain   9 starting handle   10 steering brake for left
track   11 engine   12 drinking water tank

are eight of us. Four work the guns and four drive the tank.' *'Do you need four men to drive?'* 'Oh yes. There is one man for each of the tracks and the commander and I have to work the other controls.'

'What is it like to fight from a tank?' 'Pretty terrible, I can tell you. The first thing you notice is the noise. You can't even shout above it. I signal to the other drivers by banging with a hammer. After a while the heat becomes dreadful, too. I have had to drink a gallon of water in a day. We can't take off our clothes either. When bullets hit us we get ''splash'', which is bits of hot metal flying off the inside. We only move at about four miles an hour, but we pitch and roll like a ship in a storm. I have seen men come out of a tank, sick and raving like lunatics. One of the worst problems is that we can't see through these little slits. Sometimes the commander walks ahead of the tank. He is lucky still to be alive. As soon as the Germans see a tank they fire everything they have at it.'

When the Germans first met tanks, many of the troops were terrified. Some ran away screaming, 'The Devil is coming.' British soldiers were delighted of course, and came behind the tanks shouting and cheering. Some tanks did remarkably well. There was a light tank that its crew called 'Musical Box'. This tank went into the German lines, destroyed guns, blew up lorries, killed large numbers of enemy soldiers and fought a battle with a train. Musical Box did a great deal of damage before the Germans set her on fire and captured her crew.

At one time it looked as if tanks would win the War. That was at the battle of Cambrai in 1917. The Germans had built some powerful defences called the Hindenburg Line after one of their generals. There were three rows of trenches, miles of barbed wire and

a tank in Peronne during the Battle of St. Quentin

hundreds of guns. To stop tanks, they had dug wide ditches. Nothing could halt the British attack, though. Their guns pounded the German artillery, while smoke bombs blinded the German gunners. Aircraft swept low over the infantry in their trenches, bombing and maching gunning. Then came the tanks. Each carried a huge bundle of brushwood, called a fascine, and when the tank came to an anti-tank ditch, it just dropped in its fascine and crossed easily. The tanks crushed the barbed wire and, when they came to the trenches, they turned their machine guns on the terrified soldiers inside. The British infantry came close behind, killing and capturing the Germans before they could recover from the shock of the attack. The British tore a gap in the Hindenburg Line six miles wide. At home, the church bells rang to celebrate the victory.

a Mark IV female tank destroyed by a direct hit

The bells rang too soon. There were 476 tanks, but most of them broke down on the first day of the battle. All the British could send through the gaps in the Hindenburg Line was cavalry. German machine guns mowed them down without difficulty. A few days later, the Germans counter-attacked and won back most of the ground they had lost.

The War dragged on until the end of 1918. Tanks won other battles, but the end came mostly because the German nation was worn out after four years of terrible fighting. The people rebelled, the sailors in the fleet mutinied, and the German Emperor fled to Holland. Germany then surrendered and had to accept very harsh terms under the Treaty of Versailles.

5 Dreadnought

It is the year 1906. We will visit Admiral Sir John Fisher. He is the First Sea Lord, which means he is the most important man in the Royal Navy. He tells us what he has done for the Navy.

'Let's just go back to 1897. That was the year of Queen Victoria's Diamond Jubilee. There was a splendid naval review at Spithead, you remember, and I must say the fleet certainly *looked* fine. All the paintwork was clean and new, and the brasswork was shining. There were 165 ships in three lines each 30 miles long, and that was just the home fleet. We had as many ships again guarding the Empire all over the world. We made sure our fleet was as big as the two largest foreign navies put together. The "two-power standard" we called it. No wonder foreigners were jealous. "Rule Britannia," we sang, "Britannia rule the waves!" Some of us knew better though. Admiral Beresford put his finger on it, "The fleet is not ready to fight, or nearly ready to fight," is what he said. I agreed with him.

'The Russians had a fleet like ours – a lot smaller of course, but the same kind of vessel. You know what happened when they fought against the splendid modern ships of the Japanese navy. The Japanese sank nearly the whole fleet in just one battle. The same thing would have happened to *us* if we had been foolish enough to fight.'

'What was wrong with the British fleet, Sir John?'
'Well, in the first place, there were too many useless old ships. Do you know that there were some old tubs at the Spithead review that had to be towed there? Did you hear about H.M.S. *Galatea*? That was a ship we had on service in the Far East. There was nothing wrong with the shine on her brass, but she was full of rot and rust. She was also full of dead rats and cockroaches. When at last they got round to clearing out her holds it took a gang several days to shovel out all the corpses.

'We didn't take care of the sailors either. Their lavatories stank and the air in their quarters was so stuffy they could hardly breathe. In winter they froze, and in summer they were nearly cooked alive. Do you know, we didn't even give them knives and forks! They used to eat with clasp knives and their fingers.'

'What frightens me most,' continues Sir John, 'is

Spithead review, 1897

to remember how bad the naval gunnery was. They could only put one shot in three on the target. The crews used to practise cutlass drill. I have no doubt that they would have done very well in cutlass fights, but in modern navies we fight with guns and torpedoes. That's another thing. The admirals didn't seem to know about the torpedo, even though it was an English invention. Foreigners knew about it and they knew about submarines, too. As for our people, Admiral Wilson was typical. He used to say that submarines weren't proper weapons of war, and that if he caught any he would hang their crews as pirates.

'Well, I've put a stop to all that nonsense. I've scrapped any number of old ships, and saved money for better uses. I've got rid of a lot of useless people too. The sailors are a lot more comfortable now. They have knives and forks. There are bakeries on the ships as well, so they have bread to eat instead of "hard-tack" – you know, those things that looked like oversized dog biscuits, but tasted worse. Have you heard of the Royal Naval College at Dartmouth? I started that. What's more, we let ordinary lads go there, as long as they are clever enough. It's no use making a man an officer, just because his father is a gentleman. Because you have breeding, it doesn't

the *Dreadnought*

cutlass drill

mean you must have brains. Ships have practised their gunnery too, until they are sick of it. They hit the target much more often these days.

'All that is nothing compared with my new ship. My motto is "Hit first! Hit hard! Keep on hitting!", but we didn't have the ships that could do that. We do now. People wanted me to go carefully and try all sorts of experiments with models, but I say that the best scale for experiments is twelve inches to the foot. I made them get on with it, and the builders finished my new ship in just a year and a day. Now every other battleship in the world is out of date.'

'*What do you call this wonderful new ship, Sir John?*' 'Well, I don't expect you've counted, but the words "Fear not" appear in the Bible eighty times. That gave me the idea. We call the ship *Dreadnought*. What makes her so good? There are her guns for one thing. Other battleships have four twelve-inch guns. *Dreadnought* has ten. Even if an enemy managed to hit her, it wouldn't do much damage. On the waterline, where it matters, she has armour plate eleven inches thick. She is heavy, of course, some 18,000 tons, but she is fast. She is the first battleship to have Parsons turbines instead of piston engines and can do 22 knots.'

'*What would happen if the* Dreadnought *took part in a battle?*' 'In a battle the *Dreadnought* would train all her guns on the waterline of the enemy ship and blast a hole in it with eight tons of shells. Then she would deal with the next ship and the next, and the next. She can out-sail and out-gun anything afloat,' replies Sir John.

6 Jutland

You saw in the last section how Admiral Fisher built the *Dreadnought* and how it made every other battleship in the world out of date. But there was a problem. Not only were all foreign battleships out of date, but so were all other British ships as well. The Germans realized this. They began to build Dreadnoughts of their own, and all the old British battleships became useless. The only thing the British could do was to build more Dreadnoughts than the Germans. Luckily, Britain was able to win this ship-building race, because the Germans had to concentrate more on their army. None the less, the German navy was a powerful modern force, and the British were scared of it.

The First World War began in 1914. At that time, most of the German High Seas Fleet was in its harbours in North Germany, while the British Grand Fleet was at Scapa Flow in the Orkneys. They were there to stop the Germans from sailing round the north of Scotland and into the Atlantic. If they had done that, they would have been able to sink the merchant ships bringing Britain the food and supplies she needed to fight the war. The British admiral, Sir John Jellicoe, was worried. He knew that the Germans had dangerous new weapons – mines, torpedoes and submarines. He knew also that if the Germans destroyed his ships they could at once invade Britain with a large army and they could easily win the War. Sir Winston Churchill said that Jellicoe 'was the only man who could lose the War in an afternoon.' No

John Cornwall by his gun

wonder Admiral Jellicoe was careful! On the other hand, the Germans saw that the British outnumbered them by two to one, so they were not anxious to have a battle. Both sides wondered what to do. For a long time they did nothing.

What the Germans wanted was to catch a part of the British fleet on its own. In May 1916 they thought their chance had come. Admiral Scheer led their High Seas Fleet after a squadron of battle cruisers commanded by Admiral Beatty. Scheer then discovered to his horror that the whole of the British Grand Fleet was close by. What was worse, Jellicoe's ships were between him and his home ports. The Germans had to fight. The battle that followed is known as the Battle of Jutland.

Every man in the British fleet had been longing for the day when they would at last meet the German fleet and destroy it. They thought it would be a second Trafalgar, a great victory for the British. However, Jutland was not at all like that. There was plenty of action. When a Dreadnought fired all her guns, her stokehold filled with coal dust, and the crockery flew everywhere. As shells came crashing into the ships

map of the Battle of Jutland

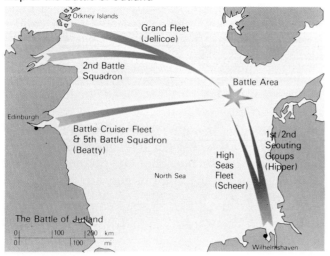

on both sides, more and more men were killed or wounded. On one of the British ships John Cornwell, a boy of sixteen, was mortally wounded. He stayed by his post while the rest of the gun crew lay dead and dying around him. He was given a posthumous V.C.

Few of the sailors could see what was happening, so on another British ship a young officer they called Mr. Johnston gave his men a running commentary and handed round mugs of tea. Mr. Johnston was really Prince George, the future George VI and the father of our Queen Elizabeth.

The battle did not go well for the British. Three of their battle cruisers blew up, which happened all too easily because they were badly designed. On the other hand, the German ships were difficult to sink because they were so well built. The British gunners were not nearly as accurate as the enemy gunners. The Germans scored far more hits. Many of the British shells were duds and did not explode as they should have done. The great battleships were frightened of the little German destroyers. They had good reason, because the destroyers fired torpedoes which could do more damage than the biggest guns.

At the start of the battle, the British had the Germans in a trap, and they outnumbered them two to one. However, the Germans fought so well that they were able to escape. Not only that, they lost far less shipping than the British and less than half as many men. None the less both fleets were almost as strong after the battle as they had been before, because, of the 250 ships that took part, only 25 were sunk. The Germans went back to their ports, and the British went back to Scapa Flow. Neither navy did very much surface fighting after Jutland.

However the German navy did come near to winning the War, and Jellicoe came near to losing it, though not in an afternoon. While the German High Seas Fleet stayed safely at home, German U-boats, or submarines, went all over the Atlantic. They sank so many merchant ships that it looked as if Britain would run out of food supplies and starve. The only sensible thing was to put the merchant ships in convoys and protect them with warships. At first Jellicoe refused to do this. He said that if large numbers of merchant ships sailed together then the U-boats would be able to sink even more of them. What he did not realize was that if the U-boats attacked a convoy they would have to sail close to the warships defending it. That meant the warships could find the U-boats and destroy them, which they had not been able to do before. In April 1917, the British lost 420 merchant ships. At last Jellicoe allowed convoys and from that time far fewer merchant ships were sunk.

You might like to know what happened to Admiral Fisher's *Dreadnought*. She was in harbour for repairs at the time of the Battle of Jutland. She did very little all through the War, and was scrapped in 1922.

What happened to the German High Seas Fleet? When the War ended the Germans were ordered to send it to Scapa Flow to surrender. The sailors took the ships to Scapa Flow but were determined that the British should not have their splendid fleet. When they arrived they opened the sea cocks and their ships filled with water. Every one of them sank to the bottom.

Jutland

survivors of the battle cruiser *Invincible* being picked up by a
British destroyer — detail from a painting by Robert H. Smith

Souvenir
OF THE
VICTORY OF JUTLAND

FOR YOUR SPLENDID WORK I THANK YOU

MAY 31ST 1916.

7 The Treaty of Versailles

When the First World War ended the leaders of the countries which had won it met at Versailles, near Paris. There they drew up a peace treaty, which they made their defeated enemies sign. You can see that this treaty brought a great many changes. Study the map and then answer the questions:

1 What provinces did Germany lose to France?
2 What provinces did Germany lose to Poland?
3 What did the Polish Corridor do to Germany?
4 What new countries were there instead of Austria–Hungary?
5 What countries and provinces joined together to form Yugoslavia?
6 What other countries took lands that had once belonged to Austria–Hungary?
7 From which countries did Poland take lands?

8 What was the reason for the Polish Corridor?
9 What port stood at the end of it?
10 Which countries, around the Baltic Sea, won their freedom from Russia?

There were other things in the treaty which cannot be shown on the map. Germany had to surrender her navy, destroy all her warplanes and keep only a tiny army of no more than 100,000 men.

Also, Germany was forced to admit that she had started the war and told that she would have to pay for it as a punishment. The cost was put at £6,600 million.

The Germans were very angry about the Treaty of Versailles. They felt it was particularly unfair that they should be blamed for the war. Many of them were determined that, if ever they had the chance, they would take their revenge.

signing the Treaty of Versailles

Right: changes made by the Treaty of Versailles

Formerly Austria-Hungary

Territory lost by Germany

Territory lost by Russia

NORWAY

SWEDEN

FINLAND

DENMARK

ESTONIA

LATVIA

LITHUANIA

SOVIET RUSSIA

To Denmark →

Polish Corridor

• Danzig

WEST PRUSSIA →

EAST PRUSSIA

POSEN

← To Poland

POLAND

NETHERLANDS

GERMANY

BELGIUM

GALICIA
(To Poland)

CZECHOSLOVAKIA

Alsace and
Lorraine
To France

BESSARABIA
(To Rumania)

AUSTRIA

HUNGARY

SWITZERLAND

RUMANIA

↑
To Italy →

FRANCE

Croatia

YUGOSLAVIA

Bosnia

BULGARIA

Serbia

Montenegro
(Joins Yugoslavia)

ITALY

ALBANIA

TURKEY

GREECE

Chapter Fourteen   The Second World War

1 How the Second World War Began

The Second World War was really two conflicts. One was against Germany and Italy, and the other was against Japan.

First we will talk with a retired German officer.

'Why did Germany fight a Second World War?' 'We wanted our revenge for the Treaty of Versailles and we also wanted to be the most powerful country in Europe. Hitler promised us both these things, after he came to power in 1933.'

'What did he do?' 'First of all he started to rearm. According to the Treaty of Versailles our army was to be only 100,000 men. Hitler soon made it much bigger than that, and indeed by 1939 all our young men had had some military training. Also our factories produced large numbers of modern weapons, especially tanks and warplanes.

'Next, Hitler made Germany much bigger. He had a good excuse for doing that, because there were millions of Germans living in other countries. He said that in fairness to them they must join their Fatherland.

'There was Austria, for a start. All her inhabitants are Germans. Hitler himself was an Austrian. In 1938, he sent our army into Austria.'

'What did the Austrians think about that?' 'There was no fighting. Instead, the people greeted our soldiers with cheers. They felt their little country had no future on its own, so they were glad to join Germany.

'Next it was the turn of Czechoslovakia. There were Germans living all round her western borders in the Sudetenland. Hitler said the Sudetenland must belong to Germany. The Czechs objected, of course, and they expected France and Britain to help them. In fact, those two countries agreed to tell the Czechs they must let Germany have the Sudetenland! All Hitler gave in return was a promise of "peace in our time." Soon afterwards, he took the whole of Czechoslovakia without any real excuse at all.

'In 1939, Hitler ordered Poland to give back those parts of Germany she had taken after the First World War. When she refused, he decided to attack. He was afraid Russia might help Poland, so he made an agreement with the Russian ruler, Stalin. Hitler said Russia could have the eastern half of Poland, if she allowed Germany to have the western half. He thought Britain and France would still do nothing, but when we invaded Poland they declared war on us. By then our army and airforce were so powerful that Hitler was not frightened of them at all.'

We will now talk to a Japanese. His people's main enemy was the United States.

'Why did Japan fight the United States? She is the most powerful country in the world!' 'Our state is the most modern in Asia and we were trying to make an Empire for ourselves as Britain had done. Over the years we fought a number of wars and we took a lot of islands in the Pacific as well as Korea and Manchuria on the mainland of Asia. Then in 1937 we began our biggest adventure of all.'

territory taken by Hitler

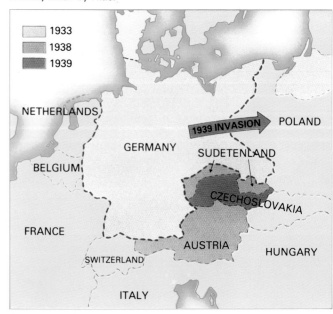

the attack on Pearl Harbor

the Japanese empire

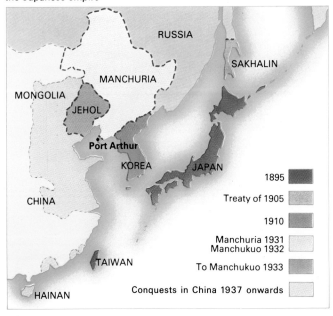

1895	
Treaty of 1905	
1910	
Manchuria 1931 Manchukuo 1932	
To Manchukuo 1933	
Conquests in China 1937 onwards	

Map labels: RUSSIA, SAKHALIN, MANCHURIA, MONGOLIA, JEHOL, Port Arthur, KOREA, JAPAN, CHINA, TAIWAN, HAINAN

'*What was that?*'   'It was the conquest of China. We fought and defeated the Chinese armies again and again, but their country is so huge we could not overrun the whole of it. The war dragged on for several years. Worse than that, the Americans decided we were becoming too powerful. In 1941 they ordered us to leave China alone. That gave us a terrible choice. Either we had to give up our conquests in China, or we had to fight America. We decided to fight America.'

'*How did you hope to win?*'   'Our greatest fear was the American Pacific Fleet. Admiral Yamamoto said it was "a dagger pointed at the throat of Japan." Our government thought that if it could be destroyed we would be safe. On December 7th, 1941 aircraft from Yamamoto's carriers attacked the fleet as it lay in Pearl Harbor. We had not declared war, so the American sailors were taken completely by surprise. We sank or crippled many of their ships.'

241

2 The Second World War, 1939–1945

The Second World War began in September 1939 with the German invasion of Poland. Britain and France, who had promised to help Poland, were not ready for war, so they could do nothing. The Germans defeated the Poles and captured Warsaw in four weeks.

In April 1940 the Germans overran Denmark and Norway. The following month they launched their main attack against France. They also invaded Holland and Belgium. The French, British, Dutch and Belgians had as many men as the Germans, and as many modern weapons, such as tanks. Nonetheless, the Germans won easily. This was partly because the Germans had such a good plan of attack, but mainly it was because they used a new way of fighting. It was the blitzkrieg, or lightning war. First of all dive bombers attacked and then came the panzer or armoured divisions. Tanks smashed the enemy defences at a number of places and motorised infantry

poured through the gaps close behind them. Other troops held the gaps open while the panzers advanced far behind the enemy lines.

You can see from the map how Guderian's thrust split the allied armies into two. Soon the Belgians surrendered and then the British fled from Dunkirk. After that, the Germans quickly defeated the French.

Hitler now expected Britain to make peace, but she refused to surrender. The only way to invade her was to have command of the air. The German airforce, the Luftwaffe, attacked and for several weeks there was fierce fighting in the skies over southern England. We call this the Battle of Britain. The British pilots beat off their enemies again and again. The Germans lost so heavily that in the end they had to stop their attacks. Hitler also gave up any hope of invading Britain for the time being.

In 1940 Italy entered the war on the German side.

The Italian dictator, Mussolini, had huge armies in North Africa and was sure he could drive the British out of Egypt. Instead, the British defeated the Italians so Hitler sent a small German army under Rommel to help them. It was not until 1942 that General Montgomery was able to defeat Rommel at the Battle of El Alamein.

In 1941 Hitler decided the time had come to attack the country he had always looked on as his main enemy, Russia. Once again the blitzkrieg was successful – but only for a time. Russia is much bigger than France, and the Russians sent millions of men against the Germans. Also they had what seemed a never-ending supply of weapons. In the winter of 1942 Marshal Zhukov won a great battle at Stalingrad. The Russians then began to roll the German armies back towards their own country.

On June 6th, 1944 American and British troops invaded northern France. They called it D-Day, or Deliverance Day. The Germans fought hard for a time. They were outnumbered, but Hitler would not allow them to retreat so they were defeated in Normandy. After that, they could not stop their enemies. In 1945 the Russian armies coming from the east met the Americans and British coming from the west. In April Hitler committed suicide and what was left of his armies surrendered.

As well as the war against Germany, there was another in the Far East, against Japan. It began, as you saw, with the Japanese attack on Pearl Harbor in December 1941. This victory gave the Japanese command of the sea for a time and they were able to advance a long way. They were only successful, though, because America had not been ready for war. Now she began to train her young men and to make enormous numbers of weapons. To fight the Japanese, what she needed most was aircraft carriers. By 1943 she had far more of these than Japan.

The Americans won their first important victory when they beat off an attack by Admiral Yamamoto on Midway Island. They then began to advance across the Pacific, 'island hopping' as they put it. They finally destroyed the Japanese navy at the Battle of Leyte Gulf in 1944. After that American submarines sank most of Japan's merchant ships, while American bombers destroyed her cities. In August 1945 the Americans dropped two atom bombs, one on Hiroshima, and one on Nagasaki. Japan surrendered on September 2nd.

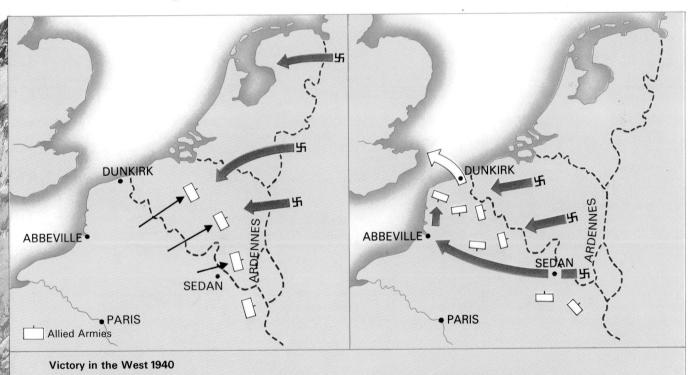

Victory in the West 1940

May 10th Germans attack. They overrun Holland and invade Belgium and Luxembourg.
British Army and best troops in French army go to help Belgians.
May 14th Panzer divisions under Guderian burst out of Ardennes where they have been hiding and break through at Sedan.

May 20th Guderian reaches the sea at Abbeville. He cuts off allied armies in Belgium from the rest of France.
May 27th Belgian army surrenders.
Late May–Early June British army and some French troops escape through Dunkirk.
Many French troops are captured.

Left: German tanks in action

The Second World War: Maps

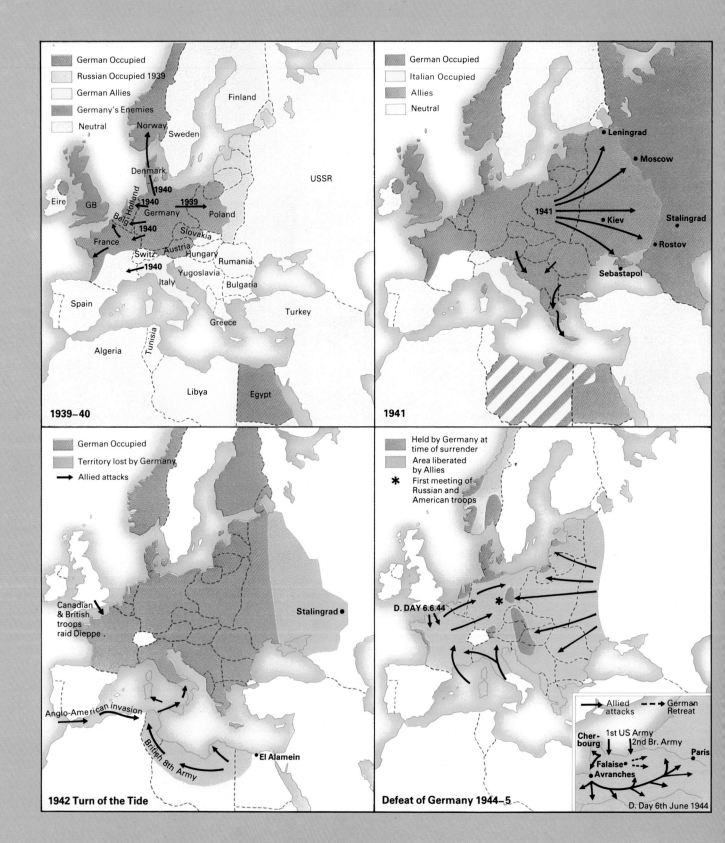

1939–40

German Occupied
Russian Occupied 1939
German Allies
Germany's Enemies
Neutral

Finland
Norway
Sweden
Denmark
1940
1940
1939
Eire
GB
Holland
Belg
Germany
Poland
France
1940
Slovakia
Switz
Austria
Hungary
Rumania
1940
Yugoslavia
Bulgaria
Italy
Spain
Greece
Turkey
Algeria
Tunisia
Libya
Egypt
USSR

1941

German Occupied
Italian Occupied
Allies
Neutral

Leningrad
Moscow
1941
Kiev
Stalingrad
Rostov
Sebastapol

1942 Turn of the Tide

German Occupied
Territory lost by Germany
→ Allied attacks

Canadian
& British
troops
raid Dieppe .
Stalingrad ●
Anglo-American invasion
British 8th Army
● El Alamein

Defeat of Germany 1944–5

Held by Germany at
time of surrender
Area liberated
by Allies
✱ First meeting of
Russian and
American troops

D. DAY 6.6.44
✱

→ Allied
attacks
--→ German
Retreat
Cher-
bourg
1st US Army
2nd Br. Army
Paris
Falaise ●
Avranches
D. Day 6th June 1944

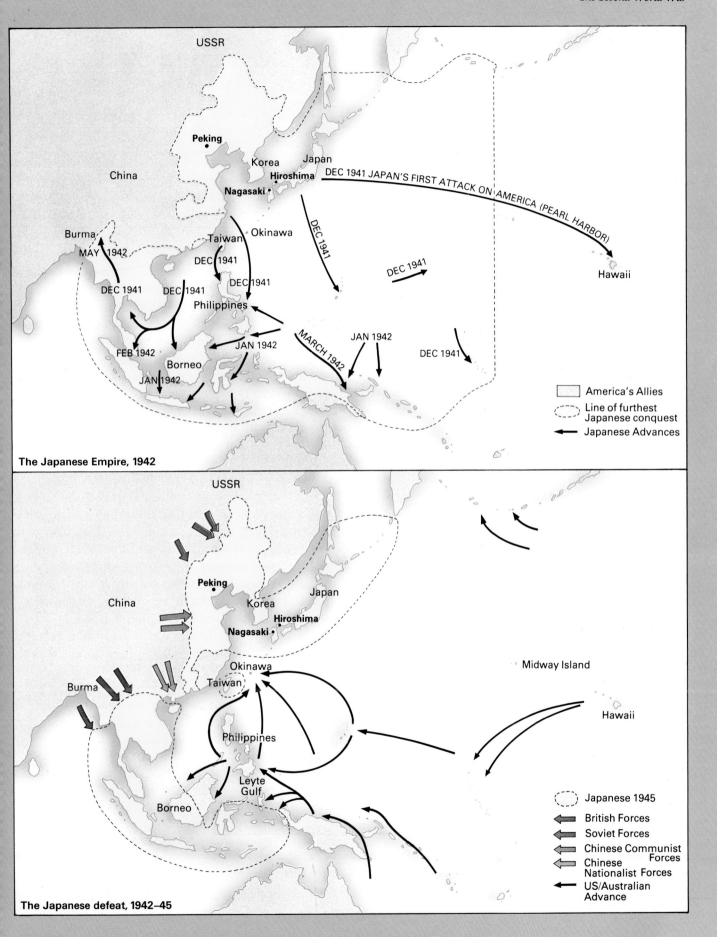

USSR

Peking
●

China

Korea

Japan

Hiroshima

Nagasaki ●

DEC 1941 JAPAN'S FIRST ATTACK ON AMERICA (PEARL HARBOR)

Burma

MAY 1942

Taiwan

Okinawa

DEC 1941

DEC 1941

DEC 1941

DEC 1941

DEC 1941

DEC 1941

Hawaii

Philippines

FEB 1942

Borneo

JAN 1942

JAN 1942

MARCH 1942

JAN 1942

DEC 1941

```
▭  America's Allies

⌐ ¬  Line of furthest
└ ┘  Japanese conquest

◄━  Japanese Advances
```

The Japanese Empire, 1942

USSR

Peking
●

China

Korea

Japan

Hiroshima

Nagasaki ●

Burma

Okinawa

Taiwan

Midway Island

Hawaii

Philippines

Leyte
Gulf

Borneo

```
⌐ ¬  Japanese 1945
└ ┘

◄◼  British Forces

◄◼  Soviet Forces

◄◼  Chinese Communist
             Forces
◄◼  Chinese
     Nationalist Forces

◄━  US/Australian
     Advance
```

The Japanese defeat, 1942–45

3 The Battle of Britain

After the First World War ended, there were twenty years of peace. In 1933, the Germans found a new leader – Adolph Hitler. He promised he would make Germany a great country once more, and take revenge for the Treaty of Versailles. First he seized Austria, then Czechoslovakia, but when he attacked Poland, the French and the British decided they must stop him. They told him he must leave Poland alone or they would fight. Hitler ignored them, and the Second World War began.

War broke out in September 1939. By the summer of 1940 the Germans had not only defeated Poland, but France as well. They were now wondering how to conquer Britain. The Germans knew they could defeat the British Army easily if they could only cross the English Channel. But they only had barges to carry their men across and the Channel was alive with ships of the Royal Navy. A man who thought he had the answer to this problem was Hermann Goering. Goering had been a fighter pilot in the First World War, and now he was in command of the German air force. Only a few weeks before, Goering's aeroplanes had destroyed the town of Rotterdam, frightening the Dutch into surrender. He was sure that Britain, too, could be defeated from the air. His bombers could do this, but he could not send them on their own because they flew too slowly to escape the British fighter planes. That did not matter, though, because Goering could protect his bombers with his own fighters. He had hundreds of *Messerschmitt 109s, and he thought they were the best fighter planes in the world.

From July 1940 onwards, German aircraft attacked Britain again and again. They soon realized that they were not going to win easily. For one thing, the British always seemed to know they were coming and were ready for them. This was because the British had radar. They had built huge aerials which sent out signals. If the signals met nothing, they just vanished into the atmosphere. But if they hit an aircraft they rebounded like a ball flung against a wall. A signal then showed up in the radar station on an instrument rather like a television screen, and so

*Willy Messerschmitt, the designer of this brilliant fighter plane, lived to be a very old man and did not die until September 1978.

gave warning that the Germans were on their way. The British had excellent fighter planes, Hurricanes and Spitfires. We will talk to Kenneth, a fighter pilot who flies a Spitfire.

'*How does your Spitfire compare with a Messerschmitt?*' 'Not badly; the German planes have two cannons and two machine guns, and Spitfires have eight machine guns, so they are about equal. Both aircraft can fly at about 400 m.p.h. I'm afraid that the Messerschmitt is better really high up. Height is very important for a fighter pilot: he likes to be able to dive down on his enemy. Above 30,000 feet, the Spitfire can't climb at all quickly, and the engine often misses a beat. I was left behind by my squadron the other day. It was frightening. The Germans like to "bounce" a stray aircraft. It was bitterly cold, and my cockpit cover steamed over, so I could hardly see a thing. Anyway, if the Germans attack, they usually fly out of the sun. I'd have been dazzled and wouldn't have spotted them until it was too late.'

'*How good are the German pilots?*' 'Much better than the British on the whole. They have all been flying and fighting for a long time. Too many of the British pilots are like me, not properly trained at all. It is as much as I can do to fly my Spitfire, let alone shoot down Germans.' '*What are you most afraid of?*'

a Hurricane fighter

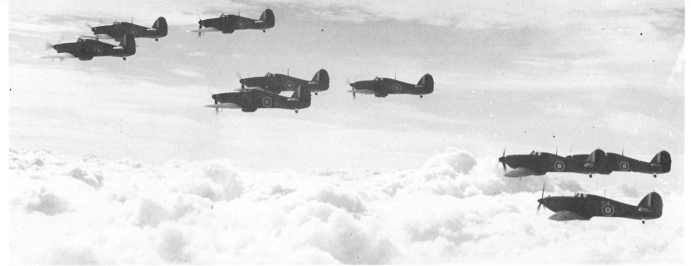
Hurricanes in flight

'Being burnt to death. The petrol tank is just in front of the cockpit. I always carry a pistol, and if ever the petrol catches fire, I shall shoot myself.' *'Do you think we are going to win?'* 'I doubt it. The trouble is I don't think Air Marshall Dowding knows what he is doing. He sends just a few of us into battle at a time. We are heavily outnumbered, but there are plenty of aircraft left on the ground doing nothing. Lots of our best pilots have been killed and we are all tired. I have seen a man fall asleep over his breakfast. He was snoring away with his face in his fried egg. Just now the Germans are attacking our airfields and when they put those out of action we are finished.'

Luckily, Ken was wrong. The Germans did not win the Battle of Britain. Why was that?

For one thing, Air Chief Marshal Sir Hugh Dowding, the man in charge of the R.A.F., knew very much what he was doing. He realized that as soon as autumn came, the weather would be too bad for the Germans to invade. In the meantime, what he had to do was to stop the Germans from destroying his

operations room of RAF Fighter Command

a German fighter shot down over southern England

fighter planes. That was why he sent them into battle only a few at a time.

Another important man was Lord Beaverbrook. His job was to see the factories made enough fighter planes. Soon we were making 400 a month in Britain, while the Germans were only making 140. Unfortunately no one could produce fighter pilots nearly as quickly.

The two men who really saved Britain in 1940 were Hitler and Goering! The reason was that they made a serious mistake. Ken was quite right when he said the Germans would win if they went on attacking airfields. However, the British bombed Berlin and Hitler and Goering wanted revenge. They ordered their airmen to leave the airfields alone and bomb London instead. The Germans attacked day and night and soon large parts of the city were blazing. Their biggest attack was on September 15th when 1,000 aeroplanes set out for London. The R.A.F. drove them back after some fierce fighting. We now call September 15th Battle of Britain Day. Really, the Battle of Britain was won as soon as the Germans decided to attack the ordinary people of London, rather than destroy the fighter planes of the R.A.F.

The Battle of Britain

a painting by Paul Nash depicting the Battle of Britain

4 The War in the Desert

From 1940 to 1943 the British Eighth Army was fighting the Germans and the Italians in the Western Desert of North Africa. The desert is a dreadful place. There is sand in places, and rocks as well, but most of it is just dust. From time to time the wind blows the dust into great billowing clouds. Vehicles on the move make their own little sandstorms as well. Here and there are mounds, but they are so low you can hardly call them hills. The most striking things are the depressions, huge pits in the ground, with sides like cliffs. The largest of these, the Qattara Depression, is 400 feet deep and 200 miles long. Maps of many parts of the desert are just blank sheets of paper. There is nothing to plot. Hundreds of square miles are empty and desolate. The climate is unpleasant. Early morning may not be too bad, but by midday the heat is unbearable. Towards sunset there is often a sandstorm. The nights are cold.

Why should anyone want to defend the Western Desert? The answer is that beyond the desert lay Egypt, the Suez Canal and the Middle East. Germany was short of oil, but if she conquered the Middle East and all its oilfields she could have all the oil she needed.

At first, the British had only the Italians to fight. The Italians were not cowards, but they had bad generals and bad equipment. In two months the British captured 130,000 Italians and lost less than 2,000 men themselves. Then General Rommel arrived with the German Afrika Korps. He drove the British back 500 miles, almost to the River Nile.

We will now talk to Bob, a commander of a tank, who is on leave in Cairo.

'What is it like fighting in the desert?' 'My father fought in the trenches in the First World War. He seems to have spent most of his time up to his knees in mud. At least we are spared that. We have dust rather than mud. It gets into our food, our clothes, our hair and our tank. Most of the time I have my head out of the top of the tank, so by the end of the day I am covered with dust. The heat is bad, too. You can fry an egg on the tank at noon. I know because I have done it. The flies are the worst thing. They get all over the food, they crawl up your nose, into your

a Crusader Mark II tank in the desert

an American Sherman Mark II tank

shot weighing only two pounds and the range is only about 600 yards. To make things even worse, Rommel has some nasty new weapons. The Germans are planting mines all over the place. "Devil's Eggs", they call them. The only way to find them is to send infantry to prod the ground with bayonets. How would you like to do that with the enemy shelling you? Rommel also has some deadly anti-tank guns. I have known one of them pick off half a dozen of our tanks on its own. What bothers me most is that no one seems to be in charge any more. The Eighth Army is breaking up, and each bit is fighting its own little war and losing it.' *'Are we going to be beaten then, Bob?'* 'If things go on like this, yes. But give us some good tanks and a good general and we will chase the Germans out of Africa.'

mouth and round the corner of your eyes. They are after the moisture you see. They will drink the sweat off your back. I have seen marching soldiers black with them. What the flies like best is blood. They swarm round the slightest cut and heaven help you if you are left wounded in the desert!'

'What do you eat?' 'Bully beef and biscuits most of the time. We have tinned milk and tea. To brew up we make a "desert fire" from sand soaked in petrol. Things were better when we were chasing the Italians. We used to capture their tinned tomatoes and vegetables. They had plenty of wine, too. Our big problem is water. Sometimes we are down to half a gallon a day each. That has to do for drinking, washing and the radiator of the tank.'

'I expect you feel safe in your tank, don't you?' 'Safe? If you had seen a roasted body hanging out of a tank, you would know how safe we feel. We are safe against a man with a rifle and that is about all. My Crusader has some thick armour at the front, but not at the sides. It is easy enough to blow off a track, and then we are stranded. What we dread most is being hit in the petrol tank, or even worse, the ammunition locker. If that happens the tank is a blazing inferno within seconds and there is no hope of getting out alive.'

'Why have the Germans defeated you so easily?' 'They have much better weapons. Take my Crusader. It *looks* strong enough, but it is always breaking down. The gun is almost useless. It throws a solid

Montgomery

In fact, both the things Bob wanted were on their way. The Americans sent 300 Sherman tanks that were more than a match for the ones the Germans had. General Bernard Montgomery took charge of the Eighth Army. On October 23rd, 1942 the Battle of El Alamein began. After more than two weeks of fierce fighting the Germans were defeated. In May the following year Rommel withdrew to Italy with the remains of his army.

5 Convoy

In Autumn 1942, some thirty ships were steaming down the St. Lawrence River. Others were coming from New York, Halifax and Cape Breton Island. Together there were over a hundred of them, all heading for a stretch of empty water near Newfoundland. They were going to form a convoy, one of the many that brought the food, weapons and other supplies that Britain needed to fight the war against Germany.

The great damage to shipping came from submarines, or U-boats. Germany had conquered France in 1940 and was able to use French ports. The U-boats could sail anywhere they wished in the Atlantic. Usually, they hunted in groups called 'wolf-packs'. In the second section you saw that during the First World War thousands of lives and hundreds of ships were lost in the Atlantic, and for a long time Admiral Jellicoe refused to allow convoys. The British had learnt their lesson over those terrible losses, and started convoys as soon as the Second World War began. Even so, the U-boats still managed to sink nearly 300 ships during the six years of war.

We will now see what happened to our convoy off Newfoundland. Each ship had a number, and as

a U-boat in the Atlantic

it arrived it took its proper place. You can see how they were arranged in the diagram:

11	21	31	41	51
12	22	32	42	52
13	23	33	43	53
14	24	34	44	54
15	25	35	45	55

You will see that ship 14 was in row 4 of column 1, and ship 31, which was the 'Commodore' ship was in row 1 of column 3, the middle column. The Commodore was an officer of the Royal Navy who had charge of the merchant ships, though he had to take orders from the Senior Naval Officer who was in charge of the escort. There were eighteen warships to protect the convoy, little ships, such as corvettes and frigates which were deadly to the U-boats. Six of the escort ships stayed close to the convoy, while the rest stayed far out, hoping to catch the U-boats before they could get close enough to make a killing. When all the ships had arrived, the convoy set off for Britain. This convoy was typical of many which braved the dangers of the North Atlantic during 1939–45.

Bill, one of the sailors who travelled with that convoy, will tell us what it was like:

'It is bad enough having to cross the North Atlantic at all. Your ship pitches and rolls as great green seas come crashing over her. Not many ship owners bother about making their crews comfortable or care about giving them decent food. Sailing in a convoy made things worse. We all had to lumber along at the pace of the slowest ship in the convoy, perhaps no more than eight or ten knots. Even so, we did not like being close to other vessels. A ship can't be driven like a car, you know. She doesn't have any brakes. If there was an attack, we had to zig-zag to confuse the submarines. We all had to do it the same way, or the whole convoy would have been bumping into each other like children rushing around in a school playground.'

'What happened during an attack?' 'The first thing you heard was a bang as some unlucky ship was hit. I remember a submarine coming right up into the

the corvette *HMS Hadleigh Castle*

middle of that convoy. She torpedoed a tanker carrying petrol, so there was a great explosion. The sea itself was a mass of flames, and all the crew were killed. Our alarm bells rang and we went to our action stations. I was a wireless operator, so I went to my cabin. The really unlucky ones were the engineers. They had to go to the engine room which was low down in the middle of the ship, just where the submarines aimed their torpedoes. As the corvettes rushed to find the U-boat, we heard the "crump" of depth charges, and huge fountains of water shot into the air. The U-boats attacked us on four days in a row. Our ship was hit on the last day and we had to take to our life-boats. We spent some very uncomfortable hours until one of the escort vessels picked us up. I still have a bad ear because of that day in the sea. We were lucky though, as most of our convoy managed to reach Britain safely.'

'*How many times were you torpedoed altogether?*' 'Three times, which was very unlucky. Some sailors crossed the Atlantic many times throughout the War and never even heard a depth charge explode. I stopped feeling sorry for myself, though, when I heard of a lad of seventeen who was torpedoed six times as well as being taken prisoner by the German battleship *Graf Spee*.

'*Could the merchant ships fight back?*' 'We couldn't fight back against submarines, but we did our best against aircraft. The Germans used to send out big Focke-Wulf Condors to work with the U-boats. We had our machine guns and pom-pom guns to fire at them. Some ships were "catapult aircraft merchantmen". They could catapult a fighter plane into the air. There was nowhere for it to land, of course, so when he had used all his petrol, the pilot came down by parachute and the plane crashed in the sea. We also had some strange devices for shooting wires up into the air. I never heard of any enemy aircraft being damaged that way, but I have known sailors lose a leg or a hand as the wire flew up.'

'*How do you feel about the War now that it's over?*' 'It's strange, but I mainly remember the good things and the funny ones, like the way we had our own back on a captain we hated. We taught his parrot to swear at him. The War left its mark though. Sometimes I have nightmares. Two torpedoes are chasing me and however I twist and turn they follow me. There is no escape. It may seem a silly dream to you, but when I have it I wake up so frightened that I cannot get to sleep again. There must be hundreds of people like me.'

Convoy

a painting by N. Wilkinson of a convoy under attack

6 The Home Front

What was it like for the people at home during the Second World War? A middle-aged man remembers. He lived in a small town in Somerset during those years.

'I was eleven when war broke out. I was so furious with Hitler that I dug my little patch of garden for all I was worth. The Government had asked us to "dig for victory", but all I managed to grow was a few radishes. I had just started at the local secondary school. The headmaster, Mr. Reid, had been a major in the First World War. When the Second World War began, he put on his uniform at once and did not take it off again, except to go to bed I suppose, until Germany surrendered. He decided to train us boys to be soldiers. As soon as we were fourteen he made us join the Army Cadet Force. There was great excitement when the uniforms arrived, and a lot more when we had our rifles, even though they had been worn out during the First World War, and were quite unsafe to fire.'

'Someone who did not always agree with the headmaster was the geography teacher, "Wally" Walker. Instead of helping with the Cadet Force, Wally became an Air Raid Warden. He said it would be more useful to learn how to look after ourselves in an air raid than to learn about old rifles. He was quite right, of course. He used to give us lectures on the different kinds of poisonous gas the Germans might use. When the time came, he issued our gas masks. We

gas mask drill

learnt to smear the inside of the window with soap to stop it steaming up. We also learnt how to put the thing on – chin in first, and then the straps were pulled over our heads. The whole class sat there, blowing beautiful raspberries through their masks, but breathing was hard work. Luckily we never had to use our masks. We were supposed to carry them the whole time and certainly we always took them to school. If Wally caught you without your gas mask, he was furious.

'I expect you have thrown a brick into a pond at some time or other. You will know that there is a big splash, and then ripples spread out. By the time they reach the edge of the pond the ripples are quite small. Living in our town during the War was a bit like that. There were big splashes in other places and only the small ripples reached us. Many other parts of the country, especially London and other big cities, were being heavily bombed, and one of the first ripples from the outside world was a trainload of evacuees from London.

'My mother went to help billet the evacuees, which meant placing them with families who had said they would have room for the children. Mother made it clear that if there were any children with nowhere to go she would bring them home with her. To my father's dismay, she came back with a miserable-looking boy called John. He was about my own age. I was delighted. Here at last was a boy to play with, instead of my tiresome younger brother.

Everything was fine for a few days, but we were soon fighting when we found we did not enjoy the same kind of things.

'John's father worked on the London Docks and his home was in an area near the docks that was bombed a number of times. I realized how lucky we were to be living in Somerset when I saw how anxiously John listened to the news to hear if there had been any bombing attacks on or near the docks. After he had been with us for several months, his mother suddenly appeared. A few days earlier she had been asleep in her bedroom when the sound of a terrible explosion woke her up. She found that the house next door had been flattened to the ground. Her own house was no longer safe to live in and so John's father made her leave London to join her·son in the country. John's mother found lodgings in our town and worked for a while in a munitions factory nearby. She was pleased to be near John, but she didn't really settle. She worried all the time about her husband and after a year she went back to London and stayed there all through the V-bomb attacks that did so much damage towards the end of the War. John was always very relieved to get letters from his parents and to know that they were still alive.

'John himself went back to London before the War was over. He was never really happy with us. He missed his parents and he found life in the country so different from the kind of life he knew. He couldn't get used to our ways or our food and was always

evacuees

homesick. Some of the other children who were evacuated with him were also unhappy and returned home after a few months, but others settled in with their families and stayed until it was safe to go back.

'There was another evacuation later, a more successful one. A whole school came from Hightown, in London, and shared our school buildings. We had our ordinary lessons in the morning, then moved out for the visitors in the afternoon. We cycled to all sorts of different church halls. It was a glorious chance for mischief. The headmaster used to shout at us that men were dying for us and all we did was misbehave. As I saw it, these men were going to die whether I was naughty or not, so I went on having my fun. I see his point now, of course.

'We were a mixed school, but the one from London was a boys' school. This meant the girls were outnumbered three to one, which pleased the girls but didn't please us at all. Of course, there were arguments and fights, but there were far more of the Hightown boys, so usually all we did was grumble. One Christmas, their school treated all of us to the cinema. It was a good film, *The Thirty-Nine Steps*, with Robert Donat, and we enjoyed it. The Hightown headmaster was standing at the door as we came out. We wondered why he was there. No one thought of saying "Thank you".

'From time to time soldiers appeared in the town. The first ones came after Germany had conquered France in 1940. Most of the British Army escaped from France via Dunkirk. A few of the soldiers were sent to us. They had no weapons, they were tired, and they talked very little. We hardly noticed when they left.

'Later, a battalion of the Welsh Guards arrived. They were giants who looked as if they could cover the length of the town in three good strides. I saw one of them step in front of an Austin Seven. The driver braked just in time. It was lucky for him that he did as he would have done serious damage to the car if he had hit the soldier. You can imagine how the girls and young women of the town felt about these visitors. Someone else who was delighted was our headmaster. He lost no time in persuading the Commanding Officer to lend him some instructors. His beloved Cadet Corps was drilled by sergeants from a regiment of Guards! Mr. Reid was a truly happy man in those days and we polished our buttons and stamped our feet as never before.

'The troops who caused most excitement in the town were the Americans. They were called G.I.s,

The Home Front

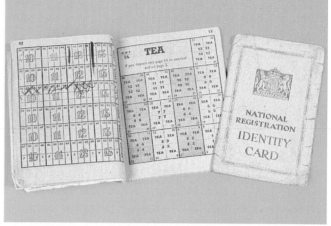

a ration book and identity card

which stood for General Infantrymen. They lived in various large houses and shops and offices that were closed because of the war. Many of the G.I.s were generous with gifts of chewing gum for the children and nylon stockings for the young women. Groups of children would call "Give us some gum, chum" and chase after the jeeps as they drove along the High Street. The black soldiers caused a lot of interest, because many people in the town had never seen a black person before. These soldiers were kind hearted too, and were pleased to bring presents of their own food whenever they were invited into English homes.

'My mother spent a lot of time worrying·during the War. At first there was little to worry about so she concentrated on the food. We had ration books which allowed us to have so many ounces of butter, meat, sugar, etc., per person. When we bought any rationed goods the grocer had to cut the coupons from the ration books. These coupons were as important as money and while rationing lasted all housewives had to plan their meals carefully. Buying clothes also became difficult. Everyone was allowed a certain number of clothing coupons and had to manage with very few new clothes. Lots of women began altering their old clothes to make them look new. This was called "Make do and mend". One of the things that worried my mother most was having to use margarine on bread instead of butter. I think we probably fed as well during the War as before it, but this was partly because we lived in the country and had fruit and vegetables from our own garden. Some foods, like fish, weren't rationed, but were in short supply. Whenever mother went shopping she had to queue for fish and other things that were hard to get. My mother found queuing very tiring, and of course it took a great deal of time. One thing we missed very much was bananas. The greengrocer had a picture of a splendid bunch of yellow bananas in his shop window and we had to pass it twice a day with our mouths watering. Even worse, sweets and chocolates were rationed after a while and even with sweet coupons you couldn't always get your favourite kinds. A shopkeeper refused me once, but I saw through a mirror that he had some boxes of the chocolates I wanted under the counter. He was keeping them for

special customers. Even in our town there were shopkeepers who kept lots of goods "under the counter" or on the "black market", which meant you could buy things without the coupons if you were willing to pay a very high price.

'When my elder brother was called up to join the Army on his eighteenth birthday, my mother really had something to worry about. We all took an even greater interest in listening to the nine o'clock news on the wireless. It was exciting when he came home on leave wearing his uniform, and it was very interesting to have his letters telling us about life in the Army. Later he fought in France but he managed to get through the War without any injury. My mother always seemed to be knitting him socks or sending him parcels.

'My father had fought in the First World War and was left with a weak chest. He could not join up in

an Anderson shelter

a painting by F. Dobson of Park Street, Bristol, during an air raid

the Second World War because of his health, but he went on working as a builder. There were no new houses to be built but he was kept busy repairing and redecorating old houses. When the Home Guard was formed he joined that and spent many evenings and weekends training with friends and neighbours so that they could help defend the country if the Germans invaded. Most of the men in the town, who had not been called up, either joined the Home Guard or became Air Raid Wardens and Fire Watchers.

'The War came closest to us when the Germans started to bomb Bath and Bristol, our nearest large cities. When the sirens wailed we came downstairs and listened for the whirr-whirr of aeroplanes. It usually came, followed by the ''crump'' of bombs and a red glow in the sky. In those days I was too young and had too little imagination to be really frightened, but if it happened now I would be terrified. We had an Anderson shelter in the garden but it was cold and quite often half-full of water. We went into it the first few times there were air raids and I can still remember the damp musty smell and the strangeness of being woken up in the middle of the night and taken into the garden. After a while we stopped going

to the shelter as my father thought our old house was so strong and well built that it would stand anything but a direct hit. Luckily we never found out.

'If you look at a war memorial you will see that not nearly as many men died in the Second World War as in the First. As far as I know, only one former pupil from our school was killed in the Second World War. His name was Hugh Barrett and he had been awarded a Military Medal for bravery. His father presented his books to the school library. The headmaster had them bound in leather and in each one was an account of Hugh's brave action. I am sure that the headmaster was proud that his school had produced at least one war hero.'

Chapter Fifteen   World Problems since 1945

1 Nuclear Weapons

During the Second World War the Americans started what they called the Manhattan Project – to develop the atomic bomb. Its leader was Robert Oppenheimer. The first explosion, a test, was at Alamagordo in New Mexico, on July 10th, 1945. By then Germany had surrendered, but Japan was still fighting. Soon the Americans had two bombs ready to use against her, 'Little Boy' and 'Fat Man'. On August 6th, 1945 they dropped 'Little Boy' on Hiroshima. It killed 60,000 people and injured 100,000 more. When President Truman heard the news he exclaimed, 'This is the greatest thing in history.' Three days later 'Fat Man' fell on Nagasaki.

The first atomic bombs each had a force of 14,000 tons of T.N.T. Then, in 1952 the Americans produced the hydrogen bomb and one of these has the force of 20 megatons of T.N.T. – that is 20 million tons. A scientist will tell us about it.

'What will happen if a hydrogen bomb falls on London, say on Trafalgar Square?' 'There will be a huge fire ball, as hot as the sun. You know how the gas under your kettle makes the water boil and turn to vapour. Well, this fire ball will be so hot that it will turn everything it touches to vapour – people, houses, and even solid rock. That, and the force of the explosion, will make a crater half a mile across. It will stretch as far south as Downing Street, as far west as Piccadilly Circus and as far east as the Thames. It will be 600 feet deep which is nearly four times Nelson's Column. The heat from the fire ball will also start fires in places twenty miles away, such as Brentwood, St. Albans, Weybridge and Gravesend.

'As well as the fire ball there will be an enormous explosion. A powerful shock will flatten every building within fifteen miles, which means the whole of London and Greater London. There will be serious damage

probable results of dropping a hydrogen bomb on London

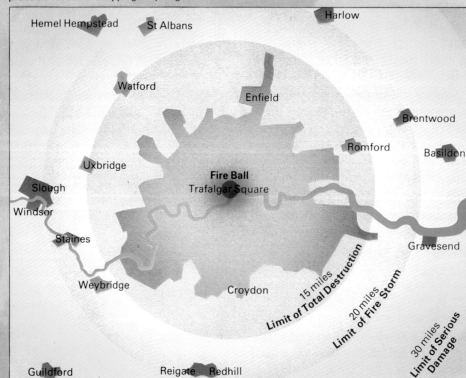

what 'Little Boy' did to Hiroshima

even in towns 30 miles away, like Basildon, Luton and Guildford. Behind the shock wave will come a wind, travelling, when it starts, at a thousand miles an hour. It will make a vacuum at the centre of the explosion, so soon afterwards air will come rushing back to fill it. These winds will fan the blaze started by the fire ball. London will not only be in ruins. It will be a raging inferno.'

'How many people will die?' 'At least six million. But those left will still be in great danger and so will others, perhaps hundreds of miles away.'

'Why is that?' 'You will remember I told you the fire ball will turn a mass of rock into vapour. This will rise for several miles, spread out and condense to form a huge mushroom shaped cloud. A rain cloud is made of droplets of water: this one will be dust and tiny fragments of rock. We call it fall-out. It will land wherever the wind takes it and as it will be radioactive it will be highly dangerous. It will give millions of people radiation sickness. They will lose their hair, they will go blind, they will vomit, they will lose all their energy and, in the end, they will die.

'In a nuclear war London will not be the only place to suffer. Hydrogen bombs will fall on other cities, perhaps Bristol, Birmingham, Liverpool, Hull and Glasgow. There will be devastation everywhere.'

'Will anyone survive?' 'I imagine so. But how will they live? The land will be poisoned, and so will the rivers and lakes. People will have to hunt for food among the ruins of the shops, and probably they will fight each other for any that is left.'

'Will much larger countries escape more lightly?' 'I'm afraid not. America and Russia have enough nuclear weapons to destroy each other several times over.'

The only nuclear bombs ever used on an enemy were the two America dropped on Japan in 1945. There have been many wars since then, but no two countries owning nuclear weapons have ever fought each other. They know only too well that it would mean total ruin for both sides. Probably it is this fear

which has prevented a Third World War between Russia and the West. But there are still very great dangers. Countries other than Russia and America are making atomic and hydrogen bombs, so their number is growing all the time. Could a nuclear war start by accident? What would happen if a maniac like Hitler came to power in a state that had nuclear weapons?

Almost everyone says that the nuclear weapons we have should be broken up and no new ones made, but the world's leaders have been unable to reach an agreement, although they are still trying. Each side is afraid it will give the other an advantage. Many countries still spend vast sums of money on less dangerous weapons, like tanks. They feel they must be able to fight a war without using nuclear weapons, except as a last resort.

nuclear submarine HMS *Warspite*

2 The Iron Curtain, 1946

Molotov

Russia and the United States are very different countries with very different points of view. Even when they were allies, fighting against Germany, they did not really trust one another. As soon as the war ended in 1945 they began to quarrel openly. A Russian and an American will tell us about it. First we will talk to the Russian foreign minister, Vyacheslav Molotov.

'What is your main worry now that the war is over?' 'During the war the Germans overran our country as far east as the River Volga. As they retreated they destroyed everything they could – farms, factories, hospitals, schools, entire villages and towns. Worse than that, they killed 20 million of our people. We are determined nothing like this shall ever happen again.'

'How are you going to stop it?' 'Fortunately, towards the end of the war, our victorious Red Army occupied many of the countries of Eastern and South-Eastern Europe. They are now a buffer between us and our enemies in the west. The Red Army will stay with them to protect them.'

'Do you really think America or any of the Western powers want to invade you?' 'Well, they have very strange ideas on Germany. We promised during the war to divide the country between us but now they will not work with us. I will give you an example. The Germans have done such terrible damage in our country that it has been agreed we should have machines from factories all over Germany to help us rebuild our industry. The Western powers are now refusing to send us machines from their zones. Instead, they are helping the Germans to start their factories working again. Do they want to make Germany rich and powerful once more, so that she can start a third World War?

'Also, we cannot forget that the Americans have the atom bomb. Because of that we have to keep the Red Army at full strength. Our young men are badly needed at home, but we dare not let them return.'

Now we will talk to an American senator.

'Why do you distrust the Russians?' 'They want to turn the whole world communist, that's why.'

'What makes you think so?' 'Look what happened in Poland towards the end of the war. The people of Warsaw rebelled against the occupying Germans.

Eastern European countries occupied by Russia

Communist not under Russian control

Iron Curtain

Russian Satellite States

Territory added to Russia

victory parade in Moscow 1945

'During the war the Red Army took all of Eastern Europe. It should clear out now and let those people alone, but it stays put. The only reason for that is to make sure that all those countries go communist and stay communist.

'Another thing, why have they still got millions of men under arms? The war is over, isn't it? What they want is to overrun the whole of Europe, right up to the Atlantic. It sure is a good thing for Europe that we have the atom bomb. That has made Stalin stop and think.'

'There have been problems with Germany, haven't there?' 'Yes Sir, there certainly have! Most of the big cities are in the American and British zones and the Russians promised they would send food from their zone which has the best farmland. They didn't play ball. They haven't sent any food, so it has had to come from Britain and the United States. Meantime, the Russians have been robbing German factories of their machinery as fast as they could go. Germany has been just like a cow, with Britain and the United States feeding her, while the Russians have milked her dry. We have told the Russians that if they don't send food, they won't get any machines. Instead we have helped the Germans start up their factories again. That way they can earn the money to buy their own food.'

Stalin's armies were a few miles away. Did he send those armies to help the Poles? No Sir! He halted them where they were. He didn't want a free, independent Poland. He wanted her crushed and broken. When he saw what Hitler was doing to Warsaw, he thought, "Fine, that saves us a job." Only when Warsaw was destroyed did Stalin order his armies forward.

'Why don't you try to reach an agreement with the Russians?' 'We have tried just that, but all Stalin has ever said was "Niet", and that means "No". You can't do business with the Russians. As Churchill has said, they have put down an iron curtain, right across Europe. The communists are on one side and the free countries of the west on the other.'

damage done by Germans in Russia

3 America and Her Allies

It is 1952. An English M.P. will tell us about his country's problems after the war.

'When Germany was defeated in 1945, all Britain went wild with joy. We soon realised, though, that we still had plenty to worry us. We had done our best to work with the Russians during the war, but it wasn't easy. When it was over they seemed to turn completely hostile. They are communists and they want the whole world to be communist too.

'Communists believe in taking power by force, you know, as they did in Russia itself in 1917. You could see what was going to happen as soon as the war ended. The Russians kept their armies in all the countries they had occupied and then they stirred up a revolution in Greece. We sent troops to help the Greek government fight the rebels.

'We were even more worried about our near neighbours, France and Italy. There are a lot of communists in those two countries. Suppose they had started a revolution and called in the Red Army to help them? We should have had Russians on the other side of the Channel and in the Mediterranean, which would have been as bad as having Germans there.

'Another of our problems was that we had spent nearly every penny we had to fight the war. Food was still rationed, and do you know, those rations were lower than during the war. It wasn't just the food, either. We didn't have enough raw materials for our factories. Imagine a man who has a shoe factory, but no money to buy leather. Our whole country was like that. We didn't have the cash to get going again.

'Meanwhile, there was the war in Greece. Even though we were worried about communists, we could not afford to go on with it. In 1947 we told the Americans we simply had to pull out of Greece.

'In a way we had been worried about the Americans, too. After the First World War they took all their soldiers home, vowing they would never return. They said they would leave the Old World of Europe to "stew in its own juice." They did nothing to help us stop Hitler, and they only entered the Second World War when the Japanese booted them into it by attacking Pearl Harbor. What would they do now? Would they go home, as they had done before, and leave us at the mercy of the Russians?

Truman   Marshall

'We soon had our answer. When we pulled our troops out of Greece, the Americans at once sent help. The Greek communists have now been crushed. Also, in 1947, President Truman made a speech. He said that it was America's duty to help free peoples all over the world. We called this the Truman Doctrine. The President didn't mention the Russians, and he didn't mention communists, but we knew what he meant.

'The Truman Doctrine was good news, but better followed. In 1948 the American Secretary of State, George Marshall, said his government was going to give the countries of Western Europe billions of dollars to put them back on their feet. This was known as Marshall Aid. You remember what I said about Britain being like a shoe manufacturer with no money to buy leather? Now, it was as if a friend had come along and given him the money he needed. He wouldn't have to go on taking help. As soon as he was making shoes, he could buy his own leather. Marshall Aid was like that for us and all the other countries in Western Europe. It gave us the push to get started again.

'What was in it for the Americans? Well, they didn't want us to turn communist. People do that when they are poor and miserable, so the Americans decided to save us from being poor. As President Truman said, Marshall Aid and the Truman Doctrine were "two halves of the same walnut".

NATO forces on manoeuvres

'Later, in 1949, most of the important countries in the west formed an alliance – the North Atlantic Treaty Organisation (N.A.T.O.) America and Britain are in it, of course, and even little states like Iceland.

'All these plans have worked. Western Europe is now richer than before the war, so the communist parties in France and Italy aren't nearly as powerful as they were. As for Russia, she will think hard before she attacks any country in N.A.T.O.. America now has the hydrogen bomb, and Britain has nuclear weapons, too. Between us we could destroy Russia completely.'

NATO Countries at 1952

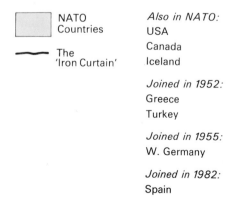

NATO Countries

The 'Iron Curtain'

Also in NATO:
USA
Canada
Iceland

Joined in 1952:
Greece
Turkey

Joined in 1955:
W. Germany

Joined in 1982:
Spain

4 Russia and Her Allies: Hungary, 1956

At the end of the Second World War Russian armies overran the countries of Eastern Europe. Stalin then forced them to have communist governments like his own in Russia, and he made them do exactly as he ordered. We call the Eastern European states Russian 'satellites'. A Hungarian lawyer tells us what happened in his country.

'After the war Hungary was ruled by a communist of the worst sort, Matyas Rakosi. The newspapers had to print only what he wanted, and no one dared to criticise him. He had a force of secret police, the A.H.V., who arrested anyone they thought might be against him. Thousands of innocent people were sent to concentration camps where many were tortured and killed. Nor was it just the victims of the A.H.V. who suffered. Because the government was so bad the country was in a dreadful state and all ordinary people were becoming poorer the whole time. Meanwhile, Rakosi and our other communist bosses were living in luxury.

'We all hated Rakosi, but we knew that the real villain was the man who had put him in power, Josef Stalin. Well, Stalin died in 1953 so we were quite hopeful. Then in 1956, Khrushchev made a speech denouncing Stalin. We thought that if Khrushchev disliked Stalin, he would not help Stalin's puppet, Rakosi. The Hungarian people rose in rebellion and there were riots all over the country. We demanded workers' councils, the right to say what we pleased and higher wages. In Budapest we pulled down the huge statue of Stalin. It fell with a great crash and everyone cheered. An old woman came rushing up, shouting "Turn him over. I want to spit on his face! Let me spit on his face!" The A.H.V. started to machine gun the crowds, but we hunted them down. Three that we wounded were taken to hospital, so we went there and demanded to have them. The hospital staff refused at first, but in the end they brought them out on stretchers. We trampled them to death. I shall always remember their bodies, lying under the trees, with the autumn leaves drifting down on them.

'Rakosi fled, and Imre Nagy became our prime minister. He was a communist, too, but quite a different kind of man. He had all the political prisoners released and he allowed the newspapers to print what they liked. He

Rakosi   Nagy

also told Khrushchev he wanted his country to be neutral. He knew that if there was a war, few Hungarians would want to fight for the Russians. I think that was his big mistake, for Russia needs Hungary as part of her shield against America. A few days later, Russian bombs were falling on Budapest, and Russian tanks were rumbling through the streets.

'Hungarians are not afraid to die. We pelted the tanks with petrol bombs and men even wrenched open their hatches to drop hand grenades inside them. Our one hope was that the Americans would do something. Our radio stations sent out frantic appeals for help, but what did the Americans do? Nothing! It seems they were scared of the Russians. In Budapest I saw Russian soldiers fleeing from Hungarian children but the American people were too frightened to act!

'The Russians were quite ruthless. I saw one of their tanks dragging two bodies behind it, just to scare us. If there was a single shot from a building, they destroyed it with gunfire. In the end they killed 20,000 of our people, and the rest of us laid down our arms. The Russians made Janos Kadar prime minister. He is just as bad as Rakosi. The members of the A.H.V. came out of hiding, and rounded up suspects in their thousands. Many were executed. I was lucky to escape across the Austrian frontier with my family. I believe that about 200,000 Hungarians fled.'

You might like to know what happened to Imre Nagy. He took refuge in the Yugoslav embassy, but after a while Kadar promised him that if he went home he would be left in peace. As soon as he left the embassy, some Russian soldiers seized him. Two years later, he was put on trial and executed.

Right: Russian tanks quelling the Hungarian uprising

5 Russia and Her Allies: Poland, 1981

Poland is the most important of Russia's satellites, and like all the others she has a communist government. Not only has it been unpopular, but it has been inefficient as well. Poland's mines, factories and farms have not produced anything like as much as they could have done, so there have been shortages of all kinds.

A worker at the shipyard at Gdansk tells us about his country and its problems in 1981.

'Of all the nations of Europe, Poland is the most unhappy. She is sandwiched between Germany and Russia, so what else can you expect?

'Look what happened in 1939. Hitler said we were ill-treating the Germans who lived in our country. It was a lie, but he used it as an excuse to invade us. Soon we heard there were Russian armies advancing from the east. We were delighted at first because we thought they were coming to help us. It was not that at all. Hitler and Stalin had agreed to divide Poland between them, and the Russians were simply grabbing their share. Our armies soon had to surrender.

'During the war we suffered terribly. Well over four million of our people died. Three-quarters of them were Polish Jews. The Germans hated the Jews and they built special concentration camps so that they could kill them, thousands at a time.

'All through the war men in our resistance movement kept up the fight against the Germans. They were a great help to the Russians when they advanced through our country in 1944. The Russians showed their gratitude by arresting and shooting many of those brave fellows. I must also tell you about the massacre of Katyn. While they were in Russia the Germans said they had found a mass grave in a wood at Katyn, near Smolensk. In it were the bodies of thousands of Polish officers, who had been murdered in cold blood. Hitler said the Russians were responsible, while Stalin said it was the Germans. They were as bad as each other. It could have been either.

'When the war ended the Russians took a great tract of our country in the east and gave us some of Germany as compensation. It was as if Poland had

changes in Poland's frontiers

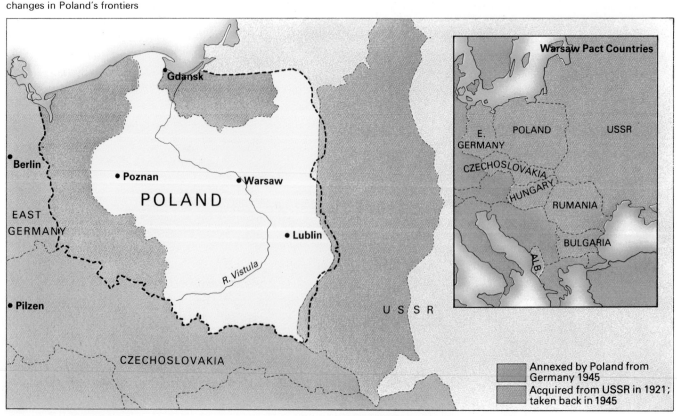

poster depicting the Katyn massacre

Les mŕtvych v **Katyne**

Pope John Paul II

Lech Walesa

been pushed westward a hundred miles. That meant of course, that there were several million Germans in Poland. We at once ordered them to leave. We remembered what had happened in 1939! Other East European countries did the same, so that four million Germans were driven from their homes. Who can blame us?

'The Russians wanted us to be on their side, so they made sure we had a communist government which was friendly to them. I look on the men in that government as traitors. Then, in 1955, the western countries were foolish enough to let West Germany join N.A.T.O. The idea that Germany would once again have an army frightened all of us in the east. The Russians made us join an alliance with them called the Warsaw Pact. I'm sure they look on Poland as a shield between them and the west. The trouble with being a shield is that in a fight you take all the knocks.

'There has been trouble at home, too. We do not like our communist government. Communists do not believe in God, and most Poles are good Roman Catholics. As you know, Pope John Paul II is a Pole. His election was an honour for all of us. More than that, life is hard under communism. Every year we grow poorer. I have to work for a day to earn enough money to buy a kilo of sausages, and then my wife has to queue for hours to buy them. We even have to queue for vinegar.

'By 1980 our patience was at an end. There were strikes all over Poland, especially here in Gdansk. The workers formed a movement called Solidarity and elected a leader, Lech Walesa. Until then our trade unions were run by communists who did just as the government said. Lech Walesa made the government agree to us having our own, free trade unions, with the right to strike. The British trade unions were quick to send us their congratulations! It was the first real piece of freedom we had won since the war. The Russians were furious, and called out their army. It was for military exercises, so they said, but really it was to threaten us. I do not think they will attack us, for they know we would fight.

'The recent troubles have not been the only ones. Back in 1970 there was a strike in this very shipyard and the communists killed 56 workers. We have now put up a memorial to them. Today, every young couple that marries in Gdansk comes to the monument to be photographed. This is the spirit we have in Poland.'

In December 1981 the Polish Commander-in-Chief, General Jaruzelski, proclaimed martial law and crushed Solidarity. Probably he was acting on orders from Moscow.

6 The Cuban Missile Crisis, 1962

The ministry which looks after America's relations with other countries is called the State Department. In this section one of its officials tells us what happened between his country and Russia in 1962. Probably, it was the closest the world has come to a nuclear war.

'We found it difficult to have any dealings with the Russians in Stalin's day. If ever we made a suggestion he usually answered "Niet" which is the Russian for "No". It seemed to be the only word in his vocabulary. We noticed a big change when Khrushchev took over in 1953. His phrase was "peaceful coexistence". That seemed to mean he wanted to make some kind of deal with us.

'Well, Khrushchev certainly tried. Stalin hardly ever left the Kremlin, let alone Russia. Khrushchev was willing to go anywhere. He visited Britain, he visited the United States and in 1960 he agreed to meet our President "Ike" Eisenhower in Paris. They were going to have a "summit conference" to settle the world's problems.

'It sure was an unlucky conference. In those days we were sending U-2 planes over Russia to take photographs. They flew very high, and for a long time the Russians couldn't touch them. Then, just as the Paris conference was beginning, they shot one of them

Fidel Castro

down. Khrushchev was spitting mad that these spy planes were flying over his country, and he told Ike he must apologise. Ike refused, so Khrushchev just packed up and went home. End of conference!

'Things got even more interesting in 1962. That was the year of the Cuban crisis. Cuba had been ruled by a dictator called Batista. No one liked him, so most Cubans felt pretty good when Fidel Castro led a

how Russian missiles in Cuba would have threatened the USA

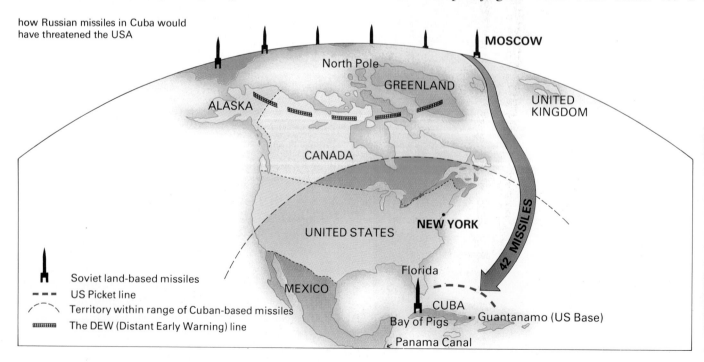

- Soviet land-based missiles
- - - US Picket line
- Territory within range of Cuban-based missiles
- The DEW (Distant Early Warning) line

Russian ships carrying missiles to Cuba

rebellion that threw him out. But we Americans weren't at all pleased with Castro. He was a communist and he made friends with the Russians.

'By this time we had a new President, John F. Kennedy. Kennedy thought it was bad enough that there were Russian satellite states in Eastern Europe, without having one on his doorstep. There were some Cuban exiles, enemies of Castro, living in the United States and Kennedy gave them weapons and boats so that they could overthrow Castro. They landed at the Bay of Pigs in 1961, but instead of licking Castro, they let his troops round them up without making a proper fight. Castro was a frightened man, though. He was afraid there would soon be a proper American invasion which would succeed. Khrushchev had a lot to worry about, too, for how could he protect his friend? In the end he decided to put some nuclear missiles in Cuba. That would make us think twice before attacking!

'In 1962 another of our U-2 spy planes photographed these missile sites the Russians were building. At the State Department we nearly went out of our minds. We knew the Russians had missiles pointed at us in their own country, but they were the other side of the North Pole, and we had an early warning system all across northern Canada to tell us when they were coming. Now the Russians were going to put these things right behind us, only ninety miles from Florida and in easy range of most of our big cities!

'This was a real test for Kennedy. If he did nothing, then the Russians would finish the missile sites and have us at their mercy. If he attacked Cuba, he risked a nuclear war with Russia. But he did neither. He told Khrushchev the U.S. navy was going to blockade Cuba to stop any ships carrying nuclear weapons there. He also said the Russians must break up their missile sites. Waiting for the answer was really tough, I can tell you. Luckily Khrushchev was as scared of nuclear war as we were. Finally, he agreed to do what President Kennedy wanted, as long as the United States promised never to invade Cuba. That was a small price to pay, so the President was quick to agree.

'We were careful not to crow about our success, and Khrushchev talked about a "victory for common sense". But the whole world knew he had had to back down. I think that must have been one of the main reasons why his buddies in the Kremlin got rid of him two years later.'

U-2 photograph of missile sites

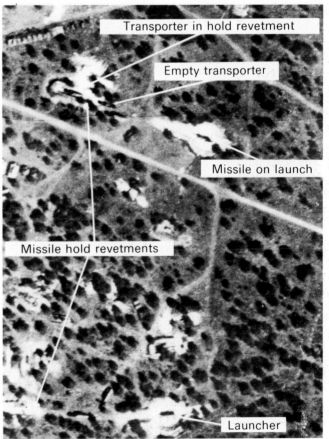

Transporter in hold revetment

Empty transporter

Missile on launch

Missile hold revetments

Launcher

7 America and Vietnam

Vietnam is a land of about 30 million inhabitants. Once it was part of a French colony called Indo-China, but after the Second World War its people rebelled. In 1954, the French had to leave. The country was then divided into two. The north had a communist government under Ho Chi Minh. The south had an anti-communist government under Ngo Dinh Diem. While Ho Chi Minh won the support of his people, Ngo Dinh Diem only bothered about the rich, and was cruel to the ordinary folk, especially the peasants. Soon, some of the South Vietnamese formed a communist party of their own, calling themselves the Vietcong, or Vietnamese Communists. They started a civil war to try and overthrow Diem.

The American government became alarmed. If the communists seized power in South Vietnam they might do so, in time, in all the countries of South-East Asia. President Eisenhower said it was like a row of dominoes – push one down, and they all go. This, the Americans were determined to prevent. At first they sent Ngo Dinh Diem weapons, but his army still could not defeat the Vietcong. They then sent soldiers of their own, and in the end 500,000 Americans were fighting in Vietnam.

It is 1970 and we will talk to an American newspaper reporter who has just come back from Vietnam.

'How is the war going for the Americans?' 'Badly. The Vietcong use guerrilla tactics, killing our men in sneak attacks and then vanishing into the jungle. If we make life too hot for them, they hide their weapons and mingle with the ordinary people of the village. Suppose a G.I. sees a peasant working peacefully in a rice field. For all he knows that man was taking pot shots at him from behind a tree the day before.'

'But don't the villagers know if the man is one of the Vietcong?' 'Sure they do. But they are on the side of the Vietcong. Our government says the V.C. destroy schools and hospitals and terrorise the people. That's all lies. The V.C. know what Mao Tse-tung said in China – guerrillas are like fish and peasants are the sea in which they swim. The V.C. treat the peasants kindly, help them with their farming and so on. Sure they kill government officials and landlords, but the peasants love that.'

'What do the American forces do?' 'Something I hate to see. They cannot tell the V.C. from the peasants, so they have as good as declared war on the whole civilian population of South Vietnam. Soldiers go on "search and destroy" operations. Their motto appears to be, "If it's yellow and it moves, kill it". They don't seem to look on Vietnamese as human beings. They call them "gooks" and "dinks". One of our generals hunts them from a helicopter, with a rifle. Back in 1968 some of our guys shot all the inhabitants of the village of My Lai – 500 of them. They killed the lot, men, women and children, and for no reason.

'Mainly our forces rely on air strikes. They spray trees with chemicals to kill the leaves, so the V.C. can't hide. They spray the rice crop with chemicals, so they can't eat – and nor can anyone else. They drop bombs

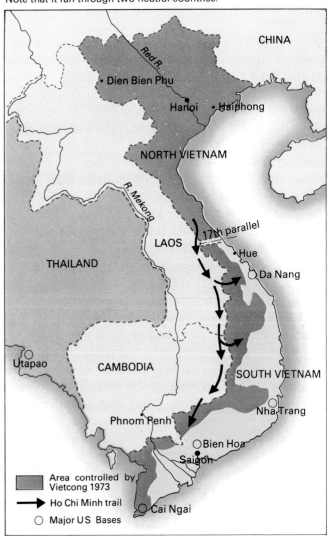

the Vietnam war. The Ho Chi Minh trail was the route along which the North Vietnamese sent weapons and supplies to the Vietcong. Note that it ran through two neutral countries.

refugees in Vietnam

of all kinds – high explosive bombs, bombs that scatter thousands of bits of sharp metal, like razor blades, and napalm bombs. I think the napalm bombs are the worst. They send out great sheets of flame. I have visited hospital wards full of the victims of napalm, covered in burns. I don't know how many were V.C., but well over half were village women.'

'*Where do the communists get their weapons?*' 'From the North Vietnamese, and they in turn get them from Russia and China.'

'*Can't your people cut off these supplies?*' 'They sure have tried. They have rained down bombs on the cities of North Vietnam, but Ho Chi Minh's answer was to send men of his regular army south to help the Vietcong. It's no use, the more we bomb the Vietnamese, the harder they fight.'

During the war in Vietnam the Americans dropped $2\frac{1}{2}$ million tons of bombs – more than fell in the whole of the Second World War. It was 70 tons for every square mile of Vietnam, or over 300 lb for each one of her inhabitants. Two million Vietnamese died, and four million were wounded. The Americans lost heavily, too, with 100,000 men killed or wounded.

Back in the United States, people saw the full horror of the war every evening on their colour television sets. Coffins and wounded soldiers came home in growing numbers. The cost rose to $2,000 million every month. There were demonstrations and angry scenes in many cities until, in 1973, the American government withdrew its forces. Within two years the communists had conquered the whole of South Vietnam.

America and Vietnam

American soldiers

2nd Lieutenant, US Infantry

Sergeant, US Special Forces

Chief Warrant Officer, US 1st
Cavalry Div. (Airmobile)

Vietnamese soldiers

'Viet Cong'

Cambodian 'Khmer Rouge'

Enlisted man, North
Vietnamese Army

Right: American helicopter gunship in action

8 America and China

capturing a Communist prisoner

In 1950 China signed a Treaty of Friendship with Russia. At that time she was on bad terms with the United States; indeed, before the end of the year the armies of the two countries were fighting each other in Korea. By the 1970s, though, China and America were the best of friends, and looked on Russia as their common enemy. Why did China change sides like that? One of her leaders Teng Hsiao-ping will tell us about it.

'Can you say why China and the United States used to be enemies?' 'To help you understand that I must explain that for over 20 years there was a bitter civil war in China. We, the communists, fought against the nationalists under Chiang Kai-shek. He was a wicked man, as were many of his followers. He was very cruel to the ordinary people of China, especially the peasants. Even so, the Americans helped him by sending him weapons.'

'Why did they do that?' 'Because he was against communists, as the Americans are themselves.'

'What happened to Chiang Kai-shek?' 'We defeated him in the end and our leader Mao Tse-tung proclaimed the People's Republic of China. Chiang fled to Taiwan with the remains of his army. The Americans sent their Seventh Fleet to protect him. He hid behind it, reorganising his forces, and threatening to come back and attack us. How could we be friends with America when she was helping our worst enemy?'

'Did you have any more quarrels with the Americans?' 'There were two that were especially serious. In 1950 there was a war in Korea. Our communist brothers in North Korea fought against the South Koreans. The Americans joined in, defeated the North Koreans and overran almost all their country. Since we did not want them right on our doorstep, we warned them to go away. They refused, so volunteers from our People's Liberation Army drove them out of North Korea.'

'What was the second quarrel?' 'That was over Vietnam. Here again was a country that was communist in the north, but had a government friendly to the United States in the south. Most of the southerners wanted a communist government themselves, so they started guerrilla warfare against their ruler Ngo Dinh Diem. He was as bad as Chiang Kai-shek, but again the

Americans helped him. We sent weapons to our friends in North Vietnam and they sent them on to their communist brothers in South Vietnam. The Americans could not defeat the guerrillas, and they dared not invade North Vietnam. They knew we would join the war if they did that. They were afraid to tangle with the People's Liberation Army a second time. In the end, the Americans had to leave Vietnam, but I think their defeat did them good.'

'Why do you say that?' It made them realise that China was too powerful for them to challenge, so it was better to have us as friends than as enemies.'

'But why did you want to become friendly with the Americans?' 'Because we quarrelled with the Russians. They are communists, as you know, so when we won our civil war, Chairman Mao Tse-tung turned to them. He wanted them to help us build modern factories to make China rich. In fact the Russians gave us very little help, and they stopped sending it altogether after a time. Also they refused to back us up against the Americans. Even after they had the hydrogen bomb themselves, they made it plain they would not help us in a war. They were afraid for their skins. Things went from bad to worse. Twice,

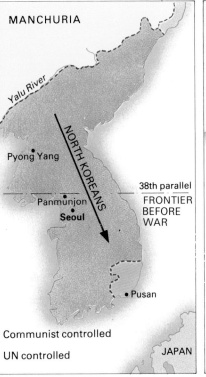

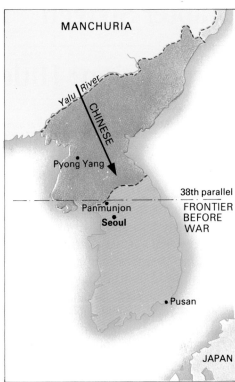

MANCHURIA

Yalu River

NORTH KOREANS

Pyong Yang

Panmunjon
Seoul

• Pusan

38th parallel
FRONTIER
BEFORE
WAR

Communist controlled

UN controlled

JAPAN

MANCHURIA

Yalu River

UN FORCES (American)

Pyong Yang

Panmunjon
Seoul

• Pusan

38th parallel
FRONTIER
BEFORE
WAR

JAPAN

MANCHURIA

Yalu River

CHINESE

Pyong Yang

Panmunjon
Seoul

• Pusan

38th parallel
FRONTIER
BEFORE
WAR

JAPAN

orea, June 1950
orth Koreans attacked in June 1950,
d occupied all but the south-east
rner of South Korea

Korea, November 1950
United Nations forces, mainly American, drove
back the North Koreans and occupied most of
their country

Korea 1950–1953
the Chinese came to the rescue of the North
Koreans, and drove the Americans back,
almost to the original frontier. An
armistice was signed in 1953

esident Nixon in China

units of the People's Liberation Army have fought
pitched battles with Russian forces on our northern
frontier.

'I'm afraid it was useless for us to try to make
friends with the Russians. We Chinese have always
distrusted them, ever since they tried to seize much of
our country back in the nineteenth century.'

'How did your friendship with America begin?' 'In a
strange way. A team of their table tennis players
visited China for some matches. We called it "ping-
pong diplomacy". That was in 1971. In 1972
President Nixon himself came, and met Chairman
Mao. Mao was pleased to see him. He realised China
could not be on bad terms with both Russia *and*
America, the two most powerful countries in the
world. I am sure, though, that Mao could never have
really trusted the Americans. They had been his
enemies for too long.'

*'But Mao is dead, so how does that affect China and the
United States?'* 'Mao died in 1976. Since then our
friendship with America has grown a great deal. We
are trading with her and she is even sending us
weapons. It is hard to realise that only a few years ago
she was doing everything she could to harm us.'

277

Chapter Sixteen   Hitler's Germany

1 Introduction: Hitler Speaks, 1932

At the end of 1918, when it was obvious that Germany had lost the war, the Kaiser fled to Holland and Germany became a Republic. The head of state was a President elected by the people. He had a lot of power since he was commander in chief of the armed forces and he chose the Chancellor or prime minister. There was also a Reichstag, or parliament, and this too was elected by the people.

We call the new form of government the Weimar Republic because the laws which brought it into being were made in the town of Weimar. After 1925 the President was Paul von Hindenburg. He was a general who had won many victories during the First World War, and was much admired by the German people.

The Weimar Republic had many problems and in the end, Hitler was able to overthrow it and make himself dictator.

In some ways Hitler was insane, as you will see from the hatred he showed different races, especially

Hitler

the Jews. In other ways he was brilliant, for example at giving speeches. He could make an audience weep, he could hold it spellbound in silence, he could make it shout with excitement or rage. He could play on it, almost as a musician plays on an instrument.

In this section, Hitler tells us about himself. It is 1932.

Hitler at a meeting of the German Workers' Party

Rohm

'I was born in Austria in 1889. As a young man I went to live in Vienna. My ambition was to become an artist, but I could find no one to help me. I made a little money painting and selling picture postcards, but I had to live among tramps and criminals. My clothes were in rags and full of lice, and I was often hungry.

'In those days Vienna was the capital of Austria–Hungary, a state made up of many different races. I soon learnt to admire the German race, to which I belong as an Austrian. I also learnt to despise all the others, particularly the Jews. There is no evil in the world for which the Jews are not responsible, at least in part. I know for a fact that they are plotting to destroy the German people. Jews are the friends of the communists, and I despise them, too. They talk a lot of nonsense about the workers in different countries being "brothers". How can a German be the brother of some inferior being like a Russian or a Pole? The Germans are a master race, as I shall one day prove.

'When the war broke out in 1914 I joined the German army. The war years were the best of my life, and I never left the trenches, even when I had leave. I won the Iron Cross for bravery, but my officers disliked me so I rose no higher than lance corporal.

'In 1918 I was gassed and was in hospital when Germany surrendered. I could not believe it. Everything went black before my eyes as I staggered back to my ward and buried my aching head between the blankets and pillows. The German army had not been defeated, of course. It had been stabbed in the back by the politicians, the communists and the Jews.

'After the war I joined a little group in Munich called the German Workers' Party. It was just a debating society, with only 40 members, but I soon changed all that. By 1920 we had hundreds of members and we renamed ourselves the National Socialist, or Nazi Party.

'Under my leadership the Nazi Party has grown. We even have a private army of brown shirted stormtroopers, the S.A. Their commander is General Ernst Rohm, a great personal friend. I am sure we shall soon be in power. There are six million unemployed in Germany. I have promised them work, so they are giving me their votes. There are many communists, but my stormtroopers are smashing them. Wealthy Germans fear the communists, so they give me money to pay the stormtroopers. Meanwhile the country is in complete chaos. President Hindenburg has had three Chancellors in one year, and none of them has been able to do anything. Soon he will have to make me Chancellor. People ask me why I don't seize power by force as I am certainly strong enough to do. But Hindenburg was our greatest general during the war, and the people worship him. Much as I despise the old cab horse, I need him. When he makes me Chancellor, my name will be linked with his and I shall have absolute control of Germany.

'When I am in power I shall destroy our enemies at home, the Jews and the communists. I shall once again make Germany the greatest country in Europe, even if it means fighting another war. I shall found an Empire which will last for a thousand years.'

2 A Member of the S.A., January 1933

The letters S.A. stand for Sturmabteilungen or 'Stormtroopers'. They were a private army which Hitler formed to terrorise his enemies. In the end it was two million strong. Here one of its members explains why he joined.

'The years just after the war were grim. First there was the peace treaty. Germany lost a lot of territories, but what made me angry was being forced to admit that we had started the war. Everyone knows it was Russia and France, encouraged by Britain, but no, we had to take the blame. Because we were supposed to be guilty, our enemies said we must pay the cost of the war – thousands of millions of marks. Of course we could not find all that money and the next thing we knew was that the French had sent an army into the Ruhr. They said that if they could not have our cash they would have our coal. Everyone in the Ruhr was determined France should have nothing at all, so they stopped work.

'With the Ruhr in French hands most of our industry ground to a halt. Worse than that, our money suddenly started to lose all its value. Prices shot up. To give you some idea, a loaf that cost half a mark in

the Ruhr

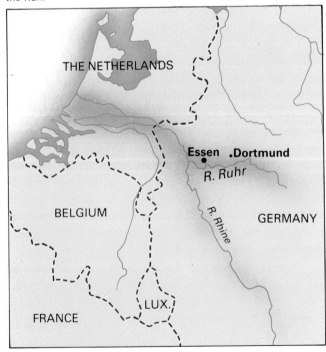

Stormtrooper

1922, cost 200,000 million marks by the end of 1923. My wages went up, of course, but not nearly as fast. I used to give my wife my pay packet at the factory gate on Friday morning, and she went shopping at once. It would have been fatal to wait until evening, for prices sometimes doubled in a single day. The people I felt sorry for were my parents. They had worked all their lives and put by enough money to buy a little house for their retirement. In the matter of a few months their life's savings dropped in value until they were only worth the price of a postage stamp.

'Then Stresemann became Chancellor. He made an agreement with the French, who took their soldiers home; he scrapped all the worthless money and we had new marks; the Americans made us generous loans. After that things weren't too bad for a few years.

'In 1930 there was another disaster. It wasn't prices this time, but unemployment. I lost my job, and so did six million other Germans. The government did not know what to do. The deputies squabbled in the Reichstag, we had one Chancellor after another, and all the time things were getting worse.

kites made from banknotes

'One day I went to hear Hitler speak. It was night time. The town square was packed with people, and huge black and red flags with swastikas hung from the buildings. In the distance we heard the clash and blare of military bands, and the steady tramp of marching feet. Hundreds of brown shirted men – stormtroopers – came into the square to take up their positions. Suddenly, a dozen search lights were switched on, their beams meeting high in the sky. At once there was complete silence. Hitler began to speak. His every word went to my heart and I listened spellbound. He talked about the unfair peace treaty, and the sufferings of the German people since the war. He laid the blame for it all where it belonged – on the feeble politicians who did not know how to govern and on the communists and Jews all over the world, who were plotting to destroy us. He promised that when he came to power he would get rid of the lot of them and make Germany

a great nation once again, feared by the rest of Europe. We clapped and cheered at everything he said, and when he had finished the band struck up the national anthem "Deutschland Uber Alles" – "Germany above All". I sang at the top of my voice, until I was quite hoarse.

'The next day I joined the stormtroopers. I am proud to wear the uniform with the brown shirt, and to be recognised as one of Hitler's most loyal followers. Our job was to see he won the election. Our most dangerous rivals were the communists, but we tore down their posters and we broke up their meetings. That was dangerous for they are a vicious lot and will fight with any weapons they can find such as chains and broken bottles. Whenever we could, we got hold of their speaker. I remember we caught one as he was escaping from the hall by a side door. We kicked him to death in the gutter.

'Well, the Nazis did win more votes than any other party, so Hindenburg has had to make Hitler Chancellor. Things will start moving now. I am sure Hitler will reward the S.A. as soon as he can. After all, we brought him to power. I expect to be in a comfortable, well-paid job before too long. A position in the Civil Service would suit me very well.'

next page: a Nazi rally

3 Field Marshal Paul von Hindenburg, March 1933

Hindenburg

Hindenburg was Germany's greatest general and a national hero. In this section he tells us what happened after the war and explains how Hitler became dictator.

'In 1918 it was the Social Democrats who formed the first government of the new Weimar Republic, for they were the largest political party in Germany at that time. The President, Ebert, was a Social Democrat, so was his Chancellor, Scheidemann, and so were many deputies in the Reichstag. The Social Democrats stand for the average German, who is neither rich nor very poor.

'I am a Nationalist. My party stands for the great landowners, the important factory owners and the high ranking army officers. In 1925 Ebert died and the German people elected me President. By this time we had recovered from the French occupation of the Ruhr in 1923 and the country prospered. Unhappily, we depended too much on American loans and when in 1930 the Americans wanted their money back we were in deep trouble. Our factories ground to a halt, and millions of people became unemployed.

'At the same time the communists were rearing their heads. They won one-sixth of the seats in the Reichstag, and their armed gangs roamed the streets. There was another threat, too. A Bohemian corporal called Hitler had formed what he called the Nazi Party. His people brawled with the communists. Many of our richest and most respectable families gave Hitler money because they thought he would save Germany from the communists. Many of the unemployed supported him because he promised them work. The man even had the impudence to stand against me in the Presidential election of 1932. He lost, of course, but millions of Germans were misguided enough to vote for him.

'Now was the time for the political parties to unite for the good of the Fatherland, but they did no such thing. We had several elections but no one party could win a majority, and the members of the Reichstag just quarrelled among themselves. In 1932 I dismissed Bruning, the Chancellor, and appointed Franz von Papen in his place. He is a real Prussian gentleman, and he and I get on very well together. Then von Papen had to resign and I appointed Schleicher. Still

Germany was in turmoil, but in the end von Papen found what he thought was the answer. He came to me and said, "You and I favour the Nationalist Party which stands for everything that is good in Germany. The trouble is that we do not win votes. It is the Nazis who do that. I suggest you make Hitler Chancellor on condition he works with the Nationalists. I will be the Vice-Chancellor, most of the Cabinet will be Nationalists, and we can use Hitler for our own ends." "Make the Bohemian corporal Chancellor!" I replied, "I wouldn't put him in charge of the post office!" '

'Finally, though, von Papen persuaded me.

'As soon as Hitler became Chancellor, there was a fire in the Reichstag. A Dutch communist, Van Der Lubbe was caught in the burning building, and the Nazis screamed that there had been a communist plot. I had to sign a decree giving Hitler power to arrest anyone he pleased. He at once rounded up all the communist members of the Reichstag.

'Shortly afterwards we had a ceremony at Potsdam church. I attended in my Field Marshal's uniform, and all the great men of Germany were present. Hitler made a most impressive speech in which he told us of his earnest wish to solve our country's problems. He then came to shake my hand, bowing low before me. For that moment at least I trusted him and so did everyone present. Two days later the Reichstag passed a law making him dictator.

'During the Potsdam ceremony I went alone to the crypt, to pray at the tomb of Frederick the Great. Through all these troubles I have done what I firmly believed was my duty. I can only hope that I will be proved right.'

Hindenburg and Hitler

4 Germany in 1939

Hindenburg died in 1934, and as no new President was elected, Hitler had complete control of Germany. He took the title of 'Fuhrer' or 'Leader'. In this section you will learn about life in Germany after he came to power.

First we will talk with the same S.A. man who spoke to us in Section 2.

'Why did you think Hitler would be grateful to the S.A.?' 'It was the S.A. that brought Hitler to power. We risked our lives fighting the communists for him, we persuaded people to vote for him, and we marched in processions shouting his praises. When he became Chancellor we were sure he would reward us by finding us jobs.'

'night of the long knives'

'*What did happen?*' 'Nothing, for a time, but then on the night of June 30th, 1934, suddenly, and without warning the S.S.* dragged all the leaders of the S.A. from their beds and murdered them! We call it the "night of the long knives". Even General Rohm our commander was killed. He was one of Hitler's best friends, but the S.S. shot him along with the rest. I went numb with horror at the time. I still can't understand it.'

Naturally the S.A. man was amazed, but Hitler had a reason for ordering the murders. He was afraid that the S.A. was becoming too strong and that its leader, Rohm, might seize power for himself.

Now we will talk to a Jewish business man.

'*How did you feel when Hitler became Fuhrer?*' 'The one thing we used to dread in the old days was that Hitler would come to power. When he did, our worst fears were realised.'

'*What happened?*' 'First of all "Jew baiting" became common. I had slogans painted on my shop window "This place belongs to a Jew. Don't shop here." Notices went up outside hotels and restaurants saying, "Jews not welcome". My little boy was attacked by some hooligans but when I complained to the police, they just ordered us away. Many shops would not serve us, and my wife found it difficult to buy milk for our baby. Then in 1935 Hitler passed the Nuremberg Laws. They said that Jews were no longer German citizens. That was a hard blow for me, for I had won the Iron Cross, First Class, fighting in the German army during the war. The real troubles began in November 1938. A Polish Jew murdered a German official in Paris, and the Nazis just went mad. They attacked and murdered our people; they set our synagogues on fire; they looted our homes and shops. So many windows were broken on November 9th that they called it "crystal night". A mob of youths set on me, while some policemen nearby pretended not to notice. An army officer told them to stop, but they just laughed at him. They beat and kicked me until I was unconscious. When the riots were over the government did not punish the criminals, but fined us Jews a billion marks!'

'*What do you think will become of you?*' 'I fear that my family and I will be sent to a concentration camp as has happened to many of our friends.'

Finally, we will talk to a factory foreman.

---

*S.S. stands for 'Schutzstaffeln' or 'protection units'. Originally they were Hitler's personal bodyguard, but later they had other duties, like running the concentration camps.

'Did you vote for Hitler in 1933?' 'Yes, and I'm sure I was right to do so.'

'Why do you think that?' 'Because the Fuhrer has made Germany prosper again. As soon as he came to power he started the "battle for work". He built motorways and public buildings which put a bit of money into the pockets of the men employed on them. They were able to buy goods, so before long all our factories sprang back into life. Soon after that we began to rearm. I work at Krupps, the armaments factory at Essen, and government orders keep pouring in. We cannot make guns and tanks fast enough. In 1933 we had six million unemployed in Germany. Now there are far more jobs than people to fill them. There is even a government scheme for every family to own a car. It will be "a people's car", or "Volkswagen".

'The Fuhrer has done more than give us back our jobs, he has given us back our pride. After the war the

early Volkswagen

allies made us give up a lot of our territory. That put millions of Germans under the rule of worthless foreigners, like Czechs and Poles. Now the Fuhrer is bringing these Germans into the Reich. Austria has joined us, we have destroyed Czechoslovakia and soon it will be the turn of Poland. Meanwhile our army and our airforce grow more powerful day by day. I hope there will not be another war, but if it comes it will not be like the last one. We will smash our enemies once and for all.'

'crystal night'

5 Germany and West Berlin since the Second World War

Hitler had boasted that his empire would last for a thousand years. It fell after twelve, with the end of the Second World War. As the bombs rained down and the allied armies came closer, Hitler realised he had lost and that he must die. He was determined, though, that as many of his people as possible should die with him, so he ordered the army to fight to the finish. Hitler committed suicide on April 30th, 1945. By then $4\frac{1}{2}$ million Germans had been killed and most German cities were in ruins.

When the fighting ended the Russians, Americans, British and French each occupied a part of Germany. They were supposed to rule the whole country between them, but the Russians and the Western Powers soon quarrelled. In 1949 the American, British and French joined their zones together to make the state of West Germany. They wanted it to grow rich and powerful and be on their side against the Russians.

That is just what has happened. Also in 1949, the Russians made their zone into the state of East Germany. They wanted it to be on their side against the Americans, and that, too, has happened. Meanwhile, many Germans are discontented about their country being split, and the most unhappy of all are the people of Berlin. Their city was treated like the rest of the country. First it was divided between the Russians, Americans, British and French, and later was split into West Berlin and East Berlin. That would have been bad enough if it had been on the frontier between West and East Germany, but it is 100 miles inside East Germany! A Berlin housewife will tell us what it was like to live there, just after the war.

'When the war ended, much of Berlin had been destroyed. Whole streets were blocked with rubble, the sewers were smashed, the water mains leaked in a thousand places and there was no gas and no

occupation zones of Germany and Berlin. In 1949 the British, French and American zones became the German Federal Republic (West Germany). The Russian zone became the German Democratic Republic (East Germany)

the ruins of Berlin

Berlin airlift

electricity. Also, the place swarmed with Russian soldiers who looted the homes that remained. Happily, the Americans, British and French soon arrived to take over their sectors and the rebuilding of the city began. Thousands of us women scraped mortar from the bricks so that they could be used again. They called us "trummerfrauen", "women of the ruins". My hands were soon red and raw, but as I scraped the bricks all I could think of was my husband who had been captured by the Russians. To this day I do not know what became of him.

'By 1948 we had gone a long way towards mending all the damage, but in that year there were new troubles. The Russians quarrelled with the Americans and refused to allow any goods in or out of West Berlin. There would be no more strawberries or asparagus from the Mark of Brandenberg and, what was far worse, there would be no more potatoes, and no more coal. Winter was coming, so we were sure we would either starve or freeze to death.

'The question everyone asked was what would the Americans and the British do? Would they abandon us to the Russians? Would they try to fight their way through and perhaps start a Third World War? We could not bear the thought of either. Then we heard

the rumble of aircraft landing at the Tempelhof Airport. We realised they were going to bring our coal and food by air. But there are over two million people in West Berlin, and we wondered if they could bring enough. During the war we dreaded the noise of American and British aeroplanes. Now we dreaded to hear it stop.

'The winter of 1948 was terrible. We had dried potatoes, which I hate, and hardly any meat, but plenty of Vitamin C tablets. Our weekly ration of coal barely filled a shopping basket, because almost all the airlifted coal went to the power stations. Even so, we were without electricity most of the time. I used to get up in the night to do my washing and ironing. But, in all that winter, dreadful as it was, I do not think a single Berliner died of cold or hunger. I cannot tell you how grateful I am to the pilots who saved us. One of them even used to drop packets of sweets for the children. He was called the "sweets bomber".

'After eleven months the Russians realised the western powers would never abandon Berlin, so they ended their blockade. We greeted the first train and lorry drivers with garlands of flowers.'

Berlin's troubles were still not over. The people of East Germany hated their communist government and many of them escaped. The frontier was closed, but they could go to West Berlin and fly from there to West Germany. By 1961 a thousand a day were doing this, so the East German government determined to stop them. To do so, it built a wall right round West Berlin. It is protected by three rows of barbed wire, and armed police with guard dogs patrol it all the time.

Other governments have built walls, but that was to keep their enemies out. The East Germans were the first to build one to keep their own people in.

Today, Germany is still divided and so is Berlin. This is part of the price of Hitler's war.

1 Introduction: Khrushchev Speaks, 1956

Russia's rulers are communists which means they are followers of Karl Marx. Marx was a German Jew, who lived in Britain in the nineteenth century. He wrote down his ideas in a book called *Capital.* Marx did not like the world of his day. He saw men, women and children working long hours, in unpleasant factories, for starvation wages. They had to do this because the factory owners wanted to make a lot of money. Marx called people like factory owners, landowners, merchants and bankers 'capitalists'. He said they were wicked because they were completely selfish.

Marx felt that for a long time things would get worse. He said that the poor people would become even poorer, and there would be far more of them. Meanwhile the rich would become richer and fewer in numbers until a handful of capitalists owned all the wealth in the world. At that point the ordinary people would join together and start a revolution. 'Workers of

Khrushchev

Russia

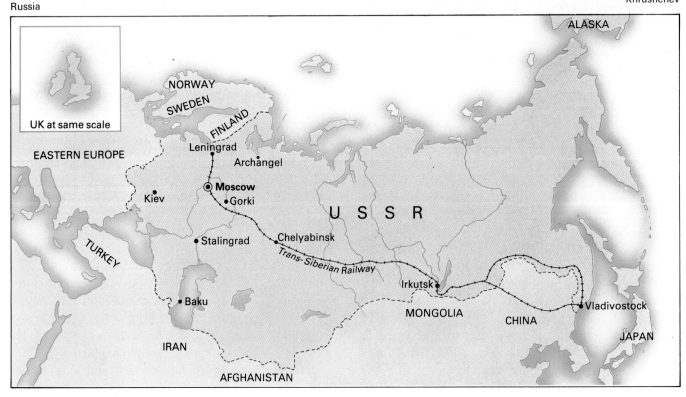

the world unite,' said Marx, 'you have only your chains to lose!' After the revolution, the workers would take over the factories, shops and offices and run them for everyone's benefit. The world would be communist and a wonderful place, for there would be no more selfishness. Also, people would give all they could and take only what they needed. The strong, healthy labourer and the skilful young doctor who were unmarried would work long hours for low wages. On the other hand, a sickly factory cleaner with a large family would have a lot of money for working, perhaps, two hours a day. 'From each according to his means, to each according to his needs,' was how Marx put it.

The world revolution never happened, but there was one in Russia in 1917. Nikita Khrushchev, who came to power there in 1956, will tell us about it.

'Earlier this century we were ruled by a tyrant of a Tsar,* Nicholas II, who kept order with the army and the secret police. The only people who had much money were the nobles and the middle classes, such as the factory owners. The Russian peasants and workers were all desperately poor.

'Then came the First World War. The Germans defeated our armies easily, mainly because the Tsar's government was so inefficient. The Tsar became more unpopular than ever until, in 1917, he was overthrown. That same year, under our great communist leader, Lenin, the workers started a revolution. After a bitter struggle they seized power so that Russia was well on the way to becoming a communist state. Then something went wrong.

'Lenin died in 1924 and Josef Stalin took his place as leader. Stalin pretended to be a good communist, but in fact he was a very wicked man. All he wanted was power for himself. He treated the Russian people with much greater cruelty than any Tsar, and he did our country a lot of harm.

'Stalin died, at last, three years ago in 1953. Now I am both leader of the communist party and Prime Minister. I mean to put right Stalin's mistakes.

'My main task, of course, is to help our people lead happier lives. They had a miserable time under Stalin because he made them produce coal, oil, steel, railway locomotives, and above all, weapons of war. Meanwhile the shops are almost empty of the goods ordinary people use. Few Russian families have a refrigerator or a washing machine and hardly any have a car. Even clothing is hard to find, and sometimes food itself is in short supply. I want our

* Tsar is a Russian word meaning *Emperor*.

people to have all these things. I ask you, what sort of communism is it that has no sausage?

'Russia is much larger than the United States. It has more minerals, more forests and more farm land. Why should we not be as rich as the Americans? I shall not rest until we are.'

Marx

Marx's tomb, Highgate cemetery, London

poster celebrating first anniversary of the Communist revolution

2 General Brusilov, 1917

We will now look back over the earlier years of Russia's history. It is 1917 and the First World War is into its fourth year. Brusilov, one of Russia's few good generals, tells us about his country.

'Russia is very unhappy. In days gone by, we conquered other nations, like the Poles. They long to be free of us and rule themselves again. Millions of our peasants are thoroughly discontented. Few of them have enough land to make a decent living, while the nobles have plenty. The peasants want to seize the land from the nobles and divide it among themselves. In the towns our workers toil long hours in dirty, dangerous factories. They draw starvation wages and live in miserable slums. Our middle classes, such as the lawyers, doctors, merchants and factory owners are wealthy enough, but they have been discontented, too.

They wanted a say in the government of the country, but until this year it was denied them.

'Indeed our government was the cause of much of our trouble. We were ruled by an Emperor, Tsar Nicholas II. He believed he had been chosen by God, so everyone was bound to obey him without question. He was a mild and pleasant man to meet, in fact rather a weak character, but terrible things were done in his name. He had his secret police, the Okhrana, who used to arrest anyone they thought was against him. Prisoners were tortured, or killed, but most were sent to Siberia. It was tragic to see them setting out on their long journey chained together. They called their manacles the "Tsar's bracelets". Then there was "bloody Sunday", back in 1905. A peaceful crowd gathered in Petrograd to complain about the sufferings of the people. Led by a priest, they made their way towards the Tsar's Winter Palace, singing "God save the Tsar". Soldiers opened fire on them, killing over 500. They even shot little boys out of the trees, where they had climbed to watch the procession.

'It took the war, though, to show how bad the Tsar's government really was. As a general, I was furious at the way my men had to suffer. We were fighting the German army, the best organised and best equipped in the world, and what did we have? Hardly

'Bloody Sunday'

Tsar Nicholas II

any artillery, hardly any machine guns and not even enough rifles! On some sectors there was only one rifle between ten men. We sent soldiers into action unarmed, telling them that if they wanted a rifle they must take one from a dead comrade! We did not have enough food, uniforms or ammunition, while many a man has been left to die because there were no bandages for his wounds.

'There is nothing wrong with the courage of the Russian soldiers. They fought like tigers, but the German artillery blasted them to pieces, and the German machine guns mowed them down in their thousands. In 1915 General Falkenhayn routed our armies, overran Poland and took one million prisoners. The Germans thought we were finished after that, but I was able to prove them wrong. I knew

better than to attack Germany, but her ally Austria–Hungary was weak. In 1916 I mounted an attack on her, through the Carpathian mountains. At first we had great success, but then the Germans sent a powerful force against us and we had to retreat. It seems that no one can beat the Germans.

'There was suffering at home as well as at the front. People in the towns were desperately hungry. There was plenty of food in Siberia, but our railways had broken down, so it was impossible to transport it. In March this year the citizens of Petrograd rebelled. The soldiers who were ordered to fire on them, joined them instead, and so did the sailors from the fleet. The rebellion spread to the rest of Russia, and the Tsar had no choice but to abdicate. We now have a Provisional Government under Alexander Kerensky. It will hold office until the war is over, when we will have free elections for a free Parliament.

'As one of the Tsar's generals I was not happy about his fall, but as I said at the time, "If I must choose between the Tsar and Russia, I shall march for Russia". I have offered my services to the Provisional Government and they have asked me to mount another offensive against the enemy. I will do my best, but I am not hopeful. Our men have lost their spirit since the defeats of 1915 and 1916. Many of them are peasants, and they are deserting. They think the nobles will soon be overthrown and they want to go home and make sure of their share of the land. Also, communist agitators are busy. I find it hard to understand these people, but I believe they are saying it is wrong for a man to be loyal to his country and that workers everywhere should unite against their masters. Anyway, they are telling our soldiers not to kill Germans, but to shoot their own officers instead.'

Russian peasants

3 Lenin, 1924

In this section Lenin, the leader of the communist revolution tells us about it.

'I was born in 1870. I became a revolutionary at the age of 17 when the police hanged my elder brother for plotting against the Tsar. In 1895, they arrested me, and sent me to Siberia for three years. It wasn't too bad. Indeed, I would say those three years were the happiest of my life. I studied, I wrote a book and I even got married. When I returned to Russia in 1898, a group of us formed the Communist Party. It was illegal – all political parties were – and I had to flee abroad.

'When the war broke out in 1914, I was in Switzerland, together with other communists. We wanted the Germans to win, because we saw that if the Russians did, it would make the Tsar stronger than ever. At first we could only wait, but then in March 1917 the Tsar was overthrown. It seemed our chance had come, but how could we return to Russia? Britain and France would not let us through because their

Lenin

governments hated communists. The Germans, though, were keen to help us as they knew we were the only Russians who wanted to make peace with them. Thirty-two of us crossed Germany in a sealed train. We then took a ship to Sweden, went from there to Finland, and home to Russia. We wondered what was going to happen when our train arrived at Petrograd. After all, we had come from Germany, Russia's most deadly enemy. We need not have worried. At the Finland Station there was a cheering crowd which carried us in triumph to communist party headquarters.

'We found a great deal of work waiting for us. The Provisional Government of Kerensky stood for the middle classes, like the factory owners. It was doing nothing for the workers and peasants and it wanted to go on with the war. It even ordered Brusilov to make a new offensive, which failed as it was bound to do. These were dreadful mistakes. For our part, we promised the people the things they wanted. "Peace! Bread! Land!" was our slogan. We sent agents to win over the soldiers, sailors and workers. When they had done so, we encouraged them to form councils, or Soviets, as we call them. We also organised a force of Red Guards.

'By November 6th, 1917 we decided our time had come. Red Guards seized all the key buildings in Petrograd, like the railway stations, the post offices and the telephone exchange. At the same time the soldiers in the Peter and Paul Fortress declared for us, and so did the sailors in the Kronstadt naval base. Kerensky fled, but there were still some members of the Provisional Government in the Winter Palace, which

the civil war

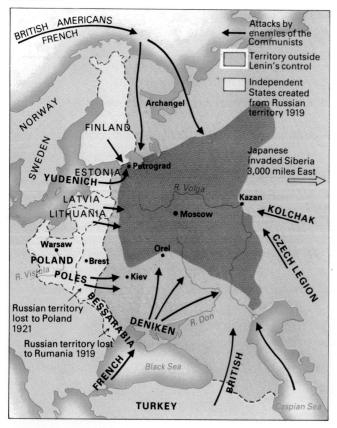

Attacks by enemies of the Communists

Territory outside Lenin's control

Independent States created from Russian territory 1919

Japanese invaded Siberia 3,000 miles East

Russian territory lost to Poland 1921

Russian territory lost to Rumania 1919

Lenin arrives at the Finland Station

was heavily defended.* The following night our brave Red Guards gathered for the attack. A shot from the cruiser *Aurora* was their signal, and they stormed the palace with the loss of only six men.

'Everything now depended on the army in the rest of Russia. Our agents had done their work well, though, and we heard from regiment after regiment that the men were on our side. The Revolution had succeeded, and we were able to form a communist government, the first one in history.

'But I'm afraid our troubles were only just beginning. We had to make peace with the Germans and they insisted on taking a quarter of our country. They had to give it back when the western powers defeated them in 1918, but then the Poles invaded us and took nearly as much. Worst of all, there was a terrible civil war. In those days, you see, only one Russian in 600 was a communist, and we had many enemies. What is more, foreign countries like America, Britain and France, sent them help. We won in the end, of course. An important reason was that in the areas we

controlled we drove out the nobles and allowed the peasants to take their lands. But the main credit for our success must go to our gallant Red Army which Leon Trotsky organised.

'The Civil War ended in 1920 and we made peace with the Poles in 1921. By then our country was ruined, with most of the factories closed. As if that was not bad enough, there was a drought in the Volga region followed by a famine. Some towns had so many dead bodies that the only thing to do was to take them away into the countryside by train and throw them beside the railway track.

'Well, our factories and farms are working again, but I fear there may be still more troubles. I had a stroke last year and if I die who will take my place as leader? I am afraid it may be Stalin. When I first knew him he seemed an unimportant little man, just a grey blur, if you know what I mean. I gave him the least important and dullest job I could think of which was Secretary of the Communist Party. Now I find he has used this position to win support all over Russia. If he should come to power he will do great harm. I must stop him if I can, but I fear I may be too late.'

*In fact the defenders of the Winter Palace were some officer cadets, who were only boys, and a regiment of women.

The attack on the Winter Palace

4 Factories and Farms under Stalin, the 1930s

Stalin

Lenin died in 1924 and as he had feared, Stalin was quick to seize power. He drove his chief rival Trotsky into exile and later sent an agent to murder him.

Stalin wanted to make Russia powerful, and he wanted to turn her into a truly communist state. In his mind, the two went together, because he thought the best way to become powerful was to become communist.

In 1924 most factories still belonged to private individuals, who ran them to make money for themselves. That was against communism, so Stalin confiscated the factories and put them under the control of his government. He then drew up a number of 'Five Year Plans', one after the other. Their aim was to give Russia the things she would need to win a war. Left in private hands the factories would have made goods to sell in the shops, but you cannot fight battles with shoes and saucepans. Stalin wanted iron, steel, coal, oil and weapons, so the Five Year Plans concentrated on them.

Stalin did his best to improve the factories Russia already had around Moscow, Leningrad and in the Ukraine. More important than that, he built entirely new industrial towns like Magnitogorsk. They are east of the Urals and well out of reach of any enemy.

Since he thought the next war might come soon, Stalin made his people work hard. A few of them were

the Baltic – White Sea Canal, built under the second Five Year Plan 1932–1937

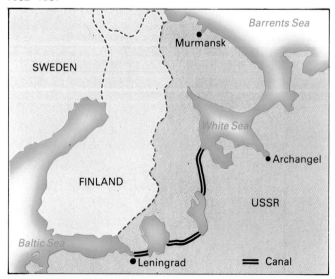

willing. There was a miner called Alexis Stakhanov, for example, who dug 100 tons of coal in just one shift. This was sixteen times what he was expected to do. Most workers, in fact, were more like the one who will speak to us now.

'What was life like under the Five Year Plans?' 'It was hard. You see, each factory had its target and if it failed to reach it, its manager was guilty of a crime against the state, and was sent to a labour camp. The government made our targets higher, year after year. We had trade union meetings where our leaders explained why we must work longer hours for the good of the Soviet Union. We always used to agree.'

'Whyever did you do that?' 'Because we knew there were spies among us. If anyone had tried to argue the secret police would have picked him up very quickly.'

'Did you earn much money?' 'No, we had miserable wages, and what was worse, there was very little to buy with them. Food was short and it was almost impossible to find even a shirt, a kettle or a blanket in the shops. All our factories were doing was preparing for a war with Germany.'

'What happened when the war was over?' 'Stalin sent us back to work harder than ever, preparing for another war, this time against America.'

Agriculture was an even greater problem for Stalin than industry. After the Civil War the nobles were killed or driven away, and the peasants were given their land. It is against communism for people to own property. Also, the farming was not well done, and Stalin felt the main reason was that most farms were too small to be efficient. In the whole country there were 24 million of them. Stalin thought the answer was to have 'collective farms.' Each was anything from 50 to 100 small farms made into one. He believed that if the peasants gave up their land they would become good communists. He was also sure that a collective farm was bound to be more efficient than all the little ones it replaced. A peasant will tell us what happened.

peasants' revolt

'Did you support the communists during the revolution?' 'Yes, because they promised to give us land.'

'What did they do when they came to power?' 'They took our land from us! They said we must work as labourers on collective farms, under communist party bosses. In our village we were determined they should have as little as possible from us. We slaughtered our cattle and refused to sow our fields.'

'What did the government do about that?' 'Stalin sent soldiers to attack us. They killed many of our people, and sent many others to labour camps in Siberia. Those of us that are left think we must at least pretend to obey, but we do as little work as we dare.'

Forcing collective farms on the peasants led to a famine. No one dared tell Stalin the truth until his wife Nadya raved at him for ruining his country. She was dead the next morning, we know not how. Stalin was so shaken that he did do something for the peasants. He said that although the collective farms must stay, each family could have its own private plot of about one acre. Naturally, the peasants work harder on their own plots than they do on the collective farms.

5 Marshal Zhukov, 1953

For reasons which you will see later, Russia had very few good generals when the Second World War began. Marshal Zhukov was one of them. Here he tells us about some of the things that happened before and during the war.

'Russia was unhappy under Stalin's rule from the day he came to power, but trouble really began in 1934. By that time Stalin was a frightened man, for he had made many enemies. How could he be rid of them? Then Sergei Kirov was shot. He was the leader of the Leningrad branch of the Communist Party, and a friend of Stalin's. We never found out who the killers were, but Stalin used Kirov's death as an excuse for murdering anyone he thought was against him.

'First of all the secret police rounded up all the members of the Communist Party that Stalin disliked. Those that had first started the party back in Lenin's day and taken part in the Revolution had formed what they called the "Old Bolshevik's Association." Stalin

Zhukov

particularly hated them, because they had ideas of their own. You would never find more loyal men, and we were amazed at first, when they confessed to all sorts of unlikely crimes. They said they had plotted to kill Stalin, plotted to overthrow the government,

T34 tanks

plotted to help foreigners invade the Soviet Union, and so on. Of course they had been tortured for weeks by the secret police until they agreed to tell these lies. They were then put on trial and sentenced to death. Stalin never appeared at the trials, but sometimes he hid behind a curtain so that he could enjoy what was going on.

'After he had finished with the Communist Party, and killed most of his old comrades, Stalin turned on the officers of the army and navy. A third of them were arrested and sent to labour camps, where many were tortured and killed. It was always the best ones, too. Stalin had nothing to fear from stupid people, so they had more chance of escaping. Next it was the civil servants and after that, the ordinary people of Russia. Once, Stalin went to a meeting. Everyone stood up, started clapping and went on clapping. They didn't dare to do anything else. But you can't clap for ever, and someone had to be the first to stop. It was the manager of a paper factory. He was a good communist, and good at his job but a few days later the secret police arrested him. They accused him of some crime or other and sent him to a labour camp for ten years. Before long no one in Russia could go to bed at night without dreading a knock on the door in the early hours of the morning. That was when the secret police called.

'We do not know how many people the secret police arrested, but it must have been millions. The country was being ruined and even Stalin himself saw he must end the purge. He wasn't going to take the blame though. He said it was all the fault of the head of the secret police, Yezhov, and he had him shot.

'When the war came I was grateful to Stalin for one thing and one thing only. He had built plenty of armaments factories beyond the Urals, and out of

reach of the Germans. Because of that, the Red Army had all the weapons it needed, especially the splendid T34 tanks. But everything else Stalin did was harmful. As I told you he had killed all our best officers. We were left with men like Stalin's drinking partner, Marshal Budenny. His soldiers called him "the general with the immense moustache and the very small brain". He had 5,000 tanks in 1941, but von Runstedt defeated him with only 600.

'Stalin spent years preparing our country for war with Germany, but when in 1941 British spies warned him Hitler was about to attack us, he refused to believe them. The Germans took our armies completely by surprise and they were in sight of Moscow before I stopped them. It was not until January 1943 that I won our first real victory at Stalingrad.

'One of my biggest problems was that Stalin insisted on taking command and he had no idea what to do. He sent millions of our brave soldiers to their deaths in useless head-on attacks. I know he never visited the front, and Comrade Khrushchev told me something even more remarkable. He said that Stalin used to make his war plans using a library globe, and working out distances with a tape measure. I can well believe it. We won the war, not because of Stalin, but in spite of him. Yet who took all the credit for the victory? Stalin did.'

Stalin planning a campaign with globe and tape-measure

6 Russia under Khrushchev, 1953–1964

You will remember that when Stalin died and Khrushchev came to power, he had ambitious plans. Now it is 1964, Khrushchev has retired and a senior member of the Communist Party talks about him and his work.

'After the war most of us living in Russia were grateful to Stalin. We all thought he had saved us from the Germans. His statue was in every town and five of our important cities were named after him. In 1956, though, three years after his death, Comrade Khrushchev made an amazing speech about him. He told us of Stalin's purges in the 1930s when so many good communists were executed for crimes they had not committed. He also described how Stalin mismanaged things during the war. So far from winning it, he almost lost it for us. Then, in 1953, Stalin had some of our leading doctors arrested, saying they were plotting to kill him. He ordered the head of his secret police to torture them saying, "If you do not obtain confessions from the doctors, we will shorten you by a head." It looked like the beginning of another purge, so it was lucky for everyone, not just the doctors, that Stalin died soon afterwards.

'Comrade Khrushchev needed to show that Stalin was wicked and made many mistakes, because he, himself, meant to rule the Soviet Union in quite a different way. Well, he certainly did.

'First of all, he cut down the powers of the secret police, ordered the judges to give fair trials, and released thousands of political prisoners from the labour camps. As long as we did not say anything too bad about the government, we no longer had any reason to dread a knock on our door at three in the morning.

'Khrushchev made new plans for our factories. "Why should Americans have motor cars, radios, television sets and washing machines but Russians nothing?" he asked. Soon we were making all these things and in quite large numbers. That pleased the ordinary people, but I'm afraid we are still a long way behind the Americans.

'Our biggest problem has always been our agriculture. We have more than enough land, so why do we not have enough food? One reason is that the peasants do not like the collective farms and will not work as hard as they should. Another reason is that the

peasants farming

Khrushchev meets a peasant woman on a collective farm

peasants are ignorant. Do you know that in some parts of Russia they think that the last few drops of milk a cow gives are magic? As a result, they milk their cows five or six times a day! Also, we are short of farm machinery. In the Soviet Union we have 600,000 tractors, while in the United States, where there is less farm land, they have five million.

'Comrade Khrushchev tried to put all that right. He went everywhere visiting collective farms. He met the peasants, laughed and joked with them and told them such things as how to grow more corn, fatten their pigs more quickly and make their hens lay more eggs. He had great faith in maize as food for animals. He advised peasants everywhere to grow it, whether or not their soil was right for it. The peasants used to laugh at Khrushchev behind his back. They even nicknamed him "maize". He didn't make them change their ways much at all.

'Khrushchev's most ambitious plan was his "virgin lands scheme". Out in Kazakhstan we have an area of grassland, as big as the prairies of North America. Khrushchev said that if it was cultivated we should have as much food as the Americans. He was warned that the soil was poor and that the weather was unreliable, but he refused to listen. Thousands of people were sent to these empty spaces, where they toiled to cultivate the land and bring in the harvest. They had to live in tents, makeshift huts, or even holes in the ground. The summers are unbearably hot there, and the winters bitterly cold. For a few years they grew some reasonable crops, but then there was a drought. The soil turned to dust, and the wind blew it around in great clouds. That was the end of the virgin lands scheme, and Kazakhstan is empty once again. What is more, we were so short of food that we had to buy wheat from America, the country we were going to overtake!'

In 1964 the other Russian leaders made Khrushchev resign. Why they did this we do not know, but probably they were afraid that he was becoming too powerful. Two men took his place, Leonid Brezhnev and Alexei Kosygin. They allowed the Russian people less freedom than Khrushchev, but they did not go back to Stalin's bad ways.

Brezhnev and Kosygin

Chapter Eighteen Mao Tse-tung's China

1 Introduction: Mao Tse-tung Speaks, 1949

'I was born in 1893 in the province of Hunan. My father was a peasant but he was not as poor as some of his kind. I had a little education whereas most children had none at all. I trained to be a teacher, but when I became a young man I went to Peking where I worked as an assistant in the library of the University.

'The China into which I was born was very different from the one we know today. She was ruled by an Emperor and nobles, all of whom were Manchus. They were descended from a race that had conquered our country in the seventeenth century. The Manchus were wicked and cared nothing for the ordinary people. What is more, they did little to resist foreigners. The great western countries, Russia, Germany, France and Britain had shared out our coastline between them. They controlled nearly all of our modern industries and much of our trade. Britain still has Hong Kong, as you know. Our worst enemies were the Japanese, and I will tell you about them later.

China

Mao Tse-tung

'Most of our people were peasants and they were very poor. What else could you expect? A quarter of the world's population is Chinese, but we have less than one-tenth of its farm land. Many a family had to scrape a living from a plot of land of less than an acre. The landlords made things even worse. Peasants did not own their farms, but had to pay rent for them. Sometimes the rent was as much as three-quarters of the crop. Most landlords were cruel and wicked, and the peasants longed to be rid of them.

'Things began to look more hopeful in the 1920s. A man called Sun Yat-sen organised a Nationalist Party, which, in the end, overthrew the Manchus and persuaded the western countries to give up their privileges in China. Sun Yat-sen also promised to give land to the peasants, but he died in 1925 and Chiang Kai-shek became leader of the Nationalists. He is as evil as any Manchu Emperor, and he was on the side of the landlords. He let them keep their estates, and they went on being as cruel as ever to the peasants.

'Also, the Japanese made trouble. In 1931 they captured Manchuria and in 1937 invaded the rest of China. Within two years they had taken all the important cities. Only the sheer size of our country stopped them from over-running it completely.

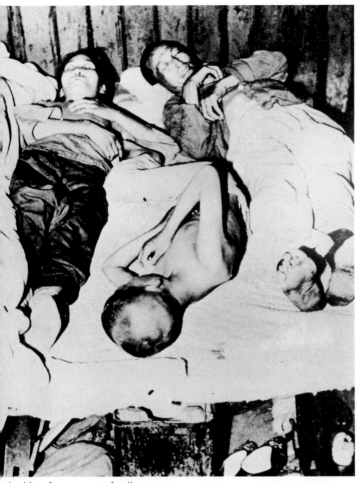

bedtime for a peasant family

Manchu family

'In the mean time, I had become a communist. In the university library at Peking I read Karl Marx's book *Capital.* In it he speaks of the great revolution which the town workers will one day make. He says that they will seize control of the government, kill their employers and run the factories for their own benefit. I knew that there had been a revolution like this in Russia, and I was sure we should have to have one in China, if we were to save our country. Accordingly, a number of us founded the Chinese Communist Party. That was in 1919. In 1928 my friend Chuh Teh organised the People's Liberation Army to fight for us. I was pleased, for I have always said that political power grows out of the barrel of a gun.

'Chiang Kai-shek decided that we communists were a bigger menace than the Japanese. He drove us into the forests of Hunan and almost destroyed us. In 1934 we managed to escape to the north and continued the struggle from there. We called our journey to the north the Long March. During the Long March two especially important things happened for me. The first was that my comrades elected me Chairman of the

Communist Party, which I still am. The second was that I decided not to imitate the Russians. Their revolution was the work of the townsfolk, just as Marx had said it should be. In China, though, we had failed miserably in the towns, while the peasants had flocked to join us. I was sure the Chinese Revolution had to be a peasant revolution, and so it has proved. I'm afraid our Russian comrades distrust us as a result, but that cannot be helped.

'During the Second World War, the People's Liberation Army fought both the Japanese and the Nationalists. When it was over, and Japan surrendered, the Nationalists turned all their strength against us. We have defeated them after a bitter struggle, and this year I proclaimed the People's Republic of China.

'Winning the Civil War is only a beginning. We must now make China a powerful country, and even more important, we must make her a Communist country. I am sure that communist ideas are the right ones, and my first duty is to persuade my people to believe in them.'

2 The Long March, 1934–1935

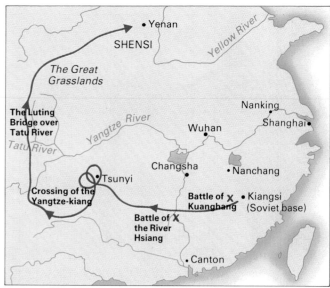

the Long March

In this section we meet a communist cadre. He describes his job later on, but first he tells us about the Long March, one of the great stories of the Communist Party.

'In 1928 Comrade Chuh Teh formed the People's Liberation Army and he and Comrade Mao took us to some out of the way hills in Hunan Province. There were only 10,000 of us so we could not fight pitched battles with the Nationalists. Instead, we lay in wait for them in the forests. Comrade Mao told us what to do when they arrived:

The enemy attacks, we retreat.
The enemy camps, we harass.
The enemy tires, we attack.
The enemy retreats, we pursue.

'Before long Chiang Kai-shek sent a huge force against us on what he called an "extermination campaign". We just melted away in front of it, but closed round behind it and cut off its supplies. We were never there when the Nationalists expected us, but we attacked them as soon as they were off their guard. We took countless prisoners, many of whom joined us. Soon, the People's Liberation Army was 300,000 strong.

'Then Chiang Kai-shek tried something different. He surrounded our hills with a ring of block houses and barbed wire. Comrade Mao's tactics were no use now. Chiang was strangling our army, and many of our men deserted. Comrade Mao made a brave decision. He would break out of the prison Chiang had made, and lead us to Yenan, in the north, where there was another communist force, like our own.

'Well, in October 1934 we smashed through Chiang's defences and we were on our way. There were 100,000 of us winding along in a column 50 miles long. From our base in Hunan to Yenan was about 700 miles, but we could not go there directly because there were powerful Nationalist armies in the way. Instead, we had to go through the remote, wild parts of southern and western China. I counted 24 rivers that we crossed as well as 18 mountain ranges, some of them snow-covered. Altogether, we walked

6,000 miles. We didn't call it the Long March for nothing.

'Of course the Nationalists did their best to stop us and we fought several battles with them. I think the most exciting was at the Tatu River. A strong Nationalist force had trapped us at a point where the river flows through a deep gorge. We simply had to cross and the only way was by an old suspension bridge. It was made from chains, with boards to walk on. There were a few enemy soldiers the other side of the bridge. They could have destroyed it quite easily, but they thought it would be good enough to remove the boards. They were wrong. Some of our men lay down on the edge of the gorge and opened up such a heavy fire on the defenders that they hardly dared raise their heads. Then thirty of our brave fellows swung across on the chains. Some were killed or wounded, and plunged into the torrent below. The rest reached the other side and killed the Nationalist soldiers. The boards were then put back for the rest of us to cross.

'The most uncomfortable time was crossing the Grasslands. In fact they are not grasslands at all, but a huge swamp. Local people showed us some paths through them, or most of us would have drowned. Even so, we dared not lie down at night. We used to sleep standing, propping each other up in groups of three or four.

crossing the Tatu River

'One good thing about the Long March was the help we had from the peasants. We treated them well, of course, and took the food we needed from the landlords.

'We reached Yenan after 368 days, at least some of us did. Three-quarters of our force had died on the march, or had been left behind.

'At Yenan Comrade Mao soon organised a new base. He won over the peasants and built up the army. He also spent a lot of time thinking about the sort of communism he wanted in China and he wrote several books. One day he was so deep in thought that he did not notice he had put his foot in the fire and his shoe was burning. After he had finished his books, numbers of us studied them and became cadres. Our job was to

be missionaries, carrying Comrade Mao's ideas to the rest of China. We did our lessons in what we called the Yenan Cave University. Nationalist aircraft raided the town so often that the only way to be safe was to burrow into the hills.

'I think the Long March was the most important event in Chinese history. If we had stayed in Hunan, Chiang Kai-shek would have wiped us out and that would have been an end to communism in our country. The Long March was a retreat, though, and you don't win wars by retreating.'

3 Fighting the Japanese and the Nationalists

It is 1949 and we talk to a communist soldier of the People's Liberation Army. He tells us about the wars with the Japanese and the Nationalists.

'What did the Red Army do during the war against Japan?' 'We fought hard against the Japanese. They tried to frighten us with their "three all's" – "burn all, slay all, loot all". In the north we drove them into the cities and they dared not show their faces in the countryside. The Nationalists were stronger than us in the south, but they didn't fight the Japanese much. Chiang Kai-shek was going to let the Americans and British defeat them for him and keep his armies intact so that he could defeat us.'

'What happened after the Japanese surrendered?' 'We tried to take the northern cities as they left, but the Americans rushed in some Nationalist groups by air, and got them there first. That gave them a big advantage. Also, the Nationalists outnumbered us by three to one, they had complete control of the air, and the Americans were sending them weapons as

Japanese troops in China

fast as they could. You should have seen our weapons! We had home-made land mines, and even some wooden cannon. Mostly we used what we captured from the Nationalists. That pleased Mao. He said, "The Nationalists have been our ammunition bearers."'

'How did the fighting against the Nationalists go?' 'Chiang Kai-shek started with some powerful attacks but we wore them down, just as we had always done. All the time his men were deserting to join us, so it was not long before our armies were as strong as his. We were able to give up our guerrilla tactics and fight pitched battles. Then, in 1948, there was a two months' battle at Huai Hai which we won. Chiang's men had no courage left after that. Earlier this year Chiang fled to Taiwan with what was left of his army. He is there now, threatening to come back and reconquer China. The problem is, how much help will the Americans give him?

'Why do you think the communists won the Civil War?' 'Because we won the most important battle in it and that wasn't Huai Hai. It was the one for the hearts and minds of the ordinary peasants.'

'How did you do that?' 'By behaving quite differently from the Nationalist forces. When I was a boy some Nationalist troops came to our village. They stole all our millet, and they told my father he must pay them taxes. When he told them he hadn't any money, they flogged him and ordered him to sell my sister. It was quite different when some Red soldiers arrived, I can tell you. They gave sweets to the children, and they put on plays to amuse everyone. What pleased people like my father most was that they chased away the landlords, and told the peasants they could share their land among themselves. I was sixteen by then, so I left home and joined the People's Liberation Army.

'One of the first things I had to learn was how to treat ordinary people when we were billetted in their homes. Mao gave us Eight Points for Attention. They are:

1 Replace all doors when you leave a house.*
2 Return and roll up the straw matting on which you sleep.

* To make a spare bed a Chinese peasant will often lift a door off its hinges and place it on wooden blocks.

Communist soldiers laying home-made land mines

3 Be courteous and polite, and help when you can.
4 Return all borrowed articles.
5 Replace all damaged articles.
6 Be honest in all dealings with the peasants.
7 Pay for all articles purchased.
8 Be clean, and especially put lavatories a safe distance from people's houses.

'In return for our kindness, the peasants helped us the whole time. When I was wounded some of them bandaged me up and hid me from the Nationalists until I was better. When my unit was lost, some peasants acted as guides to put us back on the right path. Later, a Nationalist force came looking for us, and they sent them in the wrong direction. Often the peasants have stood at the roadside with food, tea and spare sandals for us. Many times they have carried our supplies. We could not have won the war without them.'

Japanese invasion of China

4 The New China, 1958

drilling militia

Outside a factory a young woman is drilling a squad of militia. She gives her orders in a loud, clear voice and the squad is quick to obey her. When the drill is finished she talks to us, sitting with her rifle beside her.

'Is it usual for a woman to drill troops?' 'Oh yes. In China today women and men are quite equal.'

'Was that always so?' 'Not at all. You have no idea how women suffered in the past. Men used to think that for a woman to be beautiful she must have small feet. Parents used to bind the feet of girl babies with tight bandages, so that they would not grow properly. My mother's feet were squeezed into a dreadful shape, so that she never walked comfortably. She is still alive and it is pitiful to see her struggling to work in the fields. Worse than that happened. In the old days, whenever there was a famine, cartloads of girls were sent into town to be sold as slaves. Families never sold their sons. For centuries the Chinese people followed the ideas of a man called Confucius. One of the things he said was, "A door into the back yard is not a real door: a woman is not a real human being." We no longer believe in that sort of nonsense. Chairman Mao says, "Women hold up half the sky."

'All sorts of marriage customs have changed too. When a couple became engaged, the young man's family used to give an expensive gift. It was just as if they were buying the girl and it made her feel inferior. When I was engaged all I wanted as an engagement gift was a copy of the "Works of Mao Tse-tung" and this rifle. Weddings have also changed. They were once very elaborate with expensive feasts. A friend of mine was married just recently, and she rode to the ceremony on a bicycle she had borrowed. The only

wedding, Communist style

celebration was a small tea party with a few friends and a senior communist official came to wish the happy couple good luck. Chairman Mao doesn't really like us to marry young, because the population of China is too large. I shall wait another seven years, until I am twenty-five.'

'*Has family life altered at all?*' 'Indeed it has. According to Confucius a father's word was law and children had to obey him without question. Today a good communist child will question his father's wishes. Only if they agree with the teachings of Chairman Mao will he obey. The Communist Party is far more important than the family.'

'*What other changes have there been in China?*' 'Before the Revolution the important people were the landlords and the factory owners. The peasants and workers just did not count. No-one cared if they lived or starved to death. Now it is the peasants and workers who matter.'

'*What happened to the factory owners and landlords?*' 'You can see the man who used to own this factory. He is over there, the one with the broom. He wasn't fit even to look after a machine, so we made him a cleaner. In the countryside, communist cadres went to each village in turn, and questioned the peasants about their landlords. If a landlord had been good and kindly, he was allowed to keep a small farm, though no bigger than he could tend himself. But if he had been cruel, or had helped the Nationalists or the Japanese, then he was put to death.

'You will understand the new China if I tell you about Lei Peng. He was a poor peasant boy who joined the People's Liberation Army. When he was doing his training he found he could not throw a grenade far enough. The same evening he went back to the drill ground and practised again and again, until well after dark. His body ached so much he could not sleep that night. Lei led a very simple life. He patched his clothes until there was not much of the original cloth left. His cup and bowl were chipped all over. He only ever bought soap and a few books; the rest of his pay he put in the bank. Then he heard there had been a great flood near Liaoyang. He at once drew out all his money and sent it to help the people who had suffered in the disaster.

'Now the reason that Lei Peng behaved in this way was because he knew the "Works" of Chairman Mao. He used to study them every night, but so that he didn't keep the other soldiers awake, he read under the bedclothes by torchlight.

'That is the secret of the new China. Chairman Mao's thoughts are the driving force of everything.'

Lei Peng practises grenade throwing

311

5 A Commune, 1959

Today we will visit a commune in Shensi province in north-west China. Its director tells us about it.

'*What exactly is a commune?*' 'It's a group of villages whose people work together, helping one another so that they can meet nearly all their own needs. In this commune we have thirty-five villages, and about 18,000 people altogether. In the whole of China there are 23,000 communes.'

'*What work do you do?*' 'Mainly farming. We cannot grow rice here, as they do in the warmer parts of China, but we have wheat, maize, sweet potatoes, all manner of vegetables, and cotton. We also keep a great many pigs. Rabbits are valuable, too. We rear them for their fur which fetches a good price.'

'*Is there any industry?*' 'Yes indeed. Chairman Mao says we must "walk on two legs" which means producing goods as well as growing food. We don't mine coal or make such things as railway locomotives. The government looks after all the big, important industries. In the commune we concentrate on goods which people can produce without the help of com-plicated machines. We make shoes, or sandals, rather, from hemp; we make clothes and we weave baskets. Our little workshops supply many of our needs and they keep our people occupied. In Shensi the growing season is short, and in the old days a peasant was busy for no more than 190 days a year. Now he can go into the workshops when there is nothing to do on the land, so he is employed all the year round.'

'*What else does the commune do?*' 'We are improving our part of China all the time. We have terraced the hillsides to make new fields. To stop the river flooding we have strengthened its banks and built a dam. We have no bulldozers, of course. People did the work, some of them with no more equipment than their bare hands for digging and baskets to carry the earth. City folk came to help us. Thousands of men and women toiled away, all dressed in the same blue cotton clothing. We called them "blue ants". Chairman Mao was a blue ant for a time. He firmly believes that every good communist should be willing to do hard physical labour.

'The commune has other important duties, as well. We have three schools and a hospital. We look after old people, and we have a nursery where women can leave their babies while they are at work. We even have our own militia. If an enemy invaded China we would give him a very rough time. A commune, you see, can do almost everything for itself.'

'*Who runs the commune?*' 'I do as its director, but there is a Revolutionary Committee of twenty-five members to help me. The people elect them, but of course they can only choose members of the Communist Party.'

'*How long have you had communes in China?*' 'Only since last year. They are needed for Chairman Mao's "Great Leap Forward" which will make China the leading nation in the world. The other thing they will do is to make all Chinese into good communists. After the Revolution, the peasants were quick to seize the land from the landlords. Now we have persuaded them that it is wrong for a man to own a farm and cultivate it selfishly for his own benefit. Instead, the peasants have given their land to the communes and everybody works for the general good. Soon, I hope we shall give up our separate houses and eat together as big families in large dining halls. That is already happening in some communes.'

As we leave the director's office, he points to a man who is clearing manure from some pig sties and says, 'That is a university professor but he thought himself a bit too clever and dared to criticise Chairman Mao. Working with our pigs will help him change his ideas.'

peasant painting showing members of
a commune building houses

6 The Cultural Revolution, 1966–1970

Little Red Book of Mao Tse-tung

It is 1967. We are going to talk to three people. The first is Mao Tse-tung's wife, Chiang Ching.

'*What do you think was the most important change the communists made in China?*' 'We made the former landowners and factory owners equal with the rest of our people. If anyone had any privileges just after the Revolution it was the workers and the peasants. But things went wrong and before long we had a new privileged class.'

'*Who were they?*' They were the leaders of the Communist Party, the very men and women who had made the Revolution! They lived in the best houses, ate the best food, sent their children to the best schools and drove around in cars. Worst of all they gave the workers and the peasants orders, instead of seeking their advice. They were no longer good communists, for they were putting themselves first, instead of the party.'

'*What did Chairman Mao think of that?*' 'He was worried and he and I decided we must have a second

Communist rally

Revolution. The first was the Civil War, but this one was going to be different. Its aim was to change the way people were thinking, so we called it the "Cultural Revolution". It began last year, 1966.'

'How did you persuade the people to follow you?' 'Chairman Mao put all his best ideas into one compact little book that anyone could read. It is called the *Little Red Book of Mao Tse-tung.* Over 700 million copies of it have been printed. Next, Mao and I talked with three of our friends and we decided we could not trust the party bosses to make changes. So we appealed to the young. We invited them to become Red Guards, and I am delighted that millions of them answered our call.'

'How did you start the Cultural Revolution?' 'One problem was that last year Mao was 73, and some people were saying he was too old. To prove them wrong, he swam nine miles down the River Yangtze. After that he issued a poster saying "Bombard the Headquarters". By that he meant that ordinary Chinese should question their masters. Since then many exciting things have happened.'

'What are they?' 'Pupils and students have risen against their teachers and workers against their factory managers. Many party leaders have lost their posts, like that dreadful man Teng Hsiao-ping. The rest have had to go back to school, where they are studying the works of Chairman Mao and doing plenty of hard physical work.'

Now we will talk to a Red Guard.

'What part did you play in the Cultural Revolution?' 'It is hard to believe that just over a year ago I was sitting at my desk at school in Shanghai, doing just as my teacher told me. Then Chairman Mao closed all the schools and universities and invited the pupils to become Red Guards. We needed no persuading, I can tell you. In Shanghai we did all the things we felt Chairman Mao would like. We tore down the street signs of the bad old days and put up new ones like "Revolution Road", and "Mao Tse-tung Square" We attacked the department stores which were selling fancy western-style goods for the rich. We made them stock the things which workers and peasants can afford. We also attacked people if they wore the wrong clothes. The wives of the party leaders used to wear high-heeled leather shoes, silk dresses, long hair and lipstick. Overnight they went into canvas sandals, baggy cotton trousers and tunics, and cut their hair short. We ransacked private houses looking for such things as the works of Confucius or portraits of Chiang Kai-shek. If we found any we were rather unkind to

Mao swimming in the Yangtze

their owners. Then, something wonderful happened.'

'What was that?' 'We were given free railway tickets to go to Peking. Two million Red Guards from all over China paraded in front of Chairman Mao. We waved copies of his *Little Red Book* in the air and shouted slogans from it. It has been a very exciting year – much better than school.'

Finally, we will talk to a worker in an engineering factory in Peking.

'What was your factory like before the Cultural Revolution?' 'The workers had to take orders from the managers. If we dared to question them they said that they were the experts and knew best. These men weren't even good communists. They wasted money on fancy office furniture. They did only a few light jobs instead of working a proper shift on the factory floor once a week. The director even used to borrow the factory car to go fishing at the weekend. He had owned the factory in the old days and seemed to think he still did.'

'What changes were there during the Cultural Revolution?' 'We elected a Revolutionary Committee of twenty-five ordinary workers and they run the factory. Of course, they have regular meetings with all of us to decide what to do.

'One splendid idea of Chairman Mao's was that workers and peasants should exchange jobs from time to time. I am off to a commune for six weeks and a man from there will take my place in the factory.

'I have had some good family news, as well. My son will be going to Peking University when it reopens. He would not have had the chance before the Cultural Revolution because he was not too bright at school. He is such a good communist, though, that his fellow workers have nominated him for a place.'

7 China since the Death of Mao Tse-tung

Mao Tse-tung died on September 9th, 1976. Hua Kuo-feng one of his most loyal followers had already been chosen to take his place as Chairman of the Chinese Communist Party. That pleased Mao who said, 'With you in charge I am at ease.' A month after Mao's death, though, it became clear that the man who had the real power was Teng Hsaio-ping. He was one of the many leaders who had lost their jobs during the Cultural Revolution but was now back in office as Senior Vice-Premier. Teng had different ideas from Mao and he made many changes.

A government official will tell us what he thinks of Mao, five years after his death.

'Chairman Mao used to say, "We must not have blind faith in anything." But he expected everyone to have blind faith in him! Many of our people did. They

Teng Hsiao-ping

almost worshipped him as a god and his *Little Red Book* was their Bible. Well, we can now see that he made mistakes.

'One of the worst of these mistakes was the Great Leap Forward in 1958. You see, the peasants supported the communists during the Civil War because the communists promised them land. When the war was over they kept their promise and allowed the peasants to share the estates of their former landlords among themselves. The peasants were delighted. But soon communist cadres came to them and said it was wrong for anyone to own land. No good communist does that. They also said that the little farms of one acre or less were not efficient. The peasants in a village should put all their land together to make one big collective farm and work on it as a team. That way they would grow more food and everyone would be better off. The peasants grumbled but they obeyed.

'Then in 1958 Chairman Mao decided that China was going to make the Great Leap Forward. He said that if it was going to succeed, then the collective farms would have to be joined together into communes. Nearly every peasant disliked his collective farm, but at least it was his village and he understood it. Now here was Chairman Mao telling him he must sacrifice himself to this new commune which meant absolutely nothing to him!

'The Great Leap Forward was bound to fail, but what in fact ended it was a terrible drought in many parts of China, which lasted from 1959 to 1961. There was a famine, and peasants were eating bark from the trees. I am sure other countries would have sent us help, but Chairman Mao was too proud to admit anything had gone wrong. Twenty million of our people died from starvation.

'The Cultural Revolution was another disaster. Chairman Mao turned loose the Red Guards and we have no idea how many people they beat, tortured or murdered. In my province of Szechwan mobs of peasants fought back with spears, clubs and knives. There was no teaching done in the schools, no goods made in the factories, and no food grown on the farms. It was total chaos. Much the same sort of thing happened all over China. In the end the army restored order after a lot of bitter fighting. I don't think that

Red Guards

Mao himself should be blamed for the Cultural Revolution. It was the work of his wife Chiang Ching and three of her friends. We call them the Gang of Four.

'I am pleased to say things are much better now. A month after Mao died the Gang of Four was arrested.

Madame Mao on trial

Last year they were tried for their crimes and found guilty. We have also gone a long way towards mending all the harm they did. The teachers are in charge of the schools once again, instead of the pupils. Skilful managers run our factories instead of Revolutionary Committees of workers. In the country-side we have ended almost all the powers of the communes, and each village runs its own affairs. Something we have not done is to give the land back to the peasants. If we did so, China would no longer be a communist country. However, we do allow each family to have its own small plot of land. On it, they grow vegetables to eat themselves or to sell if they wish.

'I think Chairman Mao's greatest error was to think it was better to be "Red" than "expert". By that he meant the most important thing for anyone was to be a true communist. Unless you were, it was no use at all being clever. But if you were going to have your appendix out, would you rather the doctor had studied surgery or the *Little Red Book* of Mao Tse-tung? Time has shown that if China is to be a rich, powerful nation then her leaders must be "expert" rather than "Red". As Teng Hsaio-ping has said, "What does it matter if the cat is black or white as long as it catches mice?"'

317

Chapter Nineteen   Nehru's India

1 Introduction: Nehru Speaks, 1940

'I was born in 1889 at Allahabad. My father was a Brahmin which is the highest of the Hindu castes. He was a successful lawyer, so he was rich. He sent me to England to be educated, where I went first to Harrow and then to Cambridge.

'I speak English of course. I even dream in English, but I hate the British for the wrong they have done India. Their Parliament makes laws for us and their government appoints a Viceroy to rule over us. He chooses his own ministers, and until recently, none of them was Indian. The British are arrogant, too, despising us for our brown skins. In the last century there was a Viceroy, Lord Mayo, who said, "We are all British gentlemen engaged in the magnificent work of governing an inferior race." An inferior race! India was a highly civilised country when the natives of Britain were savages, dressed in animal skins. The British have robbed us, too. Just one example is the Koh-i-nor diamond. It is one of the most valuable of the British crown jewels, and it was stolen from India. Worst of all, the British have kept us poor. Our people toil for slave wages in British cotton mills and on British tea plantations.

'In spite of all these wrongs, Indians fought bravely for the British during the Great War. They guarded the Suez Canal, they helped drive the Turks out of Iraq, and they died in their thousands on the Western Front. After the war the British did allow us a little more say in the government of our country, but it was a poor reward for all our sacrifices.

'Then, in 1919, there was a massacre at Amritsar. An unarmed crowd was holding a peaceful meeting in the town square when General Dyer ordered his troops to fire on it. The people were packed so closely together that they were trapped and unable to escape. Over 400 of them were killed. Afterwards Dyer issued an order saying that anyone who went along a certain street in the town must do so crawling on his hands and knees. The Amritsar massacre made me determined to rid my country of the British.

'In 1922 I met the man whom I admire most in

Nehru

India. Before independence there were about 600 states, each ruled by its own prince. Only the important ones are shown here. The princes were under the control of the British who made sure they governed their people properly.

the world, Mahatma Gandhi. He took a liking to me and in 1929 he persuaded Congress to elect me its president. Congress, I should explain, is a political party which wants India to be united and free. Most of its members are Hindus and fairly wealthy, educated ones at that. You could say that as President of Congress I stand for these people, but the real leader of the nation is Gandhi.

'Gandhi has shown us the true road to freedom. One tremendous thing he has done is to rouse the masses. Until recent years it was only the rich, educated Indians who were interested in freedom. Now Gandhi has made the ordinary people want their freedom as well. They worship him like a saint and most of them will do anything he asks. He lives like one of them, eating very little food and wearing only a loin-cloth.

'Gandhi's work never ceases. From time to time he organises a Hartal. People refuse to work, to pay their taxes or buy foreign goods. Once he led a host of followers to the coast at Dandi where he evaporated a little sea water to make salt. By doing so, he broke the law, for only the government may make salt. It was a simple gesture, and one that the simplest Indian could understand – defy the British, but do so peacefully. Gandhi is a man of peace and against violence of any kind.

'Other Indian leaders have been glad to follow Gandhi's example. I have been arrested for picketing a shop that sold foreign goods and indeed I have spent nine years in gaol for various offences. My father gave up his law practice, and as a family we gave up our life of luxury. We all wear khaddar, or homespun cloth and we have destroyed our fine clothes. Even my little daughter, Indira, burnt her pretty dresses. ''All right, Miss Saint,'' said a visitor, ''you burn your foreign clothes, but what about your foreign doll?'' That doll was Indira's favourite toy, and to her it was a real person. For days she was in agony, but in the end she burnt it. She tells me that since then she cannot bear to strike a match.

'Now a second World War has begun. I am sure that when it is over India will be free. I am worried, though, that she will not be united. A quarter of our people are Muslims, and their leader, Jinnah, wants them to form a separate state. He calls it ''Pakistan''.'

Indira burning her doll

2 An Englishman's view of India, 1935

'I am a civil servant and I work in India. It is a difficult country to govern. There are nearly 400 million people of many different races speaking many different languages. There are many different religions, too, although three quarters of the people are Hindus and most of the others are Muslims.

'The Hindus have some strange beliefs. For example, each of them belongs to a caste. There are four castes and the lowest one is of "Sudras", or "Untouchables". It is a crime for one of them even to let his shadow fall on a high caste Hindu. They have to do all the dirty, unpleasant jobs and they are as poor as can be. Indeed, it is their religious duty to be miserable. The idea is that they were very wicked in their previous lives, and now they must be punished.

'Women suffer a great deal, as well. The Hindu believes he must have many sons to take care of his soul when he dies. An Indian girl is married before she is twelve, and is expected to have a son as soon as possible. The birth of a daughter is a disaster, so much so that in the old days girl babies were often left in the fields to die. We have stopped that, but too many little girls still die through neglect, while the boys get all the care and attention.

in "purdah". That means they spend most of their time shut up together in stuffy, unhealthy rooms. Because of that, tuberculosis is very common among Muslim women.

'In spite of all our problems we British have been able to do a great deal of good in India. Usually the rains fail one year in five, and that used to mean famine, with millions of people dying of hunger. Today, we can transport food quickly from those parts of the country which have it, to the ones which do not. In many places, especially the Punjab, we have built dams to store the precious water and we have dug thousands of miles of irrigation canals, to take it to the fields. There still are famines, I'm afraid, but they are nothing like as frequent or as bad as they used to be.

'We have encouraged farmers to grow new crops. The most important of these is tea. Thousands of tons of this are exported every year, and the trade is helping India to become more prosperous.

'There is industry too. India mines enough coal to meet all her own needs, she manufactures cotton cloth, and she makes iron and steel. The Tata Iron and Steel Works at Bihar, is the largest in the world. It is owned entirely by Indians. Most of all, I think we can be very proud of the railways. They will compare with any that you may find in Europe or North America.

'The worst fate for a married woman is to be left a widow. Her husband might have been an old man, while she was just a girl; even so the fact that he died first is taken as a sure sign that in her previous life she committed a dreadful sin. By her wickedness she has brought about the death of her husband, and must be made to suffer. Until the British forbade it, a Hindu widow would commit suttee, which meant she jumped into her husband's funeral pyre and burnt to death. Even today, a widow belongs to her husband's family, and they treat her like a slave. It is not unusual for a widow to be made so unhappy that she goes away quietly, soaks herself in oil and sets fire to herself.

'Another problem is caused because Hindus believe that cows are sacred. Hardly any give more than a quart of milk a day and there are millions of them. You see cows everywhere, even in the streets of the big cities. If all the land which grew food for these useless creatures grew food for human beings, there would be no more hungry people in India. As it is, many die of starvation each year.

'The Muslim religion is more like Christianity, so it is easier for us to understand, but even the Muslims do strange things. For example, their women have to live

'Another thing we have done is to give a good number of Indians an education. We have built schools and universities, while a few of the most favoured ones have studied in Britain. I don't see what else we could have done, but I think it will lead to the end of British rule in India. It is the educated Indians who are now agitating for us to leave, saying they are quite capable of looking after themselves. Well, we are giving them more and more say in the government, and no doubt they will be independent one day. But it would be fatal for us to go now. There would be chaos and ruin.'

3 Gandhi and Jinnah

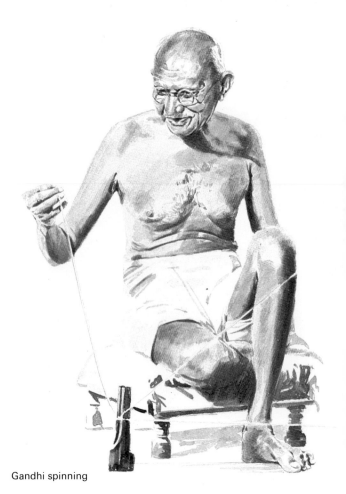

Gandhi spinning

Mahatma Gandhi, 1935

'My name is Mohandas Gandhi, and my followers have been kind enough to give me the title of Mahatma, which means "great soul".

'I was born in 1869. My parents had a little money, so they sent me to London to study law. In 1917 I returned to India. My aim is to end British rule over my country, and make her free. At first sight that should not be too difficult. There are barely 100,000 Britons governing almost 400 million Indians. They can only do that because there is a great deal wrong with the Indian people themselves. Three things worry me particularly. One is the hatred between Hindus and Muslims, the second is the ill-treatment of the Untouchables by high caste Hindus, and the third is the dreadful poverty in which most Indians live.

'Muslims number one quarter of our population and live side by side with Hindus in countless towns and villages. There must be peace between them, for if there was a war of religion hundreds of thousands of people would die.

'In India we have 60 million Untouchables, and the Brahmins, the high caste Hindus, want them to lead more miserable lives than animals. A Brahmin will object if an Englishman despises him for his brown skin, but that same Brahmin will make an Untouchable crawl on his belly! All Hindus must accept Untouchables as fellow human beings. I would sooner our religion died, than stayed as it is.

'Perhaps our greatest problem is poverty. Most of our peasants are walking skeletons, with no flesh on

beggars

their ribs. It hurts me to see them, but it hurts me even more to look into their eyes. All I meet is a blank stare. They have toiled so long with their oxen, that they have become just like them. They are so hungry that they can do nothing but worry where their next meal is coming from. How can we expect them to think about making a free India?

'There is an answer to this problem and it is the spinning wheel. India grows millions of pounds of cotton each year, and what is not exported is turned into cloth in our mills. We must give our peasants the raw cotton and they can make money by spinning it into thread in their own homes.

'The spinning wheel will do more than banish poverty from our villages. Everyone must spin, rich and poor, Brahmin and Untouchable, Hindu and Muslim, men and women. That way we will become one united people, with all our quarrels forgotten. I set an example myself, for I spin for an hour every day. It always soothes me. My wheel is the one friend on whom I can always rely.

'I have made a little progress with the leaders of the Congress Party for I have persuaded them all to wear khaddar, and some have promised me they will spin for half an hour a day. But that will not be enough to

Jinnah

bring them close to the people. How can a rich man know what it is to be poor, until he has lived in the slums of Bombay? How can a Brahmin know what it is to be an Untouchable until he has eaten scraps of food from a dustbin? How can a city lawyer know what it is to be a peasant until he has toiled for hours in the full heat of the sun?

'When all these things are done we shall throw off British rule with ease. There will be no need for violence. It is my ambition that we should win our freedom without shedding one drop of blood.'

Mohammed Ali Jinnah, 1945

'I am the President of the Muslim League, which means I am the leader of all the Muslims in India. Centuries ago our ancestors came to this country as enemies and conquerors, but many of its people were glad to adopt our religion. For the most part they were Hindu Untouchables. Who can blame them? Their own religion had nothing to offer them!

'Today a quarter of the people of India are Muslims and we have little in common with the Hindus. Very occasionally an Englishman will marry an Indian, but you never hear of a Hindu marrying a Muslim. Indeed, we Muslims have usually been on the side of the British, because we need their help to save us from the Hindus.

'Now it is certain the British will leave soon, so what will become of us? I have tried to reach an agreement with Congress but it is impossible to reason with people like Nehru and Gandhi. They are determined that India will be one country, ruled by the majority of its people – and the majority is Hindu.

'The only answer is for us to have a country of our own, quite separate from the rest of India. We already have a name for it – Pakistan. We made it up with letters from the names of the most important Muslim provinces, Punjab, Afghanis, Kashmir, Sind and Baluchistan.

'In 1940 the Muslim League passed a resolution demanding the creation of Pakistan, and I raised the cry "Islam is in danger." I am happy to say that ordinary Muslims everywhere are answering our call. If need be I shall urge them to take direct action to preserve their freedom.'

Muslim mosque

4 Independence, 1947

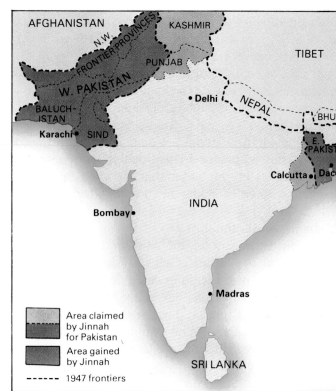

India and Pakistan

massacre of refugees

A British officer serving in the Indian Army tells us what happened when India won her independence.

'I have lived most of my life in this country. The Indians have wanted to rule themselves ever since I can remember. Often they have gone about it peacefully enough, but there has been bloodshed as well, like the time when a gang of them slaughtered some English missionaries at Amritsar. General Dyer was called a murderer for shooting a few of them. Even so, as time has gone by the British have given the Indians more and more freedom to govern themselves. We made them a first rate offer with the Government of India Act of 1935, but they were still trying to make up their minds about it when war broke out in 1939.

'Lots of Indians fought well for us during the war, especially the Gurkhas, but Nehru and his kind weren't much help. In 1942 Gandhi started a "Quit India" campaign, just when the Japanese were chasing us through Burma. We had to put the Congress leaders in gaol for a time. I think myself that our government should have promised that India would have her independence as soon as the war was over, but it didn't. I blame Churchill. He said he hadn't become Prime Minister in order to destroy the British Empire. The Americans made him change his mind. They asked him how he could expect the Indians to fight for freedom for others when they weren't going to have any themselves. In the end he sent Sir Stafford Cripps with a firm promise of independence as soon as Germany and Japan were defeated.

'You might have thought that was the end of all the trouble, but not at all. Congress and the Muslim League had never been the best of friends but now they really flew at each other's throats. Gandhi and Nehru wanted India to stay united. Jinnah wanted a separate Pakistan, and so large that there would have been millions of Hindus living in it under Muslim rule. It was bad enough to have the leaders squabbling, but worse than that happened. Until then, ordinary Hindus and Muslims had lived in peace. A Hindu procession would stop its noise as it went by a Muslim mosque. A Muslim housewife would hide her beef on the way home to avoid upsetting her Hindu neighbours. All that sort of thing ended, because Gandhi stirred up the Hindus and Jinnah did the same with the

Muslims. Both sides went hard at it, insulting each other's religion and even rioting and murdering. In 1946 Jinnah called for August 16th to be "Direct Action Day" and 4,000 people were killed in Calcutta. Before long there were thousands of people with wrongs they were burning to avenge.

'The Viceroy Lord Wavell did his best to make Congress and the League agree, but he got nowhere. In 1947 the British government lost patience and said that come what may we are going to pull out. They sacked Wavell and sent Lord Louis Mountbatten to wind things up. That brought the Indian leaders to their senses. Nehru and Gandhi said Jinnah could have his Pakistan, but Jinnah had to accept that it was going to be a lot smaller than he had hoped.

'Pakistan became independent on August 13th, 1947, and India on August 14th. Was this the end of the problems? Not a bit of it. The country was in a bigger mess than ever. When the frontiers were drawn, large numbers of Muslims realised they were

Mountbatten

going to be under Hindu rule, and many Hindus saw they would be under Muslim rule. Five million Hindus fled into India and seven million Muslims fled into Pakistan. They didn't go in peace either. We believe about 400,000 must have been killed on the way.

'Some of the worst incidents were on the refugee trains. As soon as one of them stopped, armed gangs would board it and kill everyone they could find who was of the rival religion. I was on duty at a station one day when a man came screaming to me that some hoodlums were killing his family. I only had a handful of men so it would have been suicide to interfere. I just said: "You wanted independence and now you've got it."'

5 India since Independence

Gandhi, Nehru and Jinnah led their people to independence with high hopes. We have seen that the first result was the deaths of 400,000 Indians. What happened after that?

In January 1948 Gandhi was assassinated. His murderer was a man of his own religion, a Hindu. He hated Gandhi because, in spite of all the bloodshed, Gandhi still wanted to be on good terms with the Muslims. Millions of Indians mourned him, but none more than Nehru.

Troubles between the Muslims and Hindus did not end with the division of the country. There was a quarrel as early as 1947 when the Hindu ruler of Kashmir decided that his state should join India. As three-quarters of his subjects were Muslims, the government of Pakistan said Kashmir should join

help. The trouble is that India's population is growing at the rate of ten million a year. As soon as the country has a little more wealth, there are more people to share it, so no-one is better off.

Though industry is growing, four Indians in every five are farmers. To see the sort of lives they are leading in the 1980s we will visit a village near Bangalore in the south.

There is no proper road to the village. It is just a dirt track, which becomes a mud track during the monsoon. Sometimes a bullock cart rumbles past, its huge wheels wobbling from side to side. It is not strong enough to carry more than half a ton at a time. There are better carts available, with pneumatic tyres, but as hardly any Indian farmers can afford them, it is a waste of time to make them.

Gandhi's funeral

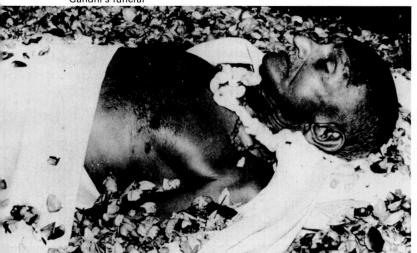

overloaded bus in Calcutta

their country. The argument went on until 1965 when there was a war. India won, and kept Kashmir.

Later, in 1971, East Pakistan rebelled against the government of West Pakistan. That pleased the Indians who entered the war on the side of East Pakistan. Again, India won, and in 1972 East Pakistan became the independent state of Bangladesh.

What has happened to India itself? Nehru was Prime Minister from 1947 until his death in 1964. He did his best to make his country richer, especially by encouraging the factories and mines to produce more. Both the Americans and the Russians gave a lot of

The village streets are just dirt, like the roads. The houses are one-room hovels, made of wood with thatched roofs. The villagers share their homes with their goats and chickens. They have no proper furniture. Indeed their only possessions that are worth anything are their pots and pans.

There are no sewers, and there is no running water in any house. The village has a pump, but it is out of order. Half the village pumps in India are out of order at any one time, simply because hardly anyone knows how to mend them. The water comes from a pond half a mile away. With any luck, this fills during the monsoon, but then it must last for the whole year. It is the women who collect the water, carrying their pots on their heads. While an English housewife just turns on a tap, the Indian village housewife must visit the pond twice a day. She walks two miles, it takes her an hour and a half and she only draws a gallon and a half of water.

There is no electricity, of course. Cooking is done on a wood fire. The children collect fallen branches and dead twigs in the countryside. It takes two and a half hours to gather enough firewood for one family for one day.

The main crop grown in the village is millet, but there is some rice and sugar-cane as well. Apart from a few crude ploughs the people have only hand tools. Every day they must toil for hours in the heat of the sun. With all their efforts they grow hardly enough to feed themselves. What is more, about one year in five the monsoon fails, and that means starvation.

The village has its own smith, wheelwright, weaver and potter. What the people cannot produce themselves, they must do without. A little machinery would make their lives a lot easier, but the simplest of windmills costs £150. They cannot afford it.

Something exciting is going to happen, though. The government has made the village a grant and it is to have a Biogas plant. Everyone will bring all the manure he can find, and the plant will take gas from it. This will be piped into the homes and people will burn it for cooking. They will use primitive little stoves made from tin cans. The farmers will even have their manure back, turned into an even richer fertiliser than it was before. It all seems like a miracle to these simple folk. Certainly it will be the most important change the village has had for generations.

An Indian village

329

Chapter Twenty   Kennedy's America

1 Introduction: Kennedy Speaks, 1961

'I have just been elected President of the United States. I am the first Catholic ever to hold that position. Also, at 44, I am the youngest man to do so.

'America is the richest and most powerful country in the world, but she has her problems. I have told the American people that we face a New Frontier. When our ancestors arrived in this country they settled the east coast. The Old Frontier was the line between them and the thousands of square miles of untamed land to the west. Gradually, they rolled it back and when they reached the Pacific it was no more. The New Frontier is even more challenging, but it is not a line drawn on a map. The things we face are not great rivers, prairies, forests and mountain ranges. What are they?

'One of the most important is poverty. It is not as bad as it was back in the 1920s when well over half of

our people had barely enough to stay alive. Many of the country people and Negroes were terribly poor. At the same time some families were very wealthy. Those were the days when our factories first produced motor cars and electrical gadgets like radios, refrigerators and washing machines. Rich families could afford all these things and they lived comfortable lives.

'Then came the great depression of the 1930s. The rich lost a lot of their money but the poor lost everything. We had millions of unemployed. President Roosevelt pulled us out of that with his New Deal, and the Second World War gave jobs to everyone. Since the war, we have not had another depression, but many of our people are still poor. I want the government to help. We must have free medical care for the elderly and we must create jobs for the unemployed.

United States of America

Former slave states

PRESIDENT KENNEDY ASSASSINATED

THREE SHOTS AT OPEN CAR IN TEXAS

We must have better schools and we must pull down the slums in the big cities and build new houses. Many Americans believe that the government should not interfere in these ways. They say people should look after themselves and make their own way by hard work. That is fine if you are young, fit and have a good job, but what if you are old, sick or unemployed? Surely, then, the government must offer you a helping hand.

'Something else we must do is to make sure all our people are equal. In years gone by, thousands of black slaves were brought from Africa to work on the cotton and tobacco plantations of the south. In 1863, after the Civil War, the slaves were set free, but in many ways they were still as badly off as ever. Many southern whites treated the Negroes very badly. At first blacks lived only in the south, but now you find them in almost every American city, and often in large numbers. What was once a problem for part of our country is now a problem for all of it.

'We have a Civil Rights Movement led by Martin Luther King. It has done much for the blacks, and has made the government take action, too. But there are still too many injustices. Let us suppose two babies, one black and one white, are born on the same day. The Negro has a third as much chance of going to college as the white baby; he has twice as much chance of being unemployed; if he has a job he will probably earn half as much, and he must expect to die seven years sooner. We cannot have such unfairness in our country.

'The New Frontier is also scientific. I am worried that America is behind Russia in the space race. The Russians put their first satellite, Sputnik 1 into orbit in October 1957. It weighed 184 pounds. Our first satellite was not ready until December. It weighed only three pounds. Khrushchev called it a grapefruit. When we tried to launch it, its rocket caught fire and it lay bleeping on the ground while the Russian Sputniks – there were two by then – were bleeping proudly from space. Soon we shall put a man into orbit, but I'm afraid the Russians may beat us to it. I am quite determined, though, that the first man on the moon will be an American, and that he will go there within the next ten years.'

President Kennedy was assassinated in November 1963. Even in his time as President his New Frontier had made little progress. Today, America still has her problems of rich and poor, black and white. She has had her successes as well though, and among them is the conquest of space.

2 America in the 1920s

We will talk to an American Negro, who has left a small town in Mississippi to live in Chicago.

'Why did you leave Mississippi?' 'To find a job. I worked on a cotton plantation for a miserable wage. Our home was a wooden shack, and we never had enough to eat. Then my boss bought a cotton picking machine and told most of his workers he didn't want them any more. He kept a couple of white men and sacked all his blacks.'

'That seems unfair.' 'It's quite usual. Long ago all Negroes were slaves. The Southern whites haven't forgotten that, and they don't let us forget it either.'

'What do they do?' 'There are a lot of "Jim Crow" laws for a start. We can't stay in certain hotels, or eat in certain restaurants. We have separate seats in buses and separate compartments on trains. Our children have to go to separate schools. Of course, the hotels, schools and everything else for whites are better than the ones for Negroes. What's worse is that we go in fear of our lives. There are people who call themselves the Ku Klux Klan. They and others like them, lynch or murder hundreds of Negroes every year. It is rare for one of them to be caught. If he is, he's sure to get off. The judges are white, the juries are white and they never convict a white man for killing a Negro.'

black railway porter

'Are you happier now you have moved to Chicago?' 'Not a lot. I'm a railway porter. My wages are much better than they ever were, but more than half of them goes on rent for these two rooms. We still don't get enough to eat, and we can't afford decent clothes.'

'Are the northern whites kinder to you?' 'I don't go in fear of being lynched up here, but the whites hate us, just the same. They won't even live in the same streets as we do. Every year, a few more white families move out of the city centre and Negro families from the south move in.'

We will now talk to a wealthy American who also lives in Chicago.

'How did you become so rich Mr. Bonnici?' 'By hard work. I started with nothing – just ran errands after I left school. But America is a land of great opportunities. That's why my parents came here from Italy. I saved hard, worked all the hours God sent and ended up with this factory in Chicago. We turned out typewriters. Since I retired I have made a fair amount playing the stock market.'

'The stock market?' 'Sure, you know, in Wall Street. When I wanted to start my business, I didn't have nearly enough money so I offered shares for sale on the stock market. People bought them and I used their cash to build up my factory. It was like each person had bought a chunk of the profits. You can buy shares in anything – railways, factories, shipping lines, banks, insurance companies, anything. Back in 1922 I invested $10,000 in Associated Gas and Electric. Last year my shares were worth $40,000 so I sold them – a

Mr. Bonnici

profit of $30,000. That's how to get rich quick. Play the stock market.'

'*But if the company does badly, what then?*' 'Then your shares drop in value and you lose money. That doesn't happen any more, though, not in America. All companies do well. Your only problem is to pick the ones that are going to do best.'

'*You have a comfortable home I see.*' 'We sure have. Plenty of rooms, plenty of good furniture and a kitchen with all the latest gadgets, even a refrigerator. President Hoover says that one day every American family will have two cars in the garage and two chickens in the pot. Well, we have four cars, one for each member of the family, and we eat what we like, any day we like.'

'*You seem to think well of America. Is there nothing that worries you?*' 'Sure there is. It's the younger generation. Take my daughter. She calls herself an "It" girl. She wears dresses that flatten her out, so she looks more like a plank than a girl. She uses make-up too. That really upsets her mother. I blame myself for buying her a car, but what can you do? Now she tears around all over the place, always at parties, always staying out to all hours of the night. She usually comes home smelling of booze. Her boyfriend is as crazy as she is. The two of them took part in a dancing marathon. Forty hours they were dancing – that's if you can call the Charleston and the Tango dancing. It wasn't as if they needed the prize money! There's this terrible jazz music too. She would like to have the phonograph pump it out all day, but I won't allow the noise in my house.

'Then there's this thing called Prohibition. Back in 1920 Congress passed a law making it illegal to buy or sell any alcoholic drinks anywhere in the United States. It was the Women's Christian Temperance Union made them do it. That's what comes of giving women the vote! No-one obeys the law. You can buy booze, no trouble at all. Instead of bars, all nice and legal, we have speakeasies with soda-pop on their counters and gin hidden underneath. That wouldn't matter so much, but the liquor trade is in the hands of gangsters who are making themselves fortunes. Pistols used to be good enough for them, but not any more. They use machine guns. In Chicago, Al Capone's got a car like a tank. It's protected with armour plate and bullet proof glass an inch and a half thick. The back window opens up for his rear gunner. The Mayor of Chicago is his buddy and the police do just as he tells them. Al Capone rules Chicago and unless something is done real quick, his kind is going to rule the whole of the United States.'

'It' girl, Miss Bonnici

333

America in the 1920s

police raiding a liquor store

3 The Great Depression

In the early 1930s America's prosperity came to an end. The first to be in trouble were those who had been 'playing the stock market'. They lost a lot of money because share prices, instead of rising, began to fall. At once, people who had been frantic to buy were frantic to sell. On just one day, October 29th, 1929, 16½ million shares were sold on Wall Street. They called it 'Black Tuesday'. But that was only the beginning of the depression. Before long, millions of Americans were suffering. Why did it happen?

Factories had been pouring out goods for people like the Bonnicis, but there was a limit to what even they wanted to buy. The shops were full of goods which did not sell, so the factories stopped making them. That meant they had to sack their workers. A man who was without a job was unable to buy a refrigerator for his wife, or even a new suit for himself. Still fewer goods were needed, and still more workers were sacked. By 1939 there were 13 million unemployed.

The depression did have just one good result. Gangsters lost money and went out of business, the same way as honest men. Also, in 1933 Congress decided Prohibition had been a mistake and made it legal once again to buy and sell alcoholic drinks.

Three Americans will tell us what life was like during the depression. First we will talk to a farmer from Montana.

'When did you realise there was a depression?' 'The first sign of trouble was strange tidings from New York. Firms were going bust and folk were jumping off skyscrapers because they had lost fortunes on the stock market. The only stock we have in Montana is cattle and sheep, so it didn't make a lot of sense to me. I didn't care much, either, until I went into town to my bank. It was all closed up, and I couldn't have any money. Then I really began to worry, but there was worse to come.'

'What was that?' 'The price of wheat and meat fell so low it wasn't worth trying to sell any of it. I left my wheat uncut. What they offered me for it wouldn't have paid for the harvesting. I killed 3,000 sheep and threw them into a canyon. It would have cost me a dollar a head, just to send them to market and I would have been lucky if they had sold for as much. While

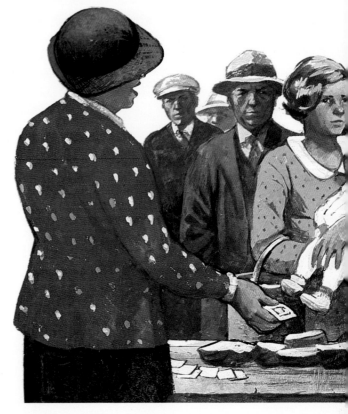

the buzzards were picking my sheep, the unemployed in Chicago were picking through the trashcans, looking for food. It didn't make any sense.'

We will now talk to a girl from one of the slum areas of Chicago.

'What happened to your family during the depression?' 'We couldn't afford our rent, so we were thrown out of our house. We went to live on some waste land, and lots of other families did the same. We built shelters with what we could find – odd bits of cardboard and wood. My father blamed our troubles on President Hoover. He called our shanty town "Hooverville", and the newspapers we slept in "Hoover blankets".'

'What did you eat?' 'Every day my young brother and I used to go to the soup line, with a bucket. There was always a long queue, right round the block. If you were among the first the man used to ladle out the greasy watery mess on the top. All the potatoes and meat were at the bottom, so we used to say, "Dip down, God damn it, dip down!" It was in the soup line that I first learnt to cuss.'

Finally, we will talk to a young man from California.

'When did you leave school?' 'At the worst time, in 1930. I walked straight into this thing, the depression.

I only had a mother – no father to help me. I had always had pretty big ideas about being a lawyer, or making a fortune in business. As it was, I had to take any job that was going. I picked apples, I washed dishes and I worked on road gangs. Soon there were no jobs at all. I was in Los Angeles at the time. One morning I went to a sugar refinery and so did a thousand others. A guy came out and said, "I got jobs for two men." All the thousand started fighting like dogs to get in. I was just a youngster and didn't stand a chance. In the end I hoboed.'

'What's that?' 'It means riding around on goods trains without paying any fare. I would wait by the rail track for a train and jump on a box car. Often I have travelled all day and all night with nothing more than a bottle of water and a hunk of bread. We used to ride in gangs, perhaps ten or fifteen of us. We dreaded the railroad police. There was one we called Texas Slim. He would draw a gun on you and make you jump from the train, no matter how fast it was moving.'

'How did your mother feel about this?' 'I was worried about my mother, wondering if she might be starving. I knew she would be worried about me too, so I used to write from the sidewalk, wherever I might be, and say I was fine. She used to tell the neighbours, "My son is up in Wisconsin. He is doing pretty fair."'

soup line

4 The New Deal

Roosevelt

In this section we talk to a government official. He tells us what was done to end the depression.

'*What did the American government do about the depression?*' 'To start with, nothing at all. Herbert Hoover was President. Like lots of Americans he believed that if you were hungry, that was your own fault – you were idle or you just weren't on the ball. He also thought that the depression would cure itself. He kept saying that prosperity was just around the corner. Well, the American people didn't believe him. He came up for re-election in 1932, and they gave his rival, Franklin D. Roosevelt, the biggest majority in our history.'

'*How were Roosevelt's ideas different?*' 'For one thing he thought that if you were on the soup line it might not be your own fault. That meant it was O.K. for the government to give you a helping hand. For another thing he didn't believe in sitting back and letting it all happen. As soon as he was elected he promised the American people what he called a "New Deal".'

'*What did he mean by that?*' 'He wasn't sure. We had never had a depression quite like the one of the

1930s. Roosevelt was like a doctor with a patient that had a new disease. He didn't know what the cure was, but he was determined to do everything he could. If he got results, fine, but if he didn't, then try something else. He was especially bothered about the ordinary folk. He knew the rich had taken a pounding, but they had something left. But what about the small time farmer who had lost his land, the house owner who had been turned out of his house and the factory worker who had lost his job? What did they have left? They were the ones Roosevelt wanted to help.

Boulder Dam

Civilian Conservation Corps

'I was one of his advisers, and I have never worked so hard as during his first three months in office. Later we called it the "hundred days". I lost count of all the measures we took.'

'Please tell us about some of them.' 'The first thing was to stop people starving, so the government gave out millions of dollars in aid to the needy. The next job was to try to cure the depression. We had all sorts of new organisations like Harry Hopkins's Works Progress Administration. Their aim was to create jobs. There were huge projects that employed hundreds of men, like building the Boulder Dam. There were little projects, like setting an unemployed artist to paint pictures on the walls of an office block. The idea was that if you gave enough people jobs, they would have wages to spend. They would want goods, and that would set the factories rolling again. They would take on workers, and the whole depression would go into reverse.'

'Did it work?' 'Something did. After the New Deal came in more and more people began to find jobs. But there are folk who say the depression would have ended anyway, with or without Roosevelt. Yes sir, there are even those who think the whole New Deal was wrong. It was un-American they say. Americans must stand on their own two feet, and the government mustn't hand out aid.'

We will now talk to an American factory worker who was a young man at the time of the New Deal.

'How did the New Deal help you?' 'My father died when I was six and my mother put me in an orphanage. I had to come out when I was seventeen. That was in 1935. There was no work, my mother still couldn't feed me, so I enlisted in the C.C.C.'

'The C.C.C.?' 'Sure, the Civilian Conservation Corps. It was one of Roosevelt's creations. The idea was to give young people something to do, so they didn't have to hobo. I was in Michigan at the time and we used to plant trees. All these trees you see at the side of the road, and a lot of the forests as well, we planted. It was all bare ground then, but we planted it. I could plant a hundred trees an hour.'

'Were you paid?' 'I had my keep and a dollar a day. I didn't need the dollar, so I sent it to my mother.'

'Did you enjoy the work?' 'Sure thing. It was hard, but it made a man of me. One thing I learnt was not to bother about the colour of the man next to me. Black and white, we were all equal in the C.C.C.'

5 McCarthy and the Communist Scare, 1950–1953

McCarthy

Eisenhower campaigning

In the 1950s certain things happened in America which later made most of her people ashamed. A newspaper editor will tell·us about them.

'What went wrong in the 1950s?' 'There was panic fear of communism. Everyone was expecting to find a Red under his bed.'

'How did it come about?' 'It started with bad news from abroad. As soon as the war ended the Russians grabbed all of Eastern Europe, and soon afterwards the communists grabbed power in China. On top of that, the Russians exploded their first atomic bomb in 1949, something we hadn't expected them to do for years. It was like a bad dream. That bad dream became a real nightmare when people began wondering if there were communists in important positions, right here in America, waiting to betray us.'

'Who put that thought in their heads?' 'It was Senator Jo McCarthy from Wisconsin.'

'Why did he do it?' 'He wanted to become famous, and he sure did. Before 1950 hardly anyone outside of Wisconsin had heard of him. Then, suddenly, he was as well known as the President. There were McCarthy Clubs in every town.'

'What did Senator McCarthy do?' 'He called all sorts of people communists – and the more unlikely they were to be so, the better, or that's how it seemed. He said the State Department was overrun with communists. He claimed he had a list of 205 of its officials who were communists. He and his henchmen attacked almost anyone likely to think for himself – trades union leaders, teachers, writers, actors and film producers. He named lots of Broadway and Hollywood stars, and he did not stop at them. He even accused Robert J. Oppenheimer.'

'The man who led the Manhattan project which produced the atomic bomb?' 'That's the guy. Oppenheimer was declared a security risk and the only evidence against him was that he had once had a communist girl friend. The craziest thing of all, though, was to say that General Marshall was hatching a plot which was too horrible to mention. Marshall was Secretary of Defence in Truman's government at the time. He had a splendid war record. I look on him as one of the greatest living Americans.'

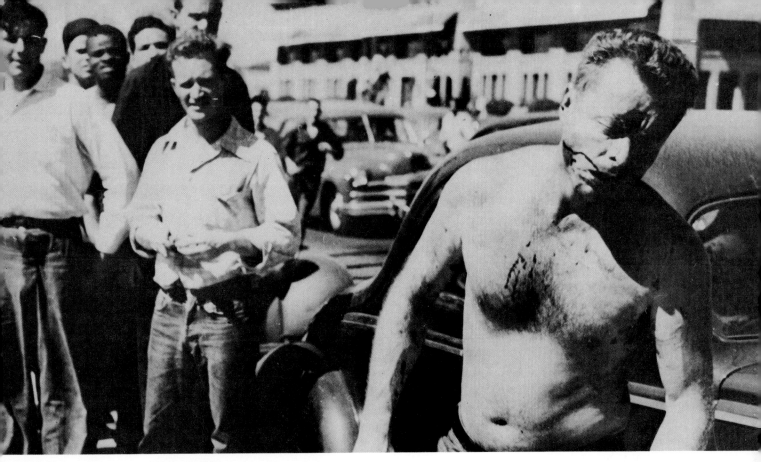

suspected Communist beaten by fellow workers

'*What happened to these people?*' 'They were "investigated" to see if they were communists or even if they had ever had anything to do with them. Over nine million Americans were investigated, some by employers and some by the state authorities. The really unlucky ones had to go before McCarthy and his sidekicks. Thousands lost their jobs and were ruined. Those who could, like the wealthy authors and actors, went abroad. Charlie Chaplin was one of them.'

'*Why did McCarthy get away with this?*' 'In those days the Democrats were in office. The Republicans wanted to win the next election and they thought McCarthy would get them votes. Their leaders must have known the guy was a phoney, but that didn't stop them using him. Eisenhower was running for President, and look what he did to Marshall! Marshall was chief of staff during the war, and he and Eisenhower were close friends. But Marshall was a Democrat, so did Eisenhower stick up for him against McCarthy? No Sir! He couldn't say anything *against* Marshall, but he was careful not to say anything *for* him. Then, when Eisenhower visited Wisconsin, he told the people there to re-elect McCarthy as their Senator. I guess Eisenhower must have wanted to be President real bad.'

'*What happened to McCarthy in the end?*' 'He had two no-goods to help him with his dirty work – Roy Cohn and David Schine. In 1953 Schine was drafted into the army and McCarthy said he should be given special privileges. Schine's officers refused. They treated him just like any other recruit. That made McCarthy hopping mad, and to get his own back he decided to investigate the army. What's more, he jumped at the idea of showing the interviews live on television. That was his big mistake. Millions of Americans were able to watch him in action. They saw him scowling, fidgeting, raving, shouting, banging on the table, bullying witnesses. They saw him as he really was. Americans are fair minded people, and they turned against McCarthy in a big way. His buddies in the Republican party had won the 1952 election – thanks to McCarthy. But they saw he would lose them the next one, so they dropped him like a hot potato. In 1953 the Senate passed a resolution saying he had "acted contrary to Senatorial ethics and tended to bring the Senate into dishonor and disrepute." It was their way of calling him a louse. That finished him. He died of drink three years later, and no one noticed he had gone. McCarthyism had become a thing of the past. We call it "McCarthywasm" now. It did our country a lot of harm, though. We had asked the whole world to support us against Russia because America was the land of the free. If that was so, how come it spawned a creature like McCarthy?'

6 Martin Luther King, 1967

Martin Luther King was leader of the Civil Rights Movement, which aims to make negroes equal with whites. Here he tells us about it.

'I have worked all my life on behalf of my fellow negroes in America. In the south, many whites still treat them as if they were no better than slaves. Partly because of that, large numbers of them have migrated to other parts of the country. Unhappily, in their new homes they have found new problems.

'Negroes have taken over the city centres. The whites have moved out, so these places have become black ghettoes. Life in the ghettoes is hard. The houses are slums, and there is a lot of unemployment and disease. Moreover, the Negro knows that out in the suburbs white people are living in luxury, and that makes his own dirt and poverty harder to bear.

'What is being done to help the Negroes? Well, we are doing a great deal to help ourselves. There was a time when we were too cowed, too frightened to fight.

Martin Luther King

black ghetto

A Negro would even step off the sidewalk when he saw a white man coming. That is over now.

'We have organised Freedom Marches in the deep south. Whites still hate the Negroes there, more than anywhere else, so a march can be dangerous. "Bull" Connor, sheriff of Birmingham, Alabama has ordered his police to club demonstrators to the ground. Numbers of our people have been shot.

'We have organised boycotts. In Montgomery, Alabama the buses had separate seats for blacks and whites. Negroes refused to use the buses until this was stopped. The company nearly went bankrupt, so in the end it had to give in.

'The Federal Government has made laws. We have had Civil Rights Acts and Voting Rights Acts. Men like "Bull" Connor have helped – without meaning to. Most Americans are decent people and they are angry if they see a television shot of four white policemen beating up a black woman. They then back the government when it tries to end injustice. The "Whites Only" signs are coming down in hotels, restaurants and airport waiting rooms. Negroes can vote at election time, the same as whites, or at least the law says they can.

'Americans have faith in education. Lots of us feel that if only the Negro child could have the same education as the white child the two would grow up to be equal. That means they must go to the same school, and the law says this must happen. But some white parents do not like their children to sit beside Negro children. In 1957 seventeen Negro children tried to attend the Central High School at Little Rock, Arkansas. This caused riots and President Eisenhower had to send 1,000 paratroopers to escort the children to school. Since then, the government has ordered "busing". Children in mainly black areas travel by bus to schools in mainly white areas, and the other way round. That means that all schools have a fair number of black children – or they should.

'We have organised demonstrations. The largest was in Washington in 1963 when 230,000 people took part. I made a speech. "I have a dream", I said, and told them my dream was of the day when all men would be free and equal.

'My dream is still a long way off. The trouble with all the new ideas that have been brought in is that they are only on paper. In real life the black man is as badly off as he ever was. It doesn't take much money to remove a "Whites Only" sign. What the Negro really needs is a decent house and a good job. Both are very expensive and the money that might have paid for them has gone on the war in Vietnam. Everywhere

Little Rock

whites break the law, especially in the Deep South. Here only two schools in every hundred have both black and white students. Parents could force all whites to accept their children as happened at Little Rock, but that takes courage. Many Negroes think it wiser to stay at home. You can hardly blame them. In the last three years alone, 40 of them have been murdered or lynched and 50 of their churches have been bombed or burnt. Not a single criminal has been punished for these acts.

'What became of President Kennedy's "New Frontier"? The Negro still has half as many of the good things of life as the white man, and double his share of the bad. That is even true of the war. A Negro soldier in Vietnam is twice as likely to be killed as a white one. How do you account for that?

'In all the years that I have led the Civil Rights Movement I have insisted that it should be peaceful, but now Negroes are losing patience. Trouble began in 1966, on a freedom march in Mississippi. Our slogan had been "Freedom Now". One of our best men, James Meredith, was shot dead. After that lots of the marchers led by Stokely Carmichael, started shouting "Black Power". Since then there have been riots in many cities.'

Martin Luther King was assassinated at Memphis, Tennessee in 1968.

7 America wins the Space Race

In this section an American scientist tells us about the exploration of outer space.

'America was slow to take any interest in the conquest of space. Before the war, we did have our rocket enthusiasts, like Robert H. Goddard, but they got no encouragement. The men in the White House and the Pentagon, who could have helped, just weren't interested.

'It was different in the Soviet Union. Tsiolkovsky started to design rockets as early as 1929. In 1933 he fired one that went three miles high. He saw a long way ahead. He said, "The earth is the cradle of humanity, but mankind will not stay in the cradle for ever."

'During the war it was the Germans that took the lead. By 1944 they were bombarding London with their V2 rockets. The V2 could have won the war for Germany if America and Britain hadn't invaded Europe pretty soon and destroyed the bases.

'After the war, lots of German scientists who had worked on rockets came to America. They included the top man, Wernher von Braun. Our government set

Yuri Gagarin

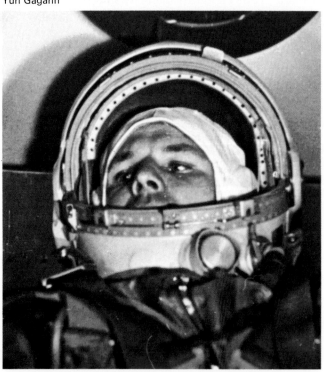

them to work designing rockets for us, but it was still half-hearted about it. Our aircraft were so good that the Pentagon didn't see the need for rockets. The Russians knew better. They realised that rockets with nuclear warheads were the weapons of the future. They saw, too, that rockets would launch space craft, and whoever commands space, can control the earth.

'In October 1957 the American people had a nasty shock. The Russians launched their first satellite, Sputnik One. Sputnik Two was orbiting round the world a month later, and, what is more, it had a dog on board.

'The Russians then won a whole lot of "firsts". In 1959 their Luna Two was the first rocket to hit the moon. In 1961 they put their first man into space, Yuri Gagarin. In 1963 they put the first woman into space, Valentina Tereshkova. In 1965 they flew their Voskhod One which had a crew of three. All satellites had been single seaters until then. In 1965 Alexey Leonov was the first man to leave his craft and "walk" in space.

'By the 1960s we Americans were nearly frantic. Sure, our own space programme was going ahead, but we were always one step behind the Russians. That was going to change, though. In 1961 John F. Kennedy was elected President and announced Project Apollo. He gave our scientists ten years to put a man on the moon and he also gave them 24,000 million dollars to spend. After 1965 the Russians only had one more "first" and it was one they didn't want. Their Colonel Komarov was the first astronaut to die in space. Until then space travel was the safest form of transportation known to man!

'Now it was America's turn. On July 16th, 1969 Apollo Eleven set off on its mission to the moon. On board were Neil Armstrong, Edwin Aldrin and Michael Collins. Their space craft landed on the moon on July 20th. The following morning Neil Armstrong stepped out of it, on to the surface of the moon. The first man on the moon was an American, just as President Kennedy had wanted.

'As for the Russians, they had already given up. I think it had something to do with the fall of Khrushchev. The men who came after him were scared of the expense.

'Of course, the space project has meant far more than putting a man on the moon. We can use satellites for all sorts of things. We can put high powered cameras in them. They will take pictures of the clouds so you can have some idea if it's going to rain on you. That will help you plan your picnic, your ploughing or whatever. You can also know whether a forest fire, a flood or a hurricane is coming your way. The cameras can pick up objects as small as a man, so it is impossible for a country to move troops or warships without the other side knowing. You can also "bounce" signals from satellites. A ship can pinpoint her position to within a hundred yards, using these signals. If you are in London you can telephone your aunt or your business partner in New York with no trouble at all. You can have a colour television programme from the other side of the world. I just long for the day when the people who write the programmes are as brilliant as the ones who make the equipment!

Is it all worth the expense? I don't know. I sometimes think that the money which has gone on the Vietnam War and on space research could have been better spent on the ordinary things we all need. Every American could now be living in a decent house and earning a decent wage in a decent job. We could have ended poverty and America would be a much better place. The big question is, though, would she have been safe from the Russians?'

Neil Armstrong on the moon

Index

WW1 *represents* First World War
WW2 *represents* Second World War

Acknowledgements

The publishers would like to thank the following for permission to reproduce photographs:

Anglo-Chinese Educational Institute; Arts Council (Peasant Paintings from Hu County, Shensi Province Exhibition); Associated Press; Austin Morris, Longbridge; Barnaby's Picture Library; Dr. Barnardo's; BBC Hulton Picture Library; Bolton Metropolitan Borough Arts Department; Chris Bonington; John Brennan; City of Bristol Museum and Art Gallery; British Leyland; British Library; British Petroleum; British Telecom; Bundesarchiv, Koblenz; Camera Press; Central Office of Information, Crown Copyright; Bruce Coleman Ltd; Colorific; Cooper-Bridgeman Library; Cunard Leisure; Darlington Museum; Department of the Environment, Slide Library; Documentation Française; J K Ellwood; Mary Evans Picture Library; Ferranti; Nick Fogden; Foster Associates; Richard Green Galleries; Robert Haas; Tom Hanley; HMSO; IBM, United Kingdom; Imperial War Museum; Institute of Agriculture and Economics, Oxford; International Computers Ltd; Raymond Irons; John Johnson Collection; Keystone Press Agency; London Art Technical Drawings Ltd; Mansell Collection; Jonathan Martin; Massey-Ferguson; Musée Carnavalet, Paris; Musée du Louvre; Museum of London; National Army Museum; National Film Archive Stills Library; National Gallery of Canada, Ottawa; National Maritime Museum; National Motor Museum, Beaulieu (courtesy of Robert Hardin Associates); National Portrait Gallery; Peter Newark's Western Americana; Northern Engineering Industries Limited; Northumberland County Council; The Observer; Paramount Pictures Corporation; Photo Library International; Popperfoto; Eliot Porter; Public Record Office; Radio Times Hulton Picture Library; Ann Ronan Picture Library; Royal Geographical Society; Science Museum; Society for Cultural Relations with USSR; Sotheby's, Belgravia; Peter Speed; Süddeutscher Verlag Bilderdienst; Tate Gallery; The Times; John Topham Picture Library; Twentieth-Century Fox; United Press International; US Navy; Victoria and Albert Museum; Volkswagen; Walker Art Gallery, Liverpool; Waterways Museum.

Illustrations by Andrew Aloof, Victor Ambrus, Robert Ayton, Dick Barnard, Norma Burgin, Jeff Burn, Stephen Cocking, Paul Crompton, Bryan Evans, Chris Fawcey, Oliver Frey, Roger Gorringe, Terry Hadler, Richard Hook, Graham Humphreys, Ivan Lapper, Tom McArthur, Malcolm McGregor, Christine Molan, Tony Morris, John Nash, Paul Nash, Mark Peppé, Leonard Rosoman, Graham Smith, Robert H. Smith, Mike Tregenza, Michael Whittlesea, N. Wilkinson, Dave Williams, and Maurice Wilson.

The cover illustration is by Richard Hook.